DOCTORS

SPIN
DOCTORS

HOW MEDIA AND POLITICIANS
MISDIAGNOSED THE COVID-19 PANDEMIC

NORA LORETO

FERNWOOD PUBLISHING
HALIFAX & WINNIPEG

362.
196
2414
00971
LOR

Editing: Lisa Frenette
Cover design: Tania Craan
Printed and bound in Canada

Published by Fernwood Publishing
32 Oceanvista Lane, Black Point, Nova Scotia, B0J 1B0
and 748 Broadway Avenue, Winnipeg, Manitoba, R3G 0X3
www.fernwoodpublishing.ca

Fernwood Publishing Company Limited gratefully acknowledges the financial
support of the Government of Canada, the Canada Council for the Arts, Arts
Nova Scotia, the Manitoba Department of Culture, Heritage and Tourism under
the Manitoba Publishers Marketing Assistance Program and the Province of
Manitoba, through the Book Publishing Tax Credit, for our publishing program.
We are pleased to work in partnership with the Province of Nova Scotia to
develop and promote our creative industries for the benefit of all Nova Scotians.

Canada   Canada Council   Conseil des arts   NOVA SCOTIA   Manitoba   Arts
     for the Arts   du Canada   NOVA SCOTIA
                                            NOUVELLE-ÉCOSSE

Library and Archives Canada Cataloguing in Publication

Title: Spin doctors: how media and politicians misdiagnosed
the COVID-19 pandemic / Nora Loreto.
Names: Loreto, Nora, 1984- author.
Description: Includes bibliographical references and index.
Identifiers: Canadiana (print) 20210259418 | Canadiana
(ebook) 20210259469 | ISBN 9781773634876
(softcover) | ISBN 9781773635064 (EPUB) | ISBN 9781773635071 (PDF)
Subjects: LCSH: COVID-19 Pandemic, 2020-—Canada. | LCSH:
COVID-19 (Disease)—Canada. | LCSH: COVID-19 Pandemic,
2020-—Press coverage—Canada. | LCSH: COVID-19 (Disease)—Press
coverage— Canada. | LCSH: COVID-19 Pandemic, 2020-—Political
aspects—Canada. | LCSH: COVID-19 (Disease)—Political aspects—Canada.
| LCSH: COVID-19 Pandemic, 2020-—Government policy—Canada.
| LCSH: COVID-19 (Disease)—Government policy—Canada.
Classification: LCC RA644.C67 L67 2021 | DDC 362.1962/41400971—dc23

MIX
Paper from
responsible sources
FSC
www.fsc.org   FSC® C013916

CONTENTS

*Dedicated to the memory of every single person whose
death could have been prevented, and in celebration of
everyone whose labour saved a life, including their own.*

ACKNOWLEDGEMENTS

Writing a book at the best of times can be a challenge. Writing one during and about the Canadian impact of a global pandemic, and in such a short amount of time, required a lot of support from others.

I have to thank the team at Fernwood for everything. When I pitched this book in August 2020, I didn't think they'd be able to take on a new project while my previous book was still being printed. Their early support for this allowed me to have as much research and writing time as possible, given the constraints of writing a book in six months. Thanks especially to Fazeela Jiwa whose fastidious editing, wonderful feedback and enthusiastic support has been a pillar in my pandemic isolation.

Thanks also to Sam Tecle and Rinaldo Walcott — online friends who first suggested that funding be crowdsourced for my nightly COVID-19 deaths research. While that research wasn't specifically for this book, it paid for work that gave me a deep understanding of how journalists and politicians had been spinning the pandemic. I have never won an award so great as the show of support from this fundraiser. Thank you to the 753 people who contributed to the fund. I would list all of your names here but then this book would be even longer than it already is.

Spin Doctors relied on a lot of other people's work. I consumed thousands of articles that were the results of hours spent in press conferences and chasing sources, gathering documents and interviews. To every journalist whose work appeared in this book, thank you. And thanks also to all journalists who wrote about COVID-19, regardless of whether I've cited you. You were working under difficult circumstances and I know many of you share the criticisms that I have highlighted in this book.

Thanks to Gabrielle Peters for her many hours of messages exchanged. Her insights and brilliance related to justice, socialism, disability theory and activism deeply impacted me. While I assume responsibility for all shortcomings in the analysis presented in these pages, I owe a lot to her in how I thought through and wrote about disability and the pandemic.

Thanks to early readers of this manuscript: David Bernans and Julia Caron. Thanks also to the optimistic early readers who didn't get a chance to get through it: don't worry about it! Thanks to Sandy Hudson who challenged me each week to think about the pandemic in different ways. The fruits of those conversations appear throughout this book. And to the DM: thanks for giving my brain ten second breaks whenever I finished writing something.

I also want to acknowledge the tens of thousands of people who died in Canada. Their legacies live on in their family members and friends, in the results of their acts and the remnants of their struggles. To every person who lost someone they loved during this pandemic, I'm so sorry. My aim in writing this book is that we will never forget that policy decisions directly led to so many deaths and that someday, there will be justice.

Finally, thanks to my partner Jes for refusing to allow the kids to bug me when I was writing and school was closed. I'd thank the kids too but they didn't contribute much.

INTRODUCTION

"The Black Death acts only as an *exaggeration* of the class relations; it *chooses*. It strikes the wretched, it spares the wealthy."
— *Jean Paul Sartre,* Search for a Method

It didn't occur to us to cancel our March Break plans. When I flew to
Toronto from Los Angeles on February 29, 2020, someone at the meeting I was attending suggested our annual conference might need to be
cancelled. She worked in the airline industry and I thought she was being
dramatic. While the world would change less than two weeks later, on
March 2, I didn't yet feel it. COVID-19 was still thousands of kilometres
away.

We left Toronto for Philadelphia on March 3. Aside from the giant jugs
of hand sanitizer in the hotel lobby, everything was normal. Museums
and bars were open. We watched the Flyers play against the Colorado
Avalanche, my first live NHL game. Like thousands of other Quebecers,
we flew home on planes that very well could have had COVID-19 cases in
the cabin, a threat from the United States that was barely evident by the
time we returned on March 7.

That next week, school was only in session three of five days. There
was a PD Day, a snow day and then nothing. School was cancelled. My
partner, who was on sabbatical at Penn State, rented a car and drove north
through Western New York State just as the border was closing, hands
clutching the steering wheel through a barrier of disinfecting wipes as he
listened to American talk radio insist that COVID-19 was just a hoax. In
the space of a year since that day he fled, of the 2.6 million residents of
Western New York, more than 2200 died from COVID-19 and more than
101,500 people caught it.[1]

We all have our own memories about where we were at the start of
the pandemic. March 2020 will be tucked away forever in our minds as a
time where everything ground to a halt and our dreams and plans for the
foreseeable future turned into dust. If I close my eyes, I can still see the May
I was supposed to have, the concerts in July, the four weddings, the fun.

But that's not how life works in a pandemic; it becomes 100% oriented towards surviving, trying to rebuild a life based on our new circumstances. I was transformed into a stay-at-home mom, with the rhythm of a day that moves slowly and very quickly at once, arriving at the end with the singular thought: *I hope I didn't get COVID-19 today.* Wake up the next morning; do it all again for as long as it takes.

Regardless of where on Earth one found themselves — whether aboard a container ship, working in a hospital, mine or factory, fleeing war, famine or injustice or in "lockdown," whatever the local version of lockdown meant — the pandemic was a giant shock to every system. It stretched social safety nets thin, left a trail of millions dead and very few unscathed communities around the globe. The United Kingdom and the United States were countries where leaders boasted about how ready and capable each were to handle a pandemic. But they were led by bumbling elitist men, both whom were infected with COVID-19 and whose individualistic, strongman approach to leadership collided with the reality that the pandemic needed a collective approach. Despite the fact that each country had healthcare systems premised on very different models (one that is primarily public versus one that is primarily private), the outcomes were both alarming: by June 30, 2021, in the U.K., there were 4,830,418 total infections (7247 infections per 100,000 people) and 128,162 deaths (192.29 deaths per 100,000 people),[2] versus 33,343,961 total infections (10,159 infections per 100,000 people)[3] and 604,656 total deaths in the U.S. (184.2 deaths per 100,000 people).[4] By comparison, Canada's infection rate death rate was 3767 per 100,000 people and 70 deaths per 100,000 people.[5]

Canada often contrasts itself to the U.S. and the U.K. and based on these figures alone, Canada fared better. Except even saying this depends on how the numbers are spun. Canada's case-fatality ratio as of July 1, 2021, was 1.9%, higher than the U.S.' rate of 1.8%. Canada may have been better able to control the spread of the virus but when people were infected, from February 2020 until July 1, 2021, the number of people who died as a result of their COVID-19 infection was slightly higher than in the U.S.[6] Unlike Australia, Canada followed infection patterns of the U.S. and the U.K. and there are important lessons to be gained from Canada's experience for both nations, just as there are lessons Canada can learn from the U.K. and the U.S. The pandemic in Canada had the potential to be an explosive moment of change: in an instant Canadians could see that money was available to help people out of poverty; that the state had the power to make massive new social programs in a matter of weeks. This demonstrated that the excuses that underpinned the previous four decades of neoliberalism were lies. There was no reason whatsoever that similarly large changes couldn't be implemented in non-pandemic times, and activists saw that the moment was ripe to start talking about these changes.

Every social problem embedded within Canadian society was torn open by the pandemic. From ableism to ageism, from racism to poverty, from the environmental crisis to healthcare, COVID-19 upended the myths that had allowed problems to fester for so long. With the right social movement structure, the right spark, or the right confluence of events, much of what underpinned Canada's status quo could have come crashing down. But governments allowed the pandemic to get worse, and in so doing, entrenched the status quo much deeper. The status quo guarantees profits for private companies, even in the provision of essential needs like food. It sees Indigenous lands as free and open for the taking to enrich a small group of white people. Its labour market is so deeply racially segmented that the lowest-income workers are the least white, the highest-income workers are the most white, and the profits extracted from the poorest workers cause incredible stress and hardship. Canada's status quo: where social services have been so viciously hollowed out over forty years of neoliberalism that the only thing holding it together is the sheer will of workers.

The neoliberal period in Canada was marked by massive divestments in Canada's social safety net. All Canadian political parties played a role in this divestment, but the turning point was the Chrétien–Martin budget of 1995. The status quo can trace its origins to that moment, where deep cuts to social spending undid years of welfare-state reforms, undermined public healthcare and created the social crises that COVID-19 so easily exploited.

This book is a snapshot of the first eighteen months of the pandemic. In the hopes that what has just happened is never erased from public consciousness, I have detailed, as best I could, the period of time from January 2020 until June 2021. In this time, according to official figures, 26,338 people died and 1,416,319 were infected. Behind these numbers, an untold number of lives were changed, new chronic illnesses developed and the course of history was profoundly altered. Any analysis needs start and end points, so even though Canadian officials are warning the population about a fourth wave at the beginning of August 2021 as I write this line, and as the pandemic rages on around the globe, I've limited my analysis to the time period in between January 2020 and June 2021. As such, it's written in the past tense, even though it's quite possible that the pandemic remains in the present tense the moment you find yourself reading this paragraph. I recognize that what comes next in fall 2021 may very well upend my educated guess that the period of mass deaths in Canada ended on July 1, 2021. Still, a critical analysis of media and politics during the first eighteen months of the pandemic in Canada can provide insights and lessons that we can and should carry forward, regardless of what the future holds.

This book examines the tension between the problems that COVID-19 laid bare and the work that politicians and media did to ensure that as little as possible would change, in spite of how badly Canadians need change. Politicians and journalists did this in very different ways, of course. There isn't evidence of widespread collusion between politicians and the press. To characterize the relationship between journalists and politicians during the pandemic as cozy would be inaccurate. They didn't have to be. Critical voices in Canadian media are systemically excluded by media owners. And so, when critical journalists were needed the most, they were mostly writing for small independent publishers, without the institutional backing that is needed to take on a government during a crisis. This was truest for opinion journalism, where the most insightful and critical opinions were most often found in the virtual pages of independent outlets. It was independent journalists who followed the death counts, factory outbreaks and local spread, and tied social services underfunding and profiteering directly to the disastrous outcomes detailed in this book. It was independent journalists who made the most compelling arguments in trying to answer why governments failed to contain COVID-19: governments failed only insofar as they failed to stop human suffering. They succeeded in their true priorities: protecting the profits and operations of corporate Canada while keeping this mostly out of sight and out of mind from Canadians suffering through pandemic measures and illness. Breaking pandemic management down into a question of protecting class interests was not something Canada's mainstream journalists were able to do, even if some of them were sympathetic. Canada's mainstream media is just as invested in protecting Canada's status quo as are Canada's politicians, and in this moment of crisis, they naturally found themselves on the same side.

Canadian media is more concentrated than it ever has been, and in 2020 it shrank even further. Media owners had a huge financial stake in how governments managed the pandemic. Most daily newspapers in Canada are owned by Postmedia. The publicly traded company is owned by Republican-linked Chatham Asset Management, hedge fund manager and Republican donor Leon Cooperman and German-based Allianz, which is an asset management and insurance company. Postmedia itself has direct connections with Conservative politics. For example, just before he ran for Ontario politics, Rod Phillips was its CEO. During 2020–2021, he held positions of Minister of Finance and Minister of Long-term Care. The other big media owners are Bell, Corus, Rogers and Québecor — all companies that rely on governments to protect their operations to be able to generate profits. Rogers and Bell in particular received a windfall with government aid programs, while also making lots of money from a subscriber base that needed telecommunication and Internet services as they isolated at home. Rogers, Bell and Québecor combined netted $8.64 billion in profits in 2020, while Corus had a $607 million loss. Media owners had a direct financial interest in how politicians reacted to the pandemic and their journalists were one way they could help spin the pandemic to their benefit.

Politicians exploited the fact that during the most confusing times of the pandemic, they would be able to get away with things that normally would have been unacceptable: making lockdown announcements at difficult times for journalists to cover, creating expensive new social programs in just a few weeks and enacting policies specifically meant to protect and enrich the business class. While some of their actions were good, on the balance, their actions would cause harm to average people while leaving Canada's elites in a better place than when the pandemic started. In choosing to protect the status quo over the safety of individuals, Canada's political emergency response could not stop COVID-19. In fact, it ensured it spread among the most marginalized people. It would be disastrous in Indigenous communities. It would ravage racialized neighbourhoods while white neighbourhoods had fewer cases and better access to testing. It would force people to put themselves and their families at risk to continue to supply Canada's beef exports to the world. It would make the rich even richer. For politicians, the stakes were high, especially as this rare moment left them exposed to a potentially historic uprising of Canadians fed up with the status quo.

Day to day, journalists were paid to explain what was happening. They replaced jargon with plain language. They reported on daily numbers, press conferences and briefings; researched, analyzed and dug into issues. But it was rarely deep enough. At the same time, there was tremendous pressure on journalists that constrained reporting even further. While many journalists did what they could in very difficult circumstances to try and extract answers from politicians, their bosses benefitted if those answers were dampened or buried. From some corners of journalism, it was clear that journalists identified more with the politicians they covered than with the population they served. Many columnists heaped praise upon provincial leaders for their steady hands and sage decisions in columns that would read as if they were written directly by political staffers.

In 2020, media bosses eliminated thousands of journalism jobs. Journalists had to work from home, with fewer resources, fewer colleagues and the same challenges as everyone else related to infection control, schooling and caring for loved ones. Where politicians had their gilded suburban lots and little threat to their existence, most journalists wrote through their own anxiety, never knowing if the hammer would fall on them when their paper was sold for the third time in just a couple of years, or if their managers would lay people off again because of persistent government underfunding. The beginning of the pandemic was the moment for journalism to demonstrate its worth in Canada and far too many media owners saw it as a good time to fire, downsize and even close up shop completely.

I imagine there will be a few journalists who will balk at the idea that they participated in spinning any part of the pandemic. But Canadian media's corporate interests didn't change during the pandemic. Issues like vaccine hesitancy and rollout were over-reported while information about ownership of private care home residences or racist healthcare systems was consistently under-reported. Canadian journalism's natural default is to defend Canada's status quo. From the CBC's vacant nationalism and nostalgia, to a refusal of media organizations like the *Globe and Mail* to accept that there has been genocide in Canada, mainstream media was not going to transform into a bastion of critical, intellectual thought overnight, especially considering prohibitive funding and resource constraints. Media owners are allergic to critical journalism at best and hostile at worst. The critical investigations that did happen should have helped to challenge how other journalists reported about workplaces, food processing, residential care and government planning, but it couldn't — it was hived off from the day-to-day, uncritical reporting that created a tsunami of media coverage so overwhelming that many people found it easier to tune out than to read everything.

Much of the analysis in this book is based on how I experienced March 2020 to June 2021 not just in my day-to-day life but also in the interpretations I read. This information formed the foundation for how I've been thinking about the pandemic, but it also created the breadth, and limits, of my own research. On April 13, 2020, after having recorded an episode of the podcast I co-host with Sandy Hudson called *Sandy and Nora Talk Politics,* I realized that deaths were increasing so quickly in long-term care that there would need to be a record of this that was easy to reference. I asked on Twitter if anyone was doing this already, and the answer seemed to be no. That night, I made a public spreadsheet that accounted for 250 deaths that I could find by searching through media reports alone.

Every night thereafter, I added to the list. To do so, I combed through news websites, public health unit data, provincial ministry websites and obituaries to try and get a picture of just how many people were dying in residential care. And to my surprise, I was the only one doing it. Every night I would read between twenty to fifty sources trying to account for Canada's dead. By the time I had finished writing this book, I had read nearly thirty thousand articles and web pages from news organizations and public health units from across Canada.

So much of COVID-19 reporting relied on two sources, at most: a public health official and a politician. If the article explored something more in-depth, it would usually feature a doctor or an academic. Isaac Bogoch, Samir Sinha, Brooks Fallis, David Fisman, Abdu Sharkawy, Jennifer Kwan, Irfan Dhalla, Michael Warner and Vivian Stamatopoulos became media regulars, explaining epidemiological curves, outbreaks within long-term care, new COVID-19 restrictions and the progression of vaccines. So did Dan Kelly from the Canadian Federation of Independent Business (CFIB), one of the loudest voices advocating to protect profits at all costs. The overwhelming focus on profits, at the expense of individual and community well-being was done through highlighting Kelly's voice specifically and consistently during 2020. In general, reporting didn't really evolve, each article reading as if it could have been written in May 2020, September 2020 or June 2021. There was no innovation in how a story was told: instead, it was a daily stream of data and some analysis, all contained in a very strict set of political parameters.

And confoundingly, the data didn't get much better over the course of the pandemic either. In some cases, it even got worse. Death statistics were often approximative, incomplete or totally absent. It made analyzing provincial data very difficult. News organizations routinely made data errors or reported on death and infection rates from a current outbreak with no mention of previous death and infections that had happened at the same facility. The data errors helped to feed the emerging anti-lockdown, anti-vaccine crowd who tried to demonstrate that foggy data was proof the pandemic was entirely made up. The pandemic started with journalists and politicians united in their criticism of China's approach to containing the virus, both levelling charges against the nation of suppressing information. And yet, data suppression was a major problem in Canada too, hiding and obscuring everything from the origins of outbreaks to the numbers of deaths from outbreaks within Canadian hospitals. Data changed from region to region, day to day. Death counts were added to and subtracted from, and data was obscured through debates about whether or not a death caused indirectly by COVID-19 should count as a COVID-19 death. The lack of information was another of many tactics that were used to distract from understanding a full picture that should have been clear and easily communicated: the oppressive structures that are baked into Canada's economy and society need to be transformed if we want to keep communities safe and secure.

While the breadth of my nightly research underpinned my understanding of the pandemic, analyzing how journalists spun the pandemic required intense research that was specific to the topics in this book. I tried to be as broad as I could in my sources referenced. I reference 579 articles from 136 news outlets, written by 423 journalists. At 115 references from 30 different regions or divisions, CBC/Radio-Canada is the most cited news source, followed by CTV national and regional stations (82) and Global national and regional stations (52). There are ten French-language sources referenced, 11 sources from B.C., 17 from the prairie provinces, seven from Atlantic Canada, 13 from Québec and four from the territories. Importantly, 29 sources are independent media outlets, many who have been founded in just the past five years. Newfoundland and Labrador and Prince Edward Island do not feature prominently, nor do the territories, partly because infection levels were so impressively kept low in each jurisdiction, and partly because Canada's population centres took up a lot of space, as they tend to do. While my research is not exhaustive, I have tried to ensure that I am fairly reflecting the way in which each chapter's theme was generally covered in the media from January 2020 until June 2021— the period of onset and mass death during Canada's pandemic.

Telling this story is impossible if it isn't told through the experiences of how we lived it. It wasn't a theoretical exercise; the pandemic had material impacts on Canadians, and analyzing these impacts required that people were understood as being connected to their work, home, family and community lives. The most common ways in which journalists spun the narrative to protect the status quo was to zoom in very closely on an individual and tell a story through them. Through this frame, the pandemic became individualized. Struggles were detached from broader social forces and therefore solutions were elusive, difficult to understand or far too complex to be seriously considered. This had a very big impact on how people came to understand the pandemic: worker deaths were explained through obituary-style features that rarely held anyone accountable for a death; deaths in residential care were broadcast through the voices of sons or daughters or friends in mourning; the plight of a frontline worker was used to illustrate the struggle of working through a pandemic, though the profits that were extracted from their labour were almost never mentioned in the same article. It atomized people, erased the connection that they had to a broader community and made it impossible to understand how COVID-19 was so deftly moving from individual to individual. After all, those community connections were so critical to being able to understand community spread. It's no wonder that community spread was one of those nebulous terms that we never really got a proper sense of, despite the fact that it was frequently talked about by politicians and journalists.

Each of these chapters follows one month from March 2020 until March 2021 and each month is anchored by a theme, though the information contained within each chapter is not limited to each month. While time felt meaningless for many people in 2020, it was often measured by waves, moments that were unique to Canada and didn't align necessarily with waves in other countries (nor did these waves even overlap from region to region within Canada). When I refer to the first wave, I mean between March and June 2020. The second wave started in September

2020, intensified in November and December 2020 and calmed down by February 2021. The third wave started before the second wave really ended in February 2021 and ended by June 2021.

The way that the pandemic was explained at the start would set in motion so much of how it would be explained throughout. In the chapter covering March 2020, I examine how the earliest discussions of the pandemic would lay the foundation for how politicians and journalists would frame COVID-19. The intense focus on China helped to obscure the responsibility that Canada held for not being prepared for a pandemic. This set off a marked rise in anti-Asian racism and made it acceptable for politicians to avoid responsibility for the actions they took or didn't take.

In the chapter covering April 2020, I explore the carnage in residential care. Residential care was in such rough shape before the pandemic that it should have been obvious COVID-19 would be devastating if it got inside the walls of Canada's thousands of residential care facilities. By April, Canada was dealing with an undeniable crisis. The confusion around what was happening, made possible especially thanks to a lack of uniform data and clear reporting that consistently named who was responsible for the operations of each facility, made it hard to understand how these facilities could have been better protected, even improved.

By May 2020, the first mass workplace outbreaks were being reported in meatpacking facilities in Alberta, and journalists placed the spotlight on food processing industries. In this chapter, I examine the combination of low-paid work, workers who have precarious status and an overrepresentation of racialized workers that created the conditions for food processing to be one of the industries hardest hit by the pandemic. Racism underpinned the brutal conditions within Canada's food industries, and I explore the racial impact of COVID-19 even further in the chapter covering June 2020. Though data was hard to come by, the impact of the pandemic on racialized communities was undeniable by June, and yet, journalists rarely wrote through a racialized lens to help explain how COVID-19 was impacting whom the most. Politicians didn't enact targeted measures either, even after data did become available that demonstrated the toll COVID-19 was taking on racialized communities in cities and small communities across Canada.

As the summer months moved people outside, politicians started talking more about the role personal responsibility played in reducing case numbers. In the chapter covering July 2020, I examine how politicians used this narrative to shift focus off workplaces and family dwellings as a source of COVID-19 spread, and onto individuals. This both rendered action ineffective, as individuals alone didn't have what they needed to stop COVID-19, and it reformulated responsibility from a collective one, tiered by how much power a group of people had in society, to solely an individual one. The COVID-19 alert app played an important role in this, sold to Canadians as an effective tool to stop the spread of the virus, while evictions continued, housing continued to be unsafe and people were forced to continue working. The personal responsibility narrative dovetailed with the government's most important aid program, the Canada Emergency Response Benefit (CERB), which was intended to help individuals weather the pandemic. When CERB was supposed to end in August 2020, it threw thousands of people into chaos, as they scrambled to try and find a way to supplement their income. In this chapter, I explore how the government managed CERB while also deciding to reward employers with a mass cash transfer called the Canada Emergency Wage Subsidy (CEWS), which came with very few strings attached and tied worker aid directly to the whims of their employers. The government did all of this while not demanding that managers take extra precautions for their workers during the pandemic or mandating paid sick leave, a rallying cry that united activists from all across Canada.

The chapter about September 2020 examines the way in which schools became a proxy war to make arguments that were both for and against public health orders. Schools became a symbol for how seriously a jurisdiction was taking COVID-19 spread. The start of school year 2020 coincided with the 2020 harvest, which put the spotlight again on seasonal migrant workers and how badly their bosses treated them, during the pandemic. In the chapter covering October 2020, I examine how the successful and relentless advocacy of migrant workers and their allies allowed this issue to pierce through a media landscape that was still mostly ignoring the role that workplaces were playing in spreading COVID-19. The Seasonal Agricultural Worker Program (SAWP) took centre stage, as advocates pushed journalists to explore horrible living and working conditions that gave rise to COVID-19 infections and employer reprimand.

By November 2020, the world had its first hope that a vaccine wasn't too far away. In this chapter, I look at how the vaccines were reported and how journalists too often promoted narratives about vaccine hesitancy more than they explained how the vaccines were being made. This helped to fuel the rise in far-right, anti-mask/anti-vaccine movements, which politicians did not take seriously as extremist movements, and which journalists gave far too much airtime to. Politicians argued over how fast vaccines could be distributed to Canadians and the Canadian government purchased more vaccines per capita than any other country in the world, lining up with other Western nations to oppose waiving IP rules around vaccine development, blocking information — and safety — from flowing to poorer countries. Neither issue received as much coverage as the anti-mask/anti-vaccine protests, and this lack of information allowed for politicians to make vaccine demands that were impossible or ridiculous simply to boost their political popularity.

In the chapter covering December 2020, I examine the pandemic through a gendered lens. Women, especially disabled and/or Black, Indigenous and racialized women, bore the brunt of the economic losses that the pandemic dealt. While this received a lot of media coverage relative to other issues, like the impact of COVID-19 on disabled people, the coverage rarely sought to put forward fundamental solutions or hold politicians to account. Politicians mostly offered platitudes, even as the statistics were showing a marked rise in gendered violence and frontline agencies were crying out for help. Disabled women were especially made to be vulnerable during the pandemic, given very little income support and few services. I explore this further in the chapter about January 2021, which looks at disability more broadly and how journalists and politicians nearly entirely erased disability from the public discussion of who is most threatened by COVID-19. Instead of disability or chronic illness, the term "comorbidity" became more popular, signalling to Canadians that avoiding the worst outcomes of a COVID-19 infection was as easy as not having an underlying health issue.

In the chapter about February 2021, I look at the role that workplaces played in spreading COVID-19. Politicians often directly or indirectly hid the impact that workplaces had on spreading COVID-19, and it wasn't until after Canada was well into the second wave that journalists finally started examining the role that large, congregant workplaces played in propagating COVID-19. But it wasn't as if workplaces were entirely erased: small businesses became the stand in for Canada's economy in media, erasing large congregant work settings and thus distorting where COVID-19 was most serious, confusing Canadians about what kind of workplaces were more susceptible to COVID-19 spread.

The final chapter, which covers March 2021, examines the elephant that is lurking in most of the pages of this book: how the media industry fared during the pandemic, trying to fulfill its mandate while bosses hacked away thousands of jobs. By March 2021, there had been one year of job losses within media agencies. Journalists were under pressure to report on the health crisis of the century while they also faced increasing attacks from their own media companies. Cuts to the media industry had profound impacts on the quality and depth of local news, the breadth of national news and the ability that media had to hold anyone to account for the existing issues laid bare by COVID-19.

There was an overreliance by some to describe the pandemic as being a moment of intense fog. This fogginess allowed politicians to spin a narrative they preferred to tell, one that shaped how Canadians understood what was happening, who to blame and, critically, how to stop it. But that narrative was incomplete, and sometimes downright misleading. And journalists, far more often than not, repeated politicians' talking points thereby contributing to this fog and making it very hard for Canadians to keep up with the news: what was happening, what did it mean and who was responsible? There were very few individuals who were able to cut through it and explain plainly what was happening, and many of those voices are featured in this book.

In her 1978 essay, "News as the reproduction of the status quo: a summary" Gaye Tuchman, a sociologist renown for her analysis of media and bias, describes how the way in which news is framed is similar to a window frame: "Characteristics of the window, its size and composition, limit what may be seen. So does its placement, that is, what aspect of the unfolding scene it makes accessible."[7] Journalism is necessary not only because it creates the frame through which people understand current affairs, but also because in so doing, journalists can create understandings and tendencies that permeate throughout a population. While straight reporting shouldn't be in the pursuit of changing politics directly, it also shouldn't be in the pursuit of not changing politics either. What it must do is give people a window with the fullest possible view of what is happening. The window that journalists construct has enormous consequences on how people understand the world around them. During the pandemic, structural and social forces meant that journalists far too often crafted a tiny window frame, looking out over only a part of the story, and Canadians were left with a small fraction of the knowledge that the moment demanded they have. Critical journalism — that is, journalism that specifically targets power — was sorely missing, and Canadians were worse off because of this. Knowledge had the power to create new political understandings and movements, or it had the power to confuse and confound an audience desperate to understand what was happening and why. Far too often, the knowledge made possible by journalism was the latter.

The spin started early — even before COVID-19 had arrived in Canada — and it set in motion a dominant media frame that didn't question fundamental problems with Canadian society, even though those problems are what allowed COVID-19 to run wild, ending lives and permanently altering others. Politicians chose to protect the status quo at all costs. And journalists covered the news in the way that they usually do — with some criticism but not much, and certainly not enough to arm people with the knowledge necessary to adequately hold their leaders to account.

March 2020

THE PANDEMIC EMERGES

Cases: 28
Deaths: 0[1]

March 2020 was the month that never seemed to end. As the world approached March 2021, across popular culture and social media, many people said we had never really left March 2020, the month where everything stopped. Plans that had been put on hold had either evaporated or, in incredible optimism, pushed ahead by one year, and then pushed ahead by another. For Canadians, March 2020 became the dividing line between the old world and the new, and people clung to this line not knowing where the next line was — whether one that demarked the end of the pandemic and the beginning of a new world, or maybe a return to the old. Or worse.

Global attention was turned to the Diamond Princess cruise ship. After the market in Wuhan China, the Diamond Princess would become the second most famous superspreader event in the world. Journalists looked for the local angle — find a Diamond Princess passenger who was a citizen or who spoke the same language, and get them live to air from their tiny quarantined cabins. COVID-19 spread among the 3711 passengers, and infected individuals from at least 11 different countries.[2] As the ship was docked in Yokohama, Japanese public health officials had the responsibility to coordinate with passengers and crew, get seriously ill passengers off the ship and impose public health measures to try and control the spread. Of the 256 Canadians on board, 47 caught the virus.[3] On February 28, the first citizen of the United Kingdom died. Nearly a month later, the first citizen of Canada died. The Diamond Princess monopolized early news of the coronavirus and showed the world early on that the virus didn't care about nations and borders. The globe was in this struggle together, whether politicians acknowledged this or not.

As journalists gathered stories related to the Diamond Princess and Wuhan, there was very little introspective reporting about how Canada was managing what would soon become a full-blown pandemic. Canadians had no idea that our response was lagging as a result of bad public policy decisions and missteps from public health and political responses. Instead, media clung to the narrative that COVID-19 and China were inextricably linked. The cover of *Maclean's* announced, "China's efforts to stop the Coronavirus have failed," in alarming font superimposed over a gas mask.[4] When COVID-19 finally came to Canada, it didn't come through the channels that we were warned to be wary of. It came from the countries Canadians travel to most, during a time of year notorious for travel.

COVID-19 was scary. It was unknown. In the fog created by these unknowns, the way in which COVID-19 was framed in early 2020 would set up how it was written about for the following 18 months. The first opportunity to frame the pandemic didn't come from journalists or politicians, though. It came through public health officials, mostly chief medical officers of health, who spoke directly to the population addressing questions about COVID-19, what it might do and how people could keep themselves safe. Except even they didn't really know the answers to these questions. The unknowns were filled in with innuendo about China and people were told to stay calm. Politicians exploited both messages for political gain and journalists reported mostly uncritically. Journalists were forced to create a new kind of journalism on the fly: pandemic journalism, which had to sort through a mix of anecdotes, ever-changing data, competing priorities and policies and experts who often agreed, but sometimes did not. This new kind of journalism became increasingly self-referential, like news that modeling predicted next month's case growth, which generated another story later on based on whether or not the models were correct. Politicians announced measure after measure and journalists became their amplifiers, teaching us about social distancing, contactless shopping and what we knew about the daily COVID-19 case counts.

We would find out later that COVID-19 entered Canada not through China, as had been what we were told to expect, but from the U.S., the U.K. and Austria. We would also find out that Canada, once a global leader in pandemic early-warning research, had effectively turned off this early alert system in 2019 through interference and mismanagement of the Global Public Health Intelligence Network (GPHIN). This created a vacuum within global pandemic monitoring that, had it been working as it was supposed to, might have found COVID-19 earlier, giving the world more time to prepare. We will never know how many lives during the first wave could have been saved, if only we had better understood the threat that faced us in February 2020, just as Québec started its March Break.

On February 29, 2020, I caught a CNN headline on a TV at Los Angeles International Airport: "Trump gives update after first coronavirus death." The man was in his 50s, from Washington State and it wasn't clear where he came in contact with the virus. He hadn't travelled. He hadn't been in contact with anyone who had had COVID-19.[5]

I was in a high-risk location: a busy international airport in the United States. Not many travellers were wearing masks, me included. Like tens of thousands of Quebecers, I had no sense of just how close we came to finding ourselves among the thousands of unlucky ones who would bring COVID-19 back to Québec from their March Break trip. British Columbia already had six cases by February 20.[6] On February 27, Québec recorded its first official case: a woman had light symptoms after returning from a trip to Iran.[7] Even though COVID-19 had reached Canada, politicians and journalists still talked about the virus as an existential threat from abroad: the Diamond Princess and Wuhan. It had barely hit Italy by then; only a few small towns had been locked down for a week by February 29.[8]

In February and March, China loomed large in COVID-19 coverage partly due to the fact that China had the most experience with this new and frightening virus. Everything known at the time about symptoms, hospital overcrowding, the seeming randomness with which the virus kills and overall case fatality rates came from China. Globally, journalists and politicians relied on medical reports and journalism from within Wuhan to translate what might happen in a local setting. The first wave of the virus in China peaked at the start of February and by the end of the month, daily new cases were considerably lower, thanks to China's aggressive pandemic mitigation policies.[9]

After February 25, cases announced outside of China exceeded the number of cases announced within the country.[10] The first cases that would propel Canada's first outbreaks came from the U.S., Austria, England, India and Italy. By the time there was another fatality outside of B.C., four people had already died at Lynn Valley Care Centre, a facility in North Vancouver that was home to Canada's first outbreak, and one of B.C.'s deadliest. Canada's fifth death happened at a Barrie Ontario hospital; a 77-year-old Muskoka man who had caught COVID-19 from a close contact.[11] Despite the intense focus on China, and the way that media and public officials focused on the possibility of spread of the virus from China, the first four people who died in Canada were victims of a long-term care system that would colossally fail over the next two months, and the fifth contracted the virus from a close contact.

OBSESSED WITH CHINA

From the start, the North American obsession with China allowed politicians to lay blame at the feet of a foreign government rather than take responsibility for how unprepared for a pandemic North America really was. This obsession also drove media analysis, justifying a deluge of coverage on Wuhan, their farmer's markets, Chinese government authoritarianism and what that government may or may not have hidden. It was easier to blame the Chinese than it was to ask why Canada's pandemic stockpiles were depleted or how many post-SARS policies were still in effect.

Death came to North America far earlier than was first reported. The first death was nearly a month earlier than the first official death announced on February 29, 2020. Patricia Cabello Dowd of California died suddenly from a heart attack on February 6. Dowd had not travelled and had no contact with someone known to have had COVID-19. Her death, announced months later at the end of April, was proof that there was some level of community spread in the United States, gone undetected by state public health officials.[12] The morning of Dowd's death, CBC Radio's *The Current* featured two segments on COVID-19: one that looked at spread on cruise ships and included an interview with Diamond Princess passenger Kent Frasure and the second focused on China. They promoted the second segment like this: "we hear from people in Wuhan who say the Chinese government has played down the coronavirus outbreak at home."[13] The intense focus on China from Canadian journalists left little room to examine North America with similar attention, including posing similar questions about the North American response, and what officials might have been holding back from the public. On February 26 in Washington State, two people died in a nursing home from COVID-19, at a location that was nearby the hospital where the February 29 death had occurred.[14] Nursing home deaths would become far more important to Canada's story than anything happening in China, and yet, nursing homes received barely any coverage in February, as I explain in the April 2020 chapter.

As the virus started to spread into other parts of the world, English-language journalists covered the pandemic as if it were a threat coming from overseas that could be battled if it appeared on a country's shores. By the time the virus had established itself in Canada, cases were mostly linked to travel, especially from the United States. But the U.S. was still not front-of-mind for public health officials, politicians or journalists. On March 5, *Global News* reported, "People travelling from China or Iran are being asked to self-isolate for 14 days, and Henry said anyone who has travelled elsewhere and is feeling ill should also stay home."[15] Even though the article mentioned that there was at least one case from Seattle and that cases there were skyrocketing, Provincial Health Officer Bonnie Henry reminded British Columbians to be careful about travel, specifically naming China and Iran, and not the United States, as locations that necessitated a 14-day quarantine. Politicians, public health agents and journalists focused on China — what Chinese officials knew, what they should have done and the ways in which Western leaders thought China had been negligent.[16] At a March 9 press conference, where Canada's first COVID-19-related death was announced, *Bloomberg* reported that B.C.'s Minister of Health Adrian Dix said that of the 32 people in B.C. who had COVID-19, only five had contact with China. Compare that to "several" transmissions related to the Lynn Valley Care Centre outbreak and 16 connected (directly and indirectly) to Iran, and it's clear that the rhetoric of where COVID-19 was coming from did not match where the vast majority of people caught it.[17]

It was a big mistake to frame this pandemic in relation to China. That was clear in February, when the World Health Organization (WHO) created the name COVID-19 to avoid linking the illness to China.[18] And even though journalists often acknowledged that focusing on China was a problematic frame, they did little to stop the racist narrative to become a key part of the pandemic story. Had journalists spent as much time focusing on the U.S. that they did on China, how would Canadians have understood this virus differently?

This racist frame gave many Canadians, including me, a false sense of security that travel that wasn't to China was safe. When a woman who was the sixth case of COVID-19 in B.C. was found to have travelled on an Air Canada flight from Montréal to Vancouver on February 14, it was becoming clear that global spread was more severe than Canadian officials expressed publicly: "officials were surprised when they learned the woman had only visited Iran, and not China or neighbouring countries that have seen the bulk of COVID-19 cases."[19] CBC News reported that around the same time, Iran only had 28 confirmed cases and five deaths. The BBC found later, in August, that Iran more likely had ten times the number of deaths at that point.[20]

It was impossible for Canadian media to know where and how the virus was spreading, but had journalists asked similar questions about Canada's response that they did about China's response, there would have been an important shift in how the dominant narrative framed the pandemic from the start. The obsession with COVID-19 and China had two important spin-off effects: it masked a much larger threat, and it gave cover to racists to spread anti-Asian sentiment. By not challenging politicians or public health officials, and instead focusing on China, Canadians had no idea just how easily COVID-19 was about to walk through our doors, thanks to people coming home from U.S. or European-based March Break vacations and rising community spread. And, as individual actions became the sole mechanism promoted by government to slow COVID-19 transmission, Canadians were primed to see COVID-19 purely as an individual threat, rather than one that would exploit the holes in social solidarity and infect whole communities of people.

COMMUNITY VERSUS INDIVIDUAL THREAT

Once COVID-19 had established itself in Canada, the first major story of the pandemic was how the virus was ravaging long-term care. The virus preyed on the cracks in Canada's social services and found its way towards the most marginalized Canadians: disabled, elderly, racialized and poor. In the early days, the rare moments of media criticism were reserved for foreign governments, while Canadian politicians in positions of power were given the benefit of the doubt.

On March 5, British Columbia announced "a major jump" in cases with eight new ones. Some cases were linked to travel from Seattle, but one was B.C.'s first case of community transmission.[21] The community transmission case was a woman who worked at Lynn Valley Care Centre, a facility where the majority of staff were Filipina care workers and who were not immediately informed that COVID-19 was circulating in their facility.[22] Lynn Valley was also the site of Canada's first COVID-19 fatality. The outbreak lasted until May 5 — one day short of two months. Fifty-two elderly residents and 26 staff were infected, and 20 people died.[23] The Lynn

Valley Care Centre outbreak should have forced media across Canada to pivot from telling an international story, based mostly aboard cruise ships or in China, to one that would focus on the capacity of an underfunded and profit-driven care system to protect Canadians from the virus. There should have been reporting about the links that these facilities have to communities and community spread. But instead, a narrative emerged from journalists that hived off long-term care from the rest of society. This created a divide between the vulnerable on the inside and the less vulnerable outside, with very little attempt at challenging government to do something before COVID-19 spread too quickly.

From the outset though, deaths were consistently reported with additional information that told the majority of Canadians to not worry too much about the virus. Under a generalized fog of pandemic-related fear, journalists rarely reported anything further than what public health had announced, and the information about whether or not someone had an "underlying health condition" would relay the message to all Canadians to absorb this information differently: be relieved if you have no underlying health conditions; be scared if you do. The rhythm of daily press briefings didn't allow for more in-depth reporting and, in March, many journalists were also stretched to their limits trying to keep themselves safe while reporting on the crisis. But the template used to report death — gender, age range and underlying health issues — got Canadians used to the idea that COVID-19 was really a problem for a specific kind of person, probably someone of a different age, gender or physical condition than they were, as I explain more in the chapter covering January 2021. Usually relying on comments made by public health, a victim's other medical issues were front-and-centre in the information about where they caught COVID-19 and how they died. *Global News* reported B.C.'s first death like this, "[Bonnie] Henry said the patient, a man in his 80s with underlying health conditions, passed away Sunday night."[24] The article only quotes Henry, a pattern that would become the norm for daily reporting.

In the early days of the pandemic, if journalists weren't talking about the virus and its evolution in China, they were reporting what Canadians could expect once it eventually came to Canada. Transmission started slowly in Canada, and in the first months of 2020, it wasn't at all obvious that the economy would grind to a halt in March. Officials walked a line between reassuring the population that basic precautions, like handwashing and not going into work sick, would be enough to slow the spread of the virus but also telling them to take the risk seriously. But they didn't impose new public policies that would make fulfilling their requests possible; they didn't mandate that employers give workers paid sick leave, even though unions had been calling for that especially in Ontario where Doug Ford cancelled the two paid sick days previously introduced by the Liberal government.[25]

Right after the B.C.'s first COVID-19 death, Adam Miller wrote a feature for CBC News arguing there was no need to panic over the virus. "While tragic for those close to the victim, the man's death should not be used as a way to justify panic for the majority of Canadians who are not at risk of severe complications from COVID-19, experts say," he wrote. Miller quoted figures from the World Health Organization (WHO) to show mortality rates were tied to the age of the patient, and older patients were far more likely to die from COVID-19. He said the overall death rate seemed to be 3.4%, then reminded readers this is still significantly higher than the seasonal flu.[26]

Miller wasn't alone in how he framed the illness. The day before Miller's article was published on March 10, Bloomberg's Amanda Lang asked Michael Gardam, a doctor who had been involved in Toronto's response to SARS and H1N1, this question:

> From the point of view of who sickens and dies from this virus … it seems for many people to be a benign event. Obviously, three percent is not an immaterial number. Do we know whether treatment has helped saved lives, or whether fatalities are a done deal, in other words there is a population that is vulnerable to begin with?[27]

Gardam reminds Lang that during a pandemic, the focus cannot be on the potential individual impact of a virus. Most important is how the collective responds to a threat to protect people who might be vulnerable to the virus. "From a population perspective," Gardam said, "it's still a very big deal."[28]

Despite this warning, many journalists had a difficult time parsing the difference between individual and collective threat, messaging that left the public confused about how serious the pandemic might be. The frame that COVID-19 wasn't all that serious further marginalized those folks for whom COVID-19 *would* be that bad. Telling Canadians that they, individually, will be fine enabled people to come to a similar conclusion as Lang: okay,

3% isn't nothing, but is it really that serious? The personal was privileged over the collective and, as Gardam pointed out, the consequences would be dire if the population couldn't find a way to understand this virus.

Within the first year, COVID-19 would kill more than 22,000 in Canada.[29] As predicted, the majority were older and living in residential facilities. Canadians didn't understand this threat from a community perspective: What does community spread actually mean? How does the virus go from household to household, through workplaces and other gathering spaces? What role does poverty, low-waged work or disability play in who is put most at risk? These questions were never entertained in March 2020. Instead risk was repackaged to be an individual calculation. As Miller's article's headline said, "80% of those infected with COVID-19 will have mild symptoms," so there was no reason for me to panic.[30] Less than one week later, Québec's school system was shut down completely.

This frame prepared Canadians for a virus that wasn't that bad — and when it turned out to be worse than "not that bad," a new genre of reporting grew from it: the life and struggles of people who had long-term COVID-19 symptoms. Journalists regularly came back to long-haulers, as they called themselves, to warn that the lingering effects of COVID-19 are mysterious and, in many cases, debilitating. The problem was that these portraits never looked at the collective impact that entire communities of people dealing with long COVID-19 might be. They never asked what the economic impact would be within an apartment complex where there had been multiple outbreaks. And the reporting rarely gave Canadians an idea of what should be done to mitigate the long-term effect of the virus. There were no national discussions about supports for people who have long-term or lingering symptoms. There were no promises of extended paid leave for people who, after months, still couldn't work. And rarely did the prospective of long-term effects make it into the discussions about why we need to protect communities from getting COVID-19 in the first place.

Every major national news outlet wrote stories that featured the struggles of one or several long-haulers. Some surveyed the scientific literature or examined where Canadian research was. They all warned Canadians to take COVID-19 seriously or else risk becoming a long-hauler, but none of them discussed what might be done for people like the ones they featured. For example, Audrey Vanderhoek told *Global News*, "I think there's a bit of a delusion that it's not going to get you until it gets you. And then your world completely changes."[31] The B.C.

nurse and COVID-19 survivor had symptoms for months after her May diagnosis. At the end of the video, she suggests that B.C. set up special medical care for long-haulers, like providing body scans to see if the virus impacted people's organs. The clip didn't pick up on the idea, instead focusing on Vanderhoek's daily struggle. *Global News* featured two other long-haulers six months into the pandemic, and each are cast in the same frame: patients talking about the frustration and difficulty of living with COVID-19 for far longer than the popular narrative had said they should have.[32] *CTV News's* Avis Favaro, Elizabeth St. Philip and Brooklyn Neustaeter interviewed two long-haulers whose neurological symptoms stopped them from working; they ended the feature examining a research initiative by Canadian neuroscientists who are hoping to learn more about the illness.[33] Rather than focusing on ideas to help people who have chronic COVID-19-related conditions, like Vanderhoek suggested, the stories stayed close to the personal narratives of the daily struggle to live with a chronic illness. These long-hauler features missed the opportunity to talk about long-term paid sick leaves, rehabilitation, public supports for long-haulers, official data collection of their experiences and symptoms. Crucially, they neither brought into the conversation voices of people who live with other chronic conditions, nor identified what they've been demanding for years to help mitigate the challenges of life with a chronic condition in Canada. There was little written to try and start a conversation about what more chronic illness among the general population will look like: what will happen to the folks who cannot work or who need workplace modifications? What about workers who caught COVID at work — what responsibility do employers have to compensate and accommodate these workers? And critically, how does government policy consider any of these questions? Even as the number of people with long COVID-19 increased, the long-hauler focus never asked any of these questions.

All of the reporting — whether it was assuring Canadians that they would probably be okay or it was analyzing individual impacts of the virus — was premised on the assumption that the most important unit in the conversation was the individual. Journalists didn't ask about how to manage the illness as a worker, or the impact COVID-19 might have on a person's ability to commute, do their job, care for their family or loved ones. It was hyper individualized, while also erasing those who would be most hurt by the illness as a sad footnote to an overall not-terrible story. It refused to look at the health of society from a larger perspective. By reporting COVID in a workplace, a seniors' residence or a low-income neighbourhood, journalists made it easier for others to ignore how COVID-19 behaved in ways that were deeply linked to larger systemic issues. For two months, even after the first victims died in long-term care, Canadians rarely heard about what a community infection might look like, even if early on experts like Michael Gardam reminded journalists that the key to understanding a pandemic is not to simply look at the potential individual effects it might have.

EMERGENCY MEASURES

Pandemic reporting focused very closely on everything that was known about the illness, but journalists also needed to cover the political response too. The images from Prime Minister Justin Trudeau's March 11, 2020 press conference capture a moment in time that would soon look completely bizarre. Trudeau was flanked by four people: federal cabinet ministers Chrystia Freeland, Patty Hadju and Bill Morneau, and Theresa Tam, Canada's top public health officer. No one was socially distanced; no one was wearing masks. Trudeau's hair was cut short — hair that would eventually come to illustrate the passage of time, as it grew longer and longer over several weeks of daily briefings. Despite the normal look of the press conference, it would be the last time ministers would stand so close together, or appear without their masks when more than one person spoke, for more than a year.[34]

That day, Trudeau announced his government was creating a billion-dollar COVID-19 response fund. "Let me be clear," he said. "No one should have to worry about their job if they have to be quarantined. No employer should feel like they have to lay off a worker because of the virus. We can support you and we will."[35] The fund would pay for short-term business loans, faster access to EI, more personal protective equipment and money for medical research. The tone was reassuring but still made it clear Canadians were facing an imminent threat. The announcement focused on economics alone and sent a signal to the corporate world that they shouldn't panic. It also tried to tell average Canadians this too, except by March 11, it wasn't clear what kind of aid people would actually need. This was a moment of rising cases and new deaths, but beyond acknowledging the pain that families were experiencing at that moment, Trudeau didn't mention anything further related to community health.

Later that day, the NBA announced that it was cancelling all games. It was the moment that the threat of COVID-19 became extremely clear. NBA officials saw what many — businesspeople, other sports league officials and politicians — didn't yet see: the time was now to shut down mass gatherings. This set off a cascade of cancelled sporting and cultural events, including other professional sports leagues. Two days later, Trudeau held his first of what would be dozens of press conferences outside, as his wife, Sophie Grégoire Trudeau caught COVID-19 during a trip to England.[36] On March 13, Trudeau announced his government would suspend cruise ship season and recommend that people limit their travel, but he didn't announce any new measures or limit large gatherings. He assured Canadians he was working for them and promised that help was on its way.[37] The same day, six of Canada's largest universities closed, parliament closed and Canada's 300,000 federal public servants were asked to work from home.[38] The next few weeks were a blur of cascading announcements: shutdowns by provincial governments and new measures that the federal government hoped would keep Canadians afloat but also locked securely away.

The pace of news in this time was dizzying, and media coverage stuck closely to reporting to government announcements. Even comments from the opposition parties were rare, perhaps related to the success with which Trudeau wielded the term "team Canada," a way to insist on national unity to get through the crisis together. The CBC's Aaron Wherry captured the general mood:

> But the potential points of stress and friction are many. What's happening now might be compared to the experience of wartime — the sort of war that includes a massive domestic effort. In a matter of days, huge portions of Canadian society have shut down, if only temporarily.[39]

Wherry pointed out that the stock market picked up 1200 points the afternoon of March 13, Trudeau's first socially distanced press conference, though warned, "But that is just one afternoon. Trudeau might need to prepare Canadians for a long and difficult haul."[40] *Might* indeed.

Trudeau controlled the message very effectively. Every day at 11:00 a.m. EST, he addressed the nation, carried live on the CBC and *Radio-Canada*. Provincial premiers started to do the same thing, later in the day, and so Canadians who were at home could tune into non-stop COVID-19 updates, with announcements separated by noon call-in shows usually asking a specific question related to how people were doing. The daily ritual of press conferences examining latest numbers and new emergency measures allowed Canadians to have a rhythm of normalcy in a chaotic and scary time — that is, Canadians who found themselves at home. Those who had to keep working outside the home through these weeks relied on their employers to implement government directives. If the directives were weak, the measures were weak too. On March 25, when the Liberals' $107-billion emergency spending bill was passed, journalists reported a new wave of stories, intended to help Canadians make sense of the aid and support that was there for them, and how they could access it.

At the same time that governments were announcing new measures at rapid speed, there were also warning signs that Canada was perhaps not as prepared as it should have been. Decisions to clear hospital beds to make way for a rush of COVID-19 patients took priority over taking stock of where Canada was most vulnerable. The dominant public health message became "do your part to plank the curve." Social distancing went from two words that had never been put together to a requirement for keeping oneself and others safe. Media played a key role in spreading this information. They examined what social distancing was intended to do and aired articles and promotional ads about handwashing and watching out for signs of COVID-19. The rapid shutdown of the economy did help to "plank the curve," but not for everyone. The differential impact of these measures were enormous: lowest income workers were shut out of aid programs; inequalities were built into the wage subsidy; disabled Canadians were given nothing despite elevated risk if exposed to COVID-19; mortgage relief was offered to businesses and landlords but not people who had rents to pay. In Toronto, one of the few jurisdictions where such data was available, planking the curve only worked to slow the spread of COVID-19 among the highest income, white residents.[41] Attention to long-term care was also inadequate — unacceptable not only because the following months would be the most deadly moment for Canadians since the Second World War but also because the first victims of COVID-19 had already died, and it was already clear that residential care would pose a significant problem for containing the virus. These were the stories that so often didn't get added to the national-level analyses of daily announcements, statistical updates or incessant reminders that we should wash our hands and not touch our faces. As the rest of this book explores, the impact of such thin analyses helped the virus to do maximum damage, while Canadians called out for help, suffered quietly or sought answers from less-than-ideal sources, especially from the organized far right.

GLOBAL PUBLIC HEALTH INTELLIGENCE NETWORK

One of the biggest barriers to a coherent and effective pandemic response was the structure of Canada in and of itself. Journalists and politicians referred to federal-provincial relations and division of power to explain, defend or justify why a measure could or could not be implemented. Jurisdictional manoeuvring was often used as the excuse for why a pandemic plan would be impossible: a federal plan either violated the constitution by encroaching on provincial jurisdiction, or a provincial plan would be impossible as it encroached on federal jurisdiction. As health-care is mostly provincial jurisdiction, funded and coordinated through the Canada Health Act, it was often not very clear how far the federal government could go with their relief measures. Governments used this unclarity to their benefit; politicians from different levels of government shadowboxed with one another through passing the buck or calling for another jurisdiction to do more. But there was one area where the federal government had full control; they were wholly responsible for the failure of the Global Public Health Intelligence Network (GPHIN), Canada's early warning pandemic system, to catch COVID-19 as soon as it likely would have been, had it been working properly.

In July, Canadians learned for the first time the extent to which the federal Liberals had altered Canada's early-warning pandemic system, thanks to in-depth reporting from *Globe and Mail* journalist Grant Robertson. Robertson reported on the GPHIN, an agency once the envy of the world, and how it was restructured and managed nearly out of existence by May 2019. The GPHIN was a little-known group of scientists who acted as an early warning system for global pandemics. Robertson wrote, "Between 2009 and 2019, the team of roughly 12 doctors and epidemiologists, fluent in multiple languages, were a prolific operation. During that span, GPHIN issued 1,587 international alerts about potential outbreak threats around the world, from South America to Siberia."[42] The group had been already established by the time SARS emerged, but Robertson described how it was still mostly an experiment — getting the right mix of machine learning and collaboration internally to spot early warning signs around the globe. The SARS outbreak created a moment for the GPHIN to become so good at what they did that, by the mid-2000s, it was able to detect outbreaks around the world from observing a change in behaviour or a price increase in a certain commodity. The WHO called the GPHIN, "a crucial service — the 'cornerstone' of Canada's pandemic response capability."[43] Its website, last updated on March 15, 2017, before the GPHIN was restructured, described the network like this: "GPHIN has a broad public health scope. Presently, it tracks events such as disease outbreaks, infectious diseases, contaminated food and water, bioterrorism and exposure to chemicals, natural disasters, and issues related to the safety of products, drugs and medical devices and radioactive agents."[44] This early warning system "went silent" in May 2019, as the department was restructured to examine domestic threats — a task it wasn't set up to do.[45]

In the first three months of 2020, as global COVID-19 infections were on the rise, nearly no Canadian news organizations reported on the GPHIN. The first mention of the network appeared in an article written for CBC *News* by Murray Brewster on April 10, 2020. It interviewed intelligence officials who argued that Canada's failure to spot the pandemic was an intelligence failure rather than a public health failure. Brewster reported that the medical intelligence division of the Department of National Defense had warned about the pandemic in January 2020. He quoted Michael Wark, a professor from the University of Ottawa: "We didn't have the early warning we needed, and we didn't have a system to deliver it." Brewster then mentioned the GPHIN: "Wark said that, despite the best intentions, the [GPHIN] is hobbled by other countries' reluctance to share data and the accuracy of open-sourced media reports in a country where an outbreak occurs."[46] Two days later, Jim Bronskill from the *Canadian Press* featured Wark in an article that asked the same questions as Brewster. Wark argued the same thing, but the article made no mention of the existence of GPHIN. Bronskill reported,

> Wark argues careful analysis of intelligence, including satellite imagery from allies, could have revealed signs such as China's military movements, the sudden setup of medical facilities and activities around funeral homes — "a picture of the crisis that clearly the Chinese authorities, in the early days, were not anxious to publicize."[47]

This would have been work that the GPHIN, when it was functioning properly, would have done.

The assumption that Canada needed to gather intelligence is rooted in understanding certain foreign entities to be hostile. While neither report explicitly states this, references to China not sharing information, being dishonest about the pandemic or possibly even trying to cover it up told Canadians that they should be wary and suspicious of China. Approaching global pandemic monitoring through this frame assumed that Canada's allies would be happy to share emerging pandemic information with Canada, and enemies would have to be surveilled for Canada to find out. Pandemics don't exist like that, though. No country is going to be immediately ready to announce to the world that they have a pandemic within their borders. Even Canada was late to announce COVID-19 as a pandemic inside its own borders, and by June 2021 could still not offer an accurate death count from the illness. GPHIN's strength was that it was established to assume that politicians in all countries are reluctant to tell the world they have a problem; they identified pandemics mainly through what they could learn about citizen behaviour rather than relying on official statements. The clash between the intelligence strategy, which views the world through the lens of ally and enemy, and the way the GPHIN collected data — by scanning thousands of data points and using machine learning to interpret them and give public health experts and the WHO an early warning of an emerging pandemic — is ideological. And unfortunately, the former fed racist, anti-Chinese campaigns that have underpinned the proliferation of conspiracy theories questioning the very existence of the pandemic at all.

The history of the GPHIN goes back to 1994, when CNN International reported that there had been an outbreak of pneumonic plague in Surat, India. Information was being reported by a 24-hour news channel before it was officially announced by a local government, and this gave the founders of the GPHIN an idea: they could analyze news from around the world to understand where pandemics might be happening before a government made any official announcement. They set up the GPHIN in 1997 as an experiment to see if a multilingual, early response monitoring team could detect an outbreak through local news reports and other information gathering before a country declared an outbreak. They worked closely with the WHO and eventually became a key partner in the Global Outbreak Alert Response Network. In a 2006 paper, it was estimated that GPHIN provided 40% of the WHO information it collected on early outbreak warnings. The paper concluded:

By internalizing health news within global health surveillance, GPHIN has made it more difficult for nations to conceal information about outbreaks of potential international significance. GPHIN's online early-warning outbreak combined with WHO verification has responded to the challenge of new forms of global health media and enhanced the effectiveness and credibility of international public health to name and act on infectious disease outbreaks.[48]

The GPHIN was supposed to do exactly what Wark said it wasn't set up to be able to do: get around the reluctance countries have to share official information about local outbreaks. And aside from this cameo in a piece about military intelligence, no other Canadian media outlet wrote about the GPHIN in English or in French until Robertson's investigation in July 2020.

The story of death of the GPHIN reads like so many other government programs that were mismanaged into destruction. In 2018, the Liberal government wanted the GPHIN to change how it worked. With such a small budget (just $2.8 million), funding was always threatened, and its international focus, wrote Robertson, left them vulnerable to being cut:

> The problem, say several past and present employees who spoke to *The Globe*, is that GPHIN was populated by scientists and doctors, yet largely misunderstood by government. Senior bureaucrats brought in from other departments believed its resources could be put to better use working on domestic projects, rather than far-flung threats that may never materialize.[49]

Scientists within the GPHIN, who were used to sending out alerts instantly, were stymied by new management that stalled alerts to the point where they eventually stopped coming out altogether. By December 30, 2019, the international aggregate news source ProMed reported that there was a mysterious respiratory virus circulating in China. Public Health Agency of Canada (PHAC) officials told Robertson at the *Globe* that senior PHAC officials had been briefed on the situation as early as December 31. Soon after, GPHIN scientists were following it, though they were more used to being the ones who officially alerted the world. Robertson reported,

> But as GPHIN analysts filed their internal reports, they began to face pushback within the department. They were told to focus

their efforts on official statements, such as data from the Chinese government and the WHO. Other sources of intelligence were just "rumours," one analyst was told. "They wanted the report restricted to only official information."[50]

There was incredible time lost between these notices and convincing PHAC officials to take the pandemic seriously. By February 26, the same day two people at a nursing home in Washington state died from COVID-19, the PHAC still listed Canada's threat level at "low." It wasn't until March 16, days after Trudeau was in isolation and Canadians were dying from community-acquired COVID-19, that the alert was raised to "high." Robertson quoted Wark in his July report, who said, "This is where GPHIN was meant to perform such an important role, as the collector and filter for decision making."[51] Easy to say perhaps in July, though obviously less clear when he was interviewed by CBC and the *Canadian Press* in April.

The impact of GPHIN's demise is impossible to gauge, but it does point to a systemic problem in journalism. Journalists relied far too much on official information and didn't look deep enough to see how Canadian officials were botching Canada's early-warning pandemic systems. Though Brewster's first article wrote about the GPHIN in such a way that it sounded as if it no longer existed, he followed up with a more in-depth piece about GPHIN on April 22, 2020, 12 days later. In this piece, a technology upgrade and funding challenges were blamed for hamstringing the GPHIN, though Robertson's investigation months later would show that that wasn't the whole picture.[52]

The failure of GPHIN after more than a decade of good work should have been the scandal that dominated much of the news that surrounded the federal government's pandemic response. In his feature, Robertson quoted epidemiologist Michael Garner who tried to gauge the impact of this systems failure: "It's not easy to know the consequences of such decisions, but Mr. Garner, the former senior science adviser at Public Health, says he believes Canada's early response to the outbreak — which has been criticized for being slow and disorganized — was a product of the many changes he saw made to the department." And then he quotes Garner directly: "'Not to be overdramatic, but Canadians have died because of this.'"[53] He's right. Canada lost two months of potential preparation time, and public health agencies found themselves scrambling when it was clear that the virus had spread much further than anyone had thought. Would Québec have cancelled March Break? Would better quarantine measures have been in place for people arriving from international travel? There would have been more time for schools, long-term care facilities and workplaces to prepare, and Canadians could have been better informed about the level of risk that was staring them down.

Despite Robertson's damning investigation, it barely made a ripple in Canadian politics. Most political reporters were obsessing over the WE Charity scandal, and aside from Brewster few other media outlets pulled at any of the threads from the *Globe* investigation. The next mention of the GPHIN in media reports came again from the *Globe and Mail* just over two weeks later, when Robertson reported that the agency has started again to issue alerts.[54] On September 8, Minister of Health Patty Hadju announced that there would be an independent review of what happened with the GPHIN, which was widely reported across media outlets. Hadju told CTV *Power Play's* Evan Solomon that not only did she not know about the changes to the GPHIN, no political staff knew either. She said the decision was purely administrative within the PHAC.[55] In November 2020, Hadju ordered a review into what happened with GPHIN. The review committee issued an interim report on February 26, 2021 that provided an overview of the history of the GPHIN, and confirmed much of what Robertson's investigation had found.[56] The committee's final report was released in July 2021, and made 36 recommendations for how to improve how GPHIN operates.[57]

We will never know the impact that a functioning GPHIN may have had on Canada's COVID-19 response, but the lack of attention this network received in the media was a good example of the danger posed by shrinking newsrooms and coverage driven by governments' official updates. Why did the GPHIN, a group whose job it was to monitor global pandemics, get so little attention from journalists during a pandemic? American news site *The Hill* featured the GPHIN in an article about how social media and other unofficial reports have become key to identifying emerging global health trends. The short piece was published on February 6, 2020, and said,

> Decades after it was created, GPHIN has become an important tool for global public health officials to monitor and track diseases quickly —sometimes before they are officially acknowledged. Some countries are reluctant to report epidemics in the earliest phases, mindful not to create a panic and also worried about possible economic impact.[58]

In doing a survey of innovative ways to track pandemics that didn't rely on official government sources, *The Hill* found the GPHIN and introduced other emerging tools that people were using. Clearly, there were at least a few journalists around the world who had their eyes on the GPHIN. But even if this little-known group eluded most Canadian journalists, Robertson's investigation should have triggered more analyses about what happened internally — but it didn't. It wasn't until politicians started talking about investigating what happened at the GPHIN that other journalists started writing about it and even then, barely. Newsrooms oriented toward covering every word that health authorities issued, or every press conference delivered by a politician, combined with fewer overall resources to report the news and folks working under stressful and bizarre conditions perhaps explain why the GPHIN wasn't investigated until July 2020. Why no other news agency picked up on the threads of Robertson's investigation, however, is much harder to explain.

During the early days of the pandemic, journalists regularly asked politicians and public health officials questions no one could answer: How long will this last? Would schools be open before June? Will we get to celebrate Ramadan with others? Will my wedding in August still be on? Public health officials answered honestly: We can't know. Politicians found more creative ways to respond, lest being honest hurt their political popularity. There were so many unknowns, and journalists were under a lot of stress to tell the story right. But media made mistakes: playing down the threat to give Canadians the false feeling that the virus was on the other side of the world; individualizing the consequences of the virus and therefore allowing the solutions to also be individualized; adhering too closely to officials who passed off COVID-19 as not being too bad for a majority of people; and not looking at what systems Canada had in place that should have given us, and the world, an early-warning alarm about the pandemic. In early 2020, journalists focused on what the Chinese government was or wasn't hiding, while never examining Canadian politicians with the same scrutiny. They kept articles narrowly focused on the idea of personal threat rather than looking more broadly at systems, clusters, workplaces and congregate settings. This narrative would collapse in the weeks and months ahead, when thousands of Canadians died in their residential care facilities thanks to a combination of systemic failures, inadequate planning and ableism. The narrative had, up until then, given able-bodied Canadians a pass to not take the threat as seriously as they should have.

Of course, it wasn't just that politicians didn't act quickly enough. They also did very little to insist that the most vulnerable locations within Canadian society were ready to withstand a pandemic. This was no more obvious, or deadly, than in residential care facilities. The lack of attention, planning and political measures intended to stop COVID-19 from spreading would lead to a death count beyond the imagination of most Canadians. Facilities already known to treat Canada's most vulnerable people — individuals who need regular care to meet their basic needs — would become locations of incredible callousness.

April 2020
DISASTER IN RESIDENTIAL CARE

Cases: 9,729
Deaths: 111[1]

In March 2020, with media attention firmly locked on China, journalists missed what the biggest story was going to be in April: residential care was so unprepared for a pandemic that thousands of residents would be sitting ducks, waiting for the virus to attack them in their beds. And politicians did nearly nothing to equip these facilities to weather the storm. Residential care, especially long-term care, was in such a precarious state of neglect before the pandemic hit that once it did, there was little staff could do to stop it. In its wake, hundreds of thousands of individuals would become sick, tens of thousands would die and residential care would become the most significant driver of COVID-19 within communities before mass vaccination started.

COVID-19 caused the most damage inside the walls of the profit-driven system of residential care. In the first wave, the overwhelming majority of people who Canada marked as official COVID-19 victims lived in residential care. Facilities became COVID-19 hubs in their communities and through staff and close family, it was exported to other parts of society. The system was not ready for a pandemic. It had grown for years outside of the public healthcare system into a complex web of private and public operators, many extracting profits from their workers' low wages and residents' care. Despite a summer lull in 2020 where conditions could have been rapidly improved, residential care was barely more prepared for fall 2020 than it had been during the spring. Only a mass vaccination campaign that started in 2021 saved the sector from a third wave. These outbreaks were not a surprise, though. They were intensified by years of poor residential conditions that were optimal for rapid transmission. After having criticized China for most of February and March for withholding information, information related to residential care outbreaks was hard to come by. It took investigative reporting and lots of work from academics to paint an image of just how bad these outbreaks were, the image of which wouldn't truly emerge until months after they were finally brought under control.

Residential care was an unmitigated disaster that unfolded before the public's eyes. Politicians made no serious interventions. In fact, their decisions often made things even worse. And the story was repeated over and over again: by the end of June 2021, there had been at least 1715 facilities where an average of ten people died in each. There was heaps of blame to shovel on managers, owners and politicians alike, and so of all the issues that the pandemic raised, none were spun as much as stories about residential care. The spin allowed politicians to sidestep blame, throw their hands in the air and say they simply couldn't do anything more, and journalists far too often followed politicians' leads and didn't dig into the underlying issues: this exploitative system that was set up to maximize profits at the expense of keeping its residents alive.

HOSPITALS VERSUS LONG-TERM CARE

Even though April 2020 would be a disaster for residents living in long-term care, long-term care was barely on the radar at all until deaths started to happen. Instead of focusing on long-term care, journalists instead reported about hospitals and their capacities to administer care if Canada had to deal with a full-blown pandemic. Flu-related hospitalizations, overcapacity, overworked staff and equipment counts all became part of regular briefings or reports about the hospital system. Hospitals were understood to be the most important node in the medical system: spaces needed to be cleared and people needed to avoid emergency rooms if they could, to be able to manage a wave of COVID-19 sick patients. In the *Ottawa Citizen*, emergency physician James Simpson argued on February 13, 2020, that Ontario's hospitals were not ready to withstand an incoming wave of patients needing care, considering how over capacity normal operations already were. He argued that much more needed to be done to avoid overwhelming the system and referenced the hospital that Chinese workers built in just ten days to help manage healthcare strain. Then, he made the important connection between hospital overcrowding and long-term care:

> This issue is entirely due to the lack of long-term beds available. During the time we had so many beds taken up in our emergency

department, we had 30 patients (out of 85 total beds) admitted to hospital who are designated "ALC" (alternative level of care) — patients who have no acute medical issues but cannot be discharged home safely and are awaiting placement in nursing homes or similar facilities. Because of this, we are over-capacity.

Furthermore, in the event of an outbreak of coronavirus, these "ALC" patients are sitting ducks. They often have significant health concerns and would be highly vulnerable to a serious viral illness. It does not make sense to keep these vulnerable patients in hospital and surrounded by other sick, contagious people.[2]

Simpson's warning about hospitals echoed the same concerns that other doctors and politicians had raised throughout February 2020. But what set his article apart from all other journalism was a rare comment on long-term care in the earliest days of the pandemic. Space was key: it needed to be rapidly built for alternate level of care patients. It wasn't as if editors were unaware of the danger posed by the conditions within long-term care. Just three days earlier in the same newspaper, Blair Crawford wrote about Maia Giller, a woman who was locked out of Hillel Lodge long-term care to wait for half an hour on the sidewalk after being sent back from the hospital at 4:00 a.m. She died ten days later.[3] If this was life in long-term care when things were normal, of course it would be a disaster during a pandemic, but journalists didn't make this connection until it was made for them by the death toll in long-term care.

On February 28, 2020, Canada's first in-depth COVID-19 feature appeared in Maclean's that looked at how far COVID-19 had spread around the world and how ready Canada was to manage the forthcoming pandemic. Writers Aaron Hutchins and Marie-Danielle Smith wrote about how, upon confirming Ontario's first positive COVID-19 case, public health, politicians and representatives from Sunnybrook Hospital called a press conference on January 25, 2020. China was not forthcoming about the virus, so went the popular narrative, and thus Hutchins and Smith argued this press conference was proof Canada was in good shape for what may come: "This type of transparency and communication from various health organizations has helped make Canada the second-least vulnerable nation in the world to outbreaks."[4] Aside from the fact that this would become painfully not true, press conferences became one of the key ways in which politicians flooded journalists with information, making it very hard to understand what was truly important to be reported, and what was noise.

Politicians all across Canada focused on clearing space in hospitals as a pandemic mitigation strategy. Nova Scotia's Chief Medical Officer of Health Robert Strang told reporters on February 27 that Nova Scotians would be hit particularly hard by a potential pandemic because they're older, on average. He said older patients would result in higher risk of needing care in a hospital, and therefore, they needed to relieve the pressure on emergency rooms already stretched from the annual flu season, but then didn't mention what protocols would be put in place to protect residents of long-term care.[5] Writing in the *National Post* on March 4, professors P.G. Forest and Jason Sutherland argued that patients who were in hospital beds and who could be moved out of a hospital needed to be sent home or, if home wasn't possible, into long-term care. They argued that moving these patients into long-term care "presents challenges for most provinces" due to long waitlists.[6] Forest and Sutherland's argument would underpin how many politicians viewed the incoming crisis: liberate hospitals at all costs, under the mistaken assumption that patients would even make it long enough to enter into a hospital room. Instead, the pandemic collided with a long-term care system that was cut to the bone.

Long-term care was barely on the radar by February 28, 2020: politicians were not talking about long-term care and journalists were not pressing them on it. But the who had already identified long-term care, as well as prisons and hospitals, as important nodes of transmission. In the final joint who-China report published on February 24, 2020, it said, "The close proximity and contact among people in these settings and the potential for environmental contamination are important factors, which could amplify transmission."[7] It wasn't until nine days later on March 4 that some Canadian journalists first wrote about long-term care. Both cbc *News* and *Global News* featured Rhonda Collins, a doctor with Revera, a private, for-profit chain owned by the federal government's pension board. Both articles quoted Collins saying Revera was preparing by assuring their facilities had "appropriate staff." Both articles highlighted handwashing, getting a flu shot and staying home if you felt sick as the most important steps that could be taken,[8] and neither examined any of the problems that plagued long-term care in Canada that would lead to thousands of people dead. Nor did the articles look deeply at government orders, and how they assisted these facilities to keep safe.[9] At least 867 people died in 60 Revera facilities from March 2020 until June 2021.[10]

The plan to liberate hospitals to be able to care for COVID-19 patients was in direct opposition to the reality that the pinch point in hospitals was actually long-term care itself. The incongruence between these two systems posed an enormous problem, and rather than reaching toward solutions that would have enabled coordination between the two, or as Simpson suggested, actually building more locations for long-term care facilities, the dominant plan across many provinces was to liberate hospital spaces. In Québec, this meant residents would only be transferred to hospital in extreme cases. The Ministère de la Santé et des Services sociaux issued a directive on April 2 that ordered COVID-19-postive patients living in long-term care to stay put, even if their conditions deteriorated. *Radio-Canada* reported that the logic behind this was to confine COVID-19 to the residence itself, rather than potentially spread it to a hospital setting.[11] There was also an order that refused to allow patients to be transferred from hospital into long-term care, creating another pressure point within the system. Infectious disease specialist from the McGill University Health Network Donald Vinh told the *Globe and Mail* that Québec's long-term care facilities, Les centres d'hébergement de soins de longue durée (CHSLD) weren't set up with the necessary equipment to care for people sick with COVID-19; many were not equipped to deliver oxygen, intravenous fluids or pain medication.[12] This ended up being a death sentence, as overworked nurses and orderlies were saddled with the incredible task of managing the pandemic's real Ground Zero in underfunded, understaffed facilities, many that were not physically set up to allow for adequate infection controls. One of the worst hit long-term care residences in Canada was the CHSLD de Sainte-Dorothée. When emergency staff were sent into the residence to help with the outbreak in March and April 2020, nurses told CBC *Montreal* that they weren't given training or appropriate personal protective equipment.[13] It got so bad that one family had to call 9-1-1 to have an ambulance come for a loved one who needed oxygen. The facility was under orders to refuse to transfer residents to hospital. When residents were in respiratory distress, they would be given morphine to manage pain, as there wasn't enough oxygen to actually treat them.[14] In his book called *Le printemps le plus long*, journalist Alex Castonguay quoted Richard Massé, a Québec senior public health adviser who said, "We underestimated potential transmission among elderly people."[15]

Compared to long-term care, hospitals controlled COVID-19 infections relatively well. But exactly how many people were infected with COVID-19 after they had been admitted to hospital was not reported publicly until August 2021 when I broke the news in the *Washington Post*. According to information gathered by the Canadian Institutes for Health Information (CIHI), 3088 Canadians were infected with COVID-19 after they had been admitted to the hospital in fiscal year 2020–2021, and there were 897 deaths, excluding Québec. When Québec is added to the total, it rises to 1640. Nearly no jurisdictions regularly reported these data, and journalists outside of Québec rarely wrote about it.[16]

Ontario's first official directive to long-term care facilities on March 9, 2020, contained no meaningful measures to stop the spread of COVID-19. The directives reminded operators to monitor residents, ask staff to monitor their symptoms and report COVID-19 cases to the local health unit. There was nothing about staffing, even though the provincial government had already established a special panel on long-term care staffing knowing it was at a crisis level.[17] By November, Nathan Stall, a physician who worked at Mount Sinai hospital in Toronto, was pleading at a press conference to not forget long-term care: "There are many people speaking specifically about the state of our health-care system as it pertains to ICU beds and hospital capacity but it's really, really critical to keep the focus as well on long-term care," he said. Indeed, even by month eight of the pandemic, it was hard to get people to focus on improving the system most vulnerable to COVID-19 spread.[18]

Why was it so difficult? Was it because hospitals hold an elevated place in society and long-term care is easy to ignore? Was it because long-term care was deeply decentralized, with lots of public and private actors involved with different and often competing interests? As mass deaths started to be reported at places like the CHSLD Hérron in Dorval, Lynn Valley Care Centre in North Vancouver, CHSLD de Sainte-Dorothée in Laval, Orchard Villa in Pickering and Pinecrest in Bobcaygeon, it was too late. By then, COVID-19 had spread through hundreds of facilities, taking advantage of broken systems that politicians had never bothered to try and fix, and journalists rarely pressed for answers.

MASS DEATHS IN LONG-TERM CARE

Residential care in Canada has been in crisis for decades and the subset of residential care called long-term care was the deadliest residential system in Canada. Long-term care (LTC) is regulated by various government ministries, whether ministries specifically dedicated to long-term care, or ministries of health. Beds, hours of care, funding and staffing are all overseen by the provinces. Outside of LTC are other kinds of residential care facilities: retirement residences, convalescent homes, residences for disabled individuals, shelters, group homes, prisons and drop-in centres. During the pandemic, residential care of all kinds were hit particularly hard, as people lived within these facilities, making them locations where COVID-19 could more easily spread than a location where individuals spent less time. LTC was particularly deadly because of the mix of for-profit providers, complex health needs of residents, facilities that were not set up to meet these needs and the age and level of disability of the residents compared to other kinds of residential care. The LTC system grew mostly outside of the Canada Health Act (CHA) — the piece of legislation that oversees public healthcare in Canada — which had to expand in scope to keep pace with Canada's rapidly expanding elderly population with increasingly complex health needs. Because Canada's constitution places most health authority in provincial hands, long-term care has mostly been controlled by the provinces, though it is impacted by federal social spending. In his book *Neglected No More*, André Picard wrote about when the CHA was passed in 1984, it covered procedures considered "medically necessary," or procedures covered by provincial public health services.[19] The CHA was intended to harmonize public healthcare, despite it being mostly a provincial responsibility. Long-term care, like so many other medically necessary but excluded services like dental or vision care, fell outside the CHA. Even though long-term care became more needed as life expectancies grew longer, it never became a priority for governments. Community researcher Madeline Ritts argued, "The LTC crisis is a result of decades of welfare-state retrenchment and the general weakness of Canada's pension-plan model," and pointed directly to Paul Martin's 1995 federal budget, where billions of dollars were pulled from Canada's social services.[20] The Martin-Chrétien budget overhauled Canada's social spending and set in motion privatization in every aspect of social services spending where money could be made. Because of the weakness of the CHA to protect healthcare, services that were considered peripheral to healthcare, long-term care especially, were opened up to private operators, who could profit off everything from artificially low wages to the land and buildings themselves through real estate holdings. When the federal government made its first major funding announcement to help the provinces through the pandemic on March 11, there was still no mention of long-term care, instead promising $500 million for "critical healthcare system needs." With long-term care mostly outside the public healthcare system, the lack of attention, political action and coordination over this sector contributed to the lack of preparedness.[21]

Many of these issues came to national attention when serial killer Elizabeth Wettlaufer admitted to murdering seven people while working at Caressant Care in Woodstock and at Meadow Park in London between 2007 and 2016 and poisoning at least six others.[22] Wettlaufer was able to murder because oversight was lax, and her crimes triggered a public inquiry into long-term care in Ontario. On July 31, 2019, an inquiry made 91 recommendations for how to improve Ontario's system of long-term care. In the report's dedication, commissioner Eileen E. Gillese addressed the families of the victims saying, "Your pain, loss, and grief are not in vain. They serve as the catalyst for real and lasting improvements to the care and safety of all those in Ontario's long-term care system."[23] Just before the pandemic, the Ontario government constituted a long-term staffing panel to review staffing and guide the implementation of some of the Wettlaufer inquiry recommendations. The committee didn't include any employee representative groups. Employees, who both have first-hand experience with the problems that plague long-term care facilities, and who are key to ensuring that protocols are implemented and followed, did not have a formal voice at a review specifically intended to oversee staffing. But the staffing review did include James Schlegel, CEO of Schlegel Villages, a large network of long-term care and retirement residences in Ontario. His company had donated $120,624 to all political parties: $2,200 to the Ontario NDP, $46,681 to the Liberals and a whopping $71,743 to the Progressive Conservatives. Journalist Zaid Noorsomer found that the Schlegel family was the largest single donor to Christine Elliott, Ontario's Health Minister during the pandemic.[24] At least 235 people died in 17 Schlegel-owned residences from March 2020 until June 2021.[25]

By 2020, 89% of Canadian long-term care was institutionalized; only 11% occurred in the home. And of that 89%, the overwhelming majority of it was within long-term care facilities — just 7% was hospital care.[26] Despite the promise written by Gillese, deaths as a result of negligence or even murder were absolutely in vain; there have always been lessons, but no politician has had the political courage, or perhaps political independence from for-profit long-term care companies, to actually rein them in. Researchers and advocates have been calling for action on these facilities for years, pointing to the fact that for-profit long-term care is deadlier than not-for-profit care. For-profit companies are often contracted and subcontracted to other companies to keep their employee costs as low as possible — diluting the quality of care possible for residents and also creating nightmarish working conditions for employees.[27] In his testimony to Ontario's Long-Term Care Commission in September 2020, elder care expert Samir Sinha argued that the staffing conditions were a key weakness of Ontario's system, leading to a situation where part-time work was rampant, which forced workers to work in multiple long-term care facilities to cobble together a living, something that was identified early on as being a key way that COVID-19 spread.[28] It wasn't until April 23 2020, that Ontario stopped workers from being able to work in multiple homes — almost a month after British Columbia made the same decision.[29] There, about a quarter of workers in long-term care worked in more than one workplace.[30] Staffing was a critical component for Saskatchewan's deadly outbreaks too. Many Saskatchewan facilities had "non-replacement" policies, which meant that if a staff person took time off, no one would replace them. This allowed facilities to save costs on overtime, as Barbara Cape told the *Regina Leader-Post*. Her union, SEIU-Healthcare, represents many workers in Saskatchewan long-term care facilities. Mont St. Joseph Home, Santa Maria and Extendicare Parkside, locations of mass outbreaks causing dozens of deaths, were short staffed during each of their outbreaks.[31] In May 2020, the federal government flowed $3 billion to the provinces specifically to boost salaries for low-wage essential workers.[32] As a result, there was a patchwork of premiums promised by provincial governments to pay low-paid essential workers more, but who was eligible and by how much varied significantly. The timelines also differed; where Québec, Ontario and B.C. had premiums in place by summer 2020, it took Alberta until February 2021 before their plan was revealed, and the one-time sum was made available to workers far beyond long-term care.[33]

Long-term care was set up to be a disaster. There was no shortage of horror stories from before the pandemic; when COVID-19 hit, not only were these facilities not ready, but they were also incapable of resisting infection. The questions were asked over and over: Who is to blame? How did this happen? How can we fix this? While the answers ranged from basic fixes to increasing worker salaries to massive systemic changes like banning for-profit care, by the time the second wave had come and gone, the proof was damning: politicians did far too little and too many residences were not supported to resist the virus. And so, despite all the warnings during summer 2020, long-term care found itself in fall 2020 and winter 2021 in much the same spot as it had been in March 2020.

ROBERTA PLACE

Even though COVID-19 spread within residential care far worse in 2020 than in 2021, 2021 started off marked by incredibly high death counts at several Ontario facilities. One of these facilities was Roberta Place, a long-term care facility in Barrie Ontario. The for-profit facility owned by Jarlette Health Services was the site of a fast-spreading COVID-19 infection in that became synonymous with the rise in COVID-19 variants of concern. From the first mention on Twitter by Mike Arsalides from CTV News on January 11, 2021, to the end of January, 72 people at Roberta Place died. At the moment of Arsalides' tweet, the Roberta Place outbreak was already Barrie's largest outbreak, with 27 of 137 residents sick with the illness. By January 12, that number had risen to two staff people and 40 residents, people whose tests had been completed days earlier.

The Roberta Place outbreak became known as Canada's first driven by the COVID-19 alpha strain. The Simcoe-Muskoka District Health Unit associate medical officer told journalists the virus was introduced by a single staff person who had close contact with someone who had travelled outside of Canada. On January 24, the health unit confirmed six people at Roberta Place had the alpha variant. By this time, 40 residents had already died and nearly every resident had caught COVID-19.

But it wasn't exactly true that cases went from zero to dozens as fast as media had reported, repeating lines from local health officials. The outbreak was declared on January 8 and by January 12, it had risen to 42. Fast, to be sure, but not unseen elsewhere, especially considering infections across Ontario were bounding thanks to the holiday season that had ended a week earlier. But the timelines were murky: two weeks later, this timeline was sped up. CP24's Chris Herhalt published an article on January 21 called, "'This has to be the variant' Barrie, Ont. long-term care home saw 55 COVID-19 cases in 2 days."[34] The two days are not explicitly identified in the article, though CBC reported the same thing, attributing the information to the local public health unit and saying 55 cases appeared "within 48 hours of the first COVID-19 case being identified."[35] The same public health unit reported however that there were 27 cases on January

11, three days after the outbreak was declared on January 8. Regardless of the exact numbers, the notion that the outbreak was so bad solely because of the alpha variant was firmly in place.[36] Every media mention of Roberta Place thereafter referenced this new coronavirus strain, often before or in place of what kind of conditions existed within the facility.

In early 2021, variants of concern were emerging around the world, and news about local variant spread put a new spin on the tired, stale story of long-term care outbreaks. By January 21, 2021, more than 13,600 people had died in residential facilities in Canada and the usual approach that media took to cover these disasters had long grown old. Surely, governments and public health units had managed to force private long-term care facility operators to tighten their practices? By 2021, surely the horrors of April 2020 were firmly in the past? But at the same time as the Roberta Place outbreak, another colossal failure would respond to these *surelys* sure enough: no, things have not improved in long-term care. Ontario had learned nothing.

Not too far from Barrie, a Scarborough long-term care facility called Tendercare was Ontario's worst outbreak site. Eighty-one residents from the 254-bed facility died in just a few weeks, at around the same time as the Roberta Place outbreak. The Tendercare outbreak was reported on through the perspective of worried family members who decried unsafe conditions, rather than through a lens that focused closely on COVID-19 variants. They held protests and media events to tell Canadians about the conditions of the facility. Tendercare had been the subject of many inspections, including six in 2019 alone: three complaint-driven inspections and three critical incident-related inspections.[37] In contrast, the reporting about Roberta Place immediately pivoted to the variant narrative, even when an article did reference the awful living conditions. One CBC *News* story featured the drummer from the band Our Lady Peace, Jeremy Taggart, whose mother Beryl lived at Roberta Place. While her COVID-19 infection did not result in critical care, he was concerned that the conditions of the place were making things worse: "Clearly, they're overwhelmed ... They've needed help for two weeks and it's a disaster and here I am, just kind of sitting and waiting." The article didn't explore this further and instead went right back to reporting about the variant strain.[38]

While journalists stayed squarely on new coronavirus variants in reporting about Roberta Place, the Ministry of Long-term Care released a report that examined the conditions of the facility, indicating that

Jarlette Health Services had not taken very basic COVID-19 mitigation measures. It was released on January 18 and found that residents who had COVID-19 were kept in the same room as residents without COVID-19, and sometimes these residents came into close contact. The facility did not employ safety precautions the moment a resident received a positive COVID-19 diagnosis, and residents who were supposed to be isolating in their rooms were moved throughout the facility. The *Barrie Advance* and other news outlets reported the details of what the inspector found on January 25.[39] And still, two days later, Canada's national political affairs radio show *The Current* did a radio segment that featured Roberta Place and the Simcoe-Muskoka District Health Unit Medical Officer Charles Gardner — but not once did either the doctor or host Matt Galloway mention the conditions of the residence. The segment, after all, was about the variants of concern.[40]

With the lion's share of death in Canada occurring within these facilities, residential care was a monster issue for journalists to write about and for politicians to dance around. The way in which infections were framed mattered: Roberta Place became about the variants due to consistent messaging from their local public health unit, even when it was clear there were significant issues that exacerbated the spread of the virus. But reporting remained thin and the solutions elusive, thanks to journalists who didn't dig deeper into what was causing these horror stories, and thanks to politicians who had no political desire to change anything. This went way beyond the story of a single location in a small Ontario city. Journalists struggled to cut through a confusing picture of failure, shifting blame and difficult answers for a system that had been built to be perpetually in crisis at the best of times. And politicians and facility owners avoided taking any responsibility.

SYSTEMS FAILURES

One of the dominant narratives during the first wave was that long-term care was caught off guard. There were staff shortages, diminished supplies that couldn't be replenished quickly because of a global run on personal protective equipment, and there was little that could be done to change the physical infrastructure of residences quickly. But the first wave was a warning. It should have been seen as such by officials in Manitoba, for example, whose first wave killed just three residents in long-term care but then infections exploded in the second wave, with 465 people killed by the time the second wave started to diminish in mid-February 2021. The warning was never heeded. Politicians avoided responsibility and didn't implement any major changes, and what was all-too predictable came to pass: the second wave was more deadly than the first and the only thing that stopped mass deaths during many provinces' third waves were mass vaccination campaigns.[41] There were several key areas that should have been the subject of intense scrutiny for journalists: staffing issues, physical space, resident safety, and much more but they didn't, likely because they were not a priority for politicians either.

Staffing was key. Long-term care facilities needed to have staffing significantly reinforced: more workers should have been promoted to full time rather than having to work at several facilities to make ends meet, and more staff should have been hired into these facilities quickly. And some of the fixes were easy, hinging only on the desire of a government to spend money. For example, elder care expert Samir Sinha argued that funding envelopes to pay nurses were very different if those nurses worked inside long-term care or if they worked in a hospital, even if their functions were more or less the same.[42] There could have been so many things done early on to save lives: ending the use of temporary agencies, forcing companies to be transparent about their COVID-19 PPE planning, cohorting COVID-19 patients, or even bringing all long-term care facilities under the management of local public health units or hospitals directly, rather than only when outbreaks became so bad that local staff couldn't manage them. The biggest advance within staffing in long-term care between the first two waves in Canada was in Québec, where the province fast-tracked training that placed more than 7000 new orderlies into the system by September 2020.[43] Ontario, instead, relied more on staffing agencies to fill the gap and some workers were even told to bring their own personal protective equipment.[44]

Ontario's Long-Term Care Commission heard testimony from September 3, 2020, to April 1, 2021, that painted a picture of a system that had long been in crisis, with zero political desire strong enough to intervene. Infectious disease specialist Allison McGeer told the commission that government officials rejected proposals made after the first wave that would have better protected residents because they would cost too much. Some of the proposals included reducing the number of people who shared rooms, or bringing hospitals closer to residential facilities to help manage the second wave. Ontario Minister of Long-Term Care

Merrilee Fullerton rejected McGreer's assertion and told the *Canadian Press* that "no expense was spared."[45] However, the proof of neglect was pretty clear: during the second wave, at Roberta Place in Barrie, residents did not have private rooms and COVID-19 infection protocols were still lax. Ontario's Long-Term Care Commission heard that Ontario had no plan to deal with an outbreak as serious as COVID-19, and Chief Medical Officer of Health David Williams told the Long-Term Care Commission he was never asked to update what had been written in the wake of the SARS pandemic. Williams didn't cooperate with the commission either, dumping 217,000 pages of documents on commissioners just one week before his testimony.[46]

In most provinces, death swept through long-term care facilities thanks to similarly lax protocols. Nova Scotia was one exception, where in the first wave 53 residents died at Northwood in Halifax, while no one died in residential care during the second wave. From the start of the pandemic until February 15, 2021, COVID-19 killed 32% of all residents in Québec long-term care. In B.C., it was 29%, Manitoba was 28% and Ontario was 25%. Only P.E.I. and Newfoundland and Labrador had no deaths in long-term care.[47] By then, mass vaccinations were underway across Canada in long-term care, and mass deaths within long-term care stopped abruptly soon after.

While staffing played a critical role in the quality delivery of care, so too did architecture. The layout of residential facilities and the prevalence of room sharing received very little attention despite being a reasonable line for journalists to follow considering close and prolonged contact was clearly a contributor to COVID-19 spread. On May 26, 2020, architect Ron Rayside wrote in *Le Devoir* that the layout of most of Québec's public long-term care facilities was terrible for a pandemic: a "very large proportion" of residents lived in settings where they shared rooms and bathrooms. "Residents of CHSLDs don't occupy a room; they occupy a bed," he wrote. He argued Québec needed to develop a ten-year plan to eliminate shared spaces in older rooms and said newer locations are already being built to provide residences private spaces, which would reduce infections in general and restore dignity and privacy to the resident.[48] In his testimony to Ontario's Long-Term Care Commission, Sinha identified problems with Ontario's infrastructure too. He told the committee that after the SARS pandemic, many countries "ensure their homes only offer single-room accommodation."[49] *CBC News Nova Scotia* looked at the role private rooms played in slowing the spread of COVID-19, and the evidence was compelling that while it might not have been the sole factor, infection control was definitely made easier when residents had their own rooms. They compared the experiences of Magnolia Continuing Care, a long-term care facility that was the site of Nova Scotia's first positive case, with Northwood, where the province's highest death count was concentrated. The 70-room Magnolia was built in 2011 and only had private rooms. Management at the Magnolia decided that everyone should wear masks two weeks before the province mandated that masks be worn. The outbreak there didn't go further than five individuals. Compare that to Northwood, a large, three-tower facility with 485 residents where the majority of beds were in shared rooms.[50] At Extendicare Parkside in Regina, the site of Saskatchewan's worst outbreak, resident rooms held up to four beds. The Saskatchewan Health Authority linked the outbreak and 41 deaths to so many residents sharing a single room. In Saskatchewan, only five residences are operated for profit, which represents 4% of all facilities. All were operated by Extendicare.[51]

The same trend was found by CBC *Marketplace* at the end of Ontario's first wave. They found a third of all beds in the province were in 1970s-era, regulated four-person shared rooms and shared dining locations. Deaths among residents within these rooms accounted for 57% of deaths in the first wave in Ontario. The majority of these beds were located in for-profit facilities, where governments have allowed these residences to continue operating as they are even in the wake of updated regulations in 1998. The changes in 1998 still allowed for two-person rooms, however. Much of the criticism that came from advocates, family members and journalists laid the blame for deaths in long-term care at those residences organized as for profit, but Extendicare blamed "the age of the home" more. Revera identified that shared bathrooms were the main predictor for outbreak outcomes, but still blamed outbreaks on community spread rather than take responsibility for spread within the facilities.[52]

Marketplace's analysis left open many questions, like how many of the newer two-person rooms were in outbreak? Just as James Simpson argued in February 2020 in the *Ottawa Citizen*, where were the new long-term care spaces? Why weren't more hotels commandeered to house people? Why didn't the physical architecture become part of the regular reporting on long-term care? When the Roberta Place outbreak took over the national airwaves, why was the focus on COVID-19 variants and not the fact that at month ten of the pandemic, COVID-19–positive patients were being housed in the same room as people without COVID-19, or that the most basic expected protocols were not being met? Long-term care was a massive problem that required many different solutions. And unfortunately, rather than press politicians and decisionmakers for these solutions, and rather than incorporating this critique into the daily grind of covering Canada's worst health crisis in 100 years, the issues that could have protected long-term care were relegated to one-off investigations. Mass outbreaks within long-term care were only stopped by vaccination campaigns, rather than mitigating measures that were widely acknowledged as being critical to slowing the spread of COVID-19 within these facilities.

There is a lot to say about long-term care and how COVID-19 wreaked havoc upon it. This pandemic will be studied and analyzed for decades to come, while people debate the best ways to fix the problems that plague Canada's systems of residential care. But these problems didn't inform coverage in the way they should have. It wasn't immediately obvious to many journalists why one long-term care facility would be hit harder than another, and in the confusion, total shock took up a lot of space that otherwise could have been dedicated to analysis. With the overwhelming number of journalists writing about COVID-19 being white, and the overwhelming number of healthcare workers hit hardest by COVID-19 being not white, it was less likely that journalists had a personal connection to workers at these facilities to centre the individuals hurt most in their stories. Politicians benefited from a population that is used to hearing about horrors in long-term care, and from the residential care system's complex regulatory regime, ownership structures and jurisdictional wrangling. Long-term care was marginal. It didn't impact everyone the way the hospital system did. It didn't need to be a core story until it was the core story due to death rates, even though the connection between long-term care hospital beds and external residences played a big role in how hospitals would manage the pandemic, and even though COVID-19 circulation within these facilities had a big impact on broader community spread. In the confusion, journalists rarely painted a clear image about what was happening in long-term care, instead asking the same questions over and over, reporting the same details again and again, priming their audience to understand facilities as unfortunate locations that simply could have not been saved.

COVERING DISASTER

Like so many other issues during the pandemic, residential care was reported in two distinct ways. The first was through daily reporting, where residential care facilities were not necessarily the main subject, but an outbreak or death counts were included in articles that told the day's news of the pandemic. Determining whether or not someone died in long-term care became a puzzle, where one piece might be gleaned from a media report, one piece might come from a facility website itself, and one from the family. In Québec, where the Ministère de la Santé et des Services sociaux gave daily reports about deaths in CHSLDs and retirement facilities, most media only reported on these outbreaks if they were newsworthy, like if there was a sharp increase somewhere, or if an outbreak was related to a particular event. *Global News Alberta*, usually concluded their daily COVID-19 articles with a list of individuals by age who had died, whether or not they had any comorbidities and if their death was related to an outbreak location. *Global News Alberta* was the only provincial media in Alberta that did this consistently. The *Calgary Herald* would mention how many people died in Calgary, and the *Edmonton Journal* would sometimes mention province-wide death counts but as 2021 advanced, this became less and less frequent. In Ontario, smaller news sites like the Torstar-owned news organizations often ran daily case counts lifted directly from local public health unit information, with little more information than what the unit had on its own website. Media outlets in Ottawa routinely did not mention if a death was related to a residential care facility, even if it had been posted to the Ottawa Public Health website. Reports were hard to find and disjointed, making it very difficult for a casual observer to stay on top of them. There was no national media organization that routinely reported residential care updates in the same place — they were all pushed out through local media, making it impossible for readers to understand the full scope of an outbreak — whether it related to a community more broadly or to province-wide or national facility chains — through daily reporting alone. With daily updates dominating daily reporting, it was easy to lose the narrative about what was happening in long-term care, who was responsible and what could be done to improve the situation.

It was this that made in-depth features that tried to explain why long-term care was the disaster that it became so important. This second kind of reporting by its very nature was rarer than the daily reports. It was critical and helped explain a lot of what seemed impossible to comprehend, especially as death counts went through the roof. But it was the former type of reporting that had the bigger impact of isolating and narrowing the scope of analysis, making it difficult to really understand the role that long-term care played in spreading COVID-19, not just to the residents and staff within a location, but to the broader community. In-depth features were not always accessible. They were often locked behind pay-walls, or they were really long, giving readers a lot of information which they would then have to contextualize. Reporting should have evolved throughout 2020 to streamline the overwhelming amount of data, even as it updated daily while telling stories about living through the pandemic from the perspectives of residents, workers, residents' families and the communities that surrounded the facilities. But in absence of this, there was little that bridged the divide between daily, data-based updates and large, deep features, and rarer still, were articles that purposefully sought to seek accountability.

By November 2020, residential care had been rhetorically transformed into a sector that was separate from general society. Ontario's Minister of Health Christine Elliott announced on November 13 that Ontario would mitigate outbreaks within long-term care by fully isolating them from the communities in which they were located. She promised to make an "iron ring" around long-term care to try and slow transmission. The day of her announcement, there were 93 residences in outbreak with 51 cases reported in them.[53] Elliott's iron ring was supposed to flow resources to residences to keep this from intensifying and yet, outbreaks would balloon in the coming weeks. Even after many residents had been vaccinated, by March 12, 2021, there were still 80 long-term care facilities with outbreaks and 183 cases reported in them, and that had dropped significantly from the holiday season. Elliott's iron ring promise was a failure, but it was always going to be a failure because it was impossible to close long-term care off from general society such that COVID-19 would have just stayed out (or stayed in). But it was this logic that confined residents to rooms for months on end, hoping to stop the spread of COVID-19 by prohibiting any movement at all among residents. The logic didn't account for the fact that these residences were part of the community, a reality that was only written about in relation to a protagonist trying to be able to see a loved one.

That was the key problem: reporting that situated these facilities within a community was rare. When it happened, it was often related to generalized analyses about why low-income and racialized communities were hit so hard. Sometimes stated and sometimes implied, the logic went that a higher concentration of long-term care workers living in these communities brought COVID-19 home more often. That was true, to an extent, but broader community connections were ignored: Where did partners work? Was there a connection between school outbreaks and long-term care, passed through a parent? Was there a ratio between long-term care outbreaks and community spread that could help explain community outbreaks or spread? No media tried to explain these forces; instead, long-term care was talked and written about as if a resident's only relationship to the outside world was the loved one whose hand was placed on the other side of their window.

There were patterns in how journalists erased the systemic forces that impacted residential care so profoundly. Sometimes, facts were simply not reported. When there was too much information on a particular day related to COVID-19, regular updates about outbreaks often took a back seat. Also, in focusing solely on what was happening, journalists too often neglected to examine why things were happening. Journalists spoke to the people most impacted — residents and workers — far less often than elder care experts, doctors and professors. Data wasn't great for any aspect of the pandemic, but it was in long-term care where data suppression had the greatest impact: rather than Canadians being able to see, in real time, the cumulative toll that COVID-19 had wreaked upon long-term care — just how many outbreaks or deaths had happened in a particular place — it was more common for updates to be doled out in periods of 24 hours, a week or across a specific outbreak.

One of the ways in which journalists didn't provide a full picture of deaths in residential care was by reporting deaths associated with a particular outbreak rather than cumulatively for an entire residence. It certainly didn't help that this was the practice of many public health units, including from Québec and Manitoba, whose daily reporting only included the number of deaths in a single outbreak or for a single day. In much of Canada, residences where cumulative deaths had climbed high into double digits would re-appear on outbreak lists with just a one or a two beside them, rather than giving the public the overall number of deaths per facility. It made tracking these deaths very difficult but not impossible for someone staying on top of them nightly. In Ontario, *Global News Hamilton* and *Inside Halton* both regularly only reported current outbreak numbers, for example reporting five deaths associated with a January 17, 2021, outbreak at Chartwell Waterford in Oakville while it actually had 17 deaths overall. This frame made it hard to get a firm handle on how dangerous life became within individual residences. Journalists should not have simply reported these figures but instead added the information available to them in the section of the public health unit's website of closed outbreaks where the numbers did exist.[54]

There was also a lack of uniform information across Canada related to deaths in residential care. B.C. reported long-term care, retirement residences and assisted living facilities more or less regularly during the first wave, but then stopped for most of the second wave, periodically reporting the overall total instead. On January 7, 2021, the B.C. Centre for Disease Control resumed regular weekly reports. They didn't include hospital outbreaks. Alberta reported this information to media, and not consistently. If journalists didn't write about the information, it would not be reported publicly for a specific day. Saskatchewan didn't report anything; outbreak and death information came through journalists who uncovered outbreak information by reporting on residences individually. Manitoba reported long-term care, retirement residences, assisted living and hospital outbreaks daily, but not cumulatively. Ontario reported long-term care daily and cumulatively, but not retirement residences, adult assisted living or hospital outbreaks. Some of Ontario's 34 public health units reported shelters, retirement residences and adult assisted living, like Toronto, Ottawa, Waterloo, Peel and Halton, but some did not, like Middlesex-London, Durham or Windsor-Essex. In Québec, the province with the best overall data, CHSLDs, retirement residences and assisted living were reported daily, though not cumulatively per residence. Through the Institut national de santé publique du Québec (INSPQ), however, data about total death by kind of residence was easy to access for any day of the year. New Brunswick and Nova Scotia both relied more on journalists to push the information out, though deaths were so low that the stories received widespread media coverage when they happened.

There was another important, confusing factor that contorted coverage —what exactly was long-term care? For experts, the definition was clear. But for laypeople, including journalists, the terms were regularly confused and mixed up. In Ontario, where retirement residence deaths were not reported by the Ministry of Health, journalists relied on long-term care numbers alone to explain how deadly COVID-19 had been, leaving out hundreds more deaths within retirement residences. In Québec where both kinds of facilities were reported daily, the public could see that the second wave was much more deadly in retirement residences than the first had been, a phenomenon that suggested that CHSLD management had made more necessary improvements to internal protocols, while overwhelmingly private, for-profit retirement residences had not.

Can journalists be forgiven for missing some of these details? The state of the data certainly made it difficult to wade through and come up with consistent, cogent analysis, especially if you were expected to write about many things, not just residential care. The lack of information and the quality of it was the fault of officials — politicians didn't mandate that public health units share the same information, and so the result was a patchwork of information disseminated that changed from region to region all across Canada. But journalists didn't do enough to challenge these problems either. After 12 months of writing about the pandemic, articles about outbreaks, case counts and errors still read as if they were written in June or September, asking the same questions and leaving out the same information in daily reporting, like facility ownership or profits made by specific residence owners. There was no evolution in the sophistication of how these stories were being told. And when the vaccines became a serious contender for ending outbreaks, and when variants took more of the spotlight in 2021, much of the coverage of residential care got even worse, or even stopped. As was the case with Roberta Place, reporting too often refused to look at the core issues that had already been known for so long.

PROFIT: THE ELEPHANT IN THE FOUR-PERSON SHARED ROOM

Québec's long-term care system was walloped by the first wave. The system had been in crisis for more than a decade, despite years and years of promises from politicians to fix it. Unlike in most of Canada, Québec's system is overwhelmingly public, though facilities were plagued by private-sector logic: operate these facilities as cheaply as possible to extract as much money from them as possible. But the fact that the system was public meant that Québec's politicians had an easier time demanding rapid changes within CHSLDs. They had direct control over most of them, unlike most other long-term care facilities in Canada.

For those residences that were privately owned and operated, there was a fundamental problem: owners and board members were politically connected and the industry was highly profitable. In Ontario, James Schlegel of Schlegel Villages was not the only individual who was connected to a political party. Many companies that operated long-term care and retirement residences had leadership with direct ties to governments. For example, Andrew Brander registered as a lobbyist for the Ontario Long-Term Care Association (OLTCA) on March 24, 2020, the industry lobby group dominated by private, for-profit operators. Brander was a former director of communications for Rod Phillips. Phillips had been Minister of Finance and Minister of Long-term Care in 2020–2021. Brander also had almost a decade of work experience inside Stephen Harper's administration and left his job with the Doug Ford government in 2019. Three days after Brander's lobby registry entry, the Ford government issued an emergency order related to long-term care. It was panned by the unions that represent staff in those facilities but praised by the OLTCA. The order gave

> employers leeway on reporting obligations, [and] allow[ed] long-term care homes to hire any staff they deem fit for a particular role. In essence, employers can shift duties from staff with higher qualifications to less-qualified staff in order to save money.[55]

While the emergency order was supposed to only last two weeks, by July 17, 2020, most of it was still in effect.[56] The *Toronto Star* framed this order negatively, with a headline that read, "Province suspends rules protecting vulnerable long-term care residents," but even then, didn't go into the connections between Ford's government and the industry.[57]

Ensuring that Canadians understood these connections was critical to being able to explain why, during a moment where residents in long-term care were dying in incredible numbers, more wasn't done to stop it. While Ontario's Long-Term Care Commission heard that cost was a big factor for why many proposals were ignored by Doug Ford, the involvement of Conservative activists who had experience both in Ontario and federal politics was not immaterial. There were so many political connections between the long-term care industry and the Ontario government. Less than a month after Brander's registration, another OLTCA lobbyist from Crestview, the same company that Brander worked for, was added to Ontario's Lobbyist Registry: Chad Rogers, a died-in-the-wool Conservative and founding partner of the agency. Christopher Chapin and Patrick Tuns lobbied for Caressant Care, a chain where at least 72 people died at seven facilities.[58] Chapin had been a member of Minister of Health Christine Elliott's Progressive Conservative Party leadership team and had worked in PC Party in various positions, and Tuns was the deputy campaign manager for Ford's leadership race and 2018 election campaign. Carly Luis lobbied on behalf of the OLTCA. Luis had been the director of strategic communication for the Ontario PCs. Paul Brown, a former adviser to Brian Mulroney was a registered lobbyist for Extendicare, a company that owned or operated 33 facilities where 684 residents died.[59] Leslie Noble lobbied on the behalf of OLTCA and federally for Chartwell. She had worked as a campaign manager for former Ontario premier Mike Harris and is "well known in Conservative circles," according to her StrategyCorp bio.[60] HCN Canadian Investment-5 LP, one of the real estate holding firms that owns Chartwell facilities, hired Jenni Byrne and Simon Jefferies to lobby on their behalf. Both have held senior positions with Stephen Harper and Ford's governments.[61]

Former Ontario premiers Ernie Eves and Bill Davis have also both been on long-term care company boards[62] and Mike Harris was the chair of Chartwell's board. Harris deregulated long-term care when he was premier, and he has made about $3.5 million over the 18 years he's been involved with Chartwell.[63] Harris made $223,000 from Chartwell for his board involvement in 2020.[64] From March 2020 until June 30, 2021, at least 429 people died at 58 Chartwell facilities across Canada.[65] Former mayor of Mississauga and Conservative politician Hazel MacCallion was Revera's "Chief Elder Officer."[66] Donna Duncan, head of the OLTCA, had previously worked in the office of a cabinet minister, according to Ontario's Lobbyist Registry. On March 15, 2021, the Ontario Lobbyist Registry reported that OLTCA received $4,197,436 from the Ontario government, a number that rose to $7,176,766 by July 5, 2021.[67]

It wasn't just Conservatives either. Chartwell lobbyists Andrew Steele and Conal Slobodin, both had ties to the Liberal Party — Steele having held senior positions within the Ontario government under Dalton McGuinty and senior campaign roles for both the Ontario and federal Liberal Party, and Slobodin as a senior consultant to the Yukon Liberal Party. Slobodin lobbied the federal government specifically, "with regards to the seeking of health sector specific changes to Employment Insurance allowing for renewed support for Chartwell staff whose employment status is affected by COVID-19," according to the federal Lobbyist Registry. Chartwell hired Liberals specifically to encourage the federal government to offer more money to pay for workers who had to stop working because of COVID-19, a curious demand, considering how high-profile the call for paid sick days had become in 2021.[68] When the Liberals were in power in Ontario, the OLTCA engaged Philip Dewan, John Duffy and Bob Lopinsky as lobbyists, all men who had roles with the Liberal Party. Dewan was McGuinty's chief of staff.[69]

There was no shortage of political connections between politicians, lobbyists and the representatives of Canada's largest long-term care facilities. This meant that the solution to fixing long-term care necessarily passed through a complex web of relationships, favouritism, cronyism and the pursuit of profit. On the surface, the horror within long-term care didn't make any sense: How could anyone have allowed the system to get so bad that death was sweeping the industry? That surface was defined by journalists who didn't go deep enough into these connections or the way they were parlayed into industry-friendly policies.

In a New Years Eve *Toronto Star* editorial, Torstar owners Jordan Bitove and Paul Rivett wrote an exacerbated, year-end call to arms. *This must stop*, was their message, alongside an infographic illustrating the toll of long-term care deaths. Indeed, by December 31, 2020, *this must stop* had long been on people's minds. But their piece was short on solutions. They neither named for-profit operators as the culprit for disgusting long-term care home conditions that had existed long before COVID-19, nor did they mention any of the provincial regulatory failures that have enabled the system to get worse. They promised that, in 2021, the *Toronto Star* will be "working tirelessly" to "help bring meaningful change and save lives." And then they did what a media organization isn't supposed to do: they invited their readers to take action with them. They promised that the letter would be available soon for Ontarians to sign, that "city, provincial and federal authorities" put a stop "to the inhuman treatment and needless death of our vulnerable elders." Six months later, there was no sign of the letter's demands anywhere, if you didn't use the Internet Archive's Wayback Machine to pull up the January 9 cached page.[70]

While newspapers are not normally in the business of advocacy, they are certainly in the business of framing crises, and Bitove and Rivett's letter ensured that blame was pointed in several different directions — not toward long-term care owners. They called for rapid tests to be deployed by "military health-care professionals as necessary," as if Ontario had any semblance of a rapid test regime. They called for Ontario's mandatory inspection regime to be reinstated. They called for an investment of $100 million from a combination of the provincial and federal governments to hire new staff and raise long-term care staff wages. They called for the province to create a "rapid response" unit that could be deployed to manage infection control as emergencies arise. And finally, they called for the creation of an ombudsman that could review complaints.[71] Incredible bluster for five recommendations that would amount to very little. Where was the attention on the ownership model that had organized long-term care around real estate exploitation for profit? Why did Bitove and Rivett fail to name any of the high-profile individuals who were involved in managing these organizations and their deep connections to the political parties? By the time of this editorial, the wheels were already in motion for the mass vaccination campaign within long-term care, the only intervention that would actually stop the spread of COVID-19, rendering Bitove and Rivett's call unnecessary. The urgency would soon be gone.

There were so many examples of this happening that it was normal for journalists to obscure who was really to blame. And politicians had little reason to talk about the crisis in terms of blame at all. But when advocates or the NDP called for nationalized long-term care, whether by adding long-term care to the Canada Health Act or by creating a separate, stand-alone act, the chorus from commentators, business leaders and many politicians was to outright reject it as impossible. In a question-and-answer feature looking back at Canada's first-year anniversary of the pandemic with Health Minister Patty Hadju, CBC's Aaron Wherry illustrated how easy it was to ignore broader issues and instead try and get politicians to talk about the constitution. Rather than raising any of the many examples where multiple health jurisdictions caused problems in Canada's pandemic response or vaccine rollout, Wherry asked, "But from where you sat, does it feel like federalism, and having these different jurisdictional responsibilities, was a big problem or even ... a positive in some way?" to which Hadju replied, "That's a really hard question. I feel like I'm being asked to be sort of almost a constitutional expert. What I will say is that, that is the system we exist in. We have 13 distinct health-care jurisdictions."[72] The rest of the interview then crosses between those jurisdictional lines, asking about profit in long-term care and national standards, as if the constitutional issues don't exist, as if the question of jurisdiction is only relevant when someone wants to disparage something or avoid answering a question. That's because in Canada, jurisdiction has always been used as an excuse to explain why something has not or cannot be done. This tactic was one of many during the pandemic that politicians used to avoid answering questions, columnists used to justify the status quo and corporations used to refuse responsibility for what was happening in their residences.

The house of cards that was residential care collapsed under the pressure of the pandemic. There was a great deal of blame to be shared by many people in power, from current to older governments, from current to former political operatives, from residence owners to managers. But journalists didn't really engage in blaming at all. The minor and milquetoast calls for reform never hit at the heart of the problem, which was that years of corruption had allowed for the system to become so rotten that horror stories from within the walls of long-term care were normal. When COVID-19 swept through these facilities, it was more likely the case that "of course" would be the response rather than actual shock. And when Chartwell announced their 2020 year-end operating situation, very few people noticed that they significantly increased their net income over 2019 from $1,067,000 to $14,879,000. While their Funds for Operations (FFO), a measure for Real Estate Investment Trusts, which Chartwell is, dipped from just under $200 million in 2019 to almost $166 million in 2020, the company demonstrated that it was still financially healthy, paying out shareholders all the profits it managed to extract from its staff and residents and giving their leadership even bigger bonuses.[73] Clearly, the system wasn't broken. It was built to be like this, and nothing short of a radical intervention will fix it.

The deaths and illness in long-term care during the first and second waves of the COVID-19 pandemic were overwhelming. Residents confined to their rooms, rendered invisible due to age and disability, are the forgotten victims of this pandemic. They lived in the care of others, and those people failed to keep them safe. Where to place the blame was rarely clear, thanks to politicians whose direct actions made these residences so unsafe, and journalists who were either unable or unwilling to go deeper in how they wrote about this crisis. The result was untold suffering in thousands of peoples' final hours, dying alone or being shut away from family and friends. There was no political will to improve their lives during the pandemic; indeed, there wasn't even the political will to protect them from what was known for years to be dangerous.

Even though residential care was treated as separate from communities, it was deeply integrated within them: personal care workers were often living with workers in other kinds of low-income jobs. It meant that COVID-19 spread within lower-income communities faster than within higher-income communities where workers tended to be more white. The infection rate in Canada was not equally distributed, and COVID-19 ravaged industries where workers were more likely to be poor and low income, particularly in the food services industry. The government's refusal to treat residential care as a part of broader communities allowed COVID-19 to spread quickly, in defiance of public health directives intended to slow spread.

May 2020
COVID-19 HITS FOOD PROCESSING INDUSTRIES

Cases: 55,061
Deaths: 3,391[1]

There were some curious similarities between Canada's system of long-term care and its food processing industries. Years of profit maximization in residential care and food processing meant that both industries relied on low-waged, precarious workers to run their operations. The jobs are physically gruelling, and immigrant or refugee workers are overrepresented in both fields. Low incomes paid to these workers forced many of them to travel between several worksites to afford to survive, a pattern that would be particularly deadly for this virus. Just as COVID-19 swept through residential care facilities, so it also swept through food industry workers.

While journalists could easily make the connection between COVID-19 and the conditions within residential care that made it such a dangerous location to live and work within, the same kind of connection was more elusive for food industry workers. Journalists and politicians alike lionized food industry workers like never before. From grocery to food production, these workers were both hailed as frontline heroes and treated as if they were expendable. Food processing facilities, especially meat packing plants, were the sites of some of Canada's largest outbreaks and from March 2020 until June 2021, and at least 22 workers died as a result of COVID-19 infection acquired within them. COVID-19 exploited these congregate settings while politicians warned of the disaster for Canada's food supply chain if these facilities shut down in case of an outbreak. Journalists rarely challenged this narrative, and so while surgeries were being postponed and most businesses closed, food processing remained mostly untouched by government directives. All so the profits anticipated by shareholders or owners would not be disrupted by a pesky factory shutdown intended to stop COVID-19's rapid spread.

BENITO

Benito Quesada was a 51-year-old Cargill employee, a father of four and a local shop steward. As a shop steward, he represented his fellow workers to management, bringing day-to-day concerns to local supervisors of the large, international corporation. Quesada had moved to High River, Alberta, from Mexico with his wife Maria Mendoza-Padron and their children. In the spring of 2020, Benito, along with nearly half of his 2000 coworkers at the Cargill plant, developed a COVID-19 infection as the virus tore through the plant's workforce. On May 12, his union UFCW Local 401 announced that Benito had died from complications related to COVID-19. The union said Benito had contracted COVID-19 sometime mid-April and spent "a considerable amount of time" in a medically-induced coma.[2] A GoFundMe set up by Maria, with a goal of $1000, surpassed $15,000.[3]

Two weeks later, through tears, his eldest daughter told *Global News*, "We haven't touched anything. His boots are still in the entryway. His toothbrush. His cologne. Everything is still there." Benito's three other children, aged five, ten and 12, each talked about how much they miss their father, and how hard he worked for the family. He worked so hard, his family said, that he accepted a $500 bonus from Cargill to continue working during the pandemic. Sixteen-year-old Ariana said Cargill did not send condolences or follow-up with the family; the only contact they had was to work out a loss of life workplace claim. Cargill claimed to have tried to reach the family to send condolences.[4]

From March 2020 until June 2021, at least 169 workers died from COVID-19 contracted on the job. Sixty-two of these workers worked in healthcare settings — hospitals, residential care or home care — and 32 died after contracting the virus in their food industry workplace: meatpacking facilities, dairy and food processing factories, grocery, restaurants or agricultural work.[5] These workers were overwhelmingly racialized, and worked in precarious, low-waged, difficult and dangerous jobs. Many also had precarious status in Canada, leaving them vulnerable to management and owners whose inaction would lead to the propagation of COVID-19.

Early on in the pandemic, it was clear that workplaces were an important source of COVID-19 infections and the food industry was particularly vulnerable, especially for seasonal migrant workers, which I explore deeper in the chapter covering October 2020. But information about workplace outbreaks was extremely difficult to get from politicians and public health officials, even as Canada entered fall 2020. There was no moment of reckoning between journalists and public health officials that forced officials to collect or release better data. And so, stories about outbreaks within food processing facilities were most often told by whistleblower employees and workers' rights groups who could anonymize and share information. Many family members who lost loved ones spoke to journalists to raise awareness about their loved ones' working conditions and how preventable these deaths really were. Ariana told *Global News*: "We want other people to know what they did, because I want every time that someone looks up the name Cargill or just Googles it, I want my dad's name to pop up."[6] The highly profitable international company based in Minnesota no doubt did not want this negative PR and prepared for this: if you entered Cargill into Google two months after Benito's death, an ad appeared inviting you to a page at Cargill's website called, "Cargill's Commitment To Safety - Get The Facts Here." The page, dated July 15, 2020, listed the measures taken to protect workers, including minimum protections like giving workers more room to work and increasing sanitary measures on the work floor. They also promised to reduce employees' use of carpooling. Carpooling was often blamed on being the source of much of the spread within congregant workplaces. Journalists regularly published comments like these, giving the impression that the only way to make workers safe was to give employers even more control over their life, including how they get to and from work. Journalists rarely explored the impact that reducing production so too many workers weren't working together at one time, or paying for workers to have access to PPE to use in their lives outside of work too would have had in helping to manage COVID-19 spread.[7] Meat factories are massive operations, employing thousands, and they were particularly vulnerable to COVID-19. Between March 2020 and June 2021, at least 21 workers of meatpacking facilities died across Canada.[8]

Despite the negative attention related to these deaths, including the poignant and tragic pleas of workers' family members, the owners of these workplaces did not feel enough pressure to improve the safety of their workplaces. There were some investigations that tried to identify who should be held responsible for these infections and deaths, but by-and-large, journalists covered plant outbreaks the same way they covered the daily updates: uncritically reporting the official line and maybe including comment from the union representing workers at the plant. Unsurprisingly, as the pandemic moved from summer into fall 2020, new outbreaks popped up in food processing facilities, indicating that the measures taken between the two waves had been insufficient.

OUTBREAKS IN LARGE FOOD INDUSTRY CONGREGANT SETTINGS

At the start of Canada's second wave, a consensus was growing internationally that COVID-19 was not likely spread equally among the people who caught the virus. The virus was easily transmissible, but not everyone would be contagious in the same way. It became more obvious that COVID-19 transmission was linked to clusters: groups of people in close contact who could catch the virus in so-called superspreader events. Journalists wrote about superspreader events around the world, with an early focus on cruise ships, religious services and choir practices. After the market in Wuhan and the Diamond Princess, superspreader incidents worldwide became headline news in Canada. One was triggered by a churchgoer in Daegu, South Korea, whose presence at four church services transmitted COVID-19 to at least 37 people.[9] Journalists would soon talk about other superspreader events: bars and clubs, festivals, fitness classes, Donald Trump rallies, Supreme Court Nomination parties at the White House Rose Garden. It was striking how many of the events media reported on happened outside of the workplace — events people voluntarily attended, where a reader could decide whether the infected individual was to blame for being careless or unlucky. It was a powerful way that journalists and politicians perpetuated the belief that COVID-19 was an individualistic problem, meaning that the power to stop this was in our hands: we just needed to stop attending activities outside of work.

Of course, this was only a small part of the problem. A workplace can have similar risks to any large gathering of people, except workers have far less ability to refuse to work if they're afraid of catching COVID-19, if they feel sick (possibly from it) or if they need to visit a testing centre. As I explain in the February 2021 chapter, large workplaces where workers are together in closed spaces became superspreader environments but were rarely talked about in the same way as those more salacious, like the karaoke night that infected at least 80 people at Quebec City's Bar Kirouac or the spin class at Hamilton, Ontario's SpinCo. The moment COVID-19 entered communities, it quickly moved to the highly precarious environment of food processing factories and left in its wake tens of thousands of infected workers. While the most compelling storytelling wove personal narratives into the workplace health and safety problems that likely created the conditions for COVID-19 to spread, reporting about outbreaks always gave prominence to the official account from public health, maybe with a politician's comment or union reaction to the news. With these two modes of reporting dominating coverage of factory outbreaks, it was very difficult for Canadians to draw larger conclusions about the problems within food processing in Canada, and therefore, call for ways to improve working conditions.

The first person to die of COVID-19 likely caught at work was reported to be Keith Saunders, a 48-year-old manager of the Great Canadian Superstore, a grocery store in Oshawa, Ontario. He died on March 25, 2020. Most of the media coverage focused on a heart-wrenching goodbye written on Facebook by his wife Katy, who wrote about how much Keith was dedicated to his coworkers and how much she will miss him.[10] By that time, Ontario had 15 COVID-19-related deaths, and Saunders was the youngest victim. CTV reported that customers were informed of the possible exposure by email, and Loblaw assured customers it would clean the store while asking customers to give each other more space. Four days later, Loblaw issued a longer list of the measures they were planning to take:

> Plexiglas shields are being installed at all checkout lanes at its stores. The company is also limiting the number of customers allowed in a store, waiving the five-cent plastic bag fee and limiting the number of checkout lanes that can accept cash payments.[11]

Despite Saunders' death being the moment when Loblaw decided to start installing safety equipment, most of the coverage about this death didn't include this information, instead focusing on the personal tragedy that his loss meant for his family. This wasn't unique to the coverage of Saunders' death. Journalism about worker deaths related to COVID-19 rarely made clear that employers could, and should, take precautions to ensure the safety of their workers. Without this relationship explicit in the reporting, Canadians had only the horror and sadness of lives lost, which likely contributed to fog and panic instead of an organized demand for robust labour standards.

This reporting pattern would be repeated again and again for the workers who died from catching COVID-19 in a food processing facility and whose identity was made public. The depth of the reporting would be related to how available the family was for comment or how compelling the family members were in an interview. With public health officials unable or unwilling to share deaths related to outbreak information, journalists relied on personal connections or social media posts. Once the story was told, the quick rhythm of pandemic reporting made it difficult for journalists to go back and see if anything had changed to stop COVID-19 from re-circulating or injuring others in that workplace. Saunders' death, for example, demonstrated the risk that frontline grocery workers took to ensure Canadians could eat, but after the initial wave of articles there was no coverage about his death that held Loblaw accountable for improved working conditions. After April 2020, no journalist returned to his place of work to see how COVID-19 precautions had been implemented.

Thousands more grocery workers would become infected over the course of the pandemic, but it's impossible to say how many, who or where. No one tracked this information centrally. Weeks after Loblaw committed to safety improvements in the wake of Keith Saunders' death, at least 18 employees at the Loblaw on Dupont in Toronto caught COVID-19. Olivia Bowden covered that outbreak for *Global News* in a feature that examined how unsafe workers felt and how little the company had been doing to actually enforce the measures in place. Responding to the claim that Loblaw wasn't doing enough to enforce social distancing, Catherine Thomas, senior director of external communication at Loblaw Companies Limited, said, "The company determines who has been in close contact with a positive case by using CCTV footage of the store along with interviewing employees."[12] So, while masks had not yet been made mandatory inside the store, management preferred to watch employees through video cameras to then inform them of COVID-19 exposure after the fact. Loblaw resisted implementing in-store mask policies until they were imposed by public health. Bowden's feature does a very good job of bringing together different themes: it discusses the personal challenges workers face working during the pandemic, uses official responses from Loblaw and, importantly, includes experts who challenge the corporate line to identify where it is insufficient.[13] As a result, it's a rare example of the kind of reporting that was so badly needed.

The important elements in this report from *Global News* should have been more common across reporting about workplace outbreaks. But the story also suffered from a lack of information too: the outbreak at Loblaw's Dupont location in Toronto was first reported on May 11 by the store on Facebook. They said that "a number" of employees had been infected. Bowden's report was published on July 2, nearly two months later. And even then, reaction from the company was added to the story in an update published a day later.[14] Putting together enough pieces to report on workplace outbreaks was a challenge, and when a journalist had to do what they could with the information they had, it was often after the outbreak had ended, or it was missing reaction from important players like management.

The lack of consistent public health-mandated COVID-19 outbreak reporting protocols for businesses helped to drive the fear and unease that many Canadians felt during the pandemic. Without knowing exactly where cases were rising, it created the illusion that risk was shared equally — that if you go outside and forget your mask, you very well may catch COVID-19, rather than the truth that exposure and infection were much more likely in congregate settings like workplaces. For employees of workplaces where people were sick from COVID-19, the fear was even more intense, turning regular experiences at work into non-stop Russian roulette. Rather than having a map of outbreaks or information from public health, Canadians most often found out their regular grocery store, Tim Horton's or McDonalds would close through direct correspondence from the store or through the press. The lack of consistent information also made telling a consistent story very difficult, as there would be weeks and months between outbreak updates in certain facilities. All of this added to the sense that public health had less control over the situation than it perhaps appeared.

THE PROFIT MOTIVE

It is impossible to understand how the food industry's inadequate actions during the pandemic without acknowledging just how powerful and wealthy the corporations that dominate this industry are. But rarely was this mentioned in reporting. Instead, outbreak stories were individualized, or told months after the fact, due to a lack of information from officials and corporate spokespeople. Too often, the way media framed outbreaks in food industries ignored broader forces that explained why corporations took (or didn't take) action. Individualizing workers by focusing on personal narratives removed them from their community, and Canadians were hardly able to see how a workplace cluster contributed to an outbreak. Thanks to uneven data, many outbreaks were simply not reported at all. Politicians could have mandated better outbreak reporting, but they did not. And because journalists adhered closely to daily updates, they rarely reported on other factors that were driving outbreaks.

Eventually, Canada's largest food companies installed barriers, created social distancing plans and adhered to public health agency guidelines. But as workers at the Loblaw's Dupont location pointed out, there was little enforcement. Without enforcement, measures could be ignored, corners could be cut and employees could be placed at risk on the whim of a manager. No government mandated that food industry businesses cut their production during the pandemic, so workers were expected to do the same work as usual, in the same space, but keep their distance from others — impossible in most workplaces. The day that Keith Saunders' infection became public, president and CEO of Loblaw Galen Weston announced they would close stores for a deep clean whenever an employee tested positive for COVID-19. He also committed to posting publicly every time there was a store outbreak. All of the measures were backward looking, though. They intended to limit spread of COVID-19 after an employee already had it. None of the measures sought to limit the contact that a potentially COVID-19 positive person would have while working, unaware that they could be contagious. Both Loblaw and fellow grocery giant Metro proactively disclosed when a worker had been on the job with COVID-19, but finding these reports required knowing where to look. Canadians needed journalists to stay on top of a disparate set of lists to know when their local store might have had an outbreak. Alberta was the notable exception to this, as it was the only province in Canada that consistently listed outbreak information for all businesses. A handful of Ontario public health units did too, but mostly that information was not easy to find.

In a CBC News feature written by Joel Dryden that tried to address what led to outbreak at the Cargill plant in High River, it was obvious that the plant's conditions were a key element. Workers were elbow-to-elbow on the factory floor and in the locker room. Cargill had announced that they brought in some measures to reduce worker-to-worker contact, but workers challenged this, saying they were as close as ever. Workers also said the company tried to push them back to work after only a few days off sick.[15] It was clear that Cargill, like other large food processors, were committed to keeping their factories open and their employees at work. "Spokesperson Daniel Sullivan said because the company has been deemed an essential service, Cargill is committed to keeping production facilities open," read the feature.[16] Employers relied on the "essential service" designation from governments to justify not slowing production as one measure to keep workers safe.

Despite the overwhelming number of racialized workers in the meat-packing industry, journalists didn't explicitly name how racism justified and permitted the spread of COVID-19 among so many low-income food industry workers. Even though Dryden's feature identified the systemic problems with working conditions that helped COVID spread, it stopped short at naming the real problem: Cargill, like all companies in this industry, are driven solely by profits, and racism allows them to extract great profits from their workers. Any slowing or stoppage of production impacts their profits. When they were labelled by governments as essential services, it meant agri-food industry corporations could accelerate their profits while the economy was otherwise shut down, making them even more attractive to investors — all off the backs of low-income, racialized workers. Rather than challenging Cargill's profits, Dryden sought comment from the Canadian Cattleman's Association (CCA) who argued the plant couldn't close because there had already been a dip in the price of beef. Quoting Dennis Laycraft from the CCA,

> "The longer the plant is closed, the more animals that were scheduled to come to market are being held back. We're also seeing plants slowed down or shut down in the United States," Laycraft said. "The first impact is really back on producers."

Laycraft, a lobbyist whose advocacy serves the owners of Cargill by ensuring that his members can move their cattle to market, is then asked about whether or not he thinks the factory safe: "So we're pretty confident that they can run that plant safely. I think it's a question of getting workers healthy again, getting them back in and available."[17] It's unclear why Dryden even asked Laycraft his opinion on plant safety when his priority is that cows can be slaughtered rather than making changes to keep workers safe.

JBS and Cargill process most of all beef that Canadians consume. Together, the plants process 8700 heads of cattle per day. Combined with the 1500-head output of Cargill's Guelph, Ontario plant, the three factories process 95% of all Canadian beef consumed in Canada, and most of what is processed in Canada is exported. By mid-May 2020, all three plants had had COVID-19 outbreaks. In a letter condemning how concentrated Canada's beef market has become, the National Farmers' Union wrote,

> Their three processing plants form a choke point that gives them undue influence over the price of cattle paid to farmers and the

price of beef paid by consumers in the grocery store. While this choke point gives Cargill and JBS tremendous power, it is also one of the weakest links in Canada's food system.

And with this tremendous power came tremendous profits. None of the articles that covered food industry outbreaks wrote about the profits at the heart of why company officials wanted these facilities kept open so badly. Harsha Walia has summed it up simply: "essential workers are essential to capitalism."[18] The workers forced to keep working through the pandemic were deemed essential, though they were far more essential to the operation of capitalism than they were to meeting our collective needs.[19] The year 2020 was a tremendous year for profits in the food industry. Loblaw netted $1.192 billion, up from $1.131 in 2019,[20] but even then, the *Canadian Press* reported their fourth quarter profits saying, "Loblaw reports Q4 profit up from year earlier, but falls short of expectations."[21] Metro made $796.4 million in their 2020 fiscal year, up from $714.4 in 2019.[22] JBS made net revenues of $15.8 billion in the third quarter alone.[23] Cargill, whose year-end is May 31, stopped reporting their annual revenues in 2020 for the first time since 1996. As a private company, they aren't obliged to make these reports public. According to *Reuters*, Cargill's 2019–2020 total revenue reached $114.6 billion USD. Their net revenues were not reported.[24] Tens of thousands of workers became sick while working for these companies while their profits soared. Not bad, for a year where hundreds of thousands of the lowest-income jobs vanished and Canada's GDP shrank by 5.4%.[25]

HIDING FOOD INDUSTRY OUTBREAKS

The outsized influence that food industry corporations have over the Canadian economy means that critical reporting during the pandemic was rare. There were barriers, technical problems and other issues that made writing about outbreaks at food processing facilities difficult, which also meant that communities touched directly by these issues were kept in the dark. Reporting on food industry outbreaks and deaths generally followed three patterns. The first was that journalists employed the same frame used in covering residential care victims: individualized, in obituary-style features. In this, journalists removed their stories from the collective, or the cluster, that led to them catching COVID-19 in the first place. The second was that there was an overreliance on officials to tell the stories of the outbreaks, which obscured who was responsible for what, and therefore who should be held accountable to make the changes necessary to make workplaces safe. The third was that there was a lack of official information from public health, politicians or the companies in question, making it hard to even tell these stories at all. Often, stories about outbreaks would be reported weeks or even months after they happened, thanks to a contact, a whistleblower or a journalist whose regular beat meant they were closer to food processing workers than most journalists. Canadians rarely had a full picture about what was happening in meatpacking factories, within communal living spaces shared by food processing workers or within common workspaces shared by many employees. As public health and politician ordinances told Canadians to stay at home and two metres away from others, workers in these industries often didn't have the option to obey the directives.

On April 21, 2020, a memo went out to workers at FGF Brands, a food processing plant in northwest Toronto saying that an employee had a confirmed COVID-19 case. The company said the worker lived with someone who worked in a nursing home. The outbreak would grow to 184 workers and was only made public months later, thanks to an investigative report by *Toronto Star* reporters Sara Mojtehedzadeh and Jennifer Yang. At least one worker died.[26] They told this story through information from workers and statements made by FGF Brands.

COVID-19 hit northwest Toronto neighbourhoods very hard. The combination of people who work in low-income jobs (especially through temp agencies), close quarters living spaces (where people must share elevators to enter and leave their apartments and use common laundry facilities) and poverty meant that these workers were the least able to follow public health guidelines to self-isolate. They had to work. They were the backbone of the food processing and long-term care systems. For FGF Brands to not announce publicly that the factory was dealing with a massive outbreak meant this remained hidden to people who lived near the factory or who may have had other connections to the area, but who would not have received any official company memo. Because outbreaks were so often hidden from the general public, reporting throughout April 2020 stuck closely to the official line — the way to reduce exposure and spread is to follow social distancing measures — with little mention of workplace safety and risk. This created the conditions for outbreaks to sweep through low-income and racialized neighbourhoods, while officials were rarely challenged about their pandemic control strategies as they related to communities most at risk. If a lockdown was supposed to slow the first wave, why did it not include the factories that were most susceptible to outbreak? If they had to remain open because the production of pastries was absolutely critical, why didn't the government intervene more firmly and insist that essential businesses reduce their workforce to give people more space, or demand that employees would get as many paid sick days off as they needed?

Was limited information a tactic intended to protect businesses from having to do more to slow the spread of COVID-19? Or was it simply the case that public health offices are disorganized because they have never been forced to use a common set of metrics? Underpinning Mojtehedzadeh and Yang's investigation was the fact that officials are simply not rendering enough information public:

> Across Ontario, there is no uniform definition of a workplace outbreak of COVID-19. And because there is no obligation for health authorities to publicly disclose them, we still don't know how many other workplaces in Toronto have suffered a similar fate.[27]

They go on to say that Toronto Public Health had not published data related to workplace outbreaks, though that of the few they've mentioned publicly, they're "mostly grocery stores."[28] This was likely thanks more to the corporate decision of both Metro and Loblaw to publicly disclose outbreaks throughout the pandemic.

It wasn't by accident that this story was broken by Mojtehedzadeh. She is one of Canada's very few labour reporters and has written extensively about abuses within the food industry. Her expertise in the industry, worker contacts and knowledge about workplace conditions made her the most likely journalist to have uncovered the FGF Brands story. Her sources and knowledge of the industry were crucial, which also meant that it would be difficult for a general assignment reporter to have enough information to do a report like this, especially if they were expected to keep up with general COVID-19 news. Politicians knew that if they started every day with updated figures, it would flood journalists with too much information to file their daily reports. It would even make it difficult to ask clear, challenging questions. Outbreaks became part of this too, and if an outbreak was announced by public health, a journalist could follow-up from there. But most times, between information about residential care, government aid packages and reactions from other politicians, there was enough to report as it was. This left outbreak reporting thin in 2020, only picked up by those journalists who have the time, resources and expertise to see beyond the lack of information and dig deeper. Things changed in 2021, when vaccines had reduced the number of people dying during the third wave. This gave journalists the space to finally examine more closely the impact of COVID-19 spread in large congregant workplaces like food processing facilities, though even then, company profits and unjust workers' conditions were rarely part of the story.

In Ontario, public health units decided what information they wanted to post about outbreaks. Some units didn't list outbreaks at all, some listed the outbreaks by an overarching category and very few listed the name of the company with the outbreak. In Québec, outbreak information was lumped together by industry. In Manitoba and Saskatchewan, there wasn't any information reported at all. In some public health units, such as Toronto and Hamilton, this changed as the pandemic advanced, with more information being reported, including naming specific outbreak sites. But many public health units didn't post this information at all, even when the third wave was pushing workplace outbreaks to levels they had not been before. On the other side of the spectrum was Alberta, the one jurisdiction that consistently named every outbreak location, subdivided in categories and regions.

Province to province, information varied significantly and changed constantly, from not reporting at all to stating which workplaces in which industries had outbreaks. Nowhere was national death data related to a workplace outbreak publicly reported. This hid the impact that outbreaks in the food processing industry had on Canadians. It also hid how workplace outbreaks led to clusters of people getting sick, and how these people were most often low-waged and precarious workers. And, because Canadians didn't know what was happening within these industries unless they were impacted directly, there was little that compelled the federal government or the provinces to force these corporations to implement measures to better protect their workers and limit how much of the pandemic in Canada was driven by spread from these industries.

WORKER ADVOCACY

Unlike most food processing outbreaks, the JBS and Cargill plants received a lot of media coverage, thanks in large part to the work that the plants' union did to promote the working conditions to local media. UFCW Local 401 represents food workers across Alberta, in grocery, food processing and other related workplaces. UFCW Local 401 made its members and the public aware of the dangers facing their members through media relations and campaigns. By mid-October 2020, they had sent nearly 200 letters to employers, pleading with them to make improvements to their employees' workplaces. Each letter contained dozens of requests for various accommodations, like allowing workers to take time off if their children are out of school, not requiring a sick note if a worker misses work due to COVID-19, local sanitary measures and so on. They also posted the responses from employers when they had them, mostly promising to do what is required of them by public health and their collective agreements.[29] The union made the workers they represented a part of the story that journalists couldn't ignore. Nor did they; most stories about factory outbreaks in Alberta included a comment from someone on behalf of workers. There is no doubt that the work UFCW Local 401 did to promote its members' demands helped to ensure journalists paid attention.

This wasn't the case elsewhere, however. Where an outbreak or death occurred and the workers were not organized, either through a union or with the help of an advocacy group, journalists either had to dig much further into the news or it passed as an update in a longer article about infection rates. When a worker died in a Montréal North food processing plant owned by Maple Leaf Foods, journalists Mike De Souza and Andrew Russell examined the conditions and location of the factory to paint a picture of what life was like inside the plant for these workers. At the time of the death, Montréal North was hit hardest of all regions in Montréal, and the plant was one of the few non-unionized facilities owned by Maple Leaf Foods. They quoted a representative from UFCW, who represents other workers in food processing facilities in Montréal. The representative said the unionized Cargill plant in nearby Chambly already had a nurse on staff, making that facility more ready to handle testing for all workers when cases started to appear in the plant. Another meat processing facility, Olymel in Yamachiche, shut down for two weeks after 129 cases were reported. Maple Leaf Foods shut down their unionized Brampton plant for two weeks after cases there were reported, but the Montréal North facility was only closed for three days. Their other non-union plant, just north of Montréal in Laval, wasn't suspended, despite rising case numbers.[30]

Maple Leaf Foods wasn't exactly consistent with how they applied their shutdown policies, and politicians never intervened to force national outbreak-mitigation standards for companies operating in multiple jurisdictions. On August 24, 2020, Migrante Manitoba called on Maple Leaf Foods to close their Brandon plant for two weeks because of a massive outbreak. While the company claimed the workers brought COVID-19 into the plant, just as they argued in the case of the Montréal North plant outbreak, the workers insisted it was far more likely that the plant itself was driving an outbreak. At the time the letter was written, 70 workers had contracted COVID-19. In their letter they wrote, "We feel the employer and the government are discriminatory toward migrant and immigrant workers, and that our health concerns are being ignored."[31] The letter outlined measures management had taken that reduced safety, like reorganizing the staff locker room months earlier in such a way that made it impossible for workers to socially distance.[32]

The outbreak was first reported earlier that month, on August 6. Many workers lived in close quarters, and the experience in other food processing facilities, including other Maple Leaf Foods plants, should have indicated to public health that infections would spread and more people would fall ill. When it was announced, Manitoba's Public Health Officer Brent Roussin played down the possibility of an outbreak and didn't even name what facility he was talking about. "To be clear, there is no evidence of workplace transmission at this time" he said. Premier Brian Pallister, reacting to a comment that many workers were afraid, said, "I think that I would say to [the workers] that they deserve to feel confident, because we are following the best health advice that we can get here in Manitoba and we're going to continue to."[33] The August 6 and 7 COVID-19 increases were the largest, single-day increases that Manitoba had seen since April 2. Workers and the opposition NDP called for the plant to be closed, as had happened elsewhere, but Maple Leaf Foods refused.

When there were more than 70 workers ill with COVID-19, Roussin and Maple Leaf Foods continued to ignore the experiences and pleas of the workers. In response to the letter from Migrante Manitoba, Roussin told *Global News*,

> There are a lot of safety measures that have been in place for quite some time, and we're working with a lot of agencies … along with

the employer, who's quite cooperative with this … The protocols in place are above and beyond what we would normally see … We're watching it very closely. We still don't have evidence of inter-facility spread, so right now there hasn't been any agency involved that suggesting we shut down that plant, but we'll continue to look at the situation.[34]

As if taking her cues from Roussin, Maple Leaf's vice president of communications and public affairs Janet Riley said, "Public Health and officials have said repeatedly that they have found no evidence of workplace transmission and the cases that have occurred among our team members appear to be linked to events and interactions within the community."[35] News of the outbreak fell out of the attention of journalists, relegated to being a footnote as part of overall COVID updates. Coverage was especially thin in the local newspaper, the *Brandon Sun*, which was surprising since the plant was Brandon's largest private employer. By September 4, cases connected to the plant reached 83, and Roussin still would not name Maple Leaf more specifically than "a business in Brandon."[36] The company and the union confirmed that nearly all cases were considered over on September 18, and that 93 workers had got sick.[37]

The story of the outbreak at Brandon's plant was told in bits and pieces, either reported in relation to the updates that Roussin gave or in reaction to the information put out by workers' advocates. In Montréal, readers got a better look at what was happening inside the plant in North Montréal thanks to the work of reporters. But even then, Maple Leaf Foods tried to downplay the possibility of spread within the facility. It's confusing that Brandon's largest private sector employer, with such a massive outbreak, got so little attention – or that so few parallels were drawn — that so few parallels were drawn between their struggle and similar outbreaks across Canada. With so many of these workers being racialized — some migrant workers, some immigrant — it does beg the question: How would their struggle have been covered had they been white? Would politicians and public health have been more ready to shut down the plant or take the workers' concerns seriously? What is it about low-income, precarious workers that sends a signal to politicians, public health and journalists to cover the case with only a passing eye? If journalists had done a better job of holding the Manitoba government and public health to account, would the plant have been shut down for a few days? Could infections have been stopped before they reached 93? The answer to these questions cannot be untied from the reality that these are powerful companies who make lots of money and who are very close to government.

GOVERNMENT REACTION AND INACTION

The considerable power the food industry has over Canada's economy, global trade and Canadians' well-being means governments must either constantly stand up to the industry or simply allow the industry to drive their political agendas. During the pandemic, their relationship was mostly the latter. When governments imposed widespread lockdowns but exempted food processing facilities, it sent a signal that they were too important to be shut down or even slowed down. But governments could have taken a range of options that wouldn't have strangled Canada's food supply. They could have mandated that food processing reduce production such that they meet the needs of domestic demand, but slow exports. They could have mandated mask wearing earlier, including for customers who might circulate within stores. They could have ordered shutdowns whenever an outbreak was declared. They could have forced companies to maintain COVID-19 wage bonuses, especially as the third wave in spring 2021 tore through these facilities. But they didn't do any of this. Rather, governments largely let the food industry regulate itself, appealing to their sense of goodwill and duty to do their part.

Canada's meat industry is intimately tied to the global meat market and international exports. Canada's closest neighbour was dealing with similarly large meatpacking outbreaks at the same time, and data from the United States demonstrated just how important the industry was to perpetuate COVID-19 infections. One study of COVID-19 spread and meatpacking facilities during the early part of the pandemic demonstrated that there was a marked increase in community spread where meatpacking facilities were located. The study found that, "residents of counties with meatpacking plants were 51% more likely to have contracted the coronavirus by July 21 and 37% more likely to die form the virus." This was true even when corrected for risk factors like race, average income, elderly population and the presence of congregant living facilities like long-term care and prisons. The study also found that nearly 8% of early COVID-19 cases could be linked directly to meatpacking. Reacting to the study, UFCW president Marc Perrone told *Bloomberg* that infection spread and deaths within the industry in the United States, "makes clear the Trump administration cares more about industry profits than protecting

America's frontline workers in the meatpacking industry."[38] But what about Justin Trudeau? If meatpacking outbreaks in Canada were also among the highest of any industry, and if they had started in comparison to other large congregant workplaces, what did these outbreaks say about the leadership of someone like Trudeau, who tried to paint himself as someone who did care about average people? And what about communities like Brooks, Brandon, London, Montréal North and Vallé-Jonction? The connections were clear, but Canadians didn't have this level of scrutiny on the role that these plants played in perpetuating community spread. Instead, Canadian public health officials and politicians tried to make it look like these outbreaks were just inevitable and unfortunate realities of living in a pandemic. Facilities were not always shut down, and in the cases they were, it was usually after dozens of cases had already been confirmed.

Despite the evidence of massive COVID-19 spread within food processing industries, the federal government guidelines during 2020 amounted to little more than advice for how to reduce COVID-19 transmission within food processing facilities, which was always accompanied by defaulting to the desires of the company. In fact, in every aspect of the economy, the private sector was mostly left to its own devices to manage COVID-19 within its workplace. Under their guidelines for how to slow transmission, the website for Agriculture and Agri-Food Canada states, "There is no single action or tool that will stop the spread of COVID-19. Each facility manager or employer should follow the hierarchy of controls using multiple measures based on their specific identified risks."[39] This, of course, wasn't quite true. If they closed these facilities entirely after positive cases of workers were identified, it would have stopped the spread of COVID-19 in these workplaces. But the government allowed corporations pick and choose the measures they wanted to implement, a decision that was usually based on what would be the least disruptive to their operations. The website states no hard rule about when to close, simply that, "Closing a business following a confirmed case of COVID-19 in the workplace is a decision that a business needs to take in consultation with its local Public Health Authority."[40] The federal government could have insisted that businesses close after an outbreak for a period of time, operate with reduced capacity or provide paid sick leave or other measures that would help sick workers avoid infecting others, but instead, it divested its authority to companies themselves. That way, the federal government never had to take responsibility for controlling outbreaks nor make enemies with owners who wanted maximum control to ensure profits could still be made. Some provinces only started to close congregant workplaces with outbreaks by April 2021, more than a year after the first death in a large congregant work setting in the food industries. Even then, most businesses with an outbreak stayed open.

Rather than forcing companies to divest some of their massive profits into basic worker protections, governments offered public money to the agri-food industry to pay for things like personal protective equipment or disinfection. The Ontario government promised up to $20,000 per business in meat processing. The federal government also created a host of other aid programs to help the food industry cope with COVID-19 disruptions.[41] For example, $42 million was earmarked for Alberta farmers to deal with delays caused by meat processing plant shutdowns due to COVID-19.

Workers, of course, got no similar aid. Justin Trudeau's government tried to maintain jobs at all costs, especially illustrated by the Canada Emergency Wage Subsidy as I explore in the chapter covering August 2020. So, workers who were deemed essential were celebrated as heroes while being seen as having had everything they needed — as long as their employers implemented basic measures. When asked about her government's position on large grocery corporations ending pandemic pay for workers, Deputy Prime Minister Chrystia Freeland told reporters,

> I think the fact that grocery stores now feel able to bring the wages back down suggests that there isn't a powerful disincentive to work out there … That is a reminder to all of us that supporting Canadian workers and supporting the Canadians that can't find jobs right now is a really essential thing to do.[42]

As reported by CBC News, reporters let this comment stand alone, unchallenged.[43] Freeland characterized this as a question of disincentive, rather than low-waged workers needing the state to help protect them at work, and the journalist didn't challenge this rhetoric.

Not only did government policy fail to protect workers, there was also no aid package for workers who were disabled by COVID-19. The most that workers who acquired COVID-19 on the job could expect to get is from structures already in place, like workplace compensation boards. But Toronto Star journalist Sara Mojtehedzadeh reported that the claims filed by October 2020 didn't match publicly available outbreak information. For example, despite the 184-person outbreak at FGF Brands, including one death, the employer filed fewer than five claims with Ontario's Workplace Safety and Insurance Board (WSIB) — until the *Toronto Star* investigation. They eventually filed 149 claims. Workers relied on their employers to submit a WSIB claim, which placed employees at the whim of their bosses.[44] As I explore in the chapter covering February 2021, there was no public accounting of how many people died from COVID-19 acquired at work, aside from my own research.

The third wave repeated all the same patterns as the previous waves before it, but this time, vaccinations reduced the deadliness of COVID-19 for older people. With long-term care and retirement facilities no longer the locations of thousands of COVID-19 infections, journalists were finally forced to look at outbreaks at work, and their impact on spreading COVID-19 within certain communities. In a Radio-Canada International feature on how Montréal avoided a third wave, Sarah-Amélie Mercure from Montréal Public Health credited the vaccine strategy of the city's public health unit for keeping cases at bay. She said that an aggressive campaign to vaccinate residents where outbreaks had been detected made the difference.[45] But in Peel Region, where vaccination was sluggish, infections in April 2021 were spiralling out of control. Despite having 20% of all COVID-19 cases in the province, Peel Region was only given 7.7% of the vaccines. In a feature for *The Local*, Fatima Syed points out that for Ontario's province-wide pharmacy vaccine pilot, Brampton only had eight pharmacies per 100,000 residents permitted to give out doses, while Kingston had 26 pharmacies per 100,000 residents.[46] Workers in the food industries, including in Peel — but pretty much no matter where they worked in Canada — were saved mostly by vaccination campaigns alone. With no improvements to their material work conditions, it was vaccination clinics, especially at their job sites, that ensured their safety to be able to continue to work. At Cargill's High River plant, 77% of the workforce had been vaccinated at the workplace site. Workers didn't need to miss any work to get their vaccines, they knew the people administering them and information was provided in many languages. And this number didn't include all the workers who instead got their vaccines through public health clinics.[47]

The lack of media attention on the food industry allowed employers to literally get away with murder. When journalists did talk about these workplaces, they were personified as being economic engines or critical links in the supply chain, and their workers were nearly entirely erased.

With only a few exceptions, this lack of attention made it possible for people to express surprise when, thanks to the third wave of infections, it was racialized, low-income, frontline workers and their families whose lives were on the line in overburdened hospital units.

The meat packing industry is one that has, from its roots, grown to rely on the low wages and exploitation of its workers, all so people can eat a cheap hamburger. North Americans rely on a network of low-waged, precarious workers to supply their food — from processing raw materials to stocking grocery stores. As most structural issues explored in this book, this was true before the pandemic, but COVID-19 has exacerbated these inequities. Just as in long-term care, COVID-19 found its way into Canada's food processing industries, injuring thousands and leaving at least 22 dead, most whom were racialized.[48]

The driving force in these industries was, and still is, profit. Every dollar that can be squeezed out of an employee's paid sick time or personal protective equipment is a little bit extra to meet or surpass last year's revenues. While politicians firmly had this in the back of their minds but had no reason whatsoever to render it visible to the electorate, this driving force was rarely mentioned by journalists, who instead focused on the individual whose life was lost in the battle against COVID-19, or who far too generously accepted the official line from politicians and health authorities. Had the systemic problems within food processing industries been tied together with the stories of individual suffering, Canadians would have had a more honest explanation for why factory outbreaks were so common, especially as corporate Canada was supposed to have learned, and done better, by the time the second wave came around.

The way in which politicians treated food industry workers and the lack of attention journalists paid to these workers — aside from daily regular reporting on outbreaks and an investigation from time to time — is deeply tied to the fact that a majority of these workers are not white. This combined with the precariousness of the jobs made these positions more deadly and meant this story was less covered than other issues during the pandemic, like opening schools. Racism played a key role in how the pandemic unfolded, how it was covered and who was ignored. And in ignoring so many racialized workers, politicians were rarely pressured to actually fix the issues that many raised as key to protecting racialized workers in not just food processing, but in all aspects of Canada's economy and society.

June 2020

SYSTEMIC RACISM AND COVID-19 SPREAD

Cases: 91,694
Deaths: 7,326[1]

In June 2020, protests erupted across Canada, bringing people out of isolation and into the streets for the first time since March, and a conversation on anti-Black racism finally hit the mainstream. While there isn't an issue related to the pandemic that can be discussed without considering race, racism and COVID-19 also required a specific lens. Canada's economic apartheid meant that racialized people were overrepresented on the front lines of the COVID-19 pandemic in long-term care and food production, but also in so many other areas considered essential. Racism underpins all of Canadian society, so it of course would be exacerbated by a public health crisis. And yet, very few voices in the media discussed how COVID-19 disproportionately caused harm to racialized people. Instead, journalists became obsessed with looking for proof of this racism; anecdotes and correlative data were not enough. For much of 2020, politicians failed to fight the pandemic through a racial lens, thereby allowing more harm against Black, Indigenous and racialized communities. But even despite the evidence, it wasn't until April 2021, when doctors took to social media to talk about how their patients were overwhelmingly, and sometimes even entirely, racialized did race finally enter a more mainstream conversation about how COVID-19 was impacting racialized communities. By then, the race-based data that had been released rendered undeniable the disproportionate impact that COVID-19 was having on racialized communities. Even still, politicians mostly ignored race too, only mentioning it when pressed or when politically convenient.

In Canada, large-scale #BlackLivesMatter protests tied the pandemic to questions of policing, and why police in Canada are able to act with such impunity. Accessible research about anti-Black racism in Canada — the work of writers like Robyn Maynard — found expression in the streets, and "defund the police" was the rallying cry. At the same time, anti-Asian racism was on the rise, in street harassment and violence, triggered by journalists and politicians' comments relating the pandemic to China. In journalism — despite the overwhelming evidence about the ways in which the pandemic was differently impacting racialized people — race would be buried, erased in daily coverage and ignored by columnists whose very jobs should have been to make connections between COVID-19, the communities it was harming most, and therefore, the most effective public policy interventions needed to help protect everyone.

MARCELIN AND OSÉNA

When Marcelin François and Oséna Charles came to Canada in 2012, they entered through Roxham Road, a crossing that separates Québec and New York State. Like so many Haitians, the couple left the United States in search of a more stable life in Canada. Marcelin and Oséna quickly started working. Oséna got work at a Cargill factory through a placement agency. A bus would pick her up every day from her Montréal North neighbourhood and bring her to one of Cargill's Québec plants where she processed meat for minimum wage. Together, they had three children: Marc-Sonder, 11; Martline, 3; and Rose-Marline, 17 months old.

Marcelin had two jobs. From Monday to Friday, he worked in a textiles factory. On the weekend, a work placement agency shuttled him between residential care facilities to work as a *préposé aux bénéficiaires*, the term used in Québec for orderlies or nursing assistants. He was not unionized and not officially recognized as a staff person at the residence where he was working when he caught COVID-19. The 40-year-old was rushed to hospital where he died not long after.

These details are from a heartbreaking feature written for *La Presse* by Yves Boisvert called "His name was Marcelin." Tipped off by workers at La Rosière, one residence where Marcelin was working, Boisvert interviewed Oséna about their story: their long path to Canada through the United States from Haiti, the agency-placed work and the pain of losing her husband.[2] Boisvert learned about Marcelin's death when he was talking with one of Marcelin's colleagues Vanne Guerrier, also a refugee from Haiti who worked in various care homes, placed by an agency. Vanne spent eight days in hospital with COVID-19, two in intensive care. Like Oséna, Vanne first started working in a meat processing facility, then found work as a *préposé*, and similarly lived in the neighbourhood of Montréal North.[3] Boisvert was one of the first journalists who tied the personal plight of refugees directly to working conditions within long-term care homes and demonstrated just how much they had sacrificed to work on the front lines of this pandemic. Between February 2017 and May 2018, just 9% of Haitians who sought refugee status were granted it. Nigerians had 34% of their claims accepted while Syrians were accepted at 84%.[4] Many Haitians who were living in Canada hoping that there would be another path to citizenship had their claims denied. And so, they kept working. On October 1, 2020, an investigation by *La Presse* found that placement agencies were still sending asylum seekers with no status to the most dangerous situations — CHSLDs in Montréal's so-called red zones, with inadequate training.[5] All three of Québec's opposition parties called on the governing Coalition Avenir Québec (CAQ) to stop allowing these agencies to operate. Vincent Marissal from Québec Solidaire called for workers to be hired directly, so they could benefit from more stable employment.[6] Anti-Black racism within the Canadian labour market has pushed hundreds of thousands of Black workers into low-paid, precarious work, especially people who have just entered Canada and who had limited work options because of restrictive and racist border and refugee policies.

On April 20, 2020, writing for the *The Conversation*, Beverly Bain, OmiSoore Dryden and Rinaldo Walcott argued that racialized workers, especially Black workers, would be the most injured by the pandemic, and they were right. Reacting to how journalists had framed the early narrative of the pandemic, they wrote,

> In our early analysis of national media coverage, those experts sharing the grim statistics of infections and deaths, those front-line workers seen as risking their lives and those who have lost loved ones are predominantly white. Black, Indigenous and racialized people, and many whose lives have been further imperiled by this pandemic, remain virtually disappeared from the Canadian landscape.[7]

The voices of the workers who were likely to be hurt the most, the ones with precarious status, who worked in the backbreaking work of long-term care or food processing, were mostly missing. Stories like Boisvert's were not the norm. Racialized workers, especially Black workers, and their communities would be the hardest hit by the virus, and this should have influenced how journalists wrote about COVID-19's impact, both anticipating it and also once the data showed just how much harder COVID-19 was hurting racialized communities. Bain, Dryden and Walcott continued: "Black people tend to be employed in low-paying and highly feminized jobs: these include clerical jobs, janitorial staff, orderlies and nursing assistants who are now determined as essential services."[8] Data about how the pandemic was hitting racialized neighbourhoods the most had not come out yet, but these professors didn't need to see data. They knew what the result would be already, thanks to the way in which Canadian society has been built: on top of colonialism and through colonial violence, with anti-Black racism deeply entwined throughout its political economy. Their foresight would be played out when meagre data would show that the racialized impact of the pandemic was clear: the measures put in place by public health agencies across Canada helped white Canadians primarily. And politicians and public health officials were never held to account for reinforcing this public health apartheid.

ERASING RACE

The Conversation was an important publication for critical perspectives on the pandemic that were absent from among Canada's opinion writers and columnists. Where most mainstream publications wrote about COVID-19 as if there was a neutral or even equitable impact of the virus, *The Conversation* published early warnings from academics whose research and experience showed clearly how the pandemic would likely unfold, and journalists writing about COVID-19 should have incorporated these warnings into how they wrote about the pandemic. On April 6, 2020, Roberta Timothy from the University of Toronto's school of public health sounded the alarm over the impact that COVID-19 would have on Black, Indigenous and racialized people, again in *The Conversation*. Data from the United States showed early on that Black Americans were dying more from COVID-19. With inadequate data, the U.S. information could help Canadian decision makers anticipate how COVID-19 would evolve in Canada and, ideally, how to address the problems within the system before COVID-19 spread too far. She wrote, "Based on my research, I believe that the actions and omissions of world leaders in charge of fighting the COVID-19 pandemic will reveal historical and current impacts of colonial violence and continued health inequities among African, Indigenous, racialized and marginalized folks."[9]

Timothy was pleading with Canadians, especially Canadian public health officials and politicians, to enact targeted interventions to help mitigate the impact that COVID-19 was going to have on racialized people. One week later, an article by Shanifa Nasser titled "Early signs suggest race matters when it comes to COVID-19. So why isn't Canada collecting race-based data?" referenced the proof that COVID-19 was circulating faster among racialized Americans and leaving more racialized Americans dead. She featured the Wellesley Institute's Kwame McKenzie, a doctor and professor who warned that Ontario's lack of race-based data would hide the worst ravages of the pandemic. She wrote, "That's the question several researchers and health professionals across the country are pressing Canada to consider as the battle against COVID-19 wages on. The fear: the virus will kill overwhelming numbers of populations we simply aren't paying attention to." Nasser then quoted McKenzie saying,

> When resources are stretched, McKenzie said, people with chronic diseases may not find themselves at the top of the list for intensive care and ventilators. He said that in some cases, people with underlying conditions have been denied access to those resources during the pandemic, with the priority going to those deemed more likely to survive.[10]

With no race-based data, early articles relied on data from the U.S. Calls for race-based data were dismissed by both chief medical officers of Canada and Ontario, who argued collecting this data wasn't necessary. The same day that Ontario's officer dismissed this, Alberta's Chief Medical Officer Deena Hinshaw said that the province needs to look seriously at collecting race-based data.[11] While Alberta did eventually start collecting race-based data, it wasn't until December 2020 that journalists confirmed this was happening. And the data was not released publicly. Instead, Premier Jason Kenney used it as part of a communications strategy to respond to criticisms that he had targeted South Asian Albertans in previous comments. Government officials claimed the data was only "preliminary," and they preferred to highlight other information instead, like whether or not an individual had other illnesses at the time of their death from COVID-19.[12]

From April until August 2020, McKenzie was quoted extensively by media outlets, especially in reaction to what race-based data showed when it was finally available in July. But his warnings, despite turning out to be true, did not influence the general coverage of the pandemic.

Journalists rarely wrote articles that centred racialized communities until they were forced to, either because the link between race and infection became undeniable or because community and public health advocates who focus on racial inequity spoke out. This lack of attention on racialized communities during the first wave, even after data was reported that made the connection undeniable, allowed politicians to sidestep the issue, never making policies that targeted the collision between systemic racism and COVID-19 infection spread.

It was not said clearly enough, whether by public health officials, politicians or journalists: the biggest burden of the pandemic was borne by racialized workers. In the first 18 months of the pandemic in Canada, 62 healthcare workers died from COVID-19. Of them, the ethnicity was known for 47 individuals, 72.3% of whom were racialized, and more specifically, 44.6% of whom were Black.[13] An article from *TVO* published in February 2021, found that despite the promises of some health units to collect racialized data, they were unable to provide a racial breakdown of the workers who died.[14] I was the only person in Canada publicly tracking this information, data that this article referenced. The percentage was similar for all workers. Even though there was far less information about the race or ethnicity of non-healthcare workers who died from contracting COVID-19 in the workplace, of the 105 deaths I had linked to a workplace outbreak, 50 individuals had their identities either fully or partially revealed. Of them, 74% were not white.[15]

As the only person collecting and reporting this information in Canada, it was very clear to me that analyzing COVID-19 deaths through the lens of race was simply not a priority for Canada's mainstream media establishment. Anecdotes and data patterns became the primary way journalists wrote about race, like looking at an overlay of neighbourhood demographic data with where cases were rising. This wasn't commonly available across Canada, but where it was, like in the City of Toronto, the overlay was near perfect, showing that the low-income quarters of the city, in which larger populations of Black Torontonians lived, aligned closely with where COVID-19 outbreaks were occurring. This was evident as early as the end of May 2020, but most news agencies waited to cover the phenomenon until public health officials that did collect data released this information, more than a month later.[16] Much earlier than that, the connection between race, income and COVID-19 infection rates were obvious in Montréal, where cases in Montréal North were the highest of any neighbourhood in that city.[17] Advocates called for race-based data to be collected and multilingual materials to be created and circulated. But the data would have confirmed what some investigative journalists had already demonstrated in May 2020: through a partnership between the *National Observer,* CTV *News* and Concordia University's Institute for Investigative Journalism, COVID-19 cases were overlaid on maps based on the socioeconomic neighbourhood information available. It was clear that COVID-19 was disproportionately impacting racialized people.[18]

On June 5, 2020, CBC *News* reported that Justin Trudeau and Ontario Minister of Health Christine Elliott would both commit to collecting race-based data.[19] When Toronto finally released the city-based racial data it had promised on July 9, 2020, the racialized impact of the virus was clear: "York University Heights, where 69 per cent of residents identify as a visible minority, has 20 times the rate of infection that The Beaches neighborhood," reported *City News* in Toronto.[20] At the end of July, City of Toronto officials revealed that 83% of everyone who had had a COVID-19 infection was racialized, despite being only half of Toronto's population. By the end of June 2021, the federal government's COVIDTrends tool still didn't report any race-based information. The only race-related information on the website of the Public Health Agency of Canada (PHAC) that is linked to its main COVID-19 data centre is an epidemiological summary from Indigenous Services Canada. It reported that the week of June 22, 2021, the rate of cases of First Nations people living on reserve was a shocking six times the rate of the general Canadian population.[21]

How much did we really know about the racial impact of COVID-19? One peer-reviewed research report that I coauthored, which was published by the Royal Society of Canada at the end of June 2021, estimated that Canada's uncounted death rate for individuals aged 45–65, adjusted for toxic drug-related deaths, was potentially 25% higher than was officially reported. These deaths, we argued, most likely happened among racialized populations at a higher rate than among white populations, based on knowing that more than 70% of workers who had died from COVID-19 they acquired through a workplace infection were racialized.[22] No journalists specifically looked at this aspect of the report.

IGNORANCE OR MALICE?

During the debate about the need to collect racialized data, journalists far too often assumed that Canadians just didn't know how COVID-19 was impacting racialized people, as if racialized Canadians weren't credible enough sources on their own experiences. Many journalists assumed in their reporting that if and when the data existed, politicians would do something about it. Except it wasn't simply a case of not knowing. More than enough indicators showed that, combined with the structural racism built into Canadian society, Black, Indigenous and racialized people were hit harder by the virus. On May 30, 2020, Kwame McKenzie told CBC Radio's *The House* that the way in which racism has operated within public health had been just as much about neglect as it had been about intention: "the fact that we haven't collected this data seems neglectful, because everybody really knew we should be collecting these data but it was never at the top of anybody's list of things to do." McKenzie said proof that the racialized impact would be disproportionate was clear; it was evident in the U.S. and the U.K., but also in how Canadians were impacted by the H1N1 virus: Southeast Asians were three times more likely to have been infected by H1N1, South Asians were six times more likely and Black people in Ontario were a staggering ten times more likely. Then, CBC editorialized: "But for some reason, nobody was collecting similar information when the COVID-19 pandemic broke out." McKenzie did not say "but for some reason." He hinted at possible reasons, including neglect, but CBC sanitized the interview and made it sound like we just don't know why this data hasn't been collected.

McKenzie made a critical point in the interview: even without data, the most important thing needed during the pandemic was action. Public health officials could have done what they could with what they knew about the racialized impact. After McKenzie's comments, white interviewer Chris Hall brought the conversation back to data and asked McKenzie if Canada needs a public inquiry to find out this information. The sleight of hand shifted attention away from discussing concrete and necessary actions that could have been and still could be taken and pushed the audience toward believing we needed more studies into why we have no data, even if we have very clear data about the impact that previous pandemics have had on non-white Canadians. By March 7, 2021, researchers from the University of Manitoba confirmed that one-third of Indigenous people had lost their jobs during the pandemic, higher than any other racialized group, and far higher than white people. They were more likely to be depressed during the pandemic and twice more likely to struggle financially.[23]

When the PHAC issued its annual report near the end of October 2020, they called it *From Risk to Resilience: An Equity Approach to COVID-19* to highlight the differential impact that COVID-19 had on marginalized communities. The data they compiled had mostly been public, like the 7000+ deaths in residential care and the correlating data that showed Black Montrealers were hit harder than others by the virus. But it offered suggestions that could give government a path forward to mitigate these issues in the future, including the very near future, as Canada was still in the middle of the second wave of the pandemic. It made broad recommendations to government for how it could strengthen the role of PHAC, encouraged politicians to share more research about the pandemic, and noted that PHAC and other public health agencies need to collect more data to "inform policy decisions to eliminate inequities and mitigate some potential long-term pandemic impacts."[24]

The problem with PHAC focusing so closely on data allowed journalists, again, to write about data at the expense of exploring what could been done in the absence of good data. This obscured that Canada already has enough evidence, experience with pandemics and experience with race-driven social inequality to have anticipated these impacts before a pandemic even hit Canada. Just before the PHAC report was released, the *Canadian Press* again covered the need for more race-based data but centred the article on comments made by Canada's Deputy Chief Public Health Officer Howard Njoo. They quoted him saying to a public health conference, "collecting data on race and ethnicity for health purposes has been neglected for a very long time but everyone recognizes its importance now."[25] This is just one example; throughout the first wave and before, when talking with journalists all the experts had said Canada's race-based inequality was well known.

The way media sanitized, obscured or ignored the racialized impact of COVID-19 by focusing on proof in the form of data ensured that Canadians did not get to hear what exactly politicians and public health were doing to address racial inequities. Politicians were able to do very little, as the pressure was always placed back onto the question of statistics rather than funding or programs that could have supported racialized people. Was there money to put more testing centres into these communities? What about offering quarantine housing for racialized workers who lived in multi-generational settings? Where was the extra programming to help keep racialized children safe when they went to school? What about mandating paid sick leave, especially for those who worked in high-risk jobs? What about insisting employers reduce production or close when needed? But the nature of Canada's economy meant racialized workers in precarious and/or low-income work, who were most vulnerable to catching COVID-19, were also the ones who didn't need incentives to keep them at their jobs: they would continue to work under intolerable situations because they had to make ends meet. And their bosses, the owners who made money off poor working conditions, were never forced to implement anything significant to keep workers safe.

The earliest and most central goal for all governments was to "plank the curve" — stop cases from rising. To do this, all governments across Canada imposed lockdowns forcing people who could work from home to stay shut in, while those who couldn't work from home (who were more likely to be deemed "essential") were forced to work. This had a sinister impact that barely got attention in national media. *Toronto Star* journalist Jennifer Yang tweeted about a data visualization project that the *Toronto Star* did with Toronto Public Health data: "Lockdown *instantly* flattened the curve for #Toronto's richest/whitest areas. For poorest/most racialized … it kept rising"[26] The graph is stark: all cases rose until the moment of the most stringent measures, then the two poorest quartiles keep rising sharply while the two richest quartiles fall. As of October 30, 2020, Black people had been hit hardest, representing 23% of all infections while only making up 9% of Toronto's population. White people, who make up 48% of Toronto's population only made up 18% of those who got sick from COVID-19 and still, this didn't change how journalists and politicians talked about the pandemic.[27] While Indigenous communities managed to keep COVID-19 at bay during the first wave, the second wave and beyond was devastating.

With everything that politicians and public health agents knew about how COVID-19 was infecting and killing racialized people in the U.S. and the U.K. — knowing how H1N1 spread, and knowing that healthcare and the economy already marginalize and cause harm to Black, Indigenous and racialized people — it is hard to see the pandemic response as anything other than racist negligence. The eventual access to data still didn't create proactive equity programs to mitigate the disproportionate impact of

COVID-19: by April 6, 2021, Nicholas Hune-Brown found that the neighbourhoods in Toronto with the highest rates of COVID-19 infection and death also had the lowest rates of vaccination. Inversely, the postal codes with the lowest rates of infection had the highest rates of vaccination. In one of the few Canadian jurisdictions that actually collected and reported race-based data, the most important intervention to the pandemic yet — vaccines — were still being administered inequitably.[28]

The way race and COVID-19 interacted in Canada's largest city was replicated across Canada, yet racism rarely figured into dominant discourses about the virus. Race was erased entirely from daily briefings, the tool that fed the majority of media coverage. When journalists did write about it, it was often a side note, a special feature or focused on the U.S. And when it was written about, racism was often put into quotation marks, like this *Global News* headline that examined what data showed in July 2020: "Black neighbourhoods in Toronto are hit hardest by COVID-19 — and it's 'anchored in racism': experts." Of course it's anchored in racism, and of course the experts said that, as they had been saying all along — the use of the colon indicated that. But *Global News* decided it still had to place racism into the realm of opinion, attributed to "experts."

Journalists should have written about how racism was central to telling the story of COVID-19, rather than relegating it to an add-on to a central story. They needed to press politicians for answers that considered how entwined COVID-19 and racism really were. For example, of the 670 media releases and advisories the Ontario government issued from February 23 (the day that Ontario had its first presumptive case of COVID-19), until the end of 2020, just one release referenced how the provincial government would combat COVID-19 through measures especially designed for racialized and/or low-income communities. In fact, of these 670 releases, race was only mentioned four times total, three of which were unrelated to the pandemic.[29] On December 21, 2020, the Ontario government promised just $12.5 million for supports like door-to-door contact where "ambassadors" would provide information, masks and sanitizer to 15 communities.[30] Even with the data, Doug Ford proved that politicians still would not move to address systemic racism. Things were not better elsewhere: Jason Kenney's government didn't release a single press release that contained the words race, racism, racial or low-income and COVID together at all in 2020 and the four releases that did mention racism (but not COVID-19), were related to rising hate incidents in the province.

The federal government was perhaps even more disappointing. They named COVID-19's impact as racialized in the September 2020 Throne Speech, and then followed the comment by announcing a strategy to combat hate, implementing minor reforms in the prison system, and creating a loan scheme run through Canada's banks to allow Black entrepreneurs to open businesses. There was nothing at all to take meaningful action on slowing the spread of COVID-19 through measures that helped those Canadians most likely to get COVID-19: Black, Indigenous and racialized people. When, at the start of the pandemic, Trudeau said: "Our government is going to make sure that no matter where you live, what you do or who you are, you get the support you need during this time," was he only speaking to white people?[31]

Had governments approached the pandemic by placing the people most impacted by it at the centre of its response, they might have been able to slow the spread, reduce the number of infections and save lives. Had they faced consistent questions from journalists, they might have felt pressure to actually do something to address the racial impact of COVID-19. As residential care workers are disproportionately racialized, an approach that placed these people at its heart would have also had the result of mitigating COVID-19 infection in residential care. As I discuss in other chapters, the racialized impact of COVID-19 was evident throughout the economy and society: within healthcare, schools, transit, large congregant work settings, and in all work deemed essential from cab drivers to migrant workers. But forcing politicians into taking these trends seriously, regardless of how good the data was, would have required that journalists treat this aspect of the pandemic with as much seriousness as the daily reported numbers or the crisis in long-term care, not an auxiliary problem that impacted a minority of people.

POLICING AND BLACK LIVES MATTER

Even though COVID-19 disproportionately hit racialized communities and workers from the start, the call for more data was the primary way through which journalists reported on racism. The first moment of reckoning between the pandemic and race did not get mainstream attention until it intersected with policing. Over the first months of the pandemic, as people were locked down, police-reported criminal events dropped. Statistics Canada reported that in the first six months of the pandemic, crime rates fell by 16%.[32] Unsurprisingly, with widespread lockdowns keeping people home or at work, there was less crime and therefore, less for police to do. This had two important results: the first was that many police were assigned to enforce public health measures. Of the 15 Canadian police forces who responded to Statistics Canada's request for information, police were involved in public health measure enforcements 41% of the time from March to May 2020. From mid-March until November 2020, police were involved in 22,867 infractions related to public health orders.[33] In March and April 2020, journalists uncritically reported that police would be asked to help enforce orders. Rarely did journalists question whether that was an effective use of resources, if there could have been other, better-suited groups of people to do this work, or what this would mean for communities that are already over-policed and overrepresented in COVID-19 infection rates. CTV *News Vancouver* ran a short article that drew heavily on a press release from the Royal Canadian Mounted Police (RCMP). In it, the RCMP insisted that they would use new powers sparingly, only arresting people as a last resort. Many news outlets carried official information directly. *Sault Online*, from Sault Ste. Marie, Ontario, published a release from the Ontario Provincial Police on March 20, explaining which activities would be fined since a lockdown order had been given.[34] Media outlets carried the official line of police detachments across Canada: police hope they don't need to arrest or fine you, but they will if you don't comply with public health orders. Journalists reporting about these new powers rarely explained who was actually being targeted by police. On September 2, 2020, in the *Halifax Chronicle Herald*, professor OmiSoore Dryden wrote about the only person to be jailed for allegedly disobeying COVID-19 public health orders: Javan Mizero Nsangira, a Congolese international student who had been living in P.E.I. for two years.[35] Compare that to the punishment that wealthy and white Rodney and Ekaterina Baker received. The pair flew to Beaver Creek, Yukon, on January 19, 2021, pretending to be locals so that they could grab an early shot of the Moderna vaccine. The White River First Nation, located at Beaver Creek, was outraged by the deception. The couple was fined a mere $2300 for violating Yukon's Civil Emergency Measures Act.[36]

While many civil advocacy organizations were immediately critical that police would be called to help enforce public health orders, it was not widely reported that this could pose problems until there were people who had been targeted by police enforcing public health measures and who could speak out after the fact. Activists created resources to track how police were interacting with Canadians during this particularly stressful period. For example, on April 4, 2020, criminology researchers Alexander McClelland and Alex Luscombe created a database called Policing the Pandemic and asked for crowdsourced examples of interactions with police enforcing public health measures.[37] They received some media attention and were called for comment when hefty fines or abusive behaviour were reported. On April 20, 2020, just as the first month of the lockdown was approaching, professors Beverly Bain, OmiSoore Dryden and Rinaldo Walcott argued,

> Public health has historically been an extension of policing for Black people that has positioned us as suspicious and nefarious in our actions and movements. In our current state of emergency, this union of policing and public health has led to more Black people being arrested, detained and physically restrained in the name of public health protection.[38]

During the first wave, journalists usually relegated race to a mention rather than being a key determinant of who police decide to target, unless something happened that they could react to, like an advocacy agency issuing a study or someone speaking out who had been racially profiled by police acting in the name of public health orders. In March 2020, for example, Ottawa's bylaw officers focused on community gatherings, not workplaces:

> The bylaw enforcement team's main focus will be educating residents about Ontario's ban on gatherings of more than five people who aren't members of the same household. The team will also monitor city parks, which are now largely closed to the public, as well as restaurants and non-essential businesses that aren't complying with provincial orders.[39]

Months later, when it was revealed that 66% of people who caught COVID-19 in Ottawa were racialized, CBC News quoted Hindia Mohamoud, director of the Ottawa Local Immigration Partnership. She said that she knew "early on" that this pandemic would disproportionately impact racialized people, because they tend to work in the jobs that are at the most risk. According to 2016 Census data, racialized people in Ottawa make up a quarter of the population.[40] CTV News' Solarina Ho reported on the disproportionate impact that fines were having on racialized people, writing that $13 million in fines that had been given out during the pandemic up until June 24, 2020, and these fines disproportionately impacted racialized and other marginalized people. Her article featured the story of a Black man being racially profiled and followed in a park in Toronto by bylaw officers, and then police.[41]

Ho's piece was published in June 2020, around the same time that narratives about policing changed sharply among mainstream journalists. Along with growing and undeniable evidence that the pandemic was disproportionately impacting racialized communities came a social uprising led by Black activists who came into the streets to say: *enough. The time is now to do away with police altogether.* The confluence of mass protest across North America with the start of warmer weather in much of Canada and the end of the total lockdown saw people drawing together the parallels of anti-Black racism as it's woven into all aspects of society. Even mainstream reporting seemed to understand how COVID-19 was simply laying bare the reality of over-policing that Black, Indigenous and racialized people experience in Canada.

In 2020, 1004 Americans were killed by police.[42] One of these murders, caught on tape, ignited international outrage and gave mainstream coverage to the abolitionist movement that called to defund police and prisons. On May 25, 2020, George Floyd was killed by a police officer who knelt on Floyd's neck while he lay on the pavement. Frustration, anger and a demand for change moved millions of people into the streets. In Canada, the action was the first time that mass mobilization emerged during the pandemic. Massive protests were held in cities across Canada, and impressive rallies were organized in dozens of small towns. Black Lives Matter took mainstream prominence again. Despite the fact that crime levels had dropped according to a Statistics Canada report that examined the first four months of the pandemic, the police did respond to an increase in calls for service during the pandemic: domestic disturbances (+11.6% increase), child welfare checks (+18.8% increase), general welfare checks (+11.5%) and mental health issues, including apprehension (+13%). The latter categories — wellness checks and mental health calls — resulted in several high-profile incidents that turned attention to how police often respond to such calls with unwarranted violence.[43] During the same months, March to June 2020, Ejaz Ahmed Choudry, Chantel Moore, D'Andre Campbell, Regis Korchinski-Paquet and at least one other unnamed man in Halifax all died either directly or indirectly from police responding to a wellness or mental health check. Police also killed many others, including Eishia Hudson, Jason Collins, Stewart Kevin Andrews, Everett Patrick, Abraham Natanine, and Rodney Levi, all of whom were Indigenous. The Statistics Canada report received very little attention from journalists, despite the nationwide calls for justice for people who had died at the hands of police. When the statistics in the report were referenced, the articles usually made it sound as if crime was not falling. In one *Prince Albert Daily Herald* article, Prince Arthur Mayor Greg Dionne warned residents that there could be a rise in petty crime once CERB was converted to Employment Insurance (EI). Readers had to get to paragraph seven before finding out that petty crime had fallen in the prairie city over the course of the pandemic.[44] Despite the mainstream coverage during the summer of 2020, the protests, insistence that Black and Indigenous Lives Matter and support for defunding the police fell out of the attention of the press just months later, and politicians were not forced act on complaints and concerns raised by movement voices.

Canada's criminal system was not just responsible to manage new public health orders; it was also expected to keep prisoners in its custody safe from COVID-19 infection. As I explore in the chapter covering November 2020, these facilities were used by Conservative politicians to argue that prisoners didn't deserve priority access to vaccines. But prisoners are in the care and custody of either federal or provincial governments, and governments largely failed to protect them from COVID-19 infection, or work with prisoners to rapidly inoculate them from COVID-19 when vaccines were available. During the first wave, from March until May 27, 2020, 3% of Canada's total prisoner population caught COVID-19. This was significantly higher than COVID-19 within the general population, which was 0.2%.[45] Social distancing was impossible for most inmates. When an infection tore through Stony Mountain in Manitoba, prisoners were locked into their cells, only given 30 minutes per day to leave to do things like shower or make a phone call. Grayson Wesley, who lived at Stony Mountain on a range where there was no COVID-19 but who eventually got infected at the end of November 2020 and had symptoms that were so bad that he was sent to hospital, told CBC *Manitoba*, "I feel like they failed miserably." Federal inmates launched a class action lawsuit alleging negligence that failed to protect them from catching COVID-19.[46] In total, as of July 1, 2021, the official tally was that nine people died in custody of a federal or provincial correctional facility, and one staff person died.[47] There were

9140 total COVID-19 infections among inmates and staff. Ontario led the provinces with 1728 prisoners infected (of 7447 in custody),[48] followed by Alberta (1483 prisoners infected of 3615 in custody) and Saskatchewan (825 prisons infected of 1923 in custody). Québec, with 4488 in custody, had 640 prisoners infected with COVID-19.[49]

Canada's prisons are locations of white supremacy, as is the institution of policing, and COVID-19 infections cannot be untied from the over-representation of racialized people within these facilities. In Ontario, one study found that Black men were five times more likely than white men to be incarcerated. They also spend more time in provincial facili-ties and more likely to be transferred to federal institutions than other men. Black women are nearly three times more likely to be incarcerated than white women.[50] The data is even more stark for Indigenous people: they represent 31% of all admissions to provincial or territorial custody, and 29% of federal custody, even though they only comprise about 4.5% of the Canadian population. Indigenous adults comprise three-quarters of admissions to correctional facilities in Manitoba and Saskatchewan, and Indigenous women make up 42% of female custody admissions.[51] Journalists didn't cover prisons very much during the first 18 months of the pandemic, from how they planned to mitigate COVID-19 or how inmates were managing, and when they did, white supremacy was never mentioned. Politicians never talked about how prisons were the locations of such devastating COVID-19 spread because of racism.

It's more or less obvious why white politicians would deny racism. To address systemic racism in Canada means fixing the core of what makes Canada, Canada. It also means challenging the power structures that give politicians their power in the first place. This makes journalism such a critical location in democracy: if journalists are not able to challenge politicians' racism, then the voices that do, often activists and advocates from civil society, are easy to marginalize and ignore. How was racism and the pandemic so ignored? The murder of George Floyd forced Canadian journalists to pay attention to racism, policing and the pandemic in a way that they hadn't been forced to before. But with racialized men dying at rates that were far higher than any other group within the working-aged population, how did this get missed by journalists? In researching this book, I referenced thousands of articles that I chose based on topic and daily coverage. And the overwhelming majority of the journalists I cited were white: of the 423 journalists whose work informs the research in this book, just 28 were racialized men. Forty-eight were racialized women. Systemic racism within journalism made it such that it was impossible for Canada's media establishment to cover racism, or challenge racist policy measures, in any meaningful or adequate way.

ANTI-ASIAN RACISM

White-centric coverage also played a fundamental role in exacerbating violence and racist attitudes thanks to an early focus on COVID-19 being a "Chinese" problem. Over the course of the pandemic, there was an intense rise in reported anti-Asian racist events. As I explore in the first chapter (March 2020), journalists linked COVID-19 to China, the location in which it was first officially discovered, in such a way that it became fundamental to the story of COVID-19. In the early days, flights from China, travellers from China, the actions of the Chinese government and daily life in Wuhan became a regular obsession of journalists. In the first weeks of the pandemic, there was a related spike in anti-Asian racism in regions across Canada. A poll conducted at the end of April 2020 found that 14% of respondents were either certain or unsure that all Chinese or Asian people carried COVID-19. Twenty-one percent of respondents didn't think it was safe to sit beside a Chinese person on a bus if they were not wearing a mask.[52] At the time of the survey in April, Canadians had not yet adopted widespread mask wearing, including on public transit.

There's little doubt that the racist narrative of the so-called China Virus was made far worse by rhetoric coming from Donald Trump, but anti-Asian racism was rarely a central story told during the pandemic until the high-profile murder of eight people, six of whom where Asian women, at three spas near in Atlanta, Georgia. Instead, stories popped up each time there was a survey or a study rather than forming the basis of a generalized analysis. This was especially true in 2021, when 2020 hate crime statistics came out. Ottawa Police reported responding to 15 incidents of anti-Asian hatred, up from just two the year before.[53] In British Columbia, hate crimes against Asian people jumped by 717%.[54] Even despite these high percentages, they were surely limited because police reporting is notoriously fraught — many people wouldn't file a report. Groups of people undertook to tell their own stories, like Project 1907. This grassroots initiative sought people's anonymous experiences of anti-Asian racism to track just how often people were being verbally harassed, assaulted or having their property vandalized. In June 2020, CTV News wrote about the group in a feature about the history of anti-Asian activities in Canada, with a focus on British Columbia as anti-Asian hate crimes continued to climb. The organization continued to track hate activity in Canada, as it climbed and the pandemic rolled on.

On March 3, 2021, Amy Chung profiled Kyungseo Min for the *Huffington Post*, a video game writer who had been collecting stories of racist events that targeted Asian Quebecers. Min tried to convince journalists that the increase in anti-Asian hate crimes should be covered by journalists but was often told "her story wasn't newsworthy." Like Project 1907, Min collected stories to create a record of these events but to also demonstrate to mostly white journalists that the rise in hate crimes was serious. Min said that during the pandemic months, the racism she experienced was "terrible" compared to the other 20 years she lived in Canada. They were so bad, she considered moving back to Korea. The South Korean consulate issued a safety warning to Koreans living in Montréal in March 2020, right after a 44-year-old research fellow was stabbed at the start of lockdown.[55] His family returned to Korea after the incident. Even after this event, journalists didn't take activists seriously when they warned of increased hate crimes. Chief Medical Officer of Health Theresa Tam faced a considerable amount of racism by anti-lockdown protesters who used the COVID-19-China connection to disparage, harass and intimidate her, including by former Conservative Party leadership candidate Derek Sloan during April 2020. In an opinion piece condemning Sloan written by the *Toronto Star*'s Bruce Arthur, he argued that China deserves to be criticized, just not in a racist way. The lack of nuance from Arthur also posed a problem, though, as it both condemned the result of tying COVID-19 and China too closely together and reinforced that they should be tied closely together.[56]

With China and COVID-19 being so tightly bound together at the start of the pandemic, the resulting rise in anti-Asian racism should have been an obvious outcome. As if a stabbing hate crime wasn't enough, activists continued to sound alarms about the rise in hate crimes, and politicians did little more than condemn it when they were (rarely) asked about it. Journalists who were already systemically incapable of writing about anti-Black racism faced the same challenges in writing about anti-Asian racism, mostly doing so in rare, longer features or responding to a police report or survey. Journalists were never forced to contend with the direct line between their coverage of COVID-19's relation to China and the rise in anti-Asian hate crimes. They certainly didn't hold politicians to account for the interventions they and public health officials made that also stoked racist flames, regardless of intent.

The long-standing problem with white supremacy within Canadian media made an already resource-strained system struggle even harder to adequately tell this story. It was just as clear with how journalism stoked anti-Asian racism as how it dealt with stories about anti-Black racism. Journalism in Canada plays a very important role in maintaining the illusion that Canada is a white country, telling stories of "minority voices" through add-ons, supplemental to the dominant narrative that imagines a white audience. In a feature that wrote with the coverage of Black Lives Matter protests in mind, journalist Hadeel Abdel-Nabi argued that systemic racism within Canadian media distorts the stories that journalists try to tell and erases experiences of racialized readers. In June 2020, she wrote,

> For years, mainstream news outlets have cozied up next to whiteness in every way. Reporting is riddled with coded language surrounding minority groups, story and source choices are dominated by racial bias, journalism programs are taught by mostly white faculty and newsrooms are overseen by often all-white executive teams. The result is deeply-rooted mistrust on behalf of non-white communities — if that trust existed in the first place — and toxic work environments for racialized journalists who are often forced to carry the burden of pushing for change within the newsroom.[57]

Inadequate, xenophobic and racist reporting is the result of both the lack of representation among journalists and also toxic newsroom cultures that actively push out racialized journalists. White supremacy within journalism also meant that there was more distance between the storyteller and average people whose story they were telling: for example, if the journalist was white and middle class, the odds were lower that they were related to someone who works in low-income, precarious work. This lack of representation, connection and attention to understanding the world as lived by racialized people showed up in reporting on COVID-19 over and over, and not just in how so many journalists were reluctant to identify the disproportionate impact that COVID-19 had on racialized communities.

WHITE COLUMNISTS

Journalism had a lot to account for in how it stoked racism, from the way in which stories about statues of white supremacists were being pulled down, to the obsession with China. In most reporting, the racism was implicit: it was usually in couched terms or mentioned through the sources that a journalist decided to include in their story. But opinion journalism was far more blatant rendering racism invisible. While opinion journalism had the flexibility to be able to move the spotlight from white-centred narratives to ones that more adequately and fairly reflected what was happening, it rarely did. There has been a steady decline of racialized opinion journalists for more than two decades. Despite shifts in Canada's demographics, opinion writing has become whiter. This is what a study done by journalism professors Asmaa Malik and Sonya Fatah found: "Our preliminary research shows that this demographic shift was not reflected in the makeup of Canadian columnists. Over the 21 years, as the proportion of white people in Canada's population declined, the representation of white columnists increased."[58] The first results were published before the pandemic, in November 2019. The concentration of writing from white columnists during the pandemic was one of the ways in which the pandemic was whitewashed. Take for example the *Toronto Star*'s senior political columnist Martin Regg Cohn. Of the 110 columns he wrote between March 1 and December 31, 2020, 50 were written about COVID either directly or indirectly. Of these 50 columns, just one mentioned race as one factor that disproportionately disadvantaged people, though it was only two sentences in a column that otherwise focused on income and homelessness.[59] He did write about six columns that dealt with race, though. In the aftermath of massive #BlackLivesMatter demonstrations in Toronto, he wrote about racism in Canada, though leads his column with this: "Never mind that America has a legacy of slavery that Canada doesn't share, for we have our own well-documented history of discrimination. The bigger difference isn't in the racism but in the responses."[60] This is factually incorrect, as scholars of slavery in Canada have pointed out numerous times. On October 4, he told on himself a little in a column that featured the Ontario NDP's Black Caucus. After having moderated a public panel with members of the Black Caucus, he wrote in his column that Ontarians needed to listen to Black voices and generalized, "When white folks confront racism, their first thought is usually slavery or strife in America — with Canada as an afterthought."[61] While the comment explained his column about historical racism from months earlier, it was a clear show of the intellectual limits he brought to his analysis. It's not too surprising that he didn't focus nearly at all on how COVID-19 was perpetuated through racist social structures and policies. The *Toronto Star*'s senior Ottawa analyst Susan Delacourt's columns were similarly limp. In one that asked if Trumpism could ever come to Canada, she interviewed two white men and didn't mention race or the rise in anti-mask movements.[62] One column, titled "Female politicians endure misogyny, racism and hurtful comments. It's time for them to talk about that," featured an interview with a white man and didn't talk about racism beyond using the word once.[63] None of her columns engaged with racism and COVID-19, though she did interview a white pollster who thought COVID-19 was having a positive influence on how white Canadians viewed Black people. In a dizzyingly what-the-fuck column, she wrote,

> The difference between 2016 and 2020 is most remarkable in positive opinions of Black people, which have seen a 10-plus percentage-point jump in both countries. In 2016, only 51 per cent of Americans said they had favourable or very favourable views on Black citizens. That's up to 62 per cent in this newest survey. The same jump has happened in Canada, from 55 per cent to 65.[64]

Delacourt wrote that the poll, done by the polling company Innovative Research was given exclusively to the *Toronto Star*, and the article featured analysis from Innovative Research's President Greg Lyle. It's hard to believe that this was even published in Canada's largest city newspaper in Canada's most diverse city, if you forget how hard media in Canada works to maintain white supremacy.[65] The article disassociates polls from the social struggle waged by Black activists who were *fighting for their humanity against a system that has been hurting and killing Black people* and boils it into how white people say they have changed their views about Black people, as if that in and of itself is an innocent or neutral poll finding. And worse, it assumes that Americans are de facto white. She didn't mention any of the Black healthcare workers who had died because of COVID-19. She didn't mention any of Canada's racist border policies, which had increased deportations during this strange year. Her only article that engaged with anti-Black racism and COVID-19, was single-sourced from a white pollster.

In covering Black Lives Matter protests and COVID-19, the *Toronto Star* was hardly an outlier in its aggressive whiteness. In the 30 columns that the *Globe and Mail*'s Toronto affairs columnist Marcus Gee wrote from the start of the pandemic until December 31, 2020, he wrote about COVID-19, either directly or adjacently, ten times. Like Regg Cohn, none examined race and the pandemic. Gee did write several columns about racism though, including defending protecting statues of Canadian genocidal leaders. One article that touched on racism condemned NDP leader Jagmeet Singh's reaction to the police investigation into the death of Regis Korchinski-Paquet. She died by falling from her balcony when police entered her apartment. Gee wrote,

> So what did Jagmeet Singh do? He pointed a finger at the police. "Regis Korchinski-Paquet died because of police intervention. She needed help and her life was taken instead. The SIU's decision brings no justice to the family and it won't prevent this from happening again," wrote the New Democrat on Twitter. That was an astonishing thing for the head of a national political party to say.[66]

Gee then defended the SIU investigation and quoted extensively from it, including how the SIU argues that she fell while trying to move from one apartment to another across balconies. Even though this indicated that yes, police presence had something to do with her falling to her death, he didn't arrive at this logical conclusion.

Gee even wrote an article on August 1, 2020, that insisted that Toronto's COVID-19 case count was low enough that, for people's mental health and the economy, businesses be opened back up:

> Any dangers of further reopening have to be weighed against the cost of prolonging a lockdown that has thrown thousands out of work. That lockdown is taking a toll not just on the economy but on human health, both physical and mental health.[67]

He failed to mention anything about race in the column, including the relevant fact that the majority of the workers who died were racialized. He didn't note the mental and physical toll that working in high-risk industries has taken on Toronto's majority non-white working class. Just two months later, Toronto would have 229 cases on October 1 alone, the highest of any other city in Ontario, and the hotspots would again be Toronto's poorest and most racialized neighbourhoods.[68]

Regg Cohn, Delcourt and Gee write in and for a city where 52% of people are not white — these people who disproportionately bore the brunt of the pandemic — and not one of their many COVID-19 columns in 2020 explored this. And these columnists are not even part of Canada's virulent right-wing columnist club. With so many columnists in Canada being aggressively right-wing, there was no shortage of outright racist columns. As race-based analyses just started to emerge in May 2020, the *Toronto Sun*'s Lorrie Goldstein wrote a column that blamed the deaths in long-term care on politicians focusing too much on racism. The column said, "One of the most infuriating blunders of Canada's political class in the ongoing pandemic was obsessing about alleged massive societal racism against Canadians of Chinese origin, when the real crisis was the looming carnage of COVID-19."[69] He didn't seem to be responding to any new data or something that happened in relation to anti-Chinese racism. He cherry-picked comments from January 29, 2020, made by Toronto City Councillor Kristyn Wong-Tam and Chief Public Health Officer Theresa Tam from before the pandemic had started in Canada. In Western Canada, Licia Corbella constantly called into question the need for lockdown measures, articles that were gleefully shared by conspiracy theorists on social media. In Québec, 2020 was the year where François Legault publicly denied racism more than he probably had in his entire life. Québec's right-to-far-right media ecosystem had a feeding frenzy on what is or is not racism. The racialized impact of COVID-19 was barely examined by mainstream columnists, and writing about racism was relegated to responding to incidents like police brutality and racial profiling, the shocking death of Joyce Echaquan in a Joliette hospital and a debate among white journalists about their right to use the n-word.

The few who tried to keep the spotlight on racism and COVID-19 became critically important. Shree Paradkar, the *Toronto Star*'s Race and Gender Columnist pushed back in her columns, consistently reminding people though various angles how COVID-19 was playing out among the city's racialized communities. Her most innovative work featured Yan, a woman who worked in a Toronto massage parlour, and who, along with Butterfly, the Asian and Migrant Sex Worker Support Network, criticized frivolous ticketing as bylaw officers were given more power in July 2020.[70] Through her column, she brought attention to a group of racialized and precarious workers that are so often shut out of Canada's mainstream media. The *Saskatoon StarPhoenix*'s Doug Cuthand used his column to talk about racism and COVID-19 regularly, including one that made a plea to protect Indigenous communities, especially Elders from the virus' deadly spread. He decried the way the community of La Loche, one of the first in Saskatchewan to have COVID-19 deaths, was left exposed because of work camps that were declared essential by the Alberta government and therefore never shut down. Niigaan Sinclair, awarded Canada's best columnist in 2018 by the National Newspaper Awards, also regularly looked at how racism, colonialism and COVID-19 intersected in Manitoba. The disproportionate number of COVID-19 cases among Indigenous people was nothing short of scandalous.[71]

White columnists writing away racism from the pandemic was bad enough, but when you consider that white columnists make up a larger proportion of columnists overall in Canada, it becomes intentional disinformation to uphold white supremacy. Columnists became even more important during the pandemic to help explain these impacts, except the perspectives of white columnists were elevated over the voices that were closer to, in experience and social location, the majority of the people who actually got COVID-19. As Malik and Fatah's research showed, even though the Canadian population has increasingly diversified, its columnists have not, allowing the few columnists who did remain in the national media more space to help scrub racism from how Canadians understood the pandemic.

The way systems in Canada are set up, built on and maintain colonial violence and white supremacy, allowed COVID-19 to easily walk in between its cracks, corridors, hallways and highways to settle into the workplaces, homes and then bodies of Black, Indigenous and racialized people. The evidence that this would happen was clear early on in the pandemic and even before, yet public health officials and politicians did nearly nothing to confront COVID-19 as it exploited systemic racism. Hundreds of thousands of Canadians suffered through COVID-19, having caught it due to a kaleidoscope of reasons related to their race, community, income and/or workplace. Journalists watched this on the front lines, and most missed this crucial part of the pandemic story.

Instead, journalists stayed close to the official line for what was really driving COVID-19. Sometimes the reason was careless young people. Sometimes it was park parties or gatherings. Most times, it was related to a lapse in good sense, collective responsibility or solidarity with others — a young person who just wanted to party or a couple who needed to spend the winter in Florida. Racism didn't need to be spoken or written about when the blame could be placed on the personal actions of individuals. As journalists lapped up this frame, racialized workers kept getting sick, racialized healthcare aides kept dying and COVID-19 continued to spread through postal code areas where the population was more Black, more Indigenous, more Asian or simply *less white* than elsewhere.

JULY 2020
THE LIE OF PERSONAL RESPONSIBILITY

Cases: 104,271
Deaths: 8,615[1]

As structural conditions of society allowed COVID-19 to spread swiftly, systemic solutions were required to limit transmissions: an end to low-waged work, cash injections into racialized communities, massive change within residential care and economic stimulus that would help the poorest people. Except politicians didn't want massive change. They didn't want to be forced into enacting systemic solutions. It was better for politicians if citizens saw themselves the way that they've wanted us to see ourselves for a generation: through an individualized, neoliberal lens. That way, we wouldn't be asked to think too hard about all the ways we are networked to others across society. Through economic and social policies that have erased our common sense of community, and instead exalted the individual as the most important unit of society, politicians knew that it would be easier to not address the underlying, systemic causes of the worst of the pandemic.

COVID-19 didn't care at all about personal responsibility and instead exploited cracks within Canadian society. The kinds of measures that helped individuals take individual action, like making hand sanitizer ubiquitous, were not extended to communities to help them take community action or to develop community protections. After months of the dominant messaging focusing on individual responses to stopping COVID-19, politicians turned their focus on the behaviours of young people in the summer of 2020.

It was clear from the start that only through social solidarity, including bringing employers to heel, would we be able to beat the virus. But instead, to protect the neoliberal status quo politicians explained, and journalists parroted, that to plank the curve or go back to normal all we needed to do was take precautions based on public health advice. This lie of personal responsibility was engrained early on in the pandemic. It even got its own app, intended to stop infection spread by notifying individuals when they had to cloister themselves, as if that was possible for someone with an employer who refused time off. To go along with this, there was intense blame levelled on young people — for being selfish and irresponsible, refusing to do what was necessary to stop the pandemic. This was a narrative that ignored the fact that many young people were essential workers forced to put themselves in danger at the service of others. It obscured the real causes of community spread: failures within residential care and large congregant workplaces to adequately protect their workers and the people they serve. In particular, journalists and politicians focused on single-unit dwellings at the expense of examining the pandemic through the lens of Canada's large population living in multiple-unit buildings.

This government narrative collided with reality as housing activists across Canada critiqued the lack of support to ensure that everyone had a safe place to socially distance. Shelter outbreaks were common, and the fight waged by thousands for people to have a dignified place to live was not just a matter of human rights and security but also important public policy to try and limit the spread of COVID-19. When COVID-19 showed up in places of work where people were poorly paid, it spread like wildfire, not just among colleagues and clients but also within the communities of people connected to the facility. If workers couldn't afford rent and had nowhere to go to at the end of the shift, some found themselves in the shelter system, creating a dangerous cycle that ensured COVID-19 could propagate over and over and over.

TWO WOMEN

"We went from opioids to COVID in a heartbeat. We deal with one disaster after the next." This is how Jeff Turnbull, medical director of Ottawa Inner City Health, explained to Ontario's Long-Term Care COVID-19 Commission why homeless shelters were ill equipped to help people during the crisis. The conditions of homeless shelters, which Turnbull described as sheltering people "cheek by jowl" in beds bunked three high, weren't optimal at the best of times.[2] Overcrowding meant that keeping COVID-19 at bay was impossible, even with lower capacity and social distancing measures. It was December 16, 2020, and Turnbull's presentation was intended to be a resource for commissioners to see if long-term care professionals could learn anything from how the shelter system managed with the pandemic.

During his testimony, he talked about two women, workers at long-term care facilities, who were staying at a shelter and who both had COVID-19. "They just can't earn enough money to afford Ottawa's rental circumstances," he said. Their jobs made them possible nodes of COVID-19 transmission from the facilities where they worked into the shelter where they lived. With the low rates of pay among personal care workers, these two found themselves unhoused in the middle of the pandemic, working on the front lines caring for others.[3]

Imagine these two women listening to public health orders: *Wash your hands, isolate, avoid contact with others.* Already, their jobs were high-risk, at the whim of an employer who may or may not have supplied adequate PPE. But once they left work, these women were at the whim of another system, one that was already under tremendous strain before the pandemic hit and where social distancing was mostly out of one's control. Is your bed far enough away from your neighbour's? It doesn't matter, you can't move it anyway. Did the woman who used the bathroom before you have COVID-19? Did she clean the sink, wipe down the faucet? Even if she did, what about aerosol transmission? What's the ventilation like?

COVID-19 moved from person to person quickly through people who travelled, and that included through workers who worked at multiple worksites. When governments promised to prohibit healthcare workers from working in multiple locations in April 2020, they didn't prohibit other workers from doing so. Worker mobility continued to pose a transmission threat as they moved from workplace to workplace to make a living. The connections between low-income work, the racialized impact of COVID-19, precarious housing and unsafe working conditions should have formed the basis of how Canadians understood COVID-19 to be spreading, as these were the principle driving factors. Instead, rather than this narrative, Canadians were told that stopping the pandemic was in their hands. If they failed to, it was a personal mistake or reckless behaviour. Rarely did we hear stories such as these two women's. When we did, they came as a result of advocates, in this case one who included their stories in testimony and it got picked up by a journalist who had read the commission transcripts. But most journalists towed the politicians' lines, explaining away the spread by blaming it on individual people, especially youth, obscured lax public health measures and hid the true culprit: precarious social structures that keep individuals hanging by a thread as they try to survive.

INDIVIDUALIZED COVID-19 RESPONSES

From the start of the pandemic, personal responsibility was at the heart of public health's messaging: if only you incorporate these things in your life, we might be able to stop the spread of COVID-19. It was epitomized in the mantra *don't touch your face*. One *Huffington Post* article offered an incredible list of ways to avoid touching your face that included: write down every time you touch your face, always carry a squeeze ball with you and squeeze it when the urge to face touch arises, always wear wool or "nubby fingerless gloves," start wearing glasses, wear nail polish that tastes disgusting, breathe differently, punish yourself for every time you touch your face with exercise, "allow yourself" to do something fun like eat popcorn or buy new nail polish if you get through a day of less face touching and the ever-helpful suggestion, "post notes around your spaces that say DO NOT TOUCH YOUR FACE." The message was clear: the power to stop this pandemic is in your hands, as long as those hands then don't touch your face.[4]

On Google Trends, "Do not touch your face" went from zero in the last months of 2019 until the week of February 23–29 and then, by March 8–14, hit the term's peak popularity, never to return to zero again in 2020.[5] Of course, as the virus was emerging and it wasn't clear how it spread, the advice to not touch one's face was practical. Canadian media was full of stories about face touching. This, combined with a barrage of other helpful personal hygiene reminders, all reminded us that we have a critical role to play in stopping the spread of the coronavirus pandemic. But while we were told to stop touching our faces, there were already hundreds of thousands of people around the world who had COVID-19 and who likely did not get the virus through touching their faces.

At the start, this narrative was less punitive and more helpful. People were not blamed for spreading illness through careless behaviour as much as they were reminded over and over to stay six feet apart from others. The personal responsibility narrative served a critical purpose: it ignored broader systemic issues, like the impact that housing had on enabling people to stay safe; it blamed youth for the spread of COVID-19; it lionized small businesses at the expense of examining the role that large, industrial facilities played in spreading the virus; it focused intensely on the role that an individualized app could play in stopping the spread of COVID-19; and it obscured the many systemic interventions that politicians should have made. Largely, these interventions were needed in workplaces, the engines of community spread, where no amount of personal responsibility was able to get past the fact that people were being forced into conditions that would perpetuate the spread of COVID-19. Despite all the airtime given to the personal responsibility narrative, it was never going to be possible to stop COVID-19 through a steady diet of handwashing and bad-tasting nail polish. But that didn't stop the personal responsibility narrative from becoming the dominant frame through which journalists wrote about COVID-19 spread.

If March, April and May 2020 were marked by a swift and high death count, confusion and anxiety, the summer months of 2020 allowed Canadians a moment to breathe. Warm temperatures expanded safe spaces to gather with others outdoors, and many provincial lockdown measures were eased. At the same time, the personal responsibility narrative that had so intensely underpinned the measures necessary to stop the spread of COVID-19 became even more present in comments from politicians, public health and journalists. This time, though, there was blame and guilt attached to not following them. Personal responsibility became typified in a single technological tool: the COVID tracking app. The app promised to keep Canadians safe by telling them when they came into contact with someone who was positive with COVID-19. The idea was that upon receiving a positive notification, an individual could self-isolate, monitor for symptoms and thereby reduce the possibility of spreading COVID-19 while pre- or asymptomatic.

The COVID-19 alert app was promised in May and delivered in July, created by volunteers from the Canadian e-commerce company Shopify. Justin Trudeau announced the government's plans to create an app on May 22, 2020, at a press conference that looked at how the federal government was planning to expand contact-tracing capacity. The app was not the only thing announced at that Friday news conference in May: Trudeau also announced that Statistics Canada had trained enough people to make up to 20,000 contact-tracing calls per day.[6] But by the end of December, Statistics Canada's capacity was still only 17,020. In the face of record-breaking case totals, from December 20 to December 26, 2020, the average daily number of contact-tracing calls was just 3245.[7] Many public health units announced they were rolling back contact-tracing efforts because they were overwhelmed, just as the second wave started to gain steam, even though Statistics Canada still had the capacity to help overwhelmed public health units.[8] But that was impossible to know in

May. The announcement of an app and more human resources for contact tracing sounded great.

If contact-tracing capacity was key to slowing the spread, then deploying human resources to do so was important. But as cases took off and public health officials admitted that contact tracing had broken down, the government's app offered journalists something new and cutting-edge to focus on as one solution to the lack of contact tracing. The app fit a very useful narrative: the pandemic was the result of people's individual actions, thereby absolving businesses and politicians from needing to take further action. If you come into contact with someone with COVID-19, you had a responsibility to keep yourself safe (through social distancing, wearing a mask, etc.). If you couldn't keep yourself safe, you had a responsibility to at least protect others and self-isolate, monitor for symptoms and not spread COVID-19 around. If you didn't know who you maybe came into contact with, the government app would help you notify them. Nowhere in the equation were the conditions of daily life: workplaces where COVID-19 spread faster than anyone would know through using an app, living situations where you would find out if your roommate had COVID-19 probably before they decided to enter anything into an app, or family relationships where your kids were infinitely more likely to sneeze directly into your mouth than they were to give you a notification about having tested positive.

The same day that Trudeau and Ford announced an app was in development, the *Globe and Mail* published analysis written by Derek Ruths, a member of the committee that offered advice to the federal government about developing an app, and professor of computer science at McGill University. Ruths described two very different kinds of apps: one that traced contacts and one that notified users of a COVID-19 exposure. The former, Ruths argued, "tend[s] to favour rapid public health response over privacy," as individuals' movement and social movements could be used to help with tracking the spread of COVID-19.[9] The latter would be more anonymous. It would rely on people voluntarily uploading a positive COVID-19 diagnosis. Ruths wrote that while only the former "can be correctly called contact-tracing," a privacy-protecting COVID-19 exposure app made more sense in Canada: less personal information required would help boost buy-in and therefore users.

There was a big problem with the latter form of app though. Ruths argued that an exposure app, which gives public health less information about the individual infected and their contacts, puts public-health workers in the uncomfortable position of having no knowledge of how a particular exposure affected the broader public, but it does give exposed individuals the knowledge they need in order to make decisions about whether they should self-quarantine. It also puts all responsibility for response squarely on our individual shoulders.[10]

Canada's COVID-19 alert app was the latter, not the former, though journalists often confused the two. CBC News regularly referred to the COVID-19 alert app as a "contact-tracing app." When the app was approved for use in the Northwest Territories, CBC News' headline was, "Federal COVID-19 contact tracing app now being rolled out in N.W.T.," and "contact tracing app" appeared throughout the article.[11] The Montreal Gazette corrected an article that featured criticisms from Yoshua Bengio, a deep learning expert from the Université de Montréal, for having called the COVID Alert app a "contact-tracing app" in a previous version of the article.[12]

Framing the app as a contact-tracing app rather than a COVID exposure app confused the purpose of the app and made it sound as if it could do something it couldn't, while also placing all the responsibility for understanding how COVID-19 was spreading on the user, as Ruths argued would happen. Aside from whether or not someone recently diagnosed with COVID-19 and languishing in bed would even think to update their app, the uptake was never high enough to have the impact that experts had hoped. There are many limits to personal responsibility, as this chapter argues, and without a robust set of social programs that would enable people to socially isolate if they received a positive app notification, its effectiveness would always be limited. In his address to Canada after September 2020's Throne Speech, Trudeau reminded Canadians again to download the app, and he drew on a hypothetical situation where someone used the app and was able to limit potential spread of COVID-19:

> Take the teacher who felt fine, but he gets a positive after the app warned her she'd been exposed. COVID Alert meant she went home instead of the classroom. It's a powerful, free tool that's easy to use and protects your privacy. So if you haven't already, download it off the App Store or Google Play.[13] [Pronoun mix-up is accurate according to the transcript.]

Trudeau's hypothetical could only work if that teacher didn't experience pressure from management to be in the classroom during an incredibly stressful and late start to the school year. For a worker in a job where they have no paid sick days, inadequate safety measures on the job or in a home shared with others, the app's utility to stop spread was extremely limited. If this teacher was exposed to COVID-19 in a workplace that was supposed to be safe and secure for them and their students, finding out several days later on the app would be too late.

The app was officially launched on July 31, almost a month after the planned release on July 2. By December 18, 2020, the federal government announced that the app had been downloaded 5,738,220 times,[14] equating to 17.9% of all Canadian adults — a far cry from the 60% that researchers argued was necessary for the app to work.[15] On March 1, 2021, it was revealed that just 5% of positive COVID-19 causes sought a user key and only 4% actually entered their code to notify their contacts of possible transmission.[16]

Journalists danced a line between being critical of the app — the privacy issues, the provincial decisions to sign up or not sign up, and its effectiveness — and not being too negative in the reporting so as to encourage (or at least not discourage) Canadians to download and use the app. This muddied coverage, giving the app an outsized air of usefulness in limiting the spread of COVID. In September 2020, as cases started to rise, politicians and public health officials reminded Canadians to download the app as a way to help limit the spread of COVID-19. It was mixed into back-to-school messaging, with *Global News* even quoting Emily Seto from the University of Toronto's Centre for Global eHealth Innovation saying that the app should be pushed on teachers and high school students as they return to school. *Global News* juxtaposed the need for Canadians to download the app with a rise in COVID-19 cases among young people: "Given that the recent rise in cases is being driven by young people — often gathering in large groups — the message about the benefit and safety of the app needs to get laser-focused, said Isaac Bogoch, an infectious disease expert from Toronto General Hospital."[17] Completely absent of context for why young people might be catching COVID-19 (which I discuss in more detail in the next section), the app was offered as an important aspect of keeping people safe. The *Global News* article ends with links for where people can download the app for Apple or Android.[18]

The COVID Alert app went a step further than the usual personal responsibility measures like social distancing and handwashing, providing journalists something that was made *for* young people. Woven into the assumptions that the app would be a critical tool was that it would be a way to reach young people, a group who were often blamed for driving the spread of COVID. Theresa Tam, responding to criticism that the app would leave people with older or no cell phones behind, argued "what if, for example, before you walked into a pub, before you walked into a nightclub or places where there may be a bunch of people you may not know, who are not in your specific social circle, where notification is particularly important?"[19] The idea of walking into a nightclub and pub at all, let alone on the same night, would soon become the stuff of nostalgia as fall lockdowns closed all restaurants, bars and lounges, a far more useful public health intervention than an app. Just like Bogoch told *Global News*, the app was seen as a solution to stop young people's apparent active and anonymous socializing. At the same time that journalists were anticipating the launch of the COVID Alert app, youth figured prominently as being the primary reason for why COVID-19 was spreading. It took the personal responsibility narrative and narrowed it even further.

BLAME THE YOUTH

There were few societal divisions as important as age in how COVID-19 interacted with the general population. Early on, it was clear that COVID-19 was less deadly for younger people and more deadly for older people. By April, this fact would be unignorable, as residential care became the site of an incredible amount of death in a rapid period of time. Older people represented the lion's share of COVID-19 casualties. By ignoring the relationship between age, disability and COVID-19 risk, journalists crafted a narrative that healthy, younger people were safer from COVID-19. As a result of who was dying, and where, many news articles, features, stock photos and profiles skewed toward painting COVID-19 as a problem for older people.

This set up a reactive narrative in summer of 2020 that the real people to blame for spreading COVID-19 were young people. The mass cohort of young and youngish people aged 20 to 39 were reckless, selfish and non-stop partying, usually shown engaging in outdoor fun on a beach or patio. In June 2020, Hamilton saw an increase in infections among twenty-somethings. Hamilton's Medical Officer of Health Elizabeth Richardson explained the spike like this: "The sense would be that we've got a group of people who are at an age and stage in life where there tends to be less thinking about how these sorts of risks can affect them ... and being very social."[20] At the same press conference, Hamilton's Mayor Fred Eisenberger said, "We were all young once and thought we were impervious and immune and can conquer anything." What was the culprit? Richardson said that they had ruled out workplaces and schools and thus zeroed in on the 'extremely reckless' behaviour of living with roommates or in family units. Richardson said it was critical that people who had COVID-19 "take precautions to isolate within the house ... ideally they have their own bathroom, wearing a mask," and then blamed the outbreak on poor handwashing. The tone was patronizing and characteristic of how many, many politicians and public health officers talked to the "younger age groups."[21] The article was based solely on comments from Eisenberg and Richardson; it didn't ask a young person what it was like to try distancing in a tiny apartment with a single bathroom or what life was like after two months of a pandemic where school was cancelled, work had dried up and roommates received conflicting messages of staying home to socially distance but also socially distance while you're at home.[22] On July 24, 2020, *CTV News* reported that Chief Medical Officer Theresa Tam, "rebuked young adults for their role in spreading the coronavirus and driving the daily case counts higher, cautioning them that they are not invincible and will make loved ones sick." The article went on to scold Canadians aged 39 and younger for not taking their "responsibility to protect others" seriously. But the article didn't mention where people under the age of 39 were getting COVID-19, instead blaming the increases on Canada Day parties and a failure of public health to communicate and engage "with that particular age group."[23]

While it was true that young people started to make up higher proportions of who was becoming infected with COVID-19 over summer 2020, the proportion was driven by a very important context: there had been specific measures taken to prevent spread for older adults living in long-term care, like widespread personal protection equipment and other safety protocols. As I mention in the April 2020 chapter, these measures were not enough to contain the deadly spread, but they did amount to more protection than the average person would have had access to. Rather than examining how certain efforts reduced spread among older people and which similar measures would be necessary to stop the spread among younger people, a narrative about personal responsibility emerged that allowed for lazy amalgams from politicians and public health officers about the folly and selfishness of youth. Crucially, those in political leadership never interrogated workplace health and safety or people's living arrangements. Journalists didn't do enough to challenge these narratives as they arose, often repeating lines from public health officials uncritically. By August, the demographic shift — people aged 40 and under being infected at higher rates than people who were older — was a global phenomenon, leading to the World Health Organization to warn that these demographics were "increasingly driving the spread."[24]

With personal responsibility the dominant strategy for prevention, it was perhaps obvious that this frame would so easily dovetail with scornful reactions to apparent youthful recklessness, aided by young people starting to make up a higher percentage of illnesses. In September, CBC News' Lauren Pelley tried to answer the question, where are young people getting COVID-19? She wrote, "They're getting infected at cottages, family gatherings, dinner parties — all kinds of indoor settings, and not always the ones with large, headline-making crowds." Pelley then bounces around headline-making superspreader events: a Windsor family with a hyperactive social life, weddings, a Toronto strip club and university students in London who, public health officials said, probably got it from London's "jam-packed downtown bar scene."[25] But the details on whether all of these cases involved people under 40 weren't clear. Was everyone at the wedding or the strip club under 40, or was Pelley using these activities as a proxy to talk about youth? The news about the family in Windsor was linked back to a *Windsor Star* article that reported the ages of the people impacted by this cluster: "Youth ages 14 to 19 make up the majority of the cluster cases with 19 out of 31. Eight are adults ages 40 to 49, three are ages 50 to 59, and one is 77 years old" — this group didn't actually include any adults aged 20 to 39 at all, the age target of her piece.[26] Pelley concludes her article by quoting neuroscientist Samantha Yammine who warned against shaming and blaming youth, even though the rest of the article read a lot like shaming and blaming.[27]

Yammine offered a far more useful analysis than assuming that the cluster events causing COVID-10 spread were parties: "living with roommates or in a multi-generational home, to working in sectors where safety measures aren't always followed."[28] CBC journalists relied on Yammine to give a critical perspective to coverage that had already argued the opposite of what Yammine was saying. The day before Pelley's article was posted, Yammine was interviewed on *The Current* where she argued that journalists needed to pay more attention to the role that workplaces played in young people outbreaks: "A lot of people who are under 40, a lot of people in their 20s, they work on the front lines in places like restaurants where they might be exposed to people not wearing a mask." Rather than pick up on the thread about the relationship that Yammine saw between COVID-19 spread, age and social location, *The Current* host Matt Galloway pivoted,

> So amongst your friends, the work thing is one part. The other assumption is that people are going out there meeting friends in restaurants or bars because we've been stuck inside for months and the weather's been nice and people can do that. Is that what you're hearing amongst your friends?[29]

He spent the rest of the segment talking about how to improve messaging geared toward younger people.[30] Galloway was not interested in discussing the factors that spread COVID-19 outside of the control of youth: work, housing, transit, debt, school and family responsibilities. Instead, young people were remixed into a caricature; individuals who simply could no longer be cooped up any longer and whose decision to meet friends in bars was driving Canada head first into a second wave.

As the fall started and the second wave became serious enough for journalists to write about other issues, the narrative that young people were to blame started to fall away, and criticisms of this frame became more common. By mid-fall, journalists turned their eye to the winter holidays, starting with Diwali celebrations and then into the Chanukah/Christmas/New Year's celebrations that families were told not to hold. Holidays replaced the focus on young people. Though, from time to time, a journalist, politician or pundit did still take a direct swing at young people. In January 2021, TVO's Steve Paikin was roasted on Twitter for blaming children for being irresponsible. While he deleted his tweet after hundreds of replies, he defended himself by saying said that he knew "plenty of 9-13-year-olds who are certainly NOT at the mercy of their parents' decisions. They make plenty of their own decisions when away from their parents and those decisions apparently have consequences on others."[31] One wonders what children he had in mind.

Individualism and youth were wrapped into one identity. Journalists and politicians alike called younger people lazy for accepting CERB and refusing to take up new employment. As I explore in the chapter covering January 2021, disability was completely erased, especially as it intersected with a young person's elevated risk for severe COVID-19 outcomes. Younger adults were demonized for not being able to avoid getting COVID, and rarely was there an attempt to understand why, or to even deconstruct how different life is for someone who is 21 versus someone who is 27 or 34 or 40. Indeed, many a 37-year-old laughed to themselves when they heard on the news that COVID-19 was spreading because people their age were partying too hard at bars that, despite the pandemic, were still open and staffed by people who were probably also called "young." Even in mid-December 2020, as COVID-19 was sweeping schools, workplaces and residential facilities, Alberta Public Health Officer Deena Hinshaw took a moment to scold youth again — "Hinshaw also reminded younger people in the province that they are still vulnerable to the virus and they should not be holding gatherings or interacting with one another" — as if, by December, the message had not been received loud and clear.[32] By then, it was obvious that the personal responsibility line could only be pushed so far — younger people were getting COVID-19 due to factors beyond their control and journalists finally started to pay attention to large congregant work settings, as I explore in chapter covering February 2021.

COVID-19 AT HOME

Age may have been what showed up in the statistics as the starkest characteristic of who was dying from COVID-19 most, but that alone could not capture the whole story. While workplaces were sites of intense outbreaks, it wasn't work where Canadians spent a majority of their time. Their homes played a critical role in slowing or accelerating the spread of COVID-19. Governments did very little to mitigate COVID-19 spread in the home and in fact made things much worse, even dangerous, when COVID-19 relief measures did nothing to support paying for housing or to protect individuals from eviction.

Housing activists were some of the first organized social movement voices to demand governments move quickly to protect renters. If the primary message coming from public health was related to isolation, it made sense that governments would give Canadians necessary supports to actually isolate. Every individual who lived in a congregate setting — whether it was long-term care, a shelter, transition housing, prison or jail, or even with roommates — was as a result more at risk of contracting

COVID-19. All these spaces were deadly, even student residences where the average age of residents was far lower than most other residential facilities. An outbreak at the Severn Court Student Residence in Peterborough, Ontario, in March 2021, killed Zachary Root, a 31-year-old Fleming College student. Root was the only person to die as a result of an outbreak within a student residence between March 2020 and July 2021. That outbreak had infected 58 other people.[33] Journalists didn't ask what role the private company that owned the residence played in not controlling spread, instead focusing on Fleming College's response.

The pandemic made people's homes Ground Zero to control spread, but journalists rarely reported about the pandemic through the lens of the home. Their uncritical reporting missed calling attention to many of the necessary interventions that could have slowed the spread of COVID-19 and focused rather on personal protocols like social distancing as well as updates to the tools we were given to do this, like masks or the COVID Alert app. Home transmission was the most likely way that someone would catch COVID-19 due to inevitably sharing bathrooms, sharing meals and often living in close quarters with someone else for days before symptom onset signalled to an individual that they might have COVID-19. This all assumed that individuals even had a place to live — an assumption that further marginalized people who had nowhere to live or who couldn't pay rent as a result of pandemic-related economic pressures that caused so many Canadians to lose income.

But the supports promised for people to protect themselves at home weren't sufficient to capture the range of situations many people live in. Families who lived in cramped, close quarters, who only had a single bathroom, or where multiple people shared a room were particularly at risk. News reported social distance orders from politicians and public health assuming their audience would mostly be living in a nuclear family inside a unit with private access to the outside: two parents, maybe some kids but with separate bedrooms, and ideally two bathrooms. Stories about the unique challenges of living in an apartment building, like sharing an elevator, masking to do your laundry and sharing central air and HVAC systems were rare and supplemental to the overarching call to stay home and self-isolate. In one article for CBC News Winnipeg, professor Michelle Dreigder suggested that people who live in apartments should be extra careful around neighbours. The article quoted her saying, "It's trying to adopt all of those kinds of protective measures that you can in a situation that you may not have full autonomy and control over your environment."[34] The key point: very few people actually do have full autonomy and control over their environments, a reality the personal responsibility narrative could not get past, rendering the loudest call from public health ineffective. For parents who lived in Toronto's high-density Thorncliffe and Flemingdon neighbourhoods, the fear of using the elevators at peak time actually kept many kids home from school in September 2020. How can you be personally responsible for your neighbours when everyone is rushing to be at work or at school on time, lest they be penalized for being late?[35]

In June 2020, a 288-unit high-rise in Calgary called The Verve was the site of 56 cases, at least three of which required hospitalization. There were many theories about what could have caused the spread: common surfaces, elevators, HVAC, AirBnB units and the building's plumbing were all raised as possibilities, but there was no conclusion and no follow-up or resulting controls to prevent another high-rise outbreak.[36] The Alberta Health Service created a committee to study what happened, and their review of other high-rise outbreaks around the world and lessons learned from the SARS outbreak found that there needed much more research. They concluded,

> As jurisdictions continue to lower the curve of COVID-19, opportunities to investigate, report and reflect on outbreaks and clusters within transmission in condos and hotels or multi-residential buildings may become available and will hopefully contribute to an understanding of the possible mechanisms of transmission in these spaces.[37]

The assessment was prepared for July 16, 2020. Despite the unknowns related to high-rise apartments, there were no new measures announced to keep these folks safe as Alberta's infection rate skyrocketed. While the Alberta government did promise free hotel rooms to enable safe self-isolation for people who had COVID-19 in Alberta's 11 most affected areas in Calgary and Edmonton, this was announced on December 16, 2020. By then, the Calgary zone, which would have 791 hotel rooms available, had 7331 active cases, and the Edmonton zone, which would have 1300 hotel rooms available, had 9946 active cases.[38]

It isn't as if people who live in apartments are rare in Canada. In Calgary and Edmonton, a quarter of each city's residents live in apartments. In

Toronto, nearly three out of ten dwellings is a high-rise — a building with five stories or more. While 53.6% of Canadians live in a single-detached dwelling, that leaves an awful lot of Canadians who don't.[39] The media attention on how to keep oneself safe in an apartment building just didn't have the attention that it warranted based on how many people live in them. Apartment buildings had the added stress of landlord control or property management decisions, where masks may not have been made mandatory or hand sanitizer available.

The lack of media attention to elevated risk in apartment buildings meant that there was also a lack of solutions coordinated by government. When journalists reported on apartment living, which was rare, it was usually tied into discussions about COVID-19's disproportionate impact on racialized, especially Black, Canadians. *iPolitcs* reported on a meeting of the Canadian Public Health Association's annual conference, where apartment living was mentioned only in response to the high concentration of cases in Toronto's Black neighbourhoods:

> Toronto's northwest neighbourhoods also have the city's largest proportion of Black residents, along with a high concentration of cramped apartments in aging buildings. Residents in the area are more likely to work industrial jobs without adequate social distancing, and are more likely to travel by public transit on some of the city's most crowded bus routes.[40]

Months earlier, CBC *News* quoted Will Prosper, an activist from Montréal North who made the same observation in his city: "We have a lot of underpaid health-care workers ... We also have a lot of front-line workers who lack their own mode of transportation. We have lots of people who live in high-density apartments, so the risk factor is greater."[41] With no strategy to address apartment dwellers, the racialized impact of COVID-19 became worse.

Apartments posed a problem for public health as cases ballooned. Middlesex-London Public Health Unit was surprised to see a cluster of cases arise from a large apartment complex in London. On December 31, 2020, the *London Free Press* reported: "The Middlesex-London Health Unit took weeks to recognize a cluster of COVID-19 cases at a northeast London apartment complex because it's a private residence and not a high-risk setting, the associate medical officer of health says."[42] Had there been a system in place to identify residential clusters in apartment buildings, interventions could have been made earlier that could have slowed the spread of COVID-19. But, as apartments were not considered "a high-risk setting," public health had to wait until there were dozens of cases before they declared an outbreak — a designation that would have been made with two cases had it been a workplace.

This was not limited to a single site in London, though news about apartments and condos was far more likely to be about how hot a housing market was than how safe residents within the building were. By February 2021, in North Bay, Ontario, a city that had relatively few COVID-19 cases, an outbreak at the Lancelot apartments infected at least 40 people and killed three people, in Ontario's highest-profile apartment-related outbreak.[43] Rebecca Towers in Hamilton became the site of another high-profile outbreak in spring 2021, infecting 110 people and killing two. The day that the outbreak at Rebecca Towers was declared over, there were two more apartment buildings in outbreak: Wellington Place where 45 people had been infected and Village Apartments, where at least 74 people had been infected. While the stories about Hamilton's apartment outbreaks focused on conditions of the apartments, like broken elevators and cramped common spaces, there was still no focus on the movements of the people living in these spaces between workplaces that may have had COVID-19 outbreaks too.[44]

HOUSING JUSTICE

It wasn't just the buildings or living settings that were unsafe; losing your place to live was a looming threat during the pandemic. Evictions that could normally send someone onto the streets, onto friends' couches or into a shelter became far more dangerous under pandemic conditions. Housing activists saw this danger from the start, and they worked very hard to build a rent relief movement to encourage politicians to halt evictions, subsidize rents and/or find alternative housing arrangements. In mid-March 2020, activists in Toronto called for a moratorium on evictions, something that Premier Doug Ford said was "on the table" with many other possibilities.[45] Eviction bans and rent freezes became the most common measure to help renters: Alberta banned evictions until the end of April; Nova Scotia, P.E.I., Québec, Saskatchewan and Yukon at various times in the summer and British Columbia, Manitoba and Ontario until September. But by the time the second wave grew into its most intense period, no Canadians were protected by eviction bans. Manitoba, B.C.

and Alberta lifted rent freezes too: Alberta in June and B.C. and Manitoba in September.[46] Most of these policies were not re-introduced, even as the third wave in 2021 became far worse than the first two. Ontario did re-implement an eviction moratorium, but advocates warned that these were barely helpful if the day after the 30-day moratorium, someone could be evicted.[47] There were no longer-term solutions put in place to protect renters anywhere in Canada.

Rent was a key factor in the crisis, and renters were given very little relief, if any at all. In mid-March 2020, a campaign spread across Canada encouraging people to withhold their April 1, 2020, rent payments. These calls were rooted in solidarity: tenants within multi-unit lodgings would withhold rent if any of their neighbours couldn't afford their April 1 rent. This collective approach, "shields people who aren't able to pay rent for all kinds of reasons from being particularly targeted by landlords for harassment or aggression," Dave Diewart from Stop Demovictions Burnaby told News 1130.[48] The pressure tactics were opposed by LandlordBC, whose CEO David Hutniak called the campaign "very destructive." The balance of power was on the side of the landlords, however, as the arbiters of who could stay and who would be evicted for not being able to pay. B.C.'s NDP government offered a $500 rent subsidy at the start of the pandemic, paid to landlords rather than to renters.[49] More than 370,000 rental subsidy payments were made directly to landlords. But the program ended on August 31, months before the second wave crested over the province.[50] Renters in that province who were in arrears had until "at least" July 2021 to pay, even though the pandemic would be far from over by then.[51] Québec similarly offered a rent subsidy program, also paid directly to landlords, though rather than giving people money in the form of a subsidy, it was a loan. That program ended on July 15, 2020.[52] Prince Edward Island created a $1 million fund for renters to access if they needed help meeting rent. Of the 1872 people who applied to the program, 1650 people received some funding, for an average of $606.[53]

Diewart understood that fighting a pandemic required a collective response. Leaving the power to landlords to make individual decisions about how to deal with their tenants would leave many renters in unsafe situations: "I think we have to think strategically and we have to think collectively for the long haul," he said.[54] That collectivity was key to understanding how COVID-19 spread, a reason why the personal responsibility narrative was so destructive: it obscured that no one can fight COVID-19 alone. Even though Justin Trudeau argued the CERB should have been enough to help Canadians with their rent, the only support that Canadians got with housing costs was the promise that banks were prepared to defer some mortgage payments. [55] The help available for homeowners, though insufficient, was still infinitely more than renters received: there were no direct aid programs to help people pay their rent. The fidelity that governments had to homeowners, who have more wealth on average than renters, while renters were told to rely on wage supplements like CERB or CEWS, demonstrated that pandemic aid packages were not intended to help the poorest Canadians.

By the latter half of 2020 and into 2021, evictions once again picked up and many anti-homelessness activists used direct action to stop people from being evicted. In an opinion piece in the *Ottawa Citizen*, Sam Hersh described what it was like trying to stop authorities from delivering an eviction notice to Amanda Proulx, an Ottawa tenant who had been evicted in December 2020. Her eviction followed a period that many called an eviction blitz, where eviction hearings ramped up after months of the moratorium. Hersh wrote that these hearings "on average last for no more than 60 seconds, in most cases without any legal defense."[56] Simply placing a moratorium on evictions was obviously going to lead to this situation. Rather than giving renters what they needed to survive the pandemic, the measures that were put into force prolonged business as usual: evictions were still inevitable, with no regard for the impact on an individual facing eviction or the person's community around them.

There was a direct line between people becoming unhoused and COVID-19 spreading within homeless shelters. Congregate settings, where multiple people shared the same room were superspreader situations. COVID-19 swept through transition housing, social services and shelters as understaffed organizations contended with social distancing protocols, PPE for users and staff and spaces that often didn't allow for the rules to be applied. A temporary shelter space set up at the Edmonton Convention Centre had to reduce its capacity from 300 to 165 as an outbreak rapidly swept over the residents. It had been set up without rapid COVID-19 test capacity, something that was identified in media after cases started to multiply.[57] Homeless Montrealers were hit by a COVID-19 wave in December 2020. Where a positivity rate of 5% anywhere would have raised alarms earlier in the pandemic, it had climbed to between 30% and 40% among shelter users.[58] The Royal Vic hospital, which had not been used as a functioning hospital for years, had been designated early on as a location for people to stay, including to isolate from COVID-19, though officials said that it hadn't been used much. As COVID-19 infections rose, the dozens of residents who did stay there were moved into a local hotel to allow space for people sick with COVID-19.[59] From March 2020 until July 2021, 14 people had died in shelters in Canada, though that number is certainly an underestimate.[60] There was no official count for deaths within congregant-setting environments across Canada, but in Ontario, there were at least 88 people who died in a group home or congregant care set-ting managed either by the Ministry of Health, the Ministry of Municipal Affairs and Housing and the Ministry of Children and Community Social Services, numbers obtained by advocate and researcher Megan Linton and me. Residents in these facilities were disabled adults.[61]

Shelters were regularly on outbreak lists across Canada. In Toronto, a group of unhoused people and their advocates challenged a bylaw that outlaws sleeping in parks. They argued that they felt safer living in parks than they did in the shelter system.[62] In November 2020, the *Toronto Star's* Tonda MacCharles quoted Andrew Bond, medical direc-tor of Inner City Health Associates in Toronto, saying that he believed that the number of unhoused people who died from COVID-19 was somewhere between 50 and 100 — probably much higher, despite the official tally by June 2021 only being nine.[63] Tent cities became vital locations for community all across Canada. In many cities, there had been a moratorium on dismantling homeless camps at the start of the pandemic, which, when lifted, saw a rush of encampments dismantled in major cities. One camp, threatened to be dismantled by the City of Winnipeg due to a lawsuit, meant that its residents saw their community destroyed, a scene that played out over and over across Canada during the first 18 months of the pandemic. In June and July 2021, Torontonians were horrified when they saw dozens of mounted police in riot gear clear Trinity Bellwoods Park and a park near Lamport Stadium of homeless encampments. The residents called for low-income housing options, and decried the wasted money spent on private security, policing and fences. Fences stayed up after the Trinity Bellwoods encampment was cleared to ensure that the lawn could grow.[64]

Nick Falvo, a homelessness researcher based in Calgary, told the *Canadian Press* that the impact of the pandemic on homelessness would not likely be fully realized for another several years, but even so, there was immediate need to give Canadians a rental subsidy (especially one that didn't go to landlords) and for CERB overpayments to not be clawed back.[65]

Reporting on these issues was rarely done at the same time as statements about the personal responsibility everyone had to keep themselves safe in their own homes. In most reporting, not only was everyone assumed to have had a home, save for a few who would land in the shelter system that was ready for them, it was also assumed that everyone had appropriate housing that would allow them to socially distance if they had COVID-19. Addressing housing issues was not seen as a solution to stopping the spread of COVID-19 as much as it was seen as a minor issue that concerned a small number of people. Its marginalization from mainstream coverage meant journalists did not focus enough on how COVID-19 spread most often in someone's living quarters, and politicians could brush off this key node of spread as being firmly in the private realm, much like how it treated workplaces as part of the corporate world. The personal responsibility narrative was rarely challenged, and worse, when housing issues related to COVID-19 spread did arise, stories never asked: what about the individual's circumstances made it difficult to respect public health orders, or was this purely a decision driven by selfishness? Rarely was it the latter.

Framing the message that planking the curve/slowing the spread/avoiding the virus was possible through personal actions alone erased the causes and therefore possible solutions necessary to slow the spread of COVID-19. Even as evidence mounted that individual actions could only go so far and that the virus was targeting people in systemic ways, we were still told to stop COVID-19 by washing our hands and coughing into our sleeves. It was clear early on that racialized communities were hit hardest by the pandemic: were they not sanitizing their hands well enough? We knew early on that outbreaks within factories spread quickly, especially among low-waged, racialized workers: were they simply touching their faces too much? There was almost no reporting that challenged the axioms from the start of the pandemic even as data improved and understanding of the virus changed. Rather, the personal responsibility narrative shifted onto other kinds of behaviour, like private gatherings and individuals "skirting the rules." The focus on personal responsibility was even more intense than the focus on how safe people were at home, or if they even had a home, which barely got a mention by politicians or journalists.

The supports that were necessary to keep people afloat needed to pay for living expenses — rent, transportation and food, especially. The Canada Emergency Response Benefit (CERB) was a critical pillar of this support, given to Canadians who lost most of their income because of the pandemic. But it, too, conveniently fit into the personal responsibility narrative — not just in that it signalled to individuals that the extent of the government's help would be through a personal cheque rather than through market controls like free rent or public transit; it also signalled that individuals were in this pandemic on their own. With your CERB cheque, you could decide where to spend your money and how to keep yourself safe. But if you relied on CERB too much, journalists and politicians alike would paint this as a failure of personal responsibility.

August 2020
THE END OF CERB

Cases: 116,551
Deaths: 8,941[1]

The personal responsibility narrative may have underpinned most of the way in which governments, public health agencies and journalists talked about keeping safe from COVID-19, but it was accompanied by an important transactional relationship with the government. At the end of March, 2020, Justin Trudeau, saucer-eyed and serious, told Canadians, "No Canadian should have to choose between protecting their health, putting food on the table, paying for their medication or caring for a family member."[2] If we all do our part, the government will give us what we need to stay housed, clothed and fed. Everyone who had lost work because of the pandemic was promised money to help weather the storm. All we had to do in return was be responsible and solemnly swear that we would keep looking for new work.

By August 2020, many Canadians were facing an uncertain future due to political wrangling over this most important personal support — the Canada Emergency Response Benefit (CERB). CERB became one of the biggest issues of the pandemic, debated by policy experts and analysts, politicians and pundits, and these debates were written about, aired, dissected and explained by news agencies across Canada. CERB got no shortage of attention, but the kind of attention it got was often inadequate, dovetailing with the personal responsibility narrative and telling people who received CERB that they were lazy, selfish or not doing enough. As the largest direct cash transfer to individuals in Canadian history, CERB was both a lifeline and a political football, and it came to symbolize the deep ideological underpinnings of politicians and journalists alike: what is more important to financially save, an individual or a business? CERB was confusing, and confusion was a key part of how it was unrolled — not universally, but through a complex and changing set of criteria that plagued the program and created a lot of anxiety among its recipients.

At the same time, the government created the Canada Emergency Wage Subsidy (CEWS), which flowed more money to Canadians than CERB did, through the hands of their employer. This meant that for thousands of Canadians, whether or not they were eligible for government aid depended on the desire of their bosses to collect and dispatch this money. As journalists obsessed over CERB, they missed examining better options, like a guaranteed income, that would have been more straightforward and induced less anxiety among the population. But this was no surprise coming from conservative Canadian media: these kinds of policies would have upended the status quo in a fundamental way. CERB was already too much for many of them.

DRUGS, GANGS AND CHEESIES

On October 19, 2020, an article published by the *Toronto Sun* made the rounds on social media. It represented the kind of scorn that CERB recipients had got from the mainstream media throughout the pandemic. "Gangsters using CERB to buy guns, protect turf: sources" was the headline. Before this, CERB had been blamed for making people lazy and triggering drug overdoses, but this *Toronto Sun* piece about CERB being used to buy guns was new anti-CERB territory. Veteran courts reporter Sam Pazzano's unnamed sources explained in detail how an increase in gun violence in Toronto was a direct result of CERB money:

> "We have learned of dozens across the GTA who are doing this. This enables them to buy more handguns, 'dirty weapons' (previously used in crimes) for between $400 and $800, and new Glocks, which are reliable and have strong stopping power, for $3,000," the source said.[3]

The piece bounced between using the word "sources" but then attributed every comment to "a source," with no indication if the source was ever different. Was the source a gangster with a soft spot for Pazzano? Was it a police officer? Impossible to say. Pazzano then focused on Toronto rappers who had been involved in gun violence. Six of the seven individuals he referenced had been shot before the pandemic even started.[4]

Pazzano's article was laughable. The story could only be conjured by a mind that was as invested in anti-Black racism as it was in opposing pandemic aid for people who need it. Were gangsters, famously known for engaging with the Canada Revenue Agency, actually buying guns with CERB money? The article certainly didn't offer any hints for readers to find out if there was any truth in it, and instead hid behind gun violence statistics in Toronto to move the reader to make up their mind with innuendo alone. It was hard to believe the only thing standing between someone and a $3000 illegal gun was saving six weeks of CERB, a benefit you could only get if you also proved that you had no other income now but had also reported income in 2019.[5]

Pazzano's CERB-pays-for-guns piece was objectively ridiculous, but it did not come from nowhere. Articles that were less sensational but just as scornful toward people who accessed CERB were common during the first seven months of the pandemic. CERB could not shake the negative narratives that surrounded it. Right-wing politicians like Alberta United Conservative Party MLA Shane Getson loved the controversy, using CERB as shorthand for laziness. Getson was slammed by the NDP when a video surfaced of him claiming that business owners couldn't hire people, "because they make more on CERB, eating cheesies and watching cartoons I guess," he told the crowd.[6] In the 28-second clip, he also said that he knows that in British Columbia, where CERB was not clawed back from people on social assistance, CERB was being used to buy drugs, and he cited his friend John "out in Vernon," who was concerned that CERB was leading to more drug use.[7] In a letter to *Maple Ridge News*, another business owner, Cory Botner, made the same point as Getson, nearly word-for-word:

> Do you know how many drugs you can buy when you don't have any bills to pay and you not only get a welfare cheque for more than $700, but then you get a $2,000 CERB cheque every month on top of that.[8]

Botner did not answer his own question of how many drugs that could buy. Concerns about CERB and drug addiction were aired regularly across Canadian media as one argument for why CERB needed to end, even after the program had been rolled into EI in October 2020.

It should have been obvious that during a pandemic, people would need help, and that people who were already struggling before the pandemic would need even more help. CERB was the most significant lifeline thrown to Canadians who had lost work during the pandemic, and it was also the most expensive immediate transfer of money to individuals the government had ever made. It was obviously going to be disparaged, especially by business owners who preferred money go to them directly rather than an aid program that would not force people into working for the lowest possible wages. CERB's critics were often powerful representatives of the business lobby who were scandalized that average people would be given a lump sum of money rather than be forced to dance for their daily bread. Even though paying people to stay home was of course the most effective COVID-19 mitigation measure, CERB critics ensured that the government would not give Canadians any more than they had already been promised, and they did this through a steady media campaign that used CERB and its recipients as punching bags. From the day it was announced on March 25, 2020, CERB was highly popular and, at the same time, the most disparaged program of the pandemic.

INTRODUCING CERB

With job losses front-of-mind, the federal government created CERB. It was announced in between the days that Ontario and B.C. went into lockdown, on March 25. By mid-March, EI claims had leaped by 500,000,[9] with Québec leading the provinces in job losses: its employment rate fell by 18.7%. Unemployment rose among single parents by a whopping 53.9% and in households where no person over the age of 15 was working, unemployment increased by 23.5%, or 1.6 million people.[10] At first glance, CERB was the perfect option for people who were either out of work or had their work significantly reduced because of the pandemic, and the government managed to create the program such that it was easy to apply and receive the money soon after. The federal government anticipated that four million people would apply for the benefit, making it the biggest federal relief program ever. But there were many restrictions on who could receive CERB. To be eligible, Canadians would have had to have made $5000 the year previous, and while on CERB their income had to stay below $1000 per 14-day period.[11] The salary ceiling was an important feature of the program, as the Liberals wanted it to be a wage replacement grant, not an emergency funding benefit.

Trudeau made CERB sound better than it actually was, and while advocates warned that the details might water down the effectiveness of the program, journalists wrote about the Liberals, at first, as if they were working-class heroes. Journalists relied on official explanations to report on CERB and played the dual role of reporting but also demystifying the process to apply. But the difference between a program that gave money to everyone who needed it in the way that Trudeau explained when introducing CERB and what was eventually announced was important: even if you had lost your job because of the pandemic, you had to have made at least $5000 the year before to be eligible for funding. Because early coverage of CERB was generally positive, it took social movement organizations to challenge the government's rhetoric and test what was known about the program and who would get it. That meant that digging into the impact of CERB was left to the Canadian Centre for Policy Alternatives (CCPA), then quoted by journalists — rather than doing any investigative journalism themselves. The CCPA analyzed the CERB requirements and concluded that one-third of unemployed Canadians — 862,000 people — would not be eligible for CERB or EI.[12] The aid that the lowest-income Canadians hoped for never came.

It cannot be overstated how important CERB was to Canadians. The way the program was designed provided people fast and easy access to emergency funding, and people were encouraged to apply. With lockdown measures in effect, people needed access to money to pay their regular expenses. If the government was not going to enact legislation that provided more fundamental measures to address the cost of living, like rent relief or debt forgiveness, CERB became an important lifeline, especially for those who were already struggling financially before the pandemic. In one poll, the *Financial Post* reported that nearly half of those surveyed said that their financial commitments were such that they couldn't afford to miss work.[13] At the start of the pandemic, Canadians' average debt as a percentage of their income was 176.9%. This meant that for every $1 Canadians were making, they owed $1.77.[14]

Even though it was a lifeline, CERB was used as a political football. In June 2020, when Prime Minister Justin Trudeau promised that CERB benefits would continue beyond the initial program period, his government tried to add language to the legislation that would have forced CERB recipients to swear they were actively searching for work and agree to not turn down "reasonable work opportunities."[15] With so many people off work because their industry had dried up during the first wave of the pandemic, this oath made it sound as if CERB was only supposed to be accessed if someone, let's say a travel agent, professed they were also searching for a job while they waited for their industry to return. CBC *News* quoted Employment Minister Carla Qualtrough saying,

> We know that Canadians are eager and ready to do their part. We expect that workers will be seeking work opportunities or

returning to work when their employer reaches out to them, provided they are able and it is reasonable for them to do so.[16]

The implication was that people collecting CERB were doing so rather than returning to their job. This frame demonized CERB recipients and telegraphed to Canadians who were not receiving CERB that there were people refusing to return to work even if it was an option for them. The plan to make CERB conditional on proof that a person had not turned down a reasonable job opportunity was eventually replaced by an attestation that the recipient had been actively looking for a job. A similar attestation was required for people who applied to the government's student benefit, and the Canada Revenue Agency (CRA) website told people to save proof of their job seeking activities, just in case they ask for it in the future.[17] While these kinds of measures made it sound like CERB was disincentivizing work, there was no proof of this happening. One CD Howe Institute study from August 17, 2020 concluded, "Because workers know the benefit is temporary, their concerns for ensuring employment in the longer term appear to be driving their behaviour. When job opportunities arise in the current uncertain climate, it is too risky to turn down those opportunities."[18]

When the government announced that it intended to roll CERB into EI, it also announced it would reduce the weekly benefit from $500 to $400.[19] Individuals would be moved to EI automatically by October 3, 2020. Thanks to pressure from the NDP, the amount was restored to $500. Part of the approval process included people needing to agree to accept work if the opportunity arises and it was "reasonable" to do so.[20] When they made this change, the government dropped the "emergency" from the name, and so CERB became CRB and was available to anyone whose income dropped by 50% or more over the year prior, as long as the individual didn't also receive any other emergency pandemic funding, EI, short-term disability benefits or Québec parental benefits. At the start of 2021, it was still expected that individuals attested that they had not turned down any work and that they are actively seeking work for the period covered by CRB.[21]

Even though CERB was easy to apply for and fast to receive, thousands of Canadians who applied for CERB would eventually find themselves in the crosshairs of the CRA, expected to pay money back that they had no ability to pay. At the same time, journalists went into overdrive writing about all the ways in which business leaders, politicians and apparent average Canadians were mad that CERB was being abused.

CONFUSION ABOUT ELIGIBILITY

Woven throughout the discussion about CERB was always a thread of distrust: could Canadians reasonably believe that their fellow citizens would not abuse free money when it was handed to them with no strings attached? The way in which journalists wrote about people receiving CERB often painted a picture that there were CERB recipients who were scamming the system and therefore, CERB needed to either be reformed or scrapped. This narrative was fed by Liberal politicians who very much preferred that people receive funding through a different program, the Canadian Employment Wage Subsidy (CEWS), which was amplified by employer lobbyists and advocacy organizations, opposition politicians and right-wing columnists. In an effort to achieve "balance," journalists often turned to employer lobbyists to provide "the other side" to a story about life during a pandemic when job prospects vanish, rather than relying on workers themselves to tell this story.

From the start, the Liberals made CERB sound like it was accessible to anyone who saw their income drop as a result of the pandemic. It was certainly easy enough to get, but the question of who was eligible was not as straightforward as the Liberals' publicity said it was. Social media was full of personal stories of people struggling to understand the CERB eligibility criteria. Many people who had first applied to EI, as they were told to do, and who were then automatically transferred to the new program received overpayments. In April, after the first phase of CERB was sent out, the *Toronto Star* talked to several people who had received multiple payments and they didn't know which one they were expected to refund. CRA agents, working from home and also impacted by the pandemic, were overloaded with calls, and recipients had a difficult time reaching anyone on the phone for answers.[22] The problems with overpayment for people who had first applied to EI were widespread, and when Canadians were expected to repay the overpayment months later, it caused even more confusion and worry among people who were already struggling to make ends meet. By the end of June 2020, the *Medicine Hat News* reported that local Hatters would be forced to miss a payment to help make up for the overpayment in April, and they were given little notice.[23] The federal government explained this as having been an "advance" that they intended to give out, "to get money in your pocket as quickly as possible" and then explained, "Because of this advance, you will not receive a payment when you complete your next report. This is equivalent to the first two-week period of the advance."[24] At the end of July, it was announced that $442 million in duplicate CERB payments were sent to more than 220,000 Canadians.[25] There were other program kinks, too. In October, CBC News featured the coordinator of a Facebook group for people who were receiving CERB who said that the problems that had plagued the system for months, especially the EI/CERB problem, had been the cause of a great deal of anxiety. For many people who had received other federal benefits, like parental leave, they found that their applications were rejected outright, sending them into a maze of CRA agents to fix the problem and get them emergency relief.[26]

Journalists didn't focus on these stories as much as they gravitated to stories that framed repayments as potentially abusive or fraudulent. One story, published by CBC News on June 10, 2020, featured CRA agents who explained that almost 190,000 CERB-related repayments had been made by Canadians who "weren't entitled to receive" the funding. That frame suggested there was nefarious intent behind why people were having to make repayments rather than the possibility that errors were made either in good faith or by CRA. The CRA had even set up a snitch line that allowed Canadians to tell on others they thought were abusing the system. By early June, there had been nearly two thousand complaints. It wasn't until the tenth paragraph that the CBC News article mentioned the confusion between CERB and EI remittances, and it was through quoting Treasury Board President Jean-Yves Duclos: "So most of these people, the vast majority of these people, are people that applied twice and therefore a double payment and they reimbursed half of those double payments." In many cases, the double-payments weren't even due to a double application, though. They were made because of the automatic switch from EI to CERB. Conservative MP Dan Albas is then quoted, saying the confusion is thanks to how the Liberals communicated the aid rather than malicious intent from people who applied. But then the story switches back to CRA saying they will "aggressively pursue tax evasion and fraud." There is no voice in the article from anyone who was caught up in the system, like the folks from Medicine Hat. There was also nothing about the added stress that clerical errors compounded on their lives, or the possibility of forgiving the overpayment because why should people in poverty suffer because of clerical errors. By October 2020, the CRA announced again that Canadians needed to pay back the money, and *Global News*, in covering CRA's announcement, placed words like "good faith" and "honest mistake" alone in quotations throughout the story when referring to people forced to repay.[27] Kelsey Catherine Schmitz, a member of the board of directors for the United Way of Stormont, Dundas & Glengarry in Ontario told the *Cornwall Standard-Freeholder* it was shameful that journalists focused on punishing people who applied for CERB but who were not eligible:

> Schmitz also deplored what she called national media articles that talked of punishing those who have falsely applied for CERB. "Why aren't we questioning why folks who don't qualify are applying to that funding?" she said. "Recognizing that cost of living, and living below the poverty line, can create desperate circumstances."[28]

The "freeloader" frame was so pervasive, it was more often reported that CERB was abused than what really happened: The Liberals wanted to make it sound like everyone would be helped but then added restrictions to their promise that actually excluded a lot of people. Worse than simply being confusing, it was actively causing harm to many people who were surprised that they needed to pay back money they thought was there to help them survive.

It was especially cruel for those people who were struggling before the pandemic, but who didn't understand that CERB was not a universal benefit. At the Annual General Meeting of Nunavut Tunngavik Inc., the legal representative of Inuit in Nunavut in treaty rights and negotiations, a motion was passed that called on the federal government to forgive any CERB overpayments that may have been given to Nunavummiut. The motion's preamble mentions the various impacts that COVID-19 has had on community health and employment, while information about CERB was not "reliably delivered in Inuktuk."[29] It also mentioned that many Inuit who live in extreme poverty and are simply not in a position to repay. The motion specifically identified the name of CERB as most confusing, as it sounded like an emergency benefit that was universal, available for everyone who has COVID-19-related needs.[30] *Nunatsiaq News* reported on the annual general meeting and their coverage led with news about this decision.[31]

Just as the tax season arrived in 2021, the federal government made a very important change to how they were deciding who would have to repay CERB. Recognizing that the language around 2019 income was unclear, the government announced they would consider the $5000 that people had to have made in 2019 to be eligible as net income rather than gross.

This meant that individuals who were self-employed and who had income of $5000 after they had netted out their taxes and expenses didn't have to repay CERB. Everyone who had already repaid CERB would be given the money back. The fact that government hadn't even decided whether that $5000 2019 salary was net or gross was proof of how confusing the program was and how easy it was for individuals to find themselves caught up in bureaucracy for just trying to access a benefit to which they were entitled.[32]

There was also a confluence of analyses that tried to link CERB to Canada's overdose crisis, a crisis that got exceedingly worse in 2020 and 2021. In June 2020, Raina Gagnon, an addictions counsellor in Ottawa, argued that CERB was simply too easy to get for people who use drugs. She concluded, "With the CERB benefit extended to October, we must urge the government to put policies in place to limit its accessibility to those who are vulnerable and ineligible but still receiving it."[33] Gagnon leveraged the news about the increasing rates of opioid overdoses, a pandemic that had already stolen thousands of lives in Canada before COVID-19 appeared, and tried to use CERB to explain why there were rising drug overdoses. In reply, Overdose Prevention Ottawa took apart the piece's logic, paragraph by paragraph, and argued,

> Gagnon's article struck a chord with the harm reduction commu-
> nity in Ottawa. "We are struggling, we're dying, and the second
> we get some relief they think we don't deserve it." These words
> from a drug user demonstrate the harm caused by Gagnon's call
> to "limit accessibility" to the CERB — a patronizing solution that
> leaves people with even fewer resources.[34]

CERB critics always took aim at the humanity of so-called CERB abusers and argued, whether it be due to guns or cheesies, drugs or sloth, they were simply unfit to receive aid.

None of the other recipients of aid programs got the same kind of attention that CERB recipients did, especially frustrating since some of the largest amounts of money went to corporations like Rogers and Bell who were still making incredible profits. Details about CERB were printed uncritically, even if what was said was untrue. *Global News* featured the executive director of the Harvest House Shelter in Moncton saying, "Once word got out to the street level that you could apply for it and there was no accountability a number of people applied for it that hadn't worked in years," even though there were several accountability measures built into the system, including CRA determining people ineligible if they had not earned $5000 the year before.[35] New Brunswick clawed provincial social assistance back from people who received CERB.

Sex workers especially found themselves in a financial conundrum thanks to program requirements. The sex workers who file taxes each year were likely eligible for CERB and may have been able to draw on the benefit until it was safe again to go back to work as normal. Sex workers who did not file taxes, though, found themselves forced to continue unsafe work as CERB disqualified them based on a lack of income.[36] Sex workers and sex worker advocates said the pandemic and the resulting financial precarity forced them to lower prices, engage in riskier contact with clients and field more calls for help from workers who found themselves unsafe. Coordinator of the Iskweu Project in Montréal, Jessica Quijano, said it had been more common to receive phone calls asking for help to get out of a situation quickly, made worse by the curfew imposed on the province in January 2021. Journalist Christopher Curtis quoted Sandra Wesley from the sex worker advocacy group Chez Stella,

> If the federal government wanted to avoid sex workers offering their services during the pandemic, they could have made us eligible for CERB ... This is a choice they made. We're an industry that lobbies the government regularly, they're aware of our concerns.[37]

Thanks to the arbitrary cut-off of income, workers whose income was not reported to CRA for whatever reason found themselves with nothing, even if the pandemic took a tremendous toll on their income. And yet, despite the impact on sex workers or even considering the role that sex work plays during a pandemic, journalists barely paid attention to their working conditions, their safety or how these policies impacted them.

On February 15, 2021, the *Canadian Press* did an analysis of where CERB payments went. The article was premised on the claim that cities soaked up more CERB payments than rural communities. Except the divide was far more important when analyzed from a racial perspective, with the poorest and most diverse neighbourhoods receiving more CERB payments than anywhere else. Areas of Canada that had higher COVID-19 case counts had higher rates of people receiving CERB. Jordan Press looked at neighbourhoods in Calgary and Brampton, two communities that had received the highest rates of CERB out of 1600 communities he analyzed. Both neighbourhoods have a high concentration of precariously employed and working-class people, and higher rates of diversity and recent immigrants. But rather than telling the story through a lens that laid out the racial divide of federal aid programs, the story focused instead on the rural-urban divide in a tone that made it sound like the program was set up to intentionally snub rural Canadians. He quoted the CCPA's David MacDonald who guessed that rural Canadians whose work relies on natural resources would have been somewhat insulated from the impact of the pandemic, as their businesses continued relatively untouched by the virus.[38] Like so much related to the pandemic, CERB was another proxy to see who was impacted hardest by COVID-19 — from layoffs and illness, to community spread and financial insecurity, CERB was a lifeline to Canada's working class.

The dominant CERB narrative was that people should have been able to find work, especially if they had been laid off for months. It didn't matter if they worked in industries like the arts, travel, airline or restaurants that were effectively shuttered by COVID-19. Many journalists, politicians and profit advocates created the illusion that people collecting CERB were simply refusing to do anything productive. This narrative was pushed especially hard by business lobbyists who wanted the government to transition people off CERB and onto another benefit, the Canada Emergency Wage Subsidy (CEWS), which was strings-free money that went immediately to businesses to help subsidize payroll. As politicians and business owners preferred CEWS, many Canadians were forced into a jam with an insufficient, confusing emergency benefit payment on one side, and a job that was impossible to do normally as long as COVID-19 was still a threat.

CERB VS. CEWS

Where CERB recipients got a lot of bad press, the other significant envelope of money designed to help Canadians through the pandemic did not. Announced on April 1, 2020, Canada Emergency Wage Subsidy (CEWS) subsidized salaries for companies that could demonstrate a 30% drop in their monthly income. Every four weeks, a company or organization could apply for a CEWS cheque by listing their payroll expenses and revenue drop, and the money would arrive soon after. When the program was announced, Finance Minister Bill Morneau told journalists that CEWS was the government's way to signal to business that they were there to support them: "My message to Canada's employers is this: get ready to rehire."[39] In the same article, journalist John Paul Tasker wrote, "Will there be penalties for abusing the system? Absolutely. The government has said it will be actively looking for instances of abuse — especially employers who pocket wage subsidies without passing them on to their employees."[40] But they built very few checks into the system. The person applying for CEWS only needed to attest that they were not lying about their figures and then the amount was approved. During the first year of the program, there had not been any reported instances of CEWS abuse. While people were outraged that CEWS had been given to profitable corporations, the program had been set up to allow for that, and that didn't amount to fraud — it's how it was supposed to work.

Many of the problems with CERB double-payments were blamed on the fact that CERB had replaced a quickly built EI program to help people who were laid off in March 2020. Many people who had applied for EI in the period between this new EI program and the launch of the CERB found themselves owing money to the CRA. Similarly, CEWS replaced a wage subsidy program that had been hastily announced in March 2020, several weeks earlier. But unlike CERB, CEWS did not have the bureaucratic mess that CERB had when it replaced the previously announced EI program. As far as the public knew, there were no similar double-payments or overpayments as a result of the wage subsidy programs being quickly designed and launched at the start of the pandemic. CRA created a hotline to receive tips about CERB and CEWS abuse, but journalists focused far more on how CERB abuses could be reported. One CTV News headline, "CRA snitch line now open to report fraudulent CERB claims," focused on "individuals" who "double-dipped" when they applied for CERB, whether inadvertently or not, and only made one passing mention of CEWS.[41]

The biggest problem with CEWS was that it gave more money to people than CERB, even if workers were laid off, but that money had to be coordinated through employers with little accountability. When CEWS was announced in April 2020, *Canadian Press* noted that a worker who was paid $17 per hour and paid through CEWS to stay home would receive $10 more per week than workers who were laid off and paid through CERB. The blatant equity differences with CERB and CEWS should have been a national scandal. One program offered just $500 per week and the other up to $847 (pegged to a worker's salary), with one difference in expectations from the individual: the one receiving CERB had to actively look for work. If an employee was laid off, waiting at home, unable to work but whose employer had applied for CEWS, he would receive $347 more, potentially, than his neighbour who lost her job as a travel agent and was drawing on CERB.[42] There was very little criticism about this difference. Instead, it was implied that CEWS was good because people were technically still working. It would boost job numbers and ensure people stayed close to their employers during the pandemic (heaven forbid that someone take the opportunity to look for a new career during the months of the pandemic!) while trying to keep the economy as normal as possible by flooding it with public money.

Employers loved CEWS. Employer lobby organizations fought hard for the government to flow aid through their members, rather than giving it to people directly, under the guise of getting the economy back on track. Except there was a key problem with this plan: many jobs simply could not come back during the pandemic at the same rate they operated at before. The idea behind CEWS was that it was better to keep people paid through their employers than for people to rely on government aid through a benefit program like CERB. Pro-business advocates were regularly asked to provide comment, insisting that CEWS was the best way to help small businesses, helping to feed the narrative that the economy had to stay open and journalists rarely challenged this logic. The way that CEWS operated, it de facto downloaded pandemic aid to employers to coordinate out of good will, and yet journalists never asked if this was the most efficient way to get money to workers who had been laid off, or whose employers were struggling to make payroll.

During 2020, journalists obsessed over small businesses. For example, the Canadian Federation of Independent Business (CFIB) was quoted extensively by CBC News, across all platforms. They wanted the money to be given to businesses with as few strings attached as possible — even arguing that attesting that your organization has seen a drop in revenue was too onerous. In a video released on October 30, 2020, where he explains some changes to business support programs, CFIB President Dan Kelly said his organization had, "appeared in the media 50,000 times since the pandemic started." He then, probably fairly, took credit for pushing the government to adopt so many business-friendly policies.[43] The agitation was successful and in July 2020, the program was expanded to offer the subsidy to any employer who had any drop in wages, related to COVID-19 or not.

CFIB may have been the most prominent pro-business organization in the news, but they were not alone. Pedro Antunes, chief economist of the Conference Board of Canada, writing in the *Globe and Mail* insisted that CERB should be ended and CEWS should be extended. He argued that CERB disincentivized returning to the lowest-paid jobs and therefore, workers should be forced to return to a new, low-paying job while they waited for their industry to get back on track. To make the argument, he calculated CERB based on a 33-hour work week to demonstrate that at $15.1 per hour, people would not return to their minimum wage jobs. It therefore needed to be cancelled.[44] Except that if CERB was calculated as an hourly wage for someone working full time at eight hours per day, it would equal $12.5 per hour — at the time, less than minimum wage in all of Canada save Saskatchewan, Manitoba and New Brunswick.[45] While Antunes should have been arguing that workers need more disposable income if Canada hoped to boost its economy, he instead took aim at the lowest-income workers and argued that it was good, actually, that they work for such low wages. He concluded, "hiring will boost household confidence and spending — creating a virtuous cycle in redressing the economy." [46] Virtuous, perhaps, for those whose pockets are filled with profits; less virtuous for the low-waged workers who were far more likely to get COVID-19 than their bosses were.

For nearly all of 2020, Canadians had no idea who was receiving CEWS, and by how much. It wasn't until December 2020 that this information was finally made public. *CBC News* did a deep dive into who received CEWS and whether or not they also paid out profits to shareholders. There were scandalous stories of certain odious organizations receiving CEWS money, like one run by neo-Nazi Paul Fromm, but there was no news about an organization or corporation that was seemingly penalized for inappropriately taking the subsidy or stories of CEWS-related corruption.[47] Indeed, the bar was set very low for what constituted fraud, and so unlike the non-stop stories of individuals accepting CERB inappropriately, there was no similar coverage of CEWS. As long as a corporation could demonstrate a drop in revenue, even if they were still paying dividends out to shareholders and making profits, they were eligible for CEWS.

There was no bigger booster of CEWS than Air Canada, and perhaps unsurprisingly, Air Canada was among the biggest winners of this money. The corporation was battered by the pandemic, forced to cancel routes and lay off thousands of staff. It became the poster child for the necessity of CEWS. When the government first announced CEWS, Air Canada was the first to publicly embrace it. On April 8, 2020, Air Canada announced that it would adopt the wage subsidy for all 36,000 Air Canada employees.[48] At the maximum rate of $847 per employee, per week (which is what CEWS is worth for any annual salary of $58,760 or higher), Air Canada was saying that it would gladly accept a massive federal subsidy: $854 million if the program was doled out for 28 weeks, as CERB had been designed to do. Air Canada received $554 million in wage subsidy money in 2020 and continued to collect it in 2021. In April 2021, the Government of Canada loaned Air Canada an additional $5.4 billion and purchased $500 million in stock. The deal forced Air Canada to finally refund money owed to travellers who had to cancel their trips 2020.[49]

The initial coverage of CEWS didn't explore just how massive a subsidy CEWS was for large employers like Air Canada. Both the *Canadian Press* and the *Toronto Star* had little detail about what the commitment to using CEWS would net financially for Air Canada, reporting only the Air Canada announcement and the reaction from one of Canada's main airline unions, CUPE.[50] As the corporation that announced its support immediately for CEWS, Air Canada's success using CEWS would be critical to the overall success of this strategy. But there were no mainstream voices asking: are we prepared to offer Air Canada hundreds of millions in subsidies? Why is there no discussion about re-nationalizing the airline industry? Should there be strings attached to this funding? Should the government have mandated Air Canada's workers to volunteer in their community's struggle against COVID-19 while being paid their salary? And aside from Air Canada, what happens when corporations who have a drop in revenue but who can still boost their profits instead subsidize their profits through CEWS? Shouldn't it be impossible for corporations to bank or pay out profits while also accepting CEWS?

Despite Air Canada being key in ginning up support for CEWS, they announced on May 21, 2020, that they were laying off 20,000 employees — more than half their workforce. The *Financial Post* quoted Air Canada saying that the layoffs were regrettable though unavoidable, and then quoted CUPE, the union that represents Air Canada flight attendants, who were furious about how Air Canada was laying off their workers because it left many ineligible for CERB.[51] Despite the massive public subsidy, Air Canada couldn't even keep its workers on payroll and when they finally decided to cut them lose, they left many in the lurch. But the news came and went, with no general stink lingering around the CEWS. By the end of June 2021, the federal government had approved

$84.56 billion CEWS claims, including making 550 payouts of more than $5 million each.[52]

There was ample evidence that CEWS would be fraught, especially for Canada's largest businesses, but it was rarely explored within the mainstream media. In a rare critical perspective on CEWS, former adviser to the Department of Finance and CRA Allan Lanthier wrote a scathing analysis for the *Globe and Mail* about how CEWS would be a "windfall" for Canadian corporations. He referenced the Royal Bank and Rogers, two corporations that had seen minor dips in profits during 2020, but could potentially receive millions from CEWS.[53] Rogers Media Inc. and Rogers Communications Canada Inc., as well as several other corporations owned by Rogers Media, received at least $82 million in CEWS payments,[54] despite having finished 2020 with $1.5 billion in net income.[55]

Rogers Media was hardly alone. Had publicly traded companies that had seen a dip in their revenue in 2020 not applied for CEWS, their shareholders could have claimed that they were negligent in not maximizing their profits by accessing funding that they were eligible for. Many of Canada's most profitable companies applied for CEWS. The *Financial Post* ran an analysis of 68 publicly traded companies who paid out shareholders and who received CEWS in December, but CRA didn't provide detailed breakdowns of how much they received. Journalists had to rely on the transparency of the companies themselves, as the report was constructed by reading financial documents and listing who had disclosed income from the federal subsidy.[56] Rogers, for example, was left off the list because they were not clear in their financial reporting about whether or not they took the subsidy. The list was topped by companies who all benefited from lax public health measures that allowed each to operate as normal, despite the fact that their large, congregant-setting workplaces were part of industries where there had been significant outbreaks: Imperial Oil ($120 million received in CEWS), Finning International ($90 million) and Aecon Group ($91.6 million).[57] Number four on their list was Extendicare, Canada's largest chain of long-term care facilities, which had been using CEWS to pay for workers in its home-care subsidiary called ParaMed. Extendicare had seen a drop in demand for home care services and, being eligible to apply for CEWS, they received $21 million. They had paid nearly the same amount — $20 million — to shareholders over the first six months of 2020, including more than half that while the pandemic ravaged long-term care.[58] Within the first 18 months of the pandemic, at least 523 people died from COVID-19 in facilities owned or managed by Extendicare. With CRA waiting until December 2020 before it published the list of employers who had received CEWS and not reporting how much each company had received, it depressed any criticism of CEWS that could be rooted in the statistics. By the time the information was released, it wasn't the bombshell that it should have been. Journalists' attention had moved beyond CEWS which, at that point, had been given out in nine 4-week phases already. The program had been normalized, and the federal government was not forced to reform CEWS or refuse to allow publicly traded companies from applying.

The power imbalance built into CEWS may have been power that many employers wanted, but it meant that employees were at the whim of their bosses' strategies in managing a program they had no control over. On October 15, 2020, there were technical changes announced to how the subsidy would be applied, the most significant of which reduced the amount of money furloughed employees could receive.[59] To adjust for these changes, WestJet announced that it was going to cut the salaries of 2300 furloughed employees by up to 53%. With no notice, furloughed WestJet employees, who had been told that CEWS was the benefit that would protect them from losing their salaries during the pandemic, had their wages cut and their lives thrown into chaos, just as the second wave was cresting over much of Canada. In a press release, CUPE representative Chris Rauenbusch said, "It is so frustrating to see the government touting CEWS while bureaucratic bumbling and ever-changing rules leave us wondering what to expect next."[60] Even then, the problems with CEWS were never projected onto the employers receiving the benefit in the same way that CERB did; its myriad bureaucratic problems, never sullied the grant program but projected its problems onto those receiving it.

RELIEF ALTERNATIVES

CERB was inadequate. It offered nothing to the poorest Canadians, it was difficult to get, it threw many people's lives into chaos when it was intended to be easy to access and it was demonized as encouraging Canadians to sit at home and do nothing rather than pitch in and do their part to fight the pandemic. The narrative suffocated what was critically necessary within Canadian society: a robust public debate about what measures could have been imposed, or should have been imposed, especially as confinement dragged on. In part, this was driven by the inherent bias of elevating employer groups who wanted to use the pandemic to ensure their corporations would lose as little money as possible. Or, in the case of the largest corporations, earn even more.

Personal finances are impacted by many costs: debt, rent, the cost of food and transit, and so on. Discussions about CERB rarely took into account how any amount offered through CERB would be rendered less effective if the other costs that Canadians had to pay during the pandemic were not addressed. There was a movement from activists demanding that rents be frozen during the pandemic, but the only rents that the government froze were related to businesses. There was no serious conversation about forcing telecom companies to reduce their fees during the pandemic, either. Despite having some of the highest telecommunication fees in the world and the subsequent billion-dollar profits these fees generate, and despite an election promise made by the Liberals in 2019 to reduce the costs of Internet and cellphone usage, the promised strategy had not reduced costs in any meaningful way.[61] In fact, Rogers, Bell and Telus made billions of dollars during the pandemic thanks to money from many Canadians who were often relying on public money to make ends meet. CERB turned out to be a massive transfer of public cash to banks and corporations through people using it to pay for their basic needs.

There was also no discussion about transit costs. At the start of the pandemic, many transit companies offered free transit as a way to keep drivers safe from potential COVID-19 exposure when riders stepped up to pay their fee. After a few months, fares were restored, with little debate of the need for free public transit to help keep household costs low.[62] Activists involved with Poverty-Free Thunder Bay surveyed locals about the impact that free transit would have on their lives, as it had been free from March to July. With overwhelmingly positive responses, local councillors expressed interest in learning more about free transit.[63] But in the south, city councillors in Mississauga were considering increased fees to transit and a host of other services to help offset budget problems caused by COVID-19, including fees for accessing parks.[64] There were also no discussions about widespread free food programs, or food boxes to help people quarantine and stay safe. Instead, the federal Liberals sent small sums of money to Canadian food banks.

Despite the efforts of many activists, alternatives to CERB did not enter into the mainstream narrative, with one notable exception: guaranteed income. Thanks to a motion served by NDP MP Leah Gazan in August

2020, there was a frenzy of attention on the idea of converting CERB into a guaranteed income at the start of fall 2020. There were dozens of opinion pieces that argued guaranteed income could be the poverty solution that everyone has dreamed of, and it was promoted by people of all political stripes. The Basic Income Canada Network was the primary social movement organization driving this debate, arguing that CERB, if made universal, would go a long way to help people through the pandemic and beyond.[65] Sudbury's board of public health endorsed transforming CERB into a universal income, saying, "A guaranteed basic income can improve economic security to support all citizens to achieve optimal health and equity."[66] Universal Basic Income got a lot of support within the media, from columnists in national newspapers to stories from local news sources about how a universal income would help locally. Writing in *Toronto Life* magazine, Ontario MPP Michael Coteau argued that a universal basic income would reduce poverty overall. He wrote,

> A basic income will allow people to prioritize spending on their needs proactively before a situation worsens. For instance, in Peterborough during the Ontario pilot, a senior citizen was able to visit an eye doctor thanks to the financial peace of mind from the basic income.[67]

His example, of course, was more of a display of why Canadians need universal eye care than a universal income, but still, these arguments represented the most significant conversation about a more complete program that could have replaced CERB and given it to more people who needed it.

The universal income discussion was sandwiched between parliamentary sessions, when the federal Liberals prorogued parliament to avoid being questioned about their decision to hand over a $1 billion contract to the WE Charity. There were hints dropped that the Liberal Throne Speech would make a major announcement related to universal income. For example, Liberal MP Neil Ellis told his local newspaper, "support among his MP colleagues for a basic income is unanimous as a stable means to recover from the worst global pandemic in more than a century."[68] When it was finally delivered, the Throne Speech didn't contain a bold plan like a universal income.

While an interesting and rare example of creating a new social program was very welcome, universal income was never the silver bullet that advocates said it would be. As David Bush argues,

> Those advocating BI want to leave the basic mechanism and relationships of capitalism in place, but alter the dynamics of the labour market. Capitalists would still own business, property and control finance. The idea that capitalists or the state would simply allow workers to achieve BI at a rate that would meaningfully alter the balance of class forces or mess with the central coercive function of the wage labour market is a fantasy.[69]

Without price controls on rent, transportation and food, basic income would rapidly be eaten up by daily spending. When the Liberals pivoted away from talking about it, it fell out of the media. Rather than turning all attention to the panacea of a universal income, there should have been just as much attention on the need to provide CERB to the lowest-income Canadians and other measures that would have reduced daily costs. The pandemic should have been a time where radical wealth reorganization became a primary focus of discussion — prohibiting profits, especially from among corporations who specifically benefit on pandemic conditions; forcing corporations to take on relief periods to not pay out shareholders while the pandemic was still on and using those profits instead to lift people out of poverty. CERB may have been a lifeline for millions of Canadians, but it also narrowed the scope of what was possible, what was necessary, to help Canadians as much as possible get through the pandemic. Instead, the rich got richer, the poor got poorer and journalists chased the story of the day — usually just as it was, manicured by government spin.

The core of the government's relief strategy was to give businesses the capital and confidence they needed to survive the pandemic, while hoping that meagre aid packages for some Canadians would be enough to help weather the storm. At its heart, the pandemic has been a story of power: those who had control over their own security and safety versus those who didn't and were left to the whims of those who did. CERB and CEWS was a proxy for this; the federal government gave employers the ability to decide who should be given a wage, who should be laid off, who should receive more through CEWS and who should jump through hoops to get CERB. Anyone without a relationship to an employer received no ongoing pandemic aid money. The non-stop stories of individuals who were forced to pay back CERB, versus no coverage about companies who were forced to repay CEWS, created the illusion that this was a pandemic where individuals were responsible for spreading the virus and business owners were respectable, benevolent individuals who were just trying to keep everything together and protect their staff — a damaging narrative that allowed many corporations to dodge any responsibility in making the pandemic worse. Clawing back CERB from individuals who were receiving other sorts of public assistance was bad enough, but it was even worse in the context of how corporations were treated by government. If a corporation was already receiving other tax breaks or public funding, whether through the federal government or from the provinces, why didn't they have their CEWS clawed back in the same way that CERB recipients did? Where were the news stories about how drug use spiked among business owners who had a fast cash injection?

CERB could have given journalists an excuse to examine different ways of doing things: free transit, lower telecommunication costs and so on. As CERB was timed to end with the end of summer 2020, another issue took over journalists' attention: students going back to school and all the ways in which school policy was inadequate or dangerous. All the while, Canadians who had been receiving CERB were glued to regular announcements to find out if, next week, they would receive enough money to cover their September rent.

September 2020
BACK TO SCHOOL

Cases: 128,948
Deaths: 9,126[1]

The end of the summer 2020 was a difficult moment for CERB recipients who didn't know what would happen to the benefit, but they were far from the only Canadians staring into the abyss of the unknown. For a majority of kids in Canada, September 2020 was the first time they would go back to school since March Break. September was a month of anxiety, for parents and students, for school staff and for communities, where increased contact within schools would create another location where COVID-19 could propagate.

During the pandemic, schools took on symbolic significance, though children were often forgotten by public health measures. Schools indicated how serious a province was taking COVID-19 outbreaks, or how well infection spread was under control. Schools were a political football, punted back and forth between staff and government, with parents oscillating between calling for schools to be closed, and their need to get their kids out of their hair. Schools also became a lens through which a province's values could be understood, with Québec being the jurisdiction more prepared to open schools even as infections were raging, and Ontario the most hesitant, while experts, including doctors, child psychologists, teachers and parents debated the balance between safety (both perceived and real) and children's mental health. Schools also became a distraction, as these particular large congregant settings were easier for all governments to close down or move online than it was politically desirable to meaningfully address other large congregant settings like workplaces.

There were three moments where students went back to school during the hottest moments of the pandemic: spring 2020, September 2020 and winter 2021. Each time was used by politicians to say something about the pandemic, either that things are going well, or things are going poorly, but above all, we are competent managers. And journalists lapped it up, covering every angle thinkable related to school. Between fall 2020 and winter 2021, enough time had passed to learn and adjust to what was known about how COVID-19 moved within schools, yet the issue was often covered as if it were all happening again for the first time. This created an anxiety-driven news cycle full of anger, fear and other powerful emotions, while politicians mostly did the bare minimum.

QUÉBEC

In May 2020, just as schools were about to open after the first lockdown, journalist Jean-François Néron from Quebec City's daily newspaper *Le Soleil* interviewed five families about whether or not they planned to send their children back to school. Three decided to send their children back to school, and each said that on the balance of risk, having their children be with their friends, stimulated in school and away from home so the parents could work made them decide to go back to school. Two decided not to send their children back: one, because a parent worked in a CHSLD with an outbreak so they decided to keep their children home "to protect everyone."[2] The other parent interviewed was Marie-Hélène Gingras who, as a single parent, worried about what happened if she got sick: "it was a simple equation: 'if I get sick, who will watch [my child]?'"[3] There were still many unknowns about COVID-19 on May 1, 2020, when Néron's article appeared, and personal circumstances played a key role in people's decisions about what to do. As COVID-19 was disproportionately impacting racialized and low-income families, the decision to send children back to school was entwined with the social location and the work/life circumstances of where families lived.

In a similar feature for CBC *Québec*, Susan Campbell surveyed English-speaking Quebecers about their decision to send or not send their children back to school, but unlike Néron, she asked the question just after the school year finished in June, after some kids had already gone back to school in May. She talked to one parent from Sherbrooke who summed up a common attitude:

> Shanna Bernier chuckles a bit when she says sending her child back to school in the middle of a worldwide pandemic was, overall, a positive experience.
>
> "I would chalk that up to magnificent resilience and creativity in our educators and not because there was a great plan," she said.

"I just hope that over the summer there's some really solid planning and thoughtfulness that goes into the return in September."[4]

The lack of a plan was a general complaint about how the government
managed back-to-school, as so much of the safety coordination and logistics fell to educators themselves to keep students in each classroom safe.
Campbell also interviewed my partner who admitted we were impressed
that the return seemed to go so well, despite our extreme skepticism and
refusal to send our kids back in May.[5]

The subject of schools was so malleable that anyone could make an
argument about the school system regardless of their personal political
orientation or goals. Schools both spread COVID-19 and slowed the spread
of COVID-19. They spread it through large classes, difficulty distancing,
poor air quality and other sanitary measures. They stopped it from spreading by taking kids away from homes where they were most likely to get
COVID-19, or from informal care arrangements, where kids might get
COVID-19 from or infect an elderly relative or friend. School is the one
location that every Canadian has some basis of experience with: while it
isn't the case that every Canadian has had direct experience with residential care, our collective experiences in the medical system vary wildly and
our workplaces are so disparate, we all have some experiences that are
generally comparable with school. This made schools a very important
location in the debate over how COVID-19 was framed, understood and
responded to.

THE RHETORICAL (AND MATERIAL) ROLE PLAYED BY SCHOOLS

From the start, the school system was at the rhetorical heart of the
pandemic, even as death and illness swept through other systems and
locations. In a *Maclean's* feature written about pandemic preparedness,
closing schools was mentioned only as a possibility. Steven Hoffman,
scientific director of the Institute of Population and Public Health at the
Canadian Institutes of Health Research, was quoted being skeptical that
such an action would be necessary:

As of late February, Hoffman would put school shutdowns in
the category of "government overreaction." "But," he adds, "if a
city in Canada faces a huge surge and it's felt to be uncontrollable, you could imagine schools being temporarily closed," he
says, through government intervention. Still, it's more likely that

schools, workplaces or communities will ask for people to stay home voluntarily as the perceived risk of infection rises. "Some of the research shows that, when people are asked to self-quarantine, there are extremely high rates of compliance."[6]

It wasn't simply shutting down schools that tied the school system to COVID-19 from the start; it was also March Break, the timing of which had a direct impact on how bad the first wave would get in each province, regardless of how many kids were actually in school. In Québec, March Break was blamed by many for why COVID-19 took off with a deadly speed that no other province experienced. With an early March Break held from March 2–6, 2020, many Quebecers travelled, especially to locations deemed to be "safe" from COVID-19, like the United States. By the time Montréal Public Health officials warned people to limit their travel — on the Friday of March Break — it was too late. Tuesday the week after, the first school in Québec was closed due to a COVID-19 outbreak, and within six days, the province's entire system was shut down.[7] By Friday, March 23, two weeks later, Québec had more cases than the rest of Canada, with 628 active cases. At his daily press briefing, Québec Premier François Legault blamed March Break on the sudden spread, as 40% to 60% of Québec's active cases had come from out-of-country travel.[8]

As Québec approached March Break, the popular understanding of global COVID-19 spread was that it was more of a threat in locations that most Quebecers didn't travel regularly to. As a result, March Break was more or less normal, and the repercussions were deadly. Even though the first reported case of COVID-19 in Québec was a woman who had just returned from Iran, infection from hotspots at the time — Iran, China and Italy — were very low: no cases came to Québec from China, only one came from Iran and six from Italy. The vast majority came from more popular travel destinations for March Break: 373 from the United States, 151 from France, 121 from Puerto Rico (a common departure country for cruises) and 117 from Austria.[9]

Closing schools was not just an emergency act to try to contain COVID-19. It was a symbolic act too — signalling to all Canadians that this virus is so serious, drastic measures needed to be taken. From a symbolic perspective, closing schools was the moment when journalists could say in no uncertain terms that this illness was serious; schools have rarely been shut down in Canada. During the Spanish Flu pandemic, schools were closed and many debates swirled about whether or not that was the best decision given the evidence of what was known about the virus and the need for children to do something during the day. And just like during the COVID-19 pandemic, people argued over whether or not schools should have been closed, especially in balance with other facilities staying open, rendering a school closure less effective. In the November 1918 edition of the *Canadian Medical Health Association Journal*, Chief Officer of Ontario's Board of Health Dr. John McCullough argued,

> the utility of closing churches, schools, theatres, etc. is obviously limited when department stores, business places and street and railway cars are allowed to carry on business as usual. There seems to be no doubt that children would be better at school than running in the streets and spending their time (as they have in large numbers in Toronto) in the shops.[10]

Many healthcare professionals argued children needed to be in school for their mental health, or even to ensure they were in a controlled environment where infection likelihood was more limited than a large-bubble home. This debate raged throughout the first year of the pandemic, with Québec tending to take a more radical approach to opening schools than Ontario, even while both provinces were in the grips of holiday-triggered infection spread in January 2021.

Widespread school closures signalled to the entire population that there was a high level of risk: COVID-19 spread was so dangerous that drastic measures needed to be taken. Schools offered a foil to Canada's broken system of long-term care: both systems were primarily created to support the circumstances of either end of life's spectrum. But where long-term care was a location of mass death, the impact of schools was much harder to gauge, and was the source of probably the pandemic's most consistent debate: how much did children spread COVID-19? From the start of the pandemic until January 29, 2021, just as mass vaccinations were starting within long-term care, the 19 years of age and under cohort comprised 16.2% of all confirmed COVID-19 infections. This was slightly more than 30–39 (15.9%), 40–49 (14.6%) and 50–59 (13.4%) age cohorts, and less than the 20–29 age cohort (18.8%). While children appeared to make up the majority of COVID-19 infections, the rate of infection among young people was lower than their proportion of Canada's population, at 21%. In fact, only the 50–59 age cohort caught COVID-19 in proportion to their population rate. Canadians aged 80 or older were overrepresented in

COVID-19 infections, comprising 7.5% of all infections[11] but only making up 4% of the total population, a fact directly linked to just how fast and far COVID-19 spread within congregate living settings.[12]

But schools were not like long-term care facilities in important ways. Children went home at the end of the day, leaving hours each day for potential contact to create an infection that could be brought to school. Schools are mostly public institutions, too, organized in large systems, unlike long-term care, which is mostly private and run by hundreds of different operators. School staff had better working conditions and wages, and had far less physical contact with students than workers in long-term care have with residents. COVID-19 was not as deadly to people who attended or worked in schools as it was for the people who lived or worked in residential care. From March 2020 until June 2021, there were seven deaths attributed to education: two educational assistants (EA) and the husband of an EA, two teachers and two daycare workers. Over the same period of time, 39 residential care workers died as a result of a COVID-19 outbreak at their workplace.[13] Outbreaks within the educational system were better managed, thanks mostly to the fact that classes could be shut down if there were several cases, unlike in long-term care where workers were at the whim of management who may or may not have followed outbreak protocols as COVID-19 swept across a facility, and who had to keep working in a facility even if there was an outbreak. But there was another big difference between how COVID-19 interacted with both cohorts: from March 2020 until June 2021, COVID-19 killed 13 people aged 0–19 while it killed 16,905 people who were 80+.[14]

In measuring the impact of COVID-19 by infection or by death, children and teens fared relatively well during this part of the pandemic. However, they were also important nodes of transmission. If a child infected a grandparent, it could have been life threatening. The interplay of personal relationships, or how connected children were to the elderly in Canada, should have oriented how journalists covered young people and COVID-19 spread within schools: what would be the reasons for why children and people who are not in their immediate household interact, and how can we limit these reasons to help keep children from spreading COVID-19? And what about children living in residential care facilities? How were they being protected from COVID-19 while also being allowed to still see parents and siblings? The answers would have generated debate about solutions like widespread forms of publicly financed and coordinated help, whether for child care or meal preparation or simply giving parents a break. But that wasn't how politicians talked about young people, and it was not the way in which journalists covered children. Instead, children and youth became one with schools themselves; school coverage became a de facto conversation about children. As a result, schools received as much media attention as did long-term care, and certainly more attention than other issues like COVID-19 workplace spread, as they could become a symbol through which to tell nearly any story a politician or a journalist wanted to tell about how good or how bad the pandemic was being managed. The way in which journalists told this story relied on how parents were feeling — an ever-changing set of emotions that were driven by the rhythm of a school year like no other, and choices made while facing a wall of unknowns.

SPRING 2020

From the March 2020 school closures until September, most students in Canada stayed at home. In Québec, Manitoba and British Columbia schools briefly re-opened in the spring, where it was not mandatory and only for several weeks. The Québec government announced that schools would return to class on Monday, May 25, just as the worst of the first wave seemed to be slowly subsiding. The return of warmer weather, plus social distancing measures and class sizes capped at 15 (made possible mostly thanks to the parents who didn't send their children back), helped create the conditions for a safe return, even while the pandemic was still new and forcing most of the economy to slow down or stop completely. Students in high schools started after elementary students, and students in Montréal, where infection spread was the most serious, went back later than the rest of Québec, with just a few weeks remaining in the school year. Even though infection was highest in Montréal, 50% of students in public school and 66% in private schools went back to school.[15] Daycares opened gradually too, first welcoming 50% capacity and slowly moving higher as the weeks passed.[16]

The May return turned out to be a very useful dress rehearsal for fall 2020. Québec's worker safety organization the CNESST developed guidelines for opening schools safely. Cafeterias were closed and children in elementary school were kept in strict group bubbles that they would maintain throughout the day, including before school care, lunchtime and after school care. The guidelines also outlined how a sick child was to be managed at the school to reduce spread and safely have them sent home.[17]

When Manitoba, British Columbia and Québec re-opened schools in spring 2020, each province had a very different prevalence of COVID-19 spread. Manitoba was in the best position, having announced no new cases on June 1, 2020, with just ten active cases in the province total.[18] That same day, British Columbia announced 24 cases over the previous weekend. They had 224 active cases across the province.[19] Québec was, by far, the province most impacted by COVID-19 at the time, and their school opening happened just as a wave of death had crested over the province's assisted living facilities. On June 1, the province reported its lowest daily increase in numbers since March, at 295 new cases, for a total of 30,096 active infections in the province. The three provinces: Québec with high prevalence, B.C. with moderate to low prevalence and Manitoba with very low prevalence of COVID-19 offered politicians, journalists, health professionals and parents three different scenarios in which schools opened; they were also the only provinces where students went back to school during the spring semester. They offered very important insights into how well it went: was there a connection between preparedness and issues within the classroom? Were parents' fears calmed by implementing specific measures? Like Campbell's article for CBC *Québec* mentioned, the experience was a treasure trove of information for nervous parents, both within the provinces who decided not to send their kids back to school in spring 2020 (like me), and parents in other provinces whose governments decided to keep these facilities closed.

But reporting that compared jurisdictions was rare. School reporting was very local, even hyper-individual, with an intense focus on issues that were mostly divorced from context. As parents were weighing their options in B.C., journalists focused tightly on the individual decisions that families found themselves making. CBC *British Columbia* quoted one father who was concerned about how faucets "that need to be pressed" would work.[20] Journalists often picked up on very small details like this, which created a confusing mix of information about whether or not going back to school would ever be possible. In the fog of spring 2020, and with limp governments who were not consistently funding the best back-to-school protocols like mandatory mask wearing, smaller classes or improved air quality, going back to school was the only way to test everything out — from bubbling children cohorts to handwashing, it all had to be practised. In absence of physically trying to open up schools, journalists were left to report parents' various fears, with little regard to how easy a workaround could have been established for whatever issue parents mentioned, like providing students with personal water bottles to avoid needing to use a water fountain. There was a distinct pattern in the reporting on school closures and openings, regardless of jurisdiction. Articles usually mentioned mask wearing, class sizes and school cleaning. Some mentioned air quality, and this issue became more and more prominent throughout the fall of 2020. There were usually one or two parent voices, a reference to how excited, though nervous a student was to go back and usually a union representative or opposition party who didn't think the government was doing enough.

Back-to-school reporting in spring and summer 2020 zoomed in on the minutiae of schools, at the expense of asking broader questions about the relationship between schools and community spread or the relationship between school infections and a parent or caregiver's exposure or risk. Schools, like long-term care facilities, were reported on as if they were separate and independent nodes unbothered by what was happening in the community around them. Schools had their own set of policies, their own government officials, different experts and a very large clientele from which to endlessly mine the same kinds of reactions. Reporting rarely sought to tease out which schools might be at higher risk for COVID than others, and instead lumped schools together into a city, region or even province as a whole.

SEPTEMBER 2020

Despite a lack of national, or even inter-provincial coordination, school reopening plans for fall 2020 mostly looked the same: cohorts for bubbling, masks for older kids, and no imposed limits to class sizes, instead allowing students to be in closer-than-2-metre contact to others within their class. New Brunswick explicitly promised to reduce class sizes "wherever possible," and several provinces had planned a rotation between days for high school students between in-person and online class to reduce students' contact.[21] In Ontario, the biggest battle was waged over class sizes, a carry-over struggle from the year before where the Ontario government moved to increase class sizes. Ontario Secondary School Teachers' Federation (OSSTF) President Harvey Bischof told CBC News in September 2019, "We're hearing from classrooms all over the province that are just jammed with kids ... The start of the school year is often a little messy, here and there, but we have never seen anything like this." The article reported that some high school classes had more than 40 students. As class sizes during the pandemic had a direct impact on how safe it was to re-open schools, teachers again demanded smaller class sizes.[22] Ontario Premier Doug Ford was particularly hostile toward teachers. Teachers claimed the Ontario government didn't consult them as they drew up their plans for back to school in 2020,[23] and the four provincial teacher unions together filed a labour board complaint requesting that the province lower class sizes and maintain, "ventilation requirements already deemed safe for the province's courthouses." *Durham Radio News* quoted the premier saying, "his 'patience for the teachers unions is running out.'"[24]

The back-and-forth over class sizes received a lot of media attention. Parents expressed fear and outrage over the Ontario government's plans, and there was tremendous anxiety, including among parents who decided to send their children back. But what was missing, again, was context: just how much community transmission needed to be in a specific location for it to have an impact on a school? And why, at month six of the pandemic, was the data such that many parts of Canada didn't really know how much COVID-19 was circulating within their neighbourhoods? Instead, articles were swift to blame back to school for a spike in infections, even though COVID-19 infections happened so quickly in some cases, it would have been impossible for school to have played a significant role in spreading the virus. For example, in Alberta, after one week of school being open, 22 schools had COVID-19 cases. In Québec, 120 schools had reported having at least one COVID-19 case within the first week back.[25] For a case to have been caught at school, a student would have had to arrive at school with COVID-19. With a three-to-five-day symptom onset period, then waiting days for a test result, the fastest COVID-19 could have spread would have been more than four days of the first week of school: Monday, a student is infected by another student, Thursday is the earliest day for symptom onset and then by the weekend, receive results back from a COVID-19 test, if you lived somewhere testing was operating quickly. Far more likely was that COVID-19 was more prevalent in the community than public health actually knew, so students were coming to school with COVID-19, causing their class to be shut down once a case was confirmed. In this way, schools actually became early-warning systems for COVID-19 spread within a community, but unlike wastewater monitoring done in many Canadian regions, schools were rarely reported on as early warnings for government action. Journalists focused on back-to-school figures in Alberta, Québec and Ontario, but rarely pressed officials on how families were supposed to access easy testing. There were no rapid testing centres established at schools before a serious cluster of cases was found, and even afterward it often didn't happen. Six weeks into the school year, testing rates were lowest among Toronto neighbourhoods that had the highest rates of COVID-19. This suggested that COVID-19 was circulating in the city, and some neighbourhoods hit hard by COVID-19 didn't have the same access to tests as other neighbourhoods.[26] In Toronto's racially segregated COVID-19 neighbourhoods (which I detail in the chapter about June 2020), access to testing had a huge impact on how safe schools were — or could have been.

Schools became a chicken-and-egg obsession: do they drive community spread or do they mirror community spread, or are they somewhere in the middle? The discussion about opening schools in fall 2020 was again framed with a detached, individualized understanding of how schools fit into a broader social fabric. Why didn't schools try to map the contacts of their students proactively to give parents a sense of how many neighbourhoods or industries were touched by specific cohorts? Why didn't governments send more money to schools where there were higher numbers of racialized and/or low-income students, as statistically, by September, the evidence was clear that COVID-19 posed a greater risk to these young people? By understanding schools as being nebulously detached from the rest of their communities, journalists were able to tell this story through the eyes of anxious parents, contrast their anxieties against other anxious parents, bring in a reassuring word from an expert, contrast that with an anxiety-inducing word from another expert and generally let government off the hook. This was the template for the average article on this topic around this time. It missed the ways in which journalists could have written about the safety of schools, including being more consistent in how they reported what was known, what was unknown, what was debatable and what was pure political posturing.

WHAT WE KNEW / WHAT WE DIDN'T

There are many factors that determined whether or not it was safe to open a school: the correct use of personal protective equipment (PPE), other safety measures in place (like distancing or ventilation) and the presence of COVID-19 within the community where a school was located, for example. Journalists spent a lot of time covering the first two, as governments announced their intention to supply PPE or improve air quality — even if these promises never actually materialized — and as parents expressed their anxiety about a lack of safety protocols within a school. But the third factor — the presence of COVID-19 within a community and therefore the likely impact on school spread — received the least amount of attention. To do an analysis like this required journalists to situate schools within a community, then connect the community with its workplaces where COVID-19 spread more easily. A school where parents were more likely to work in manufacturing, construction or residential care would be more susceptible to COVID-19 spread than a school where parents were mostly white-collar workers able to work from home, but these differences rarely accompanied outbreak or school reopening news coverage. But doing this properly was always going to be difficult: Canada has a lot of schools. Some newspapers covered regions with hundreds of schools in several different school boards. Some schools existed in regions with little to no news coverage at all.

At the end of August 2020, the *Globe and Mail*'s Kelly Grant and Chen Wang took a deep dive into the relationship between community transmission and school openings to understand what the optimal level of community spread is for schools to be relatively free of COVID-19. They referenced a document from Harvard University that created tiers of safety for school reopening based on seven-day averages, from green where there was one or fewer daily new cases per 100,000 people, up to red at more than 25 cases per 100,000 people per day. When school went back in September, most of Canada was within this green zone, except B.C., Manitoba and Alberta. Toronto was the safest city they analyzed when school was to return, and Edmonton's Northgate neighbourhood was the least safe, with 13 daily infections per 100,000 people. Grant and Wang noted that the Public Health Agency of Canada never tried to develop a similar tool.[27] By the end of August, even though we had been living with COVID-19 for five months, it still wasn't clear to many Canadians just how much COVID-19 was circulating in their communities.

Much of the lack of information could have been solved by public health units being more forthright with their data. But part of the problem was also the lack of broad-scale testing for students. After all, to follow a guide about reopening a school, public health needed to know how many cases were actually circulating in a community. Sure, the experiences of B.C., Manitoba and Québec in May and June 2020 indicated that it could be done safely, but Canadians were entering into a different pandemic moment in September 2020: rather than being at the end of a wave, we were starting the second wave. As students hadn't been in school together for months, the odds were high that viruses would spread. There was no coordinated, proactive testing regime built into the return to school, anywhere. Guidelines weren't even clear about what symptoms to even test; information varied across jurisdiction about whether or not a runny nose and a cough, for example, were enough for a family to get tested. And good luck getting to a testing centre if your family didn't have a car!

When schools re-opened, testing centres soon became flooded, both thanks to confusing information about who should and should not be tested, and to individuals being very cautious to stop themselves from potentially being a node in spread. Ottawa's testing centres were particularly over-whelmed; one testing centre, full of parents who were networked on Twitter and plugged into national media and politics, had hundreds of parents and children line up hours before the clinic opened. The West COVID-19 Care Clinic reached capacity at 9:00 a.m. and announced that it couldn't handle any more people that day. It was Friday, September 18, and by then, every student was back at school in Ottawa. Some had started on September 8 and others had staggered start dates, but the rush reflected a surge of fear and panic among parents related to back-to-school illnesses that might or might not have been COVID-19.[28] By September 18, four classes in Ottawa's public Catholic school board had been closed down because of the presence of a COVID-19 case. With a delay of up to five days to receive COVID-19 test results, parents had to, again, make arrangements to keep children at home to wait for results, even if symptoms evolved over the intervening days that made it obvious their child didn't have COVID-19. At the time of the rush on testing centres in Ottawa, there were 731 active cases — 73 cases per 100,000 people in the city, or 5.8 new cases per day, per 100,000 people (based on an average of new cases from Sept. 15–18).[29]

On September 24, just weeks after classes returned in Ontario, the province announced changes to testing: only people showing symptoms could get tested. Ontario's Associate Chief Medical Officer of Health Barbara Yaffe said,

> Your average person out there who is not exposed to a case, who is not part of an outbreak, has no symptoms, should not be going for testing. There's no value. In fact, what we found is when there's very little COVID in that group, what we end up with is false posi-tives, which just complicates things even more.[30]

This did not calm the fears of parents who were confused about how children could still pick up seasonal colds even with the social distancing and cleaning measures happening in schools. At the same time, the Government of Ontario outsourced asymptomatic testing to Shoppers Drug Mart, owned by Loblaw.[31] Anyone who was asymptomatic and who had been in close contact with a case was told to go to a pharmacy to get tested. Loblaw-owned pharmacies had already been offering asymptomatic tests in Alberta.[32] Ford promised to use $1 billion from the federal government to expand testing and contact tracing. At the time, bars, theatres, religious spaces and other businesses were permitted to operate.[33]

But there wasn't even consensus from jurisdiction to jurisdiction in Canada for what constituted a COVID-19 symptom, or what to do if you had one. All jurisdictions considered a fever a red flag symptom, but the list of potential COVID-19 symptoms was far longer than just that: cough, sore throat, loss of taste and smell and diarrhea. In B.C., the presence of a key symptom required students to stay home for 24 hours, whereas in Alberta, a student with a key symptom was expected to stay home and isolate for ten days. As the school year advanced, B.C. and Ontario amended their checklists: secondary symptoms on their own stopped being enough to keep a child home. Ontario made amendments too, reducing the threshold for having to stay home for 24 hours to a single symptom or worsening overall state. While a loss of taste and smell was a key COVID-19 symptom, it was not on its own enough to keep kids home in Alberta or the Northwest Territories (unless it appeared with other symptoms), and it didn't even appear on the list of symptoms at all in Nova Scotia. P.E.I. required students to stay home if they were sneezing and New Brunswick required students to stay home if they had a skin rash.[34]

Only Saskatchewan had a mandatory testing regime for students who were referred to testing. Québec mandated that caregivers contact public health if a student was referred to be tested. In all other parts of Canada in fall 2020, testing was just strongly encouraged. Had testing been a part of attending school, governments would have been forced to coordinate and pay for testing for students. By not making it mandatory, most governments avoided the hassle of bringing testing to schools. Caregivers had to rely on locally coordinated public health unit testing.[35] With this patchwork of policies across Canada, it was no surprise that students and parents felt frustrated and confused. And in the guidelines, again, the personal community connection was completely absent: a child who had a runny nose and whose friends all had a cold could have been exempted from staying home, if guidelines considered what caregivers knew about what was circulating among local children. Instead, extreme caution was encouraged, creating a situation where a child with a runny nose who is more likely to be suffering from allergies should be considered COVID-19 positive, just in case, even if they had never come into contact with someone who was COVID-19 positive. People were encouraged to assume that everything might be COVID-19 — probably the most stressful way for parents and caregivers to live.

By November, enough time had passed to start drawing some conclusions about COVID-19 and school spread. The *Globe and Mail*'s Les Perreaux examined what experts were saying based on just over two months of experience. One research paper found that schools were not amplifying transmission; they were reflecting what was happening within the broader community: "We don't think schools are a huge driver. We looked at growth rates in secondary and primary schools in Québec and they are not different in schools than the general community," said Caroline Colijn, a mathematician and epidemiologist at Simon Fraser University and one of the authors of the study. She cautioned against understanding this to mean that everything is fine. Her paper recommended schools need to implement rapid and regular testing and better ventilation to reduce the size of COVID-19 clusters when they do happen. Perreaux also talked to David Fisman, epidemiology professor at the University of Toronto, who said it was very hard to know how much COVID-19 circulated in Ontario schools: after the province changed its testing criteria, there was an 80% drop in how many young children were tested.[36]

That was the key problem: it was both known and not known how many cases were circulating within the schools. It was known when a student got sick and went for a test. It was known when a family member got COVID-19 and there were also cases in a student's cohort. But without testing, it was impossible to know how much asymptomatic spread there was: how often were students spreading COVID-19 who were otherwise feeling fine? Like in long-term care, asymptomatic spread became the great unknown in schools, and governments did very little to understand it. Parents were left mostly in the dark and teachers felt unsupported. Yet, governments insisted they were doing everything they could, even though that was far from true. It was a frustrating and contradictory mess, and no significantly new protocols were implemented as the semester marched on.

Even though the lack of testing left a lot of things unknown, it was very well known that some communities were hit harder by COVID-19 and therefore, some schools would have been too. Journalists did not generally drill into the differences between communities and COVID-19 spread, instead covering school boards, cities or provinces as homogeneous. If a school board announced an initiative to do something for a school that was in a low-income community, it might have got coverage, but the coverage was rarely proactive. The Hamilton-Wentworth District School Board identified 31 schools where they offered extra COVID-19 support by way of increased visits from a nursing team. CBC *Hamilton* reported on this decision but didn't dig deeper into the plan: they didn't examine if this was enough, if there would be expanded access to rapid tests, or whether or not school board members would advocate for provincial policies, like paid sick leave, that could further help families of students in these schools.[37]

Paid sick days was one of the key demands that would have helped keep people safe. Activists called for paid sick leave as a way to ensure that workers were not going to work sick. But paid sick days were critical to ensuring that COVID-19 didn't spread within the school system too: a parent who is paid to stay home is more likely to keep a sick child home. The way in which parents interacted with their workplaces — from whether or not they could work from home or keep themselves safe at the worksite, to parents' access to rapid testing, to decisions to close down workplaces if there was an outbreak — had a direct impact on how safe a school was. Where many employers were slow to admit they had an outbreak (indeed, there were many who refused to admit this at all), schools became a very important early-warning signal for COVID-19 infections. If a student had a positive test, and if a school and the local public health unit could do an epidemiological investigation into that student's contacts to determine who else should stay home to self-isolate, it stopped the spread of COVD-19 instantly. The same could not be said of workplaces, which were rarely shut down even for 24 hours when an outbreak occurred. As public bodies that are better resourced than most, schools were a critical stopgap for the spread of COVID-19, even if there was circulation within the schools as well.

In general, journalists neither reported about the connection between workplaces and school outbreaks, nor did they report on school outbreaks through this early-warning frame. There was no follow-up to the *Globe and Mail*'s August investigation into community spread metrics by other media organizations, even as community spread reached a crisis point.

School rolled on as the pandemic worsened, and then stopped: the winter holidays put on the breaks as schools shut down and students were once again at home. Depending on the province, some stayed home for three weeks while others, notably in Ontario, stayed home well into February. The same debate that happened in May and June 2020, and then again in August and September 2020, happened all over again in February and March 2021. Except unlike in September, this time, cases in most parts of Canada were very high, but falling.

WINTER 2021

December 2020 turned out to be the deadliest and most dangerous period of the second wave. As the holidays approached, new restrictions were imposed in regions across Canada, and with schools closed, one of the largest systems of congregant gatherings could not perpetuate the virus. This calmed the fears of those who believed that schools played an important role in circulating COVID-19 and gave politicians time to regroup for the new school year. But the worst locations for COVID-19 spread stayed open, untouched by new "shutdown" protocols in every province, which allowed for construction, manufacturing and other large, congregant-setting workplaces' outbreak numbers to climb. Canadians were not great at staying put during the holidays either: one poll found that 48% of people gathered with others, in-person, during the holidays. That is potentially a lot of children who otherwise would have been either at home or in school, normally.[38] B.C.'s Minister of Education Rob Fleming said he thought closing schools was "probably a mistake," as he looked back at the COVID-19 spikes that followed Thanksgiving and Halloween and looked forward to how to manage schools as cases increased.[39]

By January 2021, a better picture was emerging about just how dangerous schools really were, though gaps in data allowed many doubts to linger around the otherwise positive news. Vancouver Coastal Health said that 90% of confirmed COVID-19 cases did not lead to in-school transmission. In the Lower Mainland, CTV News reported that there were only "a handful" of outbreaks.[40] Ottawa Public Health looked at every case that had been confirmed: of 124,211 students, 888 contracted COVID-19, and 85% of these students contracted COVID-19 outside of school, even though 560 students attended school while they were contagious and a quarter were asymptomatic. Of the 55 outbreaks that were declared, half of the outbreaks only included two students total. The largest outbreak spread to 17 people. Half of the outbreaks could be confirmed as coming from a close contact of the student or staff person, outside of the school. Ottawa Public Health officer Vera Etches argued that children were most at risk of catching COVID-19 at home, due to prolonged close contact.[41] Home was certainly a location of tremendous risk, exacerbated by no extra child-care supports, no public supports for people to purchase PPE for home use and a very slow rollout of a system of self-isolation in municipally offered hotels that allowed parents to isolate away from family members. This kind of option didn't exist everywhere, nor was it helpful for adults in a household who had COVID-19 but whose children didn't. Did the obsession with schools take away from a sustained and concentrated focus on how governments could have helped minimize spread within the home?

The *Globe and Mail* again examined back to school in January 2021, though this time armed with new data as Québec, Alberta and a few other school boards went back to school the earliest. Some Ontario school boards pushed the start of school into February. That left parents in the lurch again, giving them the impression that schools are not safe, while also saddling them with child-care duties for almost two months (again, with no public policies to force their employer to reduce their workload or give them paid time off). But unlike September, a spike didn't happen. Both Alberta and Québec saw a spike in infections related to the holidays, though Alberta's was lower, and by mid-January, cases continued to fall.[42] By January 18, all residents in Alberta long-term care had received one dose of a vaccine, and nearly all residents in Québec CHSLDs had received a dose by the end of the month.[43] It was observed that the first dose of the vaccine had dropped infections by 80%.[44]

Even after ten months of living with the pandemic in Canada, governments did shockingly little to help make schools safer and this drove a lot of frustration and anger. School staff took incredible efforts to make their classrooms safer. Parents purchased masks, respected school rules and prepped their kids to be as safe as possible at school. But aside from some studies that were taken to evaluate how safe school openings were, there was always a giant unknown hanging over the data: are we really testing enough to have an adequate picture to analyze? Kate Zinszer, an epidemiologist at Université Montréal told the *Globe and Mail*,

> "It's so frustrating as a researcher to not have access to good data … We're just not responsive enough, not nuanced enough in our approach. We should be monitoring with rapid testing, saliva

samples." Dr. Zinszer said schools should be monitored much more closely to protect teachers, students and their families, but also because of the community surveillance they could provide. "Elementary schools in particular aren't the hot spots we thought they would be, but obviously there are contacts in schools and the chance for transmission ... We still don't really know their role in community transmission, and they could be such a good window into what's happening in the community."

The frustration that still, after 11 months of the pandemic, rapid tests were not being regularly done within schools was the true scandal. And politicians managed to avoid too much scrutiny over how much of a failure this really was.[45]

Rapid tests were the most important tool that should have been implemented broadly within school. In early 2021, Ontario Minister of Health Stephen Lecce called rapid testing, "a big game changer," and referenced how important it was in a few Toronto hotspots in the fall to identify how far the virus had travelled. At the start of February, he promised they had equipped public health units to do asymptomatic testing and "ultimately take action if required," a plan that was panned by OSSTF President Harvey Bischof. He referenced a program in Sudbury that had been started mid-January and said Lecce

has not laid out a program for asymptomatic testing whatsoever, they've simply abdicated their responsibility to local public health units ... If you look in jurisdictions where schools have already opened like Sudbury, they haven't come close to ramping up the asymptomatic testing program.[46]

Rapid testing was still mostly used only in situations where officials were worried about rapid spread of COVID-19 or a variant of concern, rather than being part of a regular and widespread monitoring program. But Lecce's government, always more loyal to industry than it was to students, ended up committing six times more rapid tests to businesses than it did to schools: 300,000 tests for large construction, manufacturing and energy companies versus 50,000 for Ontario schools.[47]

Rather than implement rapid testing across Québec schools, a pilot project was started in January at two Montréal high schools, where students were being monitored for the virus regularly until the school year ended. Even though Québec had rapid tests available, this was the first pilot that used them in a school in a steady and consistent manner.[48] Rapid tests also weren't used regularly in Alberta schools either. The Alberta government announced a program on February 9, 2021, to test and track cases within long-term care, but schools and other congregant settings were not included yet; plans, said Health Minister Tyler Shandro, were in the works for schools, shelters and correctional facilities. Although, one month prior, the government made available 7000 rapid tests to Suncor Energy's worksite north of Fort McMurray for ongoing COVID-19 monitoring.[49] The way in which schools were regularly sidelined to support corporations to continue their business as usual should have been reported with outrage and shock, though journalists rarely made this comparison.

Rapid tests would not become used in any regular manner in Canadian schools for the rest of the 2020–2021 school year. Vaccination campaigns took up more and more media coverage, squeezing out space to talk about other pandemic mitigation measures like rapid testing. In most of Canada, schools were only closed when there was a local surge that justified their being closed. The safety of a school or school system was intimately connected to the school's local community, and so it was difficult to truly judge how successful governments were at keeping students and staff safe versus how much of a location's success was due to broader forces. For example, the Nova Scotia Minister of Education Derek Mombourquette said that masking, hand sanitizer and $1.7 million spent on ventilation checks were enough to ensure that COVID-19 didn't spread too far within the school system.[50] But Nova Scotia embraced rapid testing like no other Canadian jurisdiction. People were encouraged to be tested, even if they were asymptomatic, and public notices about exposures were regularly posted. During the spring, rapid tests were also deployed across hundreds of workplaces.[51] Articles about workplace rapid testing should have examined the connection between workplace rapid testing, home spread and children's infections. The combination of workplace rapid testing and widespread asymptomatic testing would have been far more effective than hand sanitizer in schools. Not to mention Nova Scotia's rate of COVID-19 spread was well below many other jurisdictions in Canada, which helped keep school infections low as well. B.C., Québec and Alberta governments tried to keep schools open in spring 2021, only closing school boards where there was the highest spread. By the end of the school year, one study that examined antibodies of more than 1600 staff within the Vancouver

District School over three months showed that spread among school staff was no higher than among the general population.[52]

The outlier in Canada was Ontario, the only jurisdiction that closed all schools in the province for most of the spring in 2021. Ontario schools were closed for 25 weeks of the 2020–2021 school year, more than anywhere else. Schools were closed regardless of their proximity to high levels of spread. It became politically expedient for the Ontario government to insist that schools were dangerous and close them entirely, creating a narrow debate that clung closely to the question "open or closed?" Framing it in this way meant that there were people from all sides of the political spectrum who wanted schools to stay open, just as there were people from all sides of the political spectrum who wanted them to stay closed, with no room to have a nuanced discussion between these two poles. Ontario's own scientific roundtable, established to provide science-based advice to the Ontario government, found that, "Closures have interacted with other COVID-related hardships to disproportionately affect students with lower socioeconomic backgrounds, racialized children and youth, newcomers, and students with disabilities."[53] In shutting the system down entirely, Doug Ford marginalized already marginalized students even further, throwing families into chaotic situations where they had to juggle online school and demanding, low-waged work. For the Ontario government, children were easy to marginalize. From closing playgrounds far long after other jurisdictions had re-opened them, to instituting stay-at-home orders that even forbade children from playing together outside, children were the lowest priority group for this government. When businesses were allowed to re-open in mid-June while schools were still closed, Doug Ford sent a clear message about which constituency he was most committed to.

The online classes, juggling child care and work, stress from workplace outbreaks, lack of information, contradictory messaging and sense that COVID-19 was lurking everywhere made living through the pandemic total hell for many families. Governments, not just Ontario, most often chose the economy over schools. Work stayed open and parents had to put themselves at risk at the job site and then manage the unknowns of community spread within cramped and too-small living quarters. Or, parents that could decide to make sacrifices to keep their kids home because taking an incalculable risk felt like an impossible choice. While Canadians were overloaded with some types of data about the pandemic, it was rarely useful data for parents and students to be able to help gauge how dangerous schools really were. Parents who had the resources to keep children home, often did: the sharpest job losses over the course of the pandemic were among women with school-aged children.[54]

Young people were given nothing during the pandemic: no financial supports, no extra activities that were safe to replace the activities they couldn't regularly do and very little attention from policy makers. Children were stopped from playing with others and forced into isolation at home, with no regard to their home circumstances. And for older teens, job market numbers for them plummeted by 2021. If the pandemic was a story of who mattered and who did not, youth were among the cohorts who mattered least. They were considered lucky to not be as impacted by COVID-19 as people who were older than them. As marginalized and disenfranchised members of society, the power that youth have tends to lay in the general desire to see young people not actively harmed. Politicians knew they would not likely have students dying from COVID-19, so students became the perfect political issue when they wanted to use them, or if it was easier, simply ignore them.

Schools were both an important location to stop the spread of COVID-19 and also a tremendous distraction that politicians used as a political punching bag and journalists covered as if it were a tennis match. The endless parade of doctors and experts, anxious parents, cocksure politicians and frustrated union representatives took the place of thoughtful coverage that could have situated schools inside of communities where community spread had the biggest impact on whether or not students would get sick. A search at CBC News' website on July 8, 2021, of schools + COVID netted 1037 results; the same search with terms hospitals + COVID only brought up 781 results. Were schools that much more important or fundamental than hospitals? From March 2020 until June 2021, at least 1500 patients died from COVID-19 they had acquired from a hospital outbreak while not one student death was attributed to a school outbreak. But the fear for students' safety propagated by unclear communications and policies kept journalists coming back. The over-attention on schools didn't make them safer, and politicians still mostly dodged complaints.

In some ways, schools were a distraction from more pressing issues, especially workplaces. For migrant workers, who had more precarious status, getting their issues covered was far more difficult than getting a journalist to write about how safe riding a school bus might be.

October 2020
MIGRANT WORKERS AND COVID-19

Cases: 158,765
Deaths: 9,297[1]

With most media focused on the second wave, October 2020 passed with little regard to how migrant workers were managing during the pandemic, despite the attention that seasonal migrant workers received in the summer. By October 2020, many seasonal workers were finishing up the growing season, getting ready to go home after a very difficult and very strange year. COVID-19 exacerbated already unsafe working conditions for racialized and low-income workers. The more precarious a job was, the more susceptible workers were to becoming sick with COVID-19. While the illness disproportionately impacted racialized workers in general, migrant workers were at even more risk, as they also had to deal with uncertain or precarious status in Canada in addition to low-paid or precarious work. Journalists told migrant workers' stories through narratives that transcended a single article or investigation, allowing more complete reporting of trends of exploitation or obfuscation related to migrant workers. Journalists were able to talk to whistleblowers, air video footage of horrifying living conditions, and cover the widespread rates of illness, even death, of workers on the job. But the coverage was plagued by the same racism that plagues temporary foreign workers. Despite the increase in attention, there was frustratingly little done to address the concerns.

Migrant workers work in Canada in all industries, year-round. Workers who got the most media attention were seasonal agriculture workers who came to Canada through the Seasonal Agricultural Worker Program (SAWP), but all migrant workers were at elevated risk from COVID-19 due to precarious working and living conditions. Migrant workers working in warehouses, in people's homes and in other industries faced incredible precarity and danger, especially those workers who had no status in Canada at all. Even though they were most at risk, journalists crafted a narrative around migrant workers that usually focused squarely on agricultural workers, and their farm-owning bosses. At the same time, they erased or ignored other kinds of migrant workers from mainstream coverage.

ROGELIO

Rogelio Muñoz Santos came to Canada from Chiapas, Mexico, in February 2020. He entered the country through a tourist visa and, once here, the 24-year-old saw a social media post written in Spanish advertising jobs that paid $13 per hour according to CBC and $16 per hour according to TVO, for a 70-hour workweek. Regardless of the total, the job worked out to less than minimum wage, as his recruiter would require him to pay at least $400 per month according to TVO,[2] or $600 per month according to CBC, to live in a two-bed motel room with four other men.[3] Mary Baxter, reporting for TVO, talked with Luis Mata from the FCG Refugee Centre, who said that it was likely that Muñoz Santos, like 40 other workers his group had identified, had been trafficked into his job.[4]

By April 2020, Muñoz Santos was working in Southwestern Ontario just as the news broke that seasonal migrant workers would be allowed to work in Canada. Muñoz Santos worked for Greenhill Produce, a hydroponic farm located in Thamesville, Ontario, near Chatham, that grows different varieties of sweet peppers. The workers told CBC that they had no relationship with the farm itself, only the recruiter who had hired them. While many news stories had quoted farm owners who insisted there would be adequate COVID-19 safety measures, the workers at Greenhill Produce were not given personal protective equipment or the necessary space to socially distance.[5]

By the end of April, a COVID-19 outbreak at a bunkhouse for employees who worked at Greenhill led to 45 COVID-19–positive cases. Despite rumours within the community, local public health officials told Chatham-Kent residents the virus was not being brought from other countries to Chatham-Kent by temporary workers but likely started locally and was spreading: "The living conditions just meant it spread quickly" said David Colby, the region's medical officer of health.[6] But it wasn't only in the bunkhouses. A worker who *Radio-Canada* identified as Juan said that even though workers were sick, they were still transported to work. When he and Muñoz Santos had COVID-19 and were sick enough to be sent to isolate in a motel, Juan said they were "abandoned," and no one brought them food or supplies while they suffered through the illness.[7]

The working and living conditions at Greenhill weren't exactly a secret. Two workers wrote public letters condemning them. One, reported by *Chatham Voice* on May 4, said that a worker was calling for support from a Jamaican government official to help improve the conditions, for example, forcing management to create more separation between staff. The worker reported management saying they simply didn't have the space to do this. But Justin Geertsma, general manager of the farm, told the *Chatham Voice*,

> "We talk to our employees regularly to let them know we are here to support them and to let them know we are taking all health guidelines seriously … (Public Health) are directing all our protocols and isolation activities on farm including mandatory active screening, physical distancing, accommodation specifics, requiring all employees to wear masks and gloves at all times, instituting strict sanitation processes to be executed twice a day, and erecting physical barriers where needed."[8]

By then, Muñoz Santos's health was deteriorating. He was transferred to a local hospital at the end of May and died on June 5. He was the second of three seasonal agricultural workers to die in 2020. The first was Bonifacio Eugenio Romero, a 31-year-old Mexican worker who died on May 31, also in Windsor-Essex, and the third was Juan López Chaparro, a worker at Scotlynn Growers in Norfolk County. The 55-year-old was also Mexican.

The pandemic exploited the cracks that already existed in Canada's economy, and nowhere was that clearer than among temporary foreign workers: agricultural workers, temp agency workers, care workers and others, all whose status was precarious. Their safety was held in the hands of their employers and they depended on government policies being enforced to keep them safe. These workers received a lot of media attention, thanks largely to the tireless efforts of migrant workers support agencies across Canada, but politicians and farm owners refused to make the kind of fundamental changes that workers and advocates had been calling for years — changes that would have protected so many from illness and death, wage theft, abuse and stress.

SEASONAL MIGRANT WORKERS ARRIVE

It was mid-March 2020, at the same time that lockdowns were starting to sweep the country, that migrant workers and their issues first appeared in mainstream media. At first the coverage was basic, asking the obvious question: what happens to the 50,000 seasonal migrant workers if Canada's border is closed to international travellers?[9] It was driven by employer organizations, though migrant worker rights groups intervened in the narrative soon after. Migrant workers who enter and exit Canada over the course of a season to do their work, unlike migrant workers who work in Canada for the duration of their work visa, found themselves instantly grounded abroad.

CBC reported the border would be closed on March 16, 2020, stating that exceptions would be made for "air crew, diplomats, immediate family members of citizens" and U.S. citizens (they would be banned soon after). The article mentions, as an afterthought, that essential workers would be exempt, some even exempted from self-isolation. Reporter Kathleen Harris referred to the measures as being "beefed up," but then explains that the beefing was mostly to facilitate handing out informational flyers.[10] The day after the border was closed, farm owners called on Ottawa to commit to allowing seasonal migrant workers to enter Canada. The timing of the announcement coincided with early spring, where many growers were about to plant crops for the following season. In another article from CBC *News*, the perspective of migrant workers was nestled below the reaction from the farming industry lobby organizations, who insisted that their members' lives would be ruined by uncertainty and quarantine measures.

Seasonal migrant workers had a lot on the line too, though this perspective came only after advocates intervened in the owner-driven narrative noted in mainstream media. Chris Ramsaroop of Justice for Migrant Workers said workers want to come to Canada as many of them rely solely on the income from this work.[11] Ramsaroop argued that the federal government needed to ensure workers had safe working and living conditions when they arrived, something not mentioned by the farm-owner lobby groups. And crucially, he demanded a commitment from government that no worker would be reprimanded for having a COVID-19 infection: "Ramsaroop called on both levels of government to ensure that if any workers are brought to Canada to work, they have access to healthcare should they fall ill, and Employment Insurance if their jobs end suddenly."[12] Just three days later on March 20, the government announced exemptions to the border closure, "to protect Canadians and support the economy," but none of the changes promised to give workers access to healthcare or supports.[13] Among the first people to enter Canada under the new restrictions were workers who worked at a farm in Kelowna, B.C., 63 of whom were infected by COVID-19 by April 1, 2020.[14]

Once it was clear that seasonal migrant workers could come to Canada, the political jockeying began. Farmers wanted assurances that if seed was planted in the spring, they could harvest what they planted. But the pandemic made knowing the future even more impossible than usual, and the assurances demanded by many were unreasonable. At the end of March, just after it was announced that migrant workers would be allowed in Canada, CTV News quoted one farmer who said, "Currently, migrant workers are deemed as an essential service. However, farmers are still confused as to what essential means, and whether that can make them exempt from an isolation period."[15] The confusion wasn't completely unfair: two weeks earlier, Ontario's Agriculture Minister Ernie Hardeman had said in an email that workers who enter Canada would have to self-isolate for 14 days, and Hardeman said that Bill Blair, federal minister of public safety had confirmed this.[16]

Throughout the summer, thanks to the efforts of migrant workers advocacy organizations across Canada, journalists reported on various injustices: cramped and inadequate living arrangements, abusive practices from bosses and the three seasonal migrant workers who died. Most reporting was regional, especially in southwestern Ontario where agriculture-sector outbreaks often represented the majority of infections within local health units. The group Migrant Worker Alliance for Change (MWAC) reported that a hotline they coordinate, where workers can call and ask questions about their rights, had been "transformed into a lifeline as workers across the country call in secrecy to report poor conditions on farms."[17] By August, the Globe and Mail estimated that at least 1300 migrant workers had been sick with COVID-19.[18]

Owners regularly expressed concern for migrant workers who worked on their farms, but in the same breath would defend inadequate regulations or enforcement measures intended to keep those workers safe. They danced a line demanding more aid from governments to help them pay for worker protections and improvements and simultaneously challenging public health orders that might get in the way of their annual profits. While many articles led with the position of the farm owners, the voices of migrant workers challenging these narratives, even taking owners to court and winning, were a rare example of worker power during the pandemic, from a group of workers that Canada had tried to render powerless during extremely difficult economic situations. Inadequate federal and provincial government measures did the bare minimum to keep seasonal temporary foreign workers safe while resisting calls that demanded these workers be given access to basic rights, like healthcare, EI or a path to citizenship.

UNENFORCED PROTECTIONS

The way in which seasonal migrant workers were treated during the pandemic was predictable thanks to an unjust system that gives employers far too much power to control the lives of the people who work for them. Migrant workers' rights organizations in Canada have long called for better worker protections, improved health and safety and changes to social programs that would ensure seasonal migrant workers could access help while they were in Canada. When the pandemic hit, many of the demands that these organizations had been calling for over the years took on even more urgency. And because their advocacy had been long established, they were able to act quickly and make very clear demands.

But government had low expectations of farm owners to keep their workers safe. On March 27, 2020, the government issued guidelines for protecting seasonal temporary foreign workers from COVID-19. The guidelines mandated that employers consider all workers who entered Canada be placed in isolation as part of the employee's regular employment. This meant employees would have been paid and all other regular employer responsibilities had to be met. But if a worker was deemed essential by a chief public health officer, they could be required to work rather than quarantine. Employers were also responsible for employees' health, and they were expected to be in touch with employees daily. If a worker became ill, the employer had to isolate the worker and contact public health and local consular officials. Employers were expected to give workers hygiene products, shelter workers who had to self-isolate and maintain distancing within dwellings where workers lived together. Facilities should have been cleaned regularly.[19] None of these requirements happened consistently, at every farm. As told by Juan, the friend of Rogelio Muñoz Santos, even when workers were sick and in isolation, they didn't receive the kind of support that government had said they should expect.

Even though the guidelines seemed robust, without enforcement they were meaningless. This concerned Syed Hussan, executive director of MWAC.[20] On April 1, 2020, when it was announced that 75 agricultural workers in Kelowna, B.C., had contracted COVID-19, including 63 seasonal migrant workers, the MWAC issued an open call demanding eight improvements to seasonal temporary foreign workers' working and living conditions to keep them safe from COVID-19. The recommendations included that migrant workers be given free and easy access to healthcare and that government develop an enforcement plan.[21] Byron Cruz, from the B.C.-based group Sanctuary Health, told CTV News the same thing: "We want the government to make enforceable rules, not guidelines."[22]

But it was guidelines that they got and indeed, the government didn't ensure that enforcement would catch farm owners who skirted the rules. One Globe and Mail investigation by Tavia Grant and Kathryn Blaze Baum revealed "overcrowded accommodations, broken toilets and cockroach and bed-bug infestations. As well, sheets and cardboard were used as dividers between bunk beds. Workers also recounted not being fully paid for their initial quarantine."[23] There were videos leaked from different farms showing cramped and unsanitary living conditions. Even so, of the 32 complaints that Employment and Social Development Canada received in the period of March until July 2020, not one farm was found in violation of the government's directives. Farms were permitted to hand in three-year-old housing inspection reports, and agents stopped doing inspections entirely for the first six weeks of the pandemic. When they resumed, they were only done remotely.[24] After being criticized by advocates for the quality of inspections, the federal government announced that it would give $7.4 million to "support temporary foreign workers," most of which went to organizations who support migrant workers; $16.2 million to enhance inspections; and $35 million for improvements to housing, sanitary and safety measures which went directly to farmers to subsidize their costs in a 50-50 cost-sharing scheme. This was in addition to the $1500 per worker payment that employers received, announced in March.[25] By the end of the summer, only half of the farms that hired migrant workers had been inspected, news that was reported thanks to documents circulated in the Senate.[26]

The difficult conditions that Canadian seasonal migrant workers faced were similar to those migrant workers experienced around the world. In the United States, during the 2020 season, the Occupational Safety and Health Administration (OSHA) conducted 44% fewer inspections than they did in 2019. They also dismissed a complaint made by Maribel Hernandez and Reyna Alvarez, workers who were fired when they left their facility to seek medical assistance when their COVID-19 symptoms became unbearable. OSHA dismissed their complaint and they lost their jobs, housing and immigration status. They argued, "OSHA must stop paving the way for employers to mistreat," in a column for *USA Today* which was translated into English by Evy Peña, a worker with the migrant worker advocacy group Centro de los Derechos del Migrante.[27] Just as in Canada, the advocacy of migrant worker support groups was critical to raise injustices into the public eye.

Once the harvest season wound down and the second wave picked up in fall 2020, the calls for reforms to the program were louder than ever before, especially since there were still outbreaks happening on some farms. Outbreaks plagued southwestern Ontario farms well into 2021. In November 2020, at least 40 workers at the Martin's Family Fruit Farm in Vienna, Ontario, caught COVID-19 thanks to common sleeping quarters that did not respect public health orders. The workers were all from Jamaica and Trinidad.[28] Kevin Martin, president of the Martin's Family Fruit Farm told *Postmedia* "We're taking care of everyone," a comment nestled in an article about how a lack of employer care led to such a large outbreak.[29] About 100 workers at Schuyler Farms in Haldimand-Norfolk county were trapped in Canada due to fall outbreaks, then by travel restrictions in home countries.[30] By mid-November, Haldimand-Norfolk registered 6100 COVID-19 cases, and the vast majority of them were connected to farm-related outbreaks.[31] In mid-January, a flight carried 18 Trinidadian workers home, leaving the rest of the workers to stay. They were too worried that they might miss the next season of work if they decided to go home.[32]

In November 2020, MWAC reignited their call for immigration reform. Quoting Syed Hussan from MWAC, CTV *News* reported, "Without permanent immigration status Hussan says migrant workers face the threat of termination, homelessness or deportation if they challenge their employer." MWAC repeated their call for all temporary foreign workers to be immediately granted permanent resident status.[33] But the government chose temporary measures rather than permanent ones: the Ontario government extended health coverage and offered some financial help to stranded workers, and the federal government enacted a temporary order that would allow stranded workers to apply for temporary status to access Employment Insurance (EI). This program was set to end on February 21, 2021. Had they been Canadian workers, they'd be able to apply for EI in the off-season and then re-start their work when the next growing season started.[34]

The call from migrant workers advocates to ensure that government measures would be enforceable was never met by politicians. While money was offered, mostly to farm owners, to pay for the costs of social distancing, the lack of enforcement resources ensured that outbreaks among farm workers would continue. Even by the fall, farmers had had months of experience with the virus — a time during which they could have put measures in place that would have protected their employees — and workers still got sick and outbreaks still happened. Outbreaks were often framed as being simply unavoidable. Except they weren't: key to why outbreaks kept happening was the power imbalance that existed between employees and employers, which is the foundation of Canada's temporary foreign worker program. As Fay Faraday explained,

> Low-wage migrant workers are restricted to working for a single employer, which creates the enormous power imbalance that facilitates workplace exploitation. Their ability to remain in Canada is dependent on maintaining their employer's favour. Resisting exploitative workplace demands typically results in termination and loss of housing."[35]

Journalists who reported on both sides of the issue tried to humanize both sides equally, often in the same article. One on side, a farmer might lose his crop for the year, and on the other, a worker just wanted to make enough money to live. Both had the common goal of survival. Except, the power imbalance meant there was no way to show each sides equally. The survival of a worker who comes to Canada to make subsistence wages is not the same as a farmer who is afraid of having a bad year. In trying to humanize both sides through the same narrative of survival, media often contradicted its own coverage.

FOCUS ON FARM OWNERS

Seasonal temporary foreign workers, if compared to other precarious and low-waged workers, received in-depth, consistent and generally sympathetic coverage from journalists. Thanks to the efforts of migrant worker advocacy organizations, journalists were connected with whistleblowers, which gave Canadians a look at the brutal conditions that exist for these workers. But journalists rarely held owners to account, a group of people who, more often than not, received just as much sympathy as the workers they had total power over. Journalists moved between writing about seasonal workers through the words of the workers themselves or their advocates and writing about them through the words of their bosses, who usually referred to them as critical to their farm operations, like a piece of farming equipment or a beloved horse.

The reason for why this frame was so dominant was basic: racism. The owners — white, so-called old-stock Canadians, farming land that was probably handed to them by eager colonists in the 1800s — were always painted as simply trying to get by, like everyone else, in perilous circumstances. The workers — non-white, without citizenship and with very little structural power in Canada — all had stories about leaving family behind each year to work on Canadian farms. Migratory work was almost always framed as an act of love. Temporary work in Canada has, from its origins, been premised on bringing racialized workers to work for low wages. The SAWP, created in 1966 after Ontario farmers lobbied for access to more workers, was intended to reduce immigration from the Caribbean. Faraday quoted a federal government memo from 1965 written by the assistant deputy minister of citizenship and immigration:

> by admitting West Indian workers on a seasonal basis, it might be possible to reduce greatly the pressure on Canada to accept unskilled workers from the West Indies as immigrants. Moreover, seasonal farm workers would not have the privilege of sponsoring innumerable close relatives.[36]

Faraday argues that despite how long ago this was written, the logic still underpins the system today. This racist logic also underpinned media coverage where some journalists painted the farm owners as virtuous, even when the details in the same story made it clear that they were not.

It was far more often the case that journalists quoted farm owners warning that COVID-19 health restrictions would threaten production than challenging them on their safety plans. But even then, it wasn't exactly true that Canada's actions would lead to lower production. Blaming lower production on local health measures made it sound as if there were no barriers for workers to come to Canada from their home countries. For example, buried in one CBC article by Janyce McGregor was a mention of a significant problem causing delays in the arrival of seasonal workers — not health and safety measures, but visa processing times in other countries also battling COVID outbreaks. Visa offices around the world, working under their own locked-down conditions, had slowed the arrival of thousands of workers, especially from Mexico, where online filing was slowing the speed at which people could expect to get visas.[37]

Media's lack of attention on the global forces of the pandemic erased the reality that when Canadian food systems rely on workers from other countries to process and harvest their food, a global disruption like a pandemic would, of course, threaten the ability of those workers to both leave their country and enter Canada. This should have convinced farmers and industry organizations to call for immediate changes to Canada's immigration system, especially if the real hold up was related to visa paperwork. But that would have meant farmers giving these workers more power: more legal standing in Canada, more protections under the law and, therefore, less ability to exploit their labour. Luckily for the farmers, journalists didn't dig into this, instead focusing on a perceived threat to the food chain thanks to migrant workers who weren't coming to work fast enough. The need to control these workers is a core piece of why seasonal temporary workers were in such perilous conditions to begin with, why so many of them did get sick with COVID-19, and why farmers and their lobby groups worked so hard to ensure Canadians didn't see the injustices that have long characterized Canada's seasonal agricultural industry. Through this control, farm owners are able to maximize their profits, while workers suffer and even die to harvest their apples, asparagus and cherries.

In March 2020, when the federal government announced that the border closure would include seasonal workers, CBC *News London* introduced a story on the border closure with a quote from Ken Wall, the CEO of Sandy Shore Farms. He threatened there would be food shortages in Canada if these workers could not come. And rather than calling for health and safety protections that would allow workers to enter Canada safely, the article focused on seasonal workers as a necessary component in grower operations. The Ontario Fruit and Vegetable Growers Association tweeted, "We recognize the news yesterday came as a shock and if not solved has serious implications for individual growers and the sector as a whole. We are working vehemently with our partners to ensure growers will have the labour resources they require."[38] Bernie Solymar, executive director of the Asparagus Growers of Ontario was quoted as saying, "We can't get Canadians to take these jobs and do the type of stoop labour that is required to harvest fruit and vegetables in our farms."[39] Stoop labour requires the worker to be bent over for much of their day. Migrant workers were just too integral to farm operations to not be allowed into Canada but not important enough for farm owners to commit to fair treatment or proactively prepare for conditions that would keep them all safe during the pandemic. On July 13, 2020, more than 200 organizations signed an open letter that called on governments to offer healthcare to all migrant workers. Oftentimes, healthcare for migrant workers is dependent on one's job status, meaning that anything that might put a worker at risk with their employment might also put their health coverage at risk. In an article for the *Canadian Medical Association Journal*, Sabrina Doyle wrote,

> Migrant rights groups say overcrowded accommodations, a lack of protective gear, and pressure from employers to work while sick have contributed to the spread of the virus. Some farmers have also resisted efforts to increase testing for COVID-19 among migrant workers, out of concern that those who test positive will be unable to work.[40]

The farmers' resistance to improving local safety — from Brett Schuyler's attempts to overturn public health decisions about lodgings to industry organizations reducing migrant workers to another piece in their production line — obscured for Canadians the real danger that many seasonal temporary workers found themselves in. Canadians needed journalists to challenge these narratives and examine their claims, rather than writing about the farmers' interests and complaints as if they made equally compelling arguments as the workers' desire to work and live in safety.

The global challenge to move human capital during a pandemic was hidden within Canadian coverage about migrant workers. Rarely, did we hear about how COVID-19 was propagating in workers' countries of origin, or how their governments and public health units were reacting to their own local crises. Instead, Canadians mostly got stories told through the lens of the farmers, which often downplayed the fact that migrant workers have no power within the employer-employee relationship and instead played up the folksiness of the farmers and how tough life in 2020 was for them. Peter and Tracy Gubbels, farmers in Mt. Brydges, Ontario, were featured in the *London Free Press* about how they risked it all through the pandemic to grow their watermelons and squash. They hire 50 workers each year, 14 of whom are seasonal migrant workers from Mexico. The article called them "offshore workers," and quoted Tracy saying that they were lucky to be able to replace them with high school students: "When they shut the high schools down, that was our saving grace."[41] The farm ended up beating their anticipated production, a point that was buried near the end of the article. The Gubbelses said that the accommodations they had to make to ensure worker safety, "was quite an ordeal."[42] The workers, both the seasonal workers and the student workers, created the Gubbels' wealth, and yet were only mentioned in the story in relation to how hard it was for the Gubbelses.[43]

In another feature on migrant workers' working conditions, *Global News* introduced Lisa Bibb, the owner of an apple farm in Ontario's Durham Region. The farm usually operates thanks to the labour of four to six workers, who did not come to Canada to work in 2020. The introduction constantly talked about the workers as "hers" and even said that the Bibbs "made the decision to leave the workers — her apple specialists — at home in Mexico this year" as if these people have absolutely no agency outside of their relationship with their employer.[44] Through tears, she explained that while "her" workers are safer staying home, they will forgo income they need to survive. The article then mentioned that the workers would have been able to live in their regular cabin, as their beds were spread out. The article didn't mention by how much, or whether or not airborne transmission in the communal bunk area could still travel from one worker to another, which, by the time the feature was written, was pretty clearly the case.[45]

The folksy stories of farmers doing their best to weather the pandemic never engaged with the central questions: why do these workers get paid so little? Why are bunkhouse living conditions considered adequate at the best of times? Why do they have so few protections once they're in Canada? Instead, farmers and their lobby organizations did their best to insist that governments impose as few restrictions as they could so as to not hurt their bottom line. The farm that got the most coverage in its work to do away with some public health measures was Schuyler Farms. The *Hamilton Spectator*, in an article called, "Dispute between Norfolk farmers and public health unit threatens food security," uncritically reported Brett Schuyler's attempt to fight public health regulations that, he argued, threatened food security. The article featured a smiling Brett sitting at the end of a row of austere bunk beds in an arrangement probably no one would say they would be happy to sleep in during a pandemic. It appeared that shower curtains separated each of the bunks. Journalist J.P. Antonacci referred to seasonal temporary workers as "off-shore" workers five times, and quoted Schuyler's lawyer and other local farmers who argued that Shanker Nesathurai, Haldimand-Norfolk's chief public health officer, was making bad public health decisions because Nesathurai just didn't understand farming culture. Nesathurai told Antonacci it wasn't fair to cram so many people together in such a small space, especially since they aren't members of the same family. Vegetable grower Jason Ryder told Antonacci, "My guys are very comfortable with each other. They're a family up here. If (Nesathurai) would've asked for advice, it's simple to lay that out."[46] Antonacci's decision to quote Ryder speaking on behalf of "his guys" to discredit the local public health officer whose job was to ensure that COVID-19 protocols were being enforced had two impacts. First, it erased the agency and opinions of the workers themselves; second, it assumed that Ryder, his employees and Nesathurai all have the same interests. Whereas Ryder's interest is in ensuring his farm makes a profit, Nesathurai's interest is in slowing the spread of COVID-19. The workers probably only wanted to work and live in safety and security, though without their voices, the reader is left to guess what the workers might say.

Antonacci visited Schuyler Farms quite a few times to report — first at the start of April, then in May to cover Brett Schuyler's health and safety measures and then again in July to report on how wonderful life is for the workers at Schuyler's farm. In an article titled, "'Every day here is a little better than a good day home': Migrant farm workers lobby to work in Canada during COVID-19," Antonacci introduced Ephron Maurice and Reuben Sampson, Trinidadian workers who said they enjoyed the work and salary that come with working for Schuyler.[47] But the article ends with Sampson talking about how his young children cry when he calls them, missing him. Antonacci doesn't ask what either man thinks about their rights as workers, or whether or not they hoped to have permanent residence. Both arrived in July 2020 and were supposed to return home in November.[48] But in early November, three workers from Schuyler Farms were diagnosed with COVID-19. Everyone on the farm was tested for COVID-19 — that's 200 tests — and 20 workers who had been sharing a living space were moved to a hotel where they had to isolate by themselves. Brett Schuyler told CBC News some of the sick workers were supposed to fly home, plans that were thwarted by the illness. The issue mostly fell out of the news as

2020 marched into 2021, and a new wave of travel restrictions triggered a new wave of migrant-workers-trying-to-come-to-Canada stories.

Schuyler's attitude toward migrant workers demonstrated how farm owners intervened in public debates about keeping migrant farm workers safe: the farmers depended on their workers, yet when it came to protecting them from COVID-19 or advocating for their rights to a more stable status in Canada, the farmers instead challenged public health and made general threats about Canada's food supply, to be reported uncritically by a handful of journalists. The focus from farmers and their lobby organizations was squarely on whether or not they would be able to harvest, and the health and citizenship of migrant workers rarely figured into the equation beyond "who will pick my crop?" While the rarer, in-depth reporting features tended to centre workers' voices, shorter, more regular articles tended to rely heavily on the farm owners' voices.

STIGMA, CONTROL AND VIOLENCE

The combination of racism and control that underpins the SAWP is a potent mix for employers to wield over their employees. Farmers like the temporary work program so much because they have an incredible amount of control over their workers. The skill level, and surely the low pay, too, made finding local employees impossible. This became somewhat of an obsession among journalists who wondered why everyone out of work and receiving CERB couldn't simply sign up for a summer of farm work. Two months after Bernie Solymar from the Asparagus Growers of Ontario was quoted warning the asparagus season was under threat, on May 17, 2020, he told CBC News that hiring local workers would be impossible, especially since locals were now the ones more likely to have COVID-19 and bring it to work: "A farmer that's isolated his crew from Mexico or Jamaica has some sense of comfort that those guys are clean, that they're not infected,' he said. With locals, 'you have no idea where they've been, who they've been with, what they've been exposed to.'"[49] Under the guise of keeping COVID-19 out of the farm crew, Solymar argued that he needed total control over his workers to make sure "those guys are clean," rather than developing effective protocols at the farm to limit the inevitable spread of COVID-19. One asparagus grower posted jobs for $25/hour to hire local employees, a move that frustrated activists with MWAC as it was almost double the wage that seasonal workers were paid, and many of them had been stuck in quarantine, often sick and unsure how they would be able to pay for their living needs.[50]

Under the guise of safety, farm owners exerted even more control than ever over seasonal workers. With the spotlight on seasonal migrant workers because of COVID-19, some journalists dug deeper into the injustices that many faced, injustices that were there before the pandemic, simply exacerbated. The *Globe and Mail* found that many farm owners were restricting workers' movements off the worksite: "In an attempt to contain the spread of COVID-19 at agrifood operations, some employers are asking workers to sign agreements or conform to rules confining them to the property."[51] Chelsea Nash reported that migrant worker advocates were trying to find ways to get workers food, as confinement meant that they couldn't go and buy their own food. She interviewed Deon Castello, who dropped fresh produce to workers at two different Brantford farms in a covert location so that farm owners didn't notice. Many farm owners insisted on grocery shopping for the workers, giving them stale food in insufficient quantities.[52] Several workers quoted by the *Globe and Mail* believed they were being overcharged for the food being purchased on their behalf. No province ordered that workers should be confined to their farms, and there was also very little evidence that shopping at a grocery store is a high-risk behaviour that could result in a COVID-19 infection.[53]

The intense control exerted over migrant workers during the 2020 growing season didn't stem the tide of infections; it was more an exercise in power than measures intended to keep people safe. In June, just as infections were spiralling out of control in southwestern Ontario, Justice for Migrant Workers (J4MW) issued a call for the entire industry to be shut down so that a thorough cleaning could happen. They reiterated the long-standing demand for access to health benefits and labour standards, and permanent residence status for all workers. They had also received reports of asymptomatic COVID-19–positive workers being asked to go back to work. Farmers were likely listening closely to the rhetoric coming from Ontario Minister of Health Christine Elliott, who didn't see a problem with asymptomatic, COVID-19–positive workers staying on the job. Elliott told reporters, "We only want the people who are well, who are feeling well — they're positive but they are truly asymptomatic — to be going back to work." Chris Ramsaroop from J4MW reacted to these comments: "This is racism … This fiasco has to end."[54] COVID-19 spread thanks to health direction that came right from the top, to the pleasure of farm owners who needed workers who were not sick in bed to work.

Both Ramsaroop and Elliott's comments were made immediately following the death of migrant agricultural worker Juan López Chaparro on June 29, 2020. With infection rates rising, funds meant to help keep workers safe — and fully in the control of farm owners and increasingly strict protocols on workers' movements — it certainly seemed like a racist fiasco. Migrant rights activist Fay Faraday characterized the relationship that made this racism possible as an extreme power imbalance. She said that many seasonal workers, "don't complain when they are injured, and don't speak out when their housemates get sick."[55] And indeed, that is almost what happened to Luis Gabriel Flores Flores, a 36-year-old seasonal worker who worked at Scotlynn Sweetpac Growers. After the death of his housemate Juan López Chaparro, Flores spoke out about the negligent conditions in which Scotlynn workers were living.[56] Flores wanted to make sure it didn't happen again and their living conditions were improved. When farm owner Robert Biddle Jr. saw that Flores had spoken out, he threatened to deport Flores immediately, and Flores was fired. Flores wrote a letter to federal Immigration Minister Marco Mendicino, imploring him to intervene both in his case and to improve the working and living conditions of seasonal temporary workers.[57] Flores brought a complaint to the Ontario Labour Board (OLB), and it ruled in his favour. Scotlynn was ordered to pay $25,000 to Flores, a combination of money for lost wages and the distress the situation caused.[58] Flores had originally been seeking $40,401.35. The OLB found that:

> The power imbalance between the employer and Mr. Flores, as a migrant worker who does not speak English and relies on the employer for wages, shelter and transportation, should have been more carefully managed since a reprisal can strike a far deeper wound than might otherwise occur in the traditional employment relationship.[59]

With this power imbalance, justified by racism and discrimination based on status, at the heart of the seasonal temporary worker program, any policies that would have helped keep seasonal migrant workers safe would have had to address this. Whistleblowing is critical to ensuring employers can be held to account, and it's a basic protection when workers have few other options. Flores' horrific experience, from watching a coworker die to being fired and threatened with deportation, legally should not have happened. Scotlynn's owner Biddle obviously thought there would be no repercussions for firing Flores, or if there were, they would be minimal. Had it not been for the support and solidarity of migrant worker organizations, there may not have been any. But then Flores found himself in a difficult position, being well known as having stood up for his rights. This posed a liability for when he looked for his next job.

In late September, 2020, CTV's *W5* interviewed Erika Zavala and Jesus Molina, two workers who were fired from Bylands Nurseries in West Kelowna because they accepted a donation of food and clothes from a local migrant worker justice organization.[60] The company dismissed the pair after "multiple infractions, following orientation on the workplace policies and warnings about leaving the premises," as reported by the *Globe and Mail*.[61] The control their bosses tried to exert kept workers from being able to access food and clothing donations, all in the name of safety and security from COVID-19.

Seasonal agricultural workers received a lot of attention thanks to many factors: a cyclical news story that could be told at particular flashpoints over the course of the year; industry lobby organizations who were banging their drum to convince politicians to allow seasonal migrant workers into Canada so they could avoid financial losses; the tireless work of advocates shining light on the industry and helping workers navigate ruthless bosses, and the need for political changes to workers' status for quarantining, remaining in Canada past a growing season to be able to not miss the start of the next season and other federal regulations. But this attention meant that other migrant workers in Canada received far less attention from journalists and politicians, even though their struggle was just as important.

NON-SEASONAL MIGRANT WORKERS

The struggles and marginalization of seasonal migrant workers got a lot of attention during the pandemic, so much so that seasonal migrant workers were often seen as the quintessential migrant worker by journalists. As I explore in the chapter covering May 2020, it was non-agricultural temporary foreign workers, through a local solidarity group, who blew the whistle on the conditions that led to the plant outbreak at Maple Leaf Foods in Brandon, Manitoba, in August 2020. Workers with precarious status, including refugees, worked in essential services helping to care for people, or operating businesses deemed essential. And international students, shut out of most government aid, found themselves stuck between their home country and Canada, doing their education online regardless of the time zone in which they were located.

Filipino migrant workers were particularly impacted by the pandemic, dealing with racist bosses, unsafe working conditions and overrepresentation within temporary workplaces. John Paul Catungal from the University of British Columbia's Social Justice Institute told the *Tyee*,

> It's the health-care workers, but also those who clean facilities, especially health facilities ... It's the folks who provide us food, prepare our food, cash us out at grocery stores. It happens that Filipinos are overrepresented in these lines of work, and it happens that these are historically undervalued and underpaid lines of work. And when we've had conversations about whether to raise minimum wage, there were people who discredit these workers, saying they don't deserve it.[62]

A majority of the staff at the Lynn Valley Care Centre in North Vancouver, the site of Canada's first long-term care home outbreak, were Filipino. While not all Filipino workers in the service and food processing industries are temporary foreign workers, the impact of the program to drive instability and precarity among all Filipino workers was intensified by the pandemic: more than 42% of Filipinos who replied to a Statistics Canada survey about the impact of the pandemic said that they had been out of work — making Filipinos the ethnic group with the highest pandemic-related job losses in Canada. Of the data that is available, at least ten Filipinos died from workplace-acquired COVID-19 infection. RJ Aquino from Vancouver's Tulayan Filipino Diaspora Society told CBC, "Filipinos are particularly vulnerable to the economic impact of COVID-19 because they're 'overrepresented' in many essential industries that drastically cut temporary workers' hours, such as hospitality, retail, restaurant and food processing."[63] In meatpacking especially, conditions for migrant workers were very dangerous, as outbreaks swept the industry across Canada. Grassroots support organizations became a lifeline for temporary foreign workers at the Alberta JBS and Cargill plants when hundreds of workers caught COVID-19, especially as members of the community faced racist backlash because of the high infection rates within the plants. Community support groups like

ActionDignity offered medical advice, protective gear and groceries.[64] They even helped with funeral preparations for the family of Hiep Bui, a Canadian worker who had worked at Cargill for 20 years after having immigrated from Vietnam. She was the first worker to die from COVID-19 in Alberta's spring meatpacking cluster of infections.

Media often forgot migrant workers working outside of the seasonal migrant worker program, and politicians rarely made promises to them — the ones who worked through temporary agencies, on factory floors, in warehouses or food processing, whose precarious status was often obscured by the fact that they worked alongside workers with more, though still very little, job security. Journalist Christopher Curtis interviewed one migrant worker, called Maxime to protect his identity, who worked in a Dollarama warehouse in Montréal. He told Curtis that he raised concerns to his supervisor about a lack of physical distancing at his workplace. Despite having worked there for three years, he was fired. Dollarama denied that this happened, though Québec's workplace health and safety board, the CNESST, confirmed to the *Gazette* that they were investigating two complaints made from a Dollarama warehouse in Montréal.[65]

Maxime and other workers in the warehouse were hired through a temp agency — one of the pernicious ways in which migrant workers can find work in Canada — and this leaves them especially vulnerable. Mostafa Henaway, an organizer with the Immigrant Workers Centre in Montréal said, "They know that these are jobs filled by migrant labour, by vulnerable people who are too scared to refuse to work in dangerous conditions."[66] The associate medical officer for Peel Region emailed the Ministry of Labour in December 2020 Gayane Hovhannisyan, worried about how exposed temp agency workers were to COVID-19, asking for them to do something to protect these workers. "In almost all outbreaks, we encounter agency staff from a variety of staffing agencies … most of them don't have any paid sick benefits and may be either international students or new immigrants." The email was obtained by the *Toronto Star*'s Sara Mojtehedzadeh. The Ministry of Labour responded to say that Hovhannisyan's concerns were out of scope of the ministry.[67] Every failure to implement adequate health and safety protocols of every farm owner or any factory where the workers overwhelmingly had precarious employment status relied on this fear to convince people to stay quiet about their workplace health and safety.

Exploitation wasn't limited to large industrial worksites, either. A report released in fall 2020 by migrant care workers rights' groups detailed the extensive and brutal exploitation that migrant care workers experienced during the pandemic. They surveyed 201 migrant care workers living across Canada and found that nearly half experienced an increase to their work; more than 40% of respondents who reported that their work increased were not paid extra for working more hours; more than one-third reported that their employer controlled their movements, including being banned from using public transit; nearly 60% reported being worried about not being able to work enough to be able to apply for permanent residency. The pandemic threatened many temporary care workers' abilities to even stay in Canada, as it was harder to fulfill the necessary 24-month work requirement, especially for those who had lost work, as well as other government-mandated requirements like demonstrating English proficiency.[68]

Workers who have no legal status in Canada are at most risk of being exploited by bosses who know the incredible power imbalance that exists when the person working for you has no legal footing in Canada. Any mistake could lead to deportation. COVID-19 posed an incredible threat to these workers, which made it even harder for journalists to get them to talk about their experiences. A careless slipup or too many details that would expose a worker to a boss, and a story's source could lose everything and be deported. While most of the stories related to temporary foreign workers focused on the workers that had status to work in Canada, the few that explored life for undocumented workers truly showed the pain and violence caused by a program whose cracks many workers fall through. CBC News' Jonathon Gatehouse reported on the estimated 2000 agricultural workers in the Windsor-Essex region who were undocumented and met one man who lived in a ramshackle house with almost 20 other workers, most who also didn't have status. The father of 11 from Guatemala depended on Canadian farms hiring him so he could send money home to his family, Gatehouse wrote. He first came in 2019 and after his status lapsed, he found work moving from farm to farm. Undocumented workers are usually hired through recruiters and paid less than minimum wage. During the pandemic, because of their precarious status, many were too afraid to get tested for COVID-19, or they needed the money so badly that they worked through symptoms.[69]

Justine Taylor of Ontario Greenhouse Vegetable Growers told CBC *News* that undocumented farm workers are "very complicated" and blamed the need to hire workers with no status, who work for illegal wages, on a lack of available workers. The solution she offered was a farming registry to clamp down on unscrupulous recruiters; she did not cut to the root of the problem — the system exploits people who are already in a desperate situation.[70] While the gaps in the SAWP injured many people, the workers who were undocumented, either because their temporary work papers expired or because they found work in Canada while visiting on a visitor's visa, were in the most danger.

The most vulnerable temporary workers, whose status had lapsed and who were no longer working in Canada legally, experienced the most violence during the pandemic. From Rogelio Muñoz Santos, the migrant worker who entered into Canada through a visitor visa and found himself working on a farm in southwestern Ontario right up until his death from COVID-19, to Marcelin François, the Montrealer featured in the June 2020 chapter who was killed by COVID-19 he caught while working through a temporary agency at a long-term care facility, these were the people who bore the worst pain of the pandemic. They paid for dangerous working conditions with their lives. The thousands of others who got sick, lost wages, were threatened with deportation or being fired when they raised their voices, paid a personal toll placed on them by politicians whose actions sided with their employers. Politicians understand that racism is at the heart of the temporary foreign worker program and that if workers are given more rights, farm and factory owners will revolt. And so, they offer good words but with no action. Journalists were encouraged to tell these stories by workers and advocates exposing the abuses, but far too often they did not explore the power imbalance at the heart of why the program will never change, unless Canadians rise up and demand that it changes.

It was abhorrent the way Canada treated the most vulnerable people within its borders during the pandemic, whether they worked on the front lines of the healthcare response, in factory warehouses, food processing or agricultural work. At the best of times, Canadian regulations systemically disenfranchise temporary workers, forcing them into dangerous and difficult situations and handing near total control over to the people for who they work. During the pandemic, the systemic problems that this model creates revealed itself to be a disaster. The government's pandemic response was only as strong as its ability to protect and support the most vulnerable. If an undocumented worker got COVID-19 and spread it because they were too afraid to get tested or couldn't afford to take time off, that created a public health crisis for everyone else, too.

Just as hope was fading for the last group of seasonal migrant workers to be able to go home for a few months before the next season started, vaccines came onto the horizon. Vaccine breakthroughs were generating good news: scientists may have done the impossible and invented vaccines that could end the pandemic. The problem was that politicians were relying on vaccines to end the pandemic. For people working through SAWP, they would get access to vaccines, but their conditions would barely improve. Just the first half of 2021 would end up being even more deadly than 2020: ten migrant workers died on farms across Canada, five in quarantine before their work season started. The vaccine could not overcome the systemic dangers that had been built into the system from the beginning.

November 2020
THE RACE FOR THE VACCINE

Cases: 234,511
Deaths: 10,138[1]

In November 2020, the world finally had its first real hope that a vaccine was not only possible; it would soon be available. For the first time during the pandemic, there really was a light at the end of the tunnel — though, no one knew how long the tunnel still went. If the first eight months of the pandemic in Canada was full of hope for a vaccine, the next several were filled with debates about how fast people would be able to get it.

The way in which journalists framed vaccines from the start had a big impact on how they were discussed thereafter. Debates about whether vaccination would be mandatory helped feed some people's fears that vaccines were being developed too fast, despite more than a decade of research that predated the technological breakthrough of the mRNA vaccines. Journalists played a big role in vaccine enthusiasm but also in vaccine hesitancy by promoting and amplifying the voices and opinions of people who opposed vaccination, uncritically reporting their messages and giving them too much airtime. By June 2021, Canadians would be among the most vaccinated nationality in the world.

Once a vaccine had been approved, the first big question for most Canadians focused on how vaccines would be prioritized: when will it be my turn? Politicians used vaccine prioritization to try to win political support, and journalists passively wrote about it. All the while, internationally Canada acted selfishly, initially both hording more vaccines than any other country in the world and refusing to support waiving intellectual property related to the vaccines so that it could be shared with the world. By the time 10% of Canadians had been vaccinated, there were still dozens of countries who had yet to receive a single dose. And still, politicians demanded that Canadian doses be sent to us as soon as possible.

OSCAR

As the first wave was calming down in Québec, the Québec government announced it would fast-track education programs to train more people to become patient orderlies. Ten thousand Quebecers signed up. One of them was Oscar Anibal Rodriguez. The 58-year-old was an IT worker who traded his computer for scrubs and started working for Quebec City's public health agency on June 15, 2020. Months later, on January 2, 2021, his family in Argentina was worried that they hadn't heard from Oscar. They communicated with Diane Roy, the president of the housing cooperative where Oscar lived, to go to his door to see if he was okay. She knew that he had caught COVID-19 — he had told her on Christmas Eve — so when there was no answer at his door, she called emergency services. Oscar had died in his apartment, alone, from a virus he contracted at work. His colleagues told *Radio-Canada Québec* that his death was a shock. They were surprised and saddened to hear that they had lost their colleague.[2]

Oscar worked at the CHSLD St-Antoine, the first location to be vaccinated in all of Canada. The location was chosen because it had not been touched by an outbreak before, and with 627 residents and employees, it was a large residential care facility. But just as the Pfizer-BioNTech vaccine was making its way to Canada, residents of the CHSLD St-Antoine started to get sick. On December 11, two residents were moved from CHSLD St-Antoine to the temporary COVID-19 hospital set up at the Concorde Hotel, and a massive testing operation was started to see just how far COVID-19 had propagated.[3] The vaccination campaign started on December 14, by which time at least 15 residents had tested positive for COVID-19. The first person vaccinated in Canada, Gisèle Lévesque, caught COVID-19 two weeks after her first dose.[4]

Oscar was the first health worker to die in Quebec City. He had only lived in Quebec City for about four years, said Diane Roy. By the time the outbreak finally ended at the end of January, 263 residents and employees had been infected and 49 residents had died.[5] Even though the vaccination campaign had started mid-December, Oscar hadn't been vaccinated. As it took weeks for the first dose to be effective, it's possible that he still would have caught it after his first dose. Yet, as the first signs of relief from the pandemic showed in Quebec City, Oscar and 48 others lost their lives.[6] In the often-used metaphor, COVID-19 won the race between the virus and the vaccine and it was a warning signal to public health units everywhere: even when the vaccine is ready, it will not replace COVID-19 control measures.

CHSLD St-Antoine would be the largest outbreak of a residence that had been in the middle of a vaccination campaign, and it stood as a stark reminder that the vaccine was no silver bullet. There were no silver bullets.

A RETURN TO NORMAL?

Almost as quickly as journalists and politicians started talking about COVID-19, they were also talking about vaccines. Vaccines held within them not just the promise for individual and community protection from COVID-19 but also the promise of returning *back to normal*, a phrase that meant anything the speaker wanted it to mean. "Normal" would become the object of almost everyone's desire for most of the pandemic. Vaccines could allow us to travel again, visit together, embrace — finally. During the first seven months of the pandemic, the way in which politicians dangled vaccines in front of Canadians as a promise of a normal life — a time when there was still no vaccine — played an important role in pacifying an increasingly desperate population. Vaccination was promoted as the silver bullet that would end this pandemic, while politicians did not bring in more targeted public health measures. Politicians could hide behind the promise of a vaccine to do the bare minimum to stop the spread of COVID-19. Journalists didn't challenge this negligent rhetoric enough. Instead, a whole genre of journalism tried to answer the question: how long will this last? Had media energy been spent examining how best to live through a pandemic and which policies were necessary to make this happen, would politicians have felt enough pressure to close the economy to stop the spread of COVID-19 rather than relying on half measures that just ensured COVID-19 would continue to propagate and threaten the most vulnerable people?

Keeping Canadians in a mental headspace of being ready to jump right back to "normal" life was a key part of how politicians managed this pandemic, and vaccines played a very important role in feeding this frame. It started early, just as people were finding confinement especially boring but also as cases in the first wave accelerated. On April 1, Prime Minister Justin Trudeau hosted a press conference where journalists tried to pin an answer down from Justin Trudeau on the question "How long will this last?" as if he could know. *Global News* framed it as a "refusal" when he said COVID-19 measures could be in place for "weeks or even months," rather than saying precisely how long. *Global News* then ran an exceedingly optimistic article with the headline, "How long will coronavirus measures last in Canada? Experts say June or July," even though every expert interviewed couched their prediction by saying either how long *current* measures would be in place for or that their prediction was actually an aspirational hope.[7] This genre of journalism asking *how long* dominated for the first months of the pandemic. The press conference on April 1 triggered a wave of articles asking the same question as *Global News* did, coming up with similarly ridiculous analyses. Aaron Wherry from CBC's Parliamentary Bureau wrote about how Canadians needed to know about what was going to happen; throughout the article, he confused the difference between how government was responding based on what they did know and knowing what would happen in the future, could only be guessed. Wherry wrote, "Asked about the future on Wednesday, Trudeau declined to be precise."[8] A true surprise, surely.

While in retrospect it was ridiculous to imagine that COVID-19 restrictions would just vanish by summer or that the Prime Minister, a guy with no scientific or future-reading training, would be able to tell Canadians "the future." This frame primed Canadians to view the pandemic as a temporary problem from which we would eventually be saved by a solution — rather than a problem stemming from and exacerbating existing global and national inequities that political will could have addressed at any point before or during the pandemic. This dovetailed perfectly with conversations about vaccines, the only truly quick solution to a global pandemic. And even before any of the COVID-19 vaccines had completed human trials, Canadians were reminded constantly that our salvation was wrapped up in this medicine that didn't yet exist, that should normally take many years to develop but could surely be done in 18 months.

Canada's first vaccine commitment was made on March 23, 2020. Trudeau promised $192 million for "developing and producing vaccines." The money was spread across Canadian research groups. A month later, he promised a billion dollars more to COVID-19–related research.[9] It was a welcomed cash injection to the scientific research community, where resources are often tight. Trudeau told reporters on April 23, that, "A vaccine, obviously, arriving soon would be the best solution." In between those announcements, on April 8, Trudeau told reporters he would return to work, though modified, which prompted many questions about when Canadians could go back to normal. Trudeau said,

> We will then be in a mode until there is a vaccine, which could take many, many months if not more than a year to get to, [where]

we will be calibrating very carefully our behaviours as a country, as a society, as an economy, to managing the existence and persistence of COVID-19.

The quote appeared in one CTV article under a headline that attributed this comment to Trudeau: "'normal life' still a ways off."[10] Every time Trudeau reminded Canadians that a vaccine would be the best solution, it sent a signal that only the vaccine will save us and erased the potentially transformative structural changes that could have been made to stop the spread. As governments and journalists constantly framed the control of COVID-19 as being a personal responsibility, the vaccine became the most important way that Canadians could keep themselves safe. It put incredible pressure on vaccine distribution to happen as fast as possible, even though medical research could only progress so quickly.

The first vaccine approved was the Pfizer-BioNTech mRNA vaccine, developed in Germany. Health Canada approved it on December 9, 2020.[11] In parts of Canada where the second wave was more deadly than the first, politicians were under severe pressure to try and stop the spread, impossible thanks to weak public health orders related to large, congregant-setting workplaces. In Québec, operating rooms were ordered to cut their capacity by 50% to free up spaces for an impending rush of COVID-19 patients. In Alberta, 146 long-term care facilities were in outbreak, and the infections were five times higher than any peak during the spring or summer.[12] Average new cases in Ontario had reached 1816 per day and would rise from there thanks to the pending holiday season.[13] Vaccines could not come faster, especially for politicians who needed the distraction that vaccine news could offer. Ontario, Alberta and Canada appointed military personnel to oversee vaccine distribution, in an act of public relations that signalled to Canadians that we were at war with COVID-19. Jason Kenney was particularly enthusiastic about the vaccines, coming out early and strong in his commitment to distribute them as soon and as efficiently as possible. Alberta did have the fastest vaccine distribution plan in Canada for the first three months of 2021, but Graham Thomson writing for *iPolitics* saw beyond the legitimate reasons to be excited. He warned that by mid-December, with cases rising to critical levels, vaccines offered Kenney a very useful political tool to distract from how inadequate his policies were:

For Kenney, this is also a tacit way of defending, while also deflecting attention away from, his refusal to introduce the kind of wide-sweeping COVID-restrictions seen in other provinces. Kenney is assuring Albertans that help is on the way and as long as they obey the "minimal" restrictions he's introduced everything will be fine.[14]

Thomson estimated that the vast majority of Albertans would not likely be vaccinated any time soon, despite Kenney's promise that the vaccine program would start on January 4, 2021.

Of course, Kenney wasn't the only politician to make political hay out of the vaccine. From the moment that vaccines emerged as being viable in November 2020, all politicians engaged in some kind of jockeying around vaccine distribution. It was nice political theatre, a welcome distraction from stories about conserving oxygen in the healthcare system to make sure there would be enough or the double-digit death counts plaguing so many long-term care homes. Doug Ford greeted the first shipment of vaccines to Ontario on December 14, stating, "The province has been preparing for this day for months and we are ready for the road ahead … It's time to start vaccinating Ontarians. It's time to put an end to the COVID-19 pandemic."[15] They weren't ready for the road ahead. By January 5, 2021, in response to criticism that Ontario's vaccine ramp up was slow, Ford told journalists, "It might take us a week, maybe a couple of weeks to ramp up, but once we get the machine going, we kick butt anywhere in the country."[16] Things were still lagging at the end of February, as Ontario blamed portal testing on the delay on its launch — while CTV quoted experts saying it would have been reasonable for the Ford administration to have set up the portal and found workers to manage it months earlier.[17] It also would have been reasonable for this information to have come to light earlier too, had journalists been critically analyzing updates from public health units about what had and had not been done in the lead-up to mass vaccination efforts in March.

Federally, opposition parties tried to score some political points by challenging the government to provide more information or identifying their own plans for vaccination. On December 3, 2020, five days before the first vaccine was approved by Health Canada, Erin O'Toole introduced a motion in the House of Commons to demand the government make its vaccination plans public — something the government said would be too hard, considering how much it had been changing.[18] The arrival of vaccines in Canada signalled a new pandemic era: people were finally in reach of the inoculation that would end this nightmare.

But that proximity to the end was elusive and required not only that we individually receive our vaccines, but everyone in our communities as well. As more and more Canadians got vaccinated, COVID-19 infection rates dropped and deaths plummeted, but not before a third wave could ravage many parts of Canada, infecting and killing younger people who were unable to get the vaccine, and whose employers did not keep them safe at work. Benefits from vaccination are not individual. We are better protected when everyone in our communities are better protected, and yet, journalists spent a lot of time individualizing vaccines just as they had individualized public health orders and keeping ourselves safe. The vaccine may have arrived, but there were still months between the moment of their arrival and mass vaccination being complete. And in those intervening months, governments relied on stories about the vaccines to obscure the fact that still, not enough was being done to keep people safe. Between April 1 and June 30, 2021, the period of time where mass vaccinations were underway, at least 3293 Canadians died from COVID-19: a small percentage compared to the overall death total, but deaths that tragically happened in spite of mass vaccination.

Journalists played along and constructed a vaccine story that was hyper-individualized. They were obsessed with covering vaccine hesitancy such that they created a narrative that vaccine hesitancy threatened Canada's vaccine efforts. This narrative was pushed out at the same time that Canadians were lining up for hours, staying up past midnight to book their first doses and showing no collective sign of being hesitant. While countries around the world, including Canada's closest neighbour, were struggling with hesitancy levels that were truly worrying, Canadian journalists invented an image of a vaccine-hesitant country that was not bearing itself out in reality. As of July 1 2021, Canada was among countries leading the world in vaccination rates, with 68% of our population vaccinated with at least one dose. The U.K. was behind at 66.9% followed by Israel with 64%. Israel had been the fastest country in its vaccination campaign, until doses tapered off in early March 2021 at just under 60%. Of the 3.32 billion doses that had been administered around the world, just 1% of those doses were administered in low-income countries.[19]

By summer 2021, the global campaign to vaccinate as many people as possible coincided with the rise of several variants, notably delta. Globally, COVID-19 cases were increasing, and deaths started to increase again at the start of July. It was rapidly becoming the dominant strain of COVID-19 worldwide, and reached above 80% of all COVID-19 cases in the U.S. Despite the mass vaccine campaigns in the U.S., unvaccinated Americans posed a serious public health threat, as COVID-19 kept circulating within communities, infecting both vaccinated and unvaccinated people alike, and causing great harm to folks who were unvaccinated. Cases were doubling and hospitals were filling back up.[20] As a result, throughout July, social media was full of stories from doctors about patients who were demanding to be vaccinated on their deathbeds, or from steadfast anti-vaxxers who took their survival as proof that they did not need a dose.

The U.K. was in an even worse spot in July 2021. The kingdom had a steady incline of cases from April until July, experiencing 50,000 cases per day by the summer, and even still, the government dropped most public health restrictions. Just 55% of the population had been vaccinated, though the vaccinations were credited with why the U.K.'s death toll was staying low: 50 per day. Compare that to Indonesia, another country with 50,000 new cases per day and a vaccination rate of just 6%, and their death rate was at 1000 per day.[21] The U.K. approach to open up was made possible by the vaccines, but allowing COVID-19 to circulate among its population by dropping most public health measures was a cocktail that could lead to even more virulent variants (the alpha variant had already developed in the U.K.) that would devastate parts of the world that didn't have access to vaccines as countries like England, the U.S. and Canada did.

The pandemic showed just how important community really is, both local and national, but also globally. The pandemic could not be over in Canada unless it's over in Indonesia, and decisions to allow COVID-19 to run out of control in the U.K. would be felt all over the world. And yet, in the western nations that struggled the most with controlling COVID-19 spread, they all had an intense individualism built into the core of identity and society. That individualism was expressed most acutely in how politicians and journalists talked about vaccine hesitancy: a decision that was, above all else, a personal choice. When the time came for the personal choice narrative to be confronted by the reality that vaccines required a collective, systemic approach, it was almost too late: global English-language coverage about vaccine hesitancy, especially coming from the U.S., had transformed how individuals understood their relationship with vaccines. For Canada, journalists bombarded people with stories about hesitancy, especially ones that tried to superimpose American stories into a Canadian context, and the vaccine hesitancy narrative was born.

VACCINE HESITANCY

Vaccine hesitance in Canada goes back to the start of how politicians and journalists talked about finding a vaccine in March 2020. But the race to find a vaccine, as so many journalists and politicians called it, did not start in March 2020. It started far before that. CBC Radio's *The Current* had a segment on February 3, 2020, that looked at where global vaccine research was as the virus was emerging. Host Matt Galloway talked to Paul Hodgson from the University of Saskatchewan who said research that had been previously done for MERS and SARS had stopped because the viruses died out, but there was a good base from which to find a vaccine that could work against SARS-CoV-2. Critical work was done by Chinese scientists to sequence the virus and they made this information public. At that moment, with anti-Chinese sentiment rising in relation to COVID-19 (as I discuss in the March 2020 chapter), that could have been an interesting thread to tug further on, but host Matt Galloway pivoted instead to what kind of global cooperation was happening to develop a vaccine, finishing the interview by asking, "What's the timeline here? When do you think a vaccine would get to market?" Hodgson explained that it would be impossible to say and described the steps necessary before a vaccine would be ready for mass distribution.[22] As the pandemic grew, the necessity to improve scientific literacy and explain how vaccines are developed grew too, but segments like this one were rare. Rarer still was this kind of patience and explanation provided by guests informing daily reporting about vaccines, which could have gone a long way to both calm anti-Chinese sentiment and engage Canadians in understanding the process of creating a new vaccine.

All news organizations aired vaccine grievances without the care necessary to ensure a clear message was delivered alongside background information that could help a reader feel confident in how they understood what was written. For casual readers of the news, it would have been very easy to see the abundance of coverage of vaccine hesitancy as being a signal that there was, in fact, something to be worried about. News organizations underestimated the impact of airing these hesitations and fears over and over, even if they were nestled in articles that tried to demonstrate why these fears were unfounded. The fears were far easier to explain, and therefore far easier to spread, than were facts and evidence. The mRNA technology that made the Pfizer-BioNtech and Moderna vaccines possible was an incredible scientific advancement that, unfortunately, had not been adequately explained from the start by enough voices for this victory to be broadly understood. Even if there were special features, podcast episodes or other more in-depth reporting on the vaccines, every time a headline came out that indicated another vaccine trial death or setback, it was rarely explained as being part of a very normal process of medical testing. Journalists did a lot to feed the narrative that vaccine hesitancy was a true threat, which clashed with the other side of vaccine coverage: unabashed excitement over vaccines bringing us back to normal.

Quality vaccine reporting was absolutely critical, because from the start, vaccines would clearly be used by any force possible to push any political message. Governments could use vaccines to demonstrate their competence while refusing to go further with public health measures, especially in early 2021 when vaccines were finally so close to being available. Opposition politicians used vaccines to argue governments weren't doing enough. The far-right used vaccines to push dangerously anti-social messages, and they propagated online, spreading fear and mistrust about vaccines. And journalists, who had a tremendous responsibility to report on the vaccines with critical depth, often chose angles that were too shallow or focused on vaccine hesitancy even before a vaccine was available.

On March 23, 2020, the day that Trudeau announced vaccine funding, *Global News'* podcast *Wait There's More* featured a far-too-rare in Canadian media segment on early vaccine development. They interviewed Neil Browning, a vaccine trial volunteer who was one of just 45 adults to participate in the research coordinated by Kaiser Permanente. Host Tamara Khandaker asked him to explain what it was like being a human guinea pig, which he embraced. Because the trials were sped up, this step, he explained, took the place of animal tests. Based on everything scientists know about the body's immune system, the SARS-CoV-2's genetic sequencing and the content of the trial vaccine itself, Browning felt safe. There was no live virus in the vaccine. It included short messenger RNA (mRNA) produced in a lab to stimulate an immune response to fight off a COVID-19 infection. The trial wasn't testing whether or not the short messenger RNA could fight SARS-CoV-2 — that would come in later phases of the tests — but instead it studied how the body responded to the presence of the vaccine inside of it. Listeners of the episode must have been impressed to hear the details of this new, experimental vaccine told not by an epidemiologist or a doctor but someone who felt it was his duty to do what he could to help others. The vaccine being tested on him was the Moderna vaccine.[23] While it would have been fascinating to check in with Browning or how the trails were going over the rest of the year, the show did not follow-up with Browning or the Moderna trials, as it was cancelled in July 2020 as part of massive layoffs at *Global News* despite being one of Canada's most popular news podcasts. The impact of media layoffs on the quality of COVID-19 coverage cannot be understated, and I explore this in the chapter covering March 2021.[24]

Vaccine coverage needed to be this in-depth. It needed to balance professional expertise with comments from average people. But that was hard to do when everything else was raging around the issue, and when a common reaction to a potential vaccine was: I don't care, just get it into my arm. While not everyone needed to hear the details, describing vaccine development, updates and other related news and was difficult, especially amid the daily cycle of stats and government updates and everything else. And media outlets weren't judicious enough with what they decided to cover, either. They obsessed over all vaccine news, no matter how minor it was. Like one April 20, 2020, *Associated Press* story picked up by CTV *News* about a Facebook comment made by Novak Djokovic, the number-one ranked men's tennis player in the world at the time, saying he would refuse a COVID-19 vaccine, despite vaccines being so far down the horizon that the question was essentially theoretical.[25] *Global News* featured one anti-vaccine activist in an article about misinformation and vaccines, and quoted him saying that he's worried about, "bypassing animal studies and not taking the time that ought to be taken in order to make sure the product is safe," even though it was *Global*'s own news podcast that interviewed Browning, who was living proof that even bypassing animal studies did not mean the vaccine was less safe.[26]

Surveys received outsized coverage. Every time a survey came out that tested Canadians' vaccine opinions, it was covered. Rather than seeing little use in people's attitudes and opinions toward something so theoretical, news agencies reported the figures, which in April 2020 were very high but still left a sizable 27% saying some version of no.[27] Polling was a key way in which negative vaccine news was needlessly promoted. Through polling, Canadians opinions were plucked out of thin air and given the same seriousness as news about vaccine advancements, if not even more. One *Canadian Press* article reported that Canadians were "divided" on the entirely theoretical question about whether or not vaccines should have been made mandatory. The results were released on April 28, 2020, almost a year before any kind of serious public debate could have been had over the issue. By then, more than 2700 Canadians had died, and no vaccine was close to being approved. Yet, Lee Berthiaume wrote that the results were "setting up a potentially prickly public health debate if a vaccine becomes available."[28] Even though the poll was divided 60% to 40%, indicating a sizable amount of support for a mandatory vaccination program, 11 months later it was clear that even if Canada wanted to impose a mandatory vaccine program, they didn't have the resources or the vaccines to do this.[29]

As the second wave started, and still with no vaccine in sight, CTV News Windsor published the result of a global survey that placed support in Canada for receiving the vaccine at 77%. While very high, it was again fiction. With no vaccine available, no proof that it was safe and effective, very little information could be gleaned from the question "Would you take a vaccine?" aside from some people always saying no.[30] Until an actual vaccine became available, asking this question was a gift to the anti-vaccine movements, who knew their message would resonate with a sizable minority especially while they exploited the reality that there was still a lot of information missing. These surveys were actually gauging trust in public health — how much someone is willing to believe what a public health official promises. Of course there would be people who didn't trust, especially in absence of an actual vaccine. Would their opinion change if they caught COVID-19 between the survey and the time a vaccine was available? Would they get a shot anyway, pulled along by a partner or a friend? These kinds of forces were rendered invisible by media's obsession with asking this question before a vaccine existed, instead situating the question entirely in a hypothetical future during a very unsure year.

Public health certainly didn't do itself many favours, and journalists often highlighted comments that sounded the most sensational or worrisome. One CTV News headline read, "Safety won't be compromised for vaccine, Canada's top doctors say," making it sound like there was even a question about this. The comments were in reaction to a Russian vaccine, which Canada's Deputy Chief Public Officer of Health Howard Njoo said was created "unusually fast."[31] Explaining the processes of vaccine approval was critical in articles like these.[32] But the CTV News article said nothing more: it furthered the fear that COVID-19 vaccines were being made too fast; and it offered a headline that would easily be read suspiciously by someone who didn't think that vaccine information was abundant enough.

This kind of thing happened frequently in vaccine reporting. It was rare to hear about the processes of vaccine development or how much work had already been done to find these vaccines before the pandemic hit. On September 2, 2020, CTV News Windsor quoted Theresa Tam saying that vaccines usually take ten years to develop. She then said, "Canada and the world cannot wait 10 years for a COVID-19 vaccine … By the same token, we cannot and will not compromise safety and efficacy." Her comments were sandwiched between four Windsorites who were all hesitant about taking a vaccine that did not exist by September 2. Stacey Mills said, "I'm not anti-vaccine, I'm just cautious to who developed it and how it was tested," and Milica Kulidzan said that she didn't think there was enough time put into making the vaccine.[33] But the mRNA vaccines had been in development for a decade and more. Tam's comments, again, fed into the fear that these vaccines were being developed too quickly, even though Tam herself was likely aware of the research that had been developed prior to 2019 and that the urgency demanded by the pandemic helped to focus and fund the scientific pursuit to find the vaccines. Rather than adding any of this crucial information into the article, CTV Windsor instead ended their article with David MacKay whose comment — he won't stick a needle in his arm regardless of what's in it — suggested a fear of needles more than a fear of a new vaccine. "I don't think you can hide from the invisible boogeyman," he is inexplicably quoted as saying.[34] Perhaps the people interviewed in this article had read the CTV National News backgrounder published the day before titled, "Past vaccine disasters show why rushing a coronavirus vaccine would be 'a prescription for disaster,'" a disjointed feature that broadly looked at medical disasters from the past century.[35]

By the time vaccines were actually being distributed in December 2020, there were enough challenges getting them to everyone who needed them in the most effective order than to spend too much time debating vaccine hesitancy. The vaccines were safe, effective in curbing infections within residences that had been ravaged by the illness, but the vast majority of Canadians who wanted a vaccine had no idea when their time would come. All the debates within the press before vaccines were available didn't seemingly have any impact on hesitancy as demand for a vaccine remained high.

There was one group that benefited greatly from the manufactured worry related to vaccine hesitancy: the nascent movement of hucksters, extremists, white supremacists and new age health activists who formed the backbone of Canada's anti-vaccination movement. Deeply inspired and connected with activists in the U.S., these folks took the media's incessant attention on vaccine hesitancy and helped to mainstream the fears that underpinned regular vaccine hesitancy: is it safe, is it going to work, and so on. They were loud and pulled attention away from important aspects of the vaccine rollout process. And journalists followed their every move.

ANTI-VAXXERS

It's probably impossible to know how to assign blame accurately for the rise of the anti-mask/anti-vaccine movement. Certainly, thin reporting that didn't consider how a message would be torqued or manipulated didn't help, but there were many colliding factors that made the anti-mask/anti-vaccine movement as strong as it became and as dangerous as it was. It emerged in the summer of 2020, when masks became mandatory across Canada. While a majority of Canadians accepted the new public health measures, there was a vocal fringe who did not, and their message fit perfectly with the unknowns that circulated around the vaccine. There was a confluence between these two movements, and they found fertile ground in far-right, anti-establishment sympathizers who had been growing for years under banners like the Yellow Vests, United We Roll and La Meute and other racist groups. Politicians didn't pay enough attention to these protests and did not implement public policies that would have limited their public rallies or intervened in the distribution of their disinformation. Police were widely criticized for being too lenient on the marches even as they became more violent. Journalists should have made the connections between the rise of these anti-public health measures and the already organized far-right, but it took way too long for journalists to see these connections. By the time they did, the movements already had press — some of it negative, but it didn't matter because people seeking validation of their concerns had already found them. After one wave of protests held across Canada, on July 20, 2020, CTV News quoted one rally organizer, an activist with the far-right People's Party of Canada, saying there was no evidence that masks make people safer — but the article then didn't add anything about how there was no question that masks made people safer. Too many reporters and editors assumed that by airing the ridiculous opinions of the motivated fringe that average people would be able to reasonably see they were wrong. Instead, articles like this one became propaganda for the anti-mask movement, where its spokespeople were featured, when calling on Canadians to reject fear and join their movement.[36]

It wasn't just CTV News, of course. *Sudbury.com* literally called anti-maskers "freedom fighters" in a headline with scare quotes around it, publishing the Facebook rules of engagement from the group and some ideas for how to get around mask rules inside stores. A reader had to get past paragraphs of wild internal discussions from the group before getting to any information about mask bylaws not actually being in force or stores having the right to refuse unmasked people.[37] The *Ottawa Citizen*, in covering an August 29, 2020 anti-mask rally on Parliament Hill published an un-bylined article, mostly featuring images and uncritically reporting protesters' demands, titled "Parliament Hill protesters denounce 'tyranny,' demand end to COVID-19 restrictions." The journalist didn't put this rally in the context of local COVID-19 case data or hospitalizations, instead treating it like it was an event with no connection to the broader community around it.[38]

Who was organizing these rallies? Most of the shorter articles didn't attempt to answer this question. But when they did, the connections that rally organizers had with far-right and fascist movements became clear. A *Richmond News* feature on one of the Parliament Hill rallies irresponsibly ran this pull quote at the top of an article: "People are not afraid of a second wave because we never had a first one." The founder of Hugs not Masks, Vladislav Sobolev, compared the anti-mask movement to "uprising of Nazi Germany, as well as the Bolshevik Revolution in Russia," a comment that red-flags the speaker's fascist tendencies as no one sympathetic to communism would describe Nazis in Germany as "rising up." The article did, however, mention that Sobolev's day job was selling a kind of herbal supplement that had been connected to liver failure. While that alone should have disqualified him from being profiled like this, the Nazi nostalgia probably should have too.[39] Anti-racist activists and researchers had been sounding the alarm on these rallies from the start, and journalists should have known better if they really didn't want to help promote these far-right movements.

Articles written about anti-mask/anti-vaccine events followed the same pattern: broadcast the protesters' demands uncritically, bury or exclude fact-checking, use a headline the movement could be proud of and neglect to write about who was actually organizing these events. By the time vaccine campaigns were well under way across Canada, these rallies had grown in size and violence across Canada. In Alberta especially, politicians were routinely targeted and even attacked. Marchers were open with white pride messages, including hosting Tiki Torch rallies to call back to the racist Unite the Right rally held in Charlottesville, Virginia. *Vice* reported that among the speakers of an Edmonton rally was someone who had been charged with Islamophobic hate crimes. At the same time, hate crimes against Black Muslim women were on the rise in Edmonton.[40]

And yet, coverage of these rallies barely matured. The *Vice* article was written by Mack Lamoureaux, one of Canada's few journalists who closely watches the organized white supremacy beat. Most journalists covered these events the same way they would a Santa Claus parade. An article about a protest in Kelowna on March 20, 2021, called it a "'freedom' protest rally." It quoted Heather Friesen, a counter protester, who said that hatred in Kelowna was on the rise and pointed the blame directly at the anti-mask/anti-vaccine rally. The journalist Darrian Matassa-Fung followed Friesen's comments by saying the protesters had a right to protest, but didn't explore Friesen's analysis about the relationship between the rally and a rise in hatred in Kelowna. This was even though Matassa-Fung himself was physically harassed by protesters while reporting on the story, something he mentioned on Twitter that was embedded into the article, but not mentioned in his video report. "Do you want this reported or not," he can be heard saying in the video in response to the harassment, betraying a critical failure of media to grapple with these protests: they benefit from all press, including negative press, and they know that journalists will be there, even if there is a threat to their personal safety.[41]

Every single rally, every single Facebook group were content generation mills that used social media to push out anti-vaccine messages much further than they would have otherwise gone. And almost every story about one of these rallies lumped together freedom, opposition to public health orders, suspicion of science and politicians and suspicion of the pandemic in general. This failure of reporting had real, life-and-death impacts. For example, after the first few months of Canada's vaccination effort, the only outbreaks within residential care still happening were entering into residences through unvaccinated individuals, usually healthcare workers. At CHSLD Lionel-Émond in Gatineau, the site of one of the biggest outbreaks in Québec post-vaccination in spring 2021, only 41% of healthcare workers were vaccinated. While 96% of residents agreed to be vaccinated, 25 of them died as they only had the first dose. In a report undertaken to figure out how the outbreak happened, it was found that health workers were hesitant or fearful about the vaccines. The local health unit noted that vaccination rates among staff jumped from 41% to 61% after the outbreak and said it was committed to better communications to convince even more staff to get vaccinated.[42] It wasn't too surprising that healthcare workers would be vaccine hesitant. As workers whose employers rarely offered them adequate resources, financial or physical, to stay safe, being told to take a new vaccine may have felt like just another way that these workers were being disrespected. The vaccines became the key measure to keep people safe, rather than other ways employers and public health policies could have controlled infection.

COVID-19 exploited cracks in social solidarity, and anti-mask protests were the extreme example of where social solidarity broke down during the pandemic. The selfishness wrapped up in a concern for one's own health at the expense of the most vulnerable population's health was very difficult to break through, especially since the underlying drive of these rallies was racism. As a public health crisis that disproportionately hurt racialized communities, the need to convince everyone to get vaccinated was even more important to those same communities. But because journalists and politicians did not communicate vaccine development information as clearly as they should have, white vaccine-hesitant individuals — who were more likely than non-white individuals to have not been touched directly by COVID-19 —were more drawn toward a movement that claimed to want to protect personal health and safety. The perverse irony was that their movement hurt many people — acutely through racist violence and generally through convincing people to distrust vaccines and other public health measures. With media's focus on people refusing to get vaccines, an opposite story was being spun by advocates, unions, business leaders, politicians and public health officials: how public health and politicians decided who would be vaccinated and when.

THE POLITICS OF PRIORITIZATION

For the vast majority of Canadians who were not vaccine hesitant, the vaccine could not come soon enough. Vaccines stood in for improved workplace health and safety and could almost eliminate the incredible anxiety that living through a pandemic had elicited. But politicians who saw the vaccine as the sole solution to the pandemic problem created a scarcity rush on vaccines that generated two kinds of discussions. The first was relatively straightforward. Based on global vaccine evidence and the way COVID-19 was sweeping through residential facilities, all provinces had a policy of starting with residents in long-term care, followed by various plans to reach adults living in retirement residences or who were over 90 and lived alone. From there, public health units would release appointment dates based on age. At the same time, frontline healthcare workers were also offered vaccines. For weeks, there was a steady flow of information about what age was being vaccinated where. Each Monday, somewhere, a public health unit was vaccinating people younger and younger. Vaccine capacity slowly improved, and steadily, Canadians who were eager for a vaccine were vaccinated.

The second discussion happened at the same time as the one that prioritized individuals by birth date and became the political expression for who has value within a society and who does not. A public debate ensued about who should have priority access for vaccines: police, fire-fighters, hospital administrators and chiropractors, or people who stay in homeless shelters, inmates and disabled adults? Politicians, journalists and advocates weighed in: what was the most efficient way to carry out a mass vaccination campaign?

As had been the case throughout the pandemic, disabled people were mostly left off early vaccination schedules, even if they lived in congregant care settings. In Ontario, where disabled adults live in facilities that have similar levels of care as long-term care facilities, they were not included in the first phase of vaccinations, even though retirement residences, police, firefighters, chiropodists and dental hygienists were. The rollout focused primarily on age, but didn't take into account disability at all, despite being an aggravating factor for severe COVID-19 outcomes.[43]

For shelter users, people who were unhoused or incarcerated, the need for vaccines was obvious. Brutal pre-pandemic conditions exacerbated a public health crisis which led to at least 14 deaths within the shelter system and nine deaths in the prison system between March 2020 and June 2021. In absence of an immediate prisoner release, or instant safety measures brought to the shelter system, these individuals needed to be vaccinated as soon as possible. But there was political opposition to this. As the federal government was planning to start a pilot project where they would vaccinate 600 federal inmates who were elderly or had underlying health conditions[44] — that was out of an average of 14,071 federally-held inmates per day, or 4.2%[45] — the federal Conservatives tried to make this plan sound like it was privileging inmates over residents of long-term care. Erin O'Toole tweeted, "Not one criminal should be vaccinated ahead of any vulnerable Canadian or front line health worker," as if there weren't federally incarcerated individuals who were also vulnerable.[46] Journalists reported the issue as if the plan to only vaccinate 1.5% of the total prison population was one that would actually keep inmates safe, as if COVID-19 would somehow be controlled by only vaccinating a very small number of individuals. By 2021, the data clearly demonstrated the disproportionate impact that COVID-19 had on racialized people because of systemic discrimination, and yet, journalists failed to make the connection between systemic racism, racism within the criminal justice system and Canada's prison population. Like how Indigenous men make up more than 30% of the federal prison population. For Indigenous women, that percentage rises to 42%.[47]

By February 23, 2021, there had been more than 880 cases in federal correctional facilities and the *Canadian Press* reported that about 70% of these cases occurred in the Saskatchewan Penitentiary and Stony Mountain Institution, both locations with high Indigenous populations. By then, Correctional Services Canada had administered the 600 vaccines but said it wasn't planning to begin vaccinating the rest of the population until spring.[48] There was a very simple reason for why the federal government needed to inoculate inmates in federal custody: they have the responsibility to care for people in their protection. It wasn't more complicated than that, even if O'Toole wanted to make political hay out of the issue. Across the provinces, vaccine rollout within prisons was different from place to place, with Ontario not vaccinating anyone in a correction facility until April 2021.[49] In Alberta, anyone in a provincial jail over the age of 75 would be eligible to be vaccinated as of January, except that by January 21, 2021, there was no one older than 75 in custody of a provincial jail.[50] During spring 2021, COVID-19 outbreaks continued to plague correctional facilities. *CBC Investigates* talked with Deepan Budlakoti, an inmate at the Ottawa-Carleton Detention Centre, a provincial facility, who explained that for someone without the Internet, having basic questions about vaccines were impossible to answer. He said,

> We are a year-and-a-half into this. At this stage, they easily could have put in place safe measures, like rapid testing and proper protective equipment … If anyone gets COVID-19, it's the sole result of [the province] not ensuring we're safe.[51]

Despite assurances that the prisoner population would be prioritized for vaccines, that didn't happen. By June 2021, CBC found that 268 of 1000 prisoners in provincial jails had been infected with COVID-19. For federal facilities, that number was 126. Both figures were far higher than the Canadian average of 37 per 1000. Vaccine campaigns lagged behind the general population too, and only Québec was publicly announcing their daily vaccination rates. While in B.C., Saskatchewan, Yukon and P.E.I, 70% of prisoners had been immunized (CBC doesn't say if this meant two doses or one), just 44% of prisoners in Ontario had received a first dose. Far from being among the first to be vaccinated, many inmates found themselves at the back of the line, despite not having any control over their individual living environment to keep COVID-19 at bay.[52] The high rate of COVID-19 infections, enabled by state inaction and playing politics with prisoners' lives, left thousands of people with potentially life-impacting chronic illness that many will need support to manage for decades to come.

There was a very big danger in playing politics with the vaccine. By the time it actually arrived, much of the distribution was in the hands workers who had experience coordinating annual mass vaccination campaigns, rather than politicians. The NDP called for the military to be involved in the vaccine rollout. They presented a mass vaccination plan on February 16, 2021, and focused mostly on the human resources of distribution. Their statement was heavy on catch phrases: "Team Canada," "small businesses," "go back to some kind of normalcy," and "ensure this situation never happens again."[53] By "situation" they meant the slow state of vaccination, though this was mostly tied to supply timelines — Canada wasn't supposed to receive enough doses for mass vaccination until March, and true to this, the week before this statement, the *Canadian Press* had reported very few to no vaccine doses delivered to most provinces.[54] Vaccine delivery schedules had been negotiated and Canada was one of many countries scrambling to get doses. There were many things the federal government could have controlled but early-stage doses was not one of them. The NDP's attempt to turn this into a political question that the military could have solved was probably the least useful intervention they could have made at that moment.

The line between where politicians' actions could move things along and where they were effectively powerless was never clear. Journalists didn't dig into trying to identify where this line might be or how it moved over the course of the vaccine rollout. There were some obvious failures, like Ontario's chaotic vaccine rollout that relied on volunteer social media accounts to connect individuals to vaccine appointments, but vaccines in early 2021 were always only going to go to a few people, if we had them at all. Vaccine news took up a lot of airtime that could have been better spent examining the ways in which politicians were failing to keep people safe from COVID-19 spread. Some of that kind of critical reporting continued in 2021 — it was rare even through 2020 — but the fervour over the vaccines reformulated the arc of the pandemic from an endless problem to one on the cusp of resolution, even if it was impossible to know when that would be. A potential end date allowed politicians, again, to promise we would soon go back to normal — our old world is not that far away, just as Jagmeet Singh said in his media statement from February 16, 2021.

Just as COVID-19 infection had ravaged racialized and low-income communities, there should have been a wide-scale effort to flood vulnerable communities with vaccine doses. The inequity of the vaccine rollout, as I explain in the chapter covering June 2020, was rooted in race and class marginalization, and politicians did not make it a priority to target vaccine distribution accordingly, with few exceptions — especially in the early days when the vaccine was a precious commodity, leaving vulnerable communities in Peel and Toronto with little to no access to vaccines. There were some targeted interventions made to reach people directly to get a vaccine. But Ontario's chaotic vaccine rollout meant that the more connected you were to Twitter and the Vaccine Hunter account, an account that spat out open vaccination spots all across Canada where they were available, the more likely you were to get vaccinated. This was a highly inequitable way to manage vaccine rollout.

The order in which people were vaccinated made for major political jockeying. Even though there was compelling evidence to show that vaccines should be dispatched based on postal code to reach racialized and low-income communities, authorities mostly used age as the primary category to determine when someone could be vaccinated. As a result, by April 6, 2021, the regions within the City of Toronto that had had the highest rates of COVID-19 infection had the lowest rates of vaccination.[55] Disability groups decried that many provinces did not prioritize disabled people within Phase 1 priority groups. Unions and companies insisted that their workers needed the shot first. The jockeying for vaccine priority was made even more political by vaccine shortages thanks to the global race to secure vaccines. In this race, Canada wasn't exactly a team player. In fact, Canada was hording vaccines more than any other country in the world.

CANADA AND THE WORLD

On December 16, 2020, I wrote an opinion piece for *Passage* that examined how Canada was hoarding vaccines, to the frustration of many people within the international community, while at the same time not supporting a motion submitted to the World Trade Organization that sought to waive international IP rights for vaccine production. There had been very little news about either issue. I had been tipped off by researchers in October 2020 who were concerned that Canada was blocking poorer countries' access to IP information, and they were frustrated no one was paying attention.[56]

Both issues did gradually get more attention as Canada's vaccination efforts accelerated in early 2021. Vaccine production around the world and Canadians' hunger for vaccines pushed the federal government into procuring as many vaccines as possible. By the end of November 2020, before Health Canada had approved a single vaccine, Canada had procured 429 million doses from seven companies. It was the highest amount of any country. And still, Conservative politicians accused the federal government of being behind the ball in vaccine procurement.[57] Clearly, the Liberal government knew that vaccination would be politically popular, and they did everything they could to secure vaccines, even accessing vaccines intended for the poorest countries through the global vaccination consortium COVAX. Indeed, Liberal success in a 2021 election hinged on having a majority of Canadians vaccinated.

The race to vaccinate all Canadians brought out ugly tendencies among politicians. There was global demand for vaccines and yet, politicians in Canada acted as if there was an unlimited global supply of the vaccine and the Liberals were simply not doing enough to access them. When the NDP rightfully condemned the Liberals for accessing vaccines through COVAX, they also blamed the federal government for not having done two things to "ensure adequate supply of vaccines:" not having built vaccine manufacturing capacity, which would have been impossible to do in such a short period of time, and not doing international procurement well enough.[58] The contradiction was apparently lost on the NDP: Canada could not procure more vaccines without taking them from somewhere else. A more progressive message would have been to explain how the global race for vaccines was robbing poorer countries of doses, and we all need to be patient and wait. The NDP instead made it sound like Canada was both taking vaccines from poor countries and also not doing enough to take more vaccines from all countries. It was confusing and didn't give Canadians a global picture of the pressures on Canada in securing doses. While confusion helped the Liberals, who could always say they were at the mercy of international vaccine manufacturers regardless of whether that was always true, it did not help Canadians understand what exactly happens when Canada purchases so many extra doses that it will not be able to use. By March 2021, when 9.3% of Canadians were vaccinated with at least one dose, many countries had not yet received one dose. Egypt, Nigeria, Kenya, Vietnam and Bahamas, for example, all had only vaccinated fewer than 0.1% of the population.[59] Ninety percent of all vaccines distributed by March 22, 2021, went to wealthy nations.[60] Experts had warned this would happen; the wealthiest countries would scramble for access to the vaccine as fast as they could. The *New York Times* quoted Yale epidemiologist Gregg Gonsalves, who compared the global hoarding to the scenes from across North America during March a year earlier, "It was like a run on toilet paper. Everybody was like, 'Get out of my way. I'm gonna get that last package of Charmin … We just ran for the doses.'"[61]

Global vaccine hoarding made Canada's decision to block vaccine intellectual property waivers even more egregious. Not only had we hoarded more vaccines than any other country in the world, we were also actively stopping poorer countries from accessing them too. On March 10, 2021, a coalition of trade unions and other progressive organizations wrote a letter urging Justin Trudeau to change his mind and vote in favour of waiving the IP.[62] This got very little attention in national Canadian media, especially alongside discussions about how fast vaccines could be delivered and articles that tried to answer why vaccine rollout was not going as smoothly in some places as it was going in others. On March 22, 2021, the eve of a massive shipment of new vaccine doses, the *Canadian Press* wrote an in-depth article about how many of which vaccines Canada was about to receive and where they would be dispatched. There wasn't a single mention of Canada's COVAX order, Canada's vaccine hoarding, where the global vaccine campaign was or Canada blocking the IP waiver at the UN.[63] Canada's actions within a global context were considered to be a wholly separate issue than the more important domestic rollout, which allowed politicians to frame issues in the way that the NDP did — procurement is simply a matter of political strategy and will — rather than the crucial context of Canada being one among a sea of nations all fighting to access the same resources.

By spinning vaccines as our only hope, but also hoarding and blocking vaccines from the rest of the world, politicians remixed vaccines into a commodity that was for individual use. The vaccine was the ultimate step of personal responsibility for someone to take: after a year of social distancing and wearing a mask, it would all end once you got your second dose. But that's not how vaccines work. We are all more safe when members of our community become more safe. Vaccine campaigns that targeted neighbourhoods or cohorts helped to bring collective safety to those locations. Journalists rarely applied this logic when talking about the global vaccination campaign, instead focusing closely on Canada's procurement, next shipment or next delay. As cases spiralled out of control even while vaccines were available, the world's leaders were demonstrating that on the most important test of the pandemic, they would miserably fail, even if it meant they'd have a good shot at winning their re-election.

While everything during the pandemic was political, vaccines were perhaps the issue that was also the most confusing. How Canadians understood vaccines was deeply connected to the way in which politicians spun vaccines for political gain, and to journalists who were not scientifically literate enough to cut through the noise. The gaps left in reporting because of this, and the willingness of journalists to promote hateful and far-right movements, gave even more fuel to anti-mask/anti-vaccine campaigns. As the issue required robust international reporting, the most complete picture of what was happening internationally tended to come from international news sources, while Canadian sources simply paid very close attention to the details of domestic vaccine campaigns.

By the time that Health Canada approved the first vaccines and photos spread across media of Canadian military officials greeting the precious cargo, Canadians were coming to the end of a brutal 2020. But it wasn't brutal for everyone equally. Women, especially disabled, Black, Indigenous and/or racialized women bore the brunt of the pandemic. And for them, neither government nor journalists managed to respond to or report on their struggles in a way that would create an opening for radical and urgent change.

December 2020
THE GENDERED IMPACT

Cases: 378,139
Deaths: 12,130[1]

Even if the vaccine was offering a glimmer of hope that the pandemic might be over someday soon, the systemic issues that boiled over during the pandemic had no instant fix. December 7, 2020, was the 50th anniversary of the release of the *Final Report of the Royal Commission on the Status of Women,* a report that made hundreds of recommendations for how to improve women's lives in Canada. Looking back, a great deal of work had not yet happened, despite decades of progress. Canada still did not have a universal system of child care. Violence against women was still endemic and women's participation in the job market had still not caught up to men's. While gender equality was far from achieved before the pandemic hit, COVID-19 devastated safety, social supports and labour market access for women and nonbinary people.

Unlike other identities, journalists and politicians talked a lot about gender. There was no shortage of attention on the gendered impact of the pandemic, which stood in stark contrast with how journalists and politicians ignored or obscured the impact of COVID-19 on racialized or disabled people. Of the sources I cited for this book, where journalists were overwhelmingly white and able bodied, there was an even number of women and men reporters: 215 men and 216 women (though only a few nonbinary reporters). The critical mass of women reporters meant that reporting through a gendered lens was more possible than for other marginalized identities. And women are a sizable and important voting block, so politicians paid them a lot of attention. In fall 2020, under pressure from a Conservative Party that had just elected a new leader, the Liberals promised that child care would be their one major promise to Canadians, and it launched gendered issues into the spotlight. The spinoff effects of child care, the impacts of women withdrawing from the labour force and the money that a child-care system could generate circulated through the news cycle, spun around by pundits and columnists who loved the faux word *she-cession*. All the while, the most needed targeted help for women never came.

Early on, it was clear the pandemic would have a variety of gendered impacts. Just as COVID-19 would disproportionately impact disabled people and racialized people, it also disproportionately impacted women, though not all women equally. Through a lack of resources and emergency benefits, the poorest women — most likely to be disabled, Indigenous, Black and/or racialized — received nothing from Canada's self-declared feminist prime minister. As Canada locked down in spring 2020, there was desperate need for support services to combat gendered violence and women's labour participation walked off a cliff. Governments enacted some policies trying to mitigate these effects but there was nothing done that managed to cut to the core of the issues: systemic misogyny that plagues Canadian society. And at the heads of these governments were variations on a theme of Dad — men whose steady hand or quick rage became the defining characteristic of how they managed the pandemic.

ROWENA

When I first asked Rowena Alivio if I could talk with her for a short feature for *Chatelaine*, she immediately said yes. My assignment was to illustrate how women were surviving the pandemic, in the shadow of the 50th anniversary of the *Final Report of the Royal Commission on the Status of Women*. COVID-19 stripped away women's gains so quickly that many people wondered: what would the pandemic had looked like if we at least had a child-care system? Notable Canadian feminist Michele Landsberg wrote, "It's hard to contemplate the current wreckage of women's dreams for advancement without some bitter reflection on how long and hard we have fought to make governments pay attention to the child care crisis."[2]

When I spoke with Rowena, it wasn't child care that she was desperate for, though. The single mother was enjoying the extra time she was spending with her son and her adult daughter, whose life she had been absent from for too many years while her daughter grew up in Philippines and she worked in Canada. But as a longtime casino worker, the pandemic placed her in a bind. Her job was, for the foreseeable future, gone. When we spoke during the fall of 2020, her employer was threatening to end her health benefits, and the uncertainty created by CERB transitioning to EI, as I explain in the chapter covering August 2020, was almost too much for her to bear. Her anxiety was through the roof. Rowena was desperate for a solution that would help her gain financial stability while her industry waited out the pandemic. She told me,

> The government's shutdown orders ended our jobs. They should have a backup plan for us; they cannot leave us behind. It is their responsibility to help us to survive. As parents, we tried our best to deal with this, and some of us cannot deal with this anymore.[3]

Rowena was walloped by the pandemic's economic and social impacts. And, with very little aid money that was doled out through an intersectional frame, women and nonbinary people were largely not included in economic recovery, relying either on help from CERB and then CRB, or left out entirely and forced to manage with few to no resources. I explain the impact of government emergency benefit programs in the August 2020 chapter and the impact that the pandemic had on Filipina workers specifically in the October 2020 chapter.

Economic lockdown divided people into two categories: essential and non-essential. Women make up 81% of Canada's healthcare and social assistance workforce. They are also overrepresented as cashiers, and in cleaning, catering and clerical work which, when combined with care, are where 56% of women's work is concentrated. Men make up just 17% of these workers, though it skews higher with racialized and low-income workers.[4] So, as Canadian governments were shutting down parts of their economies and services, many women found themselves on the front lines of the pandemic, in care homes and hospitals, as orderlies, personal care workers, nurses and informal care takers of those made most vulnerable by the pandemic. While daily briefings were being made by male politicians in capital cities across Canada, women performed the day-to-day work of trying to hold together Canada's health and social services system. And the women who were not considered essential were more likely to find themselves laid off, stuck at home caring for children or other family members and scrambling to access emergency benefits to survive.

THE WOMEN IGNORED BY GENDERED IMPACT ANALYSES

At the end of March 2020, an Abacus poll showed that, in general, men were less concerned about COVID-19 than women were. This was surprising, as global reports showed that COVID-19 was disproportionately killing men.[5] Even though part of the survey questions asked if respondents had been closely following the news and 75% responded to say they had been, the percentage of men who said they were either a little or not at all concerned was 38%. Forty-seven percent of women who replied said they were extremely concerned. The same survey identified that women and poor people were more likely to report being lonely during the first weeks of the lockdown.[6]

The day after the Abacus poll news, the Canadian Centre for Policy Alternatives (CCPA) published a report that forecasted what the impact of the pandemic would be on unemployment. It found that 13% of working women in Canada were at risk of being laid off compared to 9% of working men. They also found that the risk of layoff was skewed by income: the lower income someone made, the higher their risk of layoff was. The calculation, done by CCPA economist David Macdonald, did not include workers in essential services like grocery, as it was unlikely that they would be laid off.[7] There were non-economic impacts too: stress from the Phase One lockdown translated into more depression and interrupted sleep, according to one study done by Veronica Guadagni from the University of Calgary. The difference between genders, she told CBC News, was "great."[8]

While violence was the most acute expression of the gendered impact of the pandemic, which I detail in the next section, the most profound impact of the pandemic on women was also the most fundamental — COVID-19 stopped millions of women from working, for many different reasons. By nearly every measure, women had a more difficult time during the pandemic, a fact that became generally accepted canon among journalists after the first wave, once data could back up the millions of anecdotes. One report, called Unmasking Gender Inequality, explored how COVID-19 had a gendered impact on finances, risk exposure, caregiving and safety. On every measure, women performed worse than men during the pandemic. Women's unemployment rate was higher, as they lost 60% more jobs than men in the first month of the pandemic. Women were more exposed to COVID-19 risk than men were, even when they worked in similar jobs. Working mothers in B.C. lost 12% more hours than working fathers in April 2020. The report, published by the B.C. Women's Health Foundation and Pacific Blue Cross in November 2020 demonstrated what had been long stated by feminist activists and columnists in Canada: women bore the brunt of the pandemic.[9] As many media outlets reported in Canada, the pandemic threatened to set back women's advancement by decades.

The limited recoveries possible between the first two waves also disproportionately hurt women. One study from the Royal Bank showed that while more than 20,000 women had left the workforce between February and October, 68,000 men joined it. Women with children under the age of six make up 41% of the workforce, and yet they represented two-thirds of job losses. The *Canadian Press* reported that the pandemic drove women's participation in the labour force to its lowest level in 30 years.[10]

The report blamed this divide on industries that managed to bounce back during the pandemic being mostly in science, engineering and technology, industries from which women continue to be systemically shut out. So-called women's work was much harder to come by. This phenomenon was global: one survey done by Mastercard found that 87% of women surveyed around the world reported experiencing a financial setback during the pandemic.[11] Across the G7 countries, according to an Ipsos poll, women were ten percentage points more worried about the future than men, 13 percentage points more likely to have experienced burnout or depression and ten percentage points more likely to report losing confidence in themselves.[12]

Of course, the impact on women was not borne equally. Racialized women were overrepresented in essential services, including direct care work, and therefore could not simply work from home. At a press conference where Ottawa public health announced the impact of the pandemic on Ottawa's Black and otherwise racialized populations, Hindia Mohamoud, director of the Ottawa Local Immigrant Partnership said, "People talk about, 'We are in this all together.' We are not in this all together. The risk that is faced by racialized populations is disproportionate."[13] The *Ottawa Citizen* article that quoted Mohamoud added that women were overall more likely to be infected by COVID-19 than men, and immigrant men and women were in particular danger.[14] But it was rare that journalists looked at the different impacts of different kinds of women, instead collapsing women into a universal category. Beyond dividing women based on their proximity to motherhood, journalists rarely tried to identify the disproportionate impact on racialized or poor women and never went deeper to understand the experiences of Indigenous women, even when COVID-19 was raging across Indigenous communities. Disabled women were especially ignored, even though the vast majority of people who had died from COVID-19 were disabled or had a chronic health issue. No aid was given directly to the poorest individuals — a population that skews toward racialized women — but $100 million was promised for food banks across Canada, the federal government's version of deciding to offer expired cans to someone collecting for the poor than simply giving money to them directly. Food bank usage shot up during the pandemic, and there's little doubt that extra money to help these organizations function was important. But as the sum total of the government's aid to the poorest Canadians, it was a paltry measure, especially because, as one report from Toronto's Daily Bread Food Bank found, food bank users were at higher risk of COVID-19 thanks to a combination of factors that also included health status. In a telephone survey of food bank users, nearly two-thirds of the respondents were women.[15]

The gendered frame was almost never extended to nonbinary people and stories that looked at the particular experiences of trans women were extremely rare. The paucity of reporting on how the pandemic disproportionately impacted trans women, trans men and nonbinary people erased their voices and experiences. In a feature for the *Toronto Star* on the way that COVID-19 was impacting trans healthcare, Angelyn Francis wrote, "After months of contending with COVID-19, the risk factors the trans community faces during the pandemic have scarcely been considered."[16] Data collection often erased trans and nonbinary individuals through binary gender checkbox choices and an already-hostile medical establishment became even less helpful under the strain of the pandemic. Add that queer and/or trans women are more likely to be low-income and have less access to safe and secure housing than the average population, trans women were dealt a double, triple or quadruple whammy.[17] Calgary independent media *The Sprawl* uncovered through access to information that Alberta's Ministry of Culture, Multiculturalism and Status of Women created a daily briefing in early March 2020 about the disproportionate impact the pandemic would have on women and racialized people. One of the notes said, "transgender people report high levels of discrimination and stigma in accessing healthcare settings. This may particularly be the case for those whose names and gender did not match on their official documents." But as journalist Danielle Paradis pointed out, the government didn't act on its own information to do anything to make healthcare more accessible for trans Albertans. This information was reported more than 16 months after the briefing notes were prepared.[18]

Understanding how COVID-19's gendered impact hurt women and nonbinary people generally, and different kinds of women and nonbinary people specifically, would have been critical had public officials wanted to target their relief measures to help the people most impacted by the pandemic. Except those policies rarely took aim at gender inequality, and journalists rarely wrote critically about this. When it was clear that lock-down measures were forcing women to leave the workforce, the solution from some corners was simply to re-open school: once school is open, the child-care dilemma goes away. The ways in which politicians, journalists and pundits talked about women often assumed that all women were mothers and that a lack of child care was the quintessential woman's issue. Unfortunately, the true quintessential women's issue, gendered violence, raged out of control during the first 18 months of the pandemic. And as the statistics on gendered violence were rising, politicians did what they usually do in the face of another shocking death announcement: they offer platitudes, small sums of money and pivot to something else.

GENDERED VIOLENCE

Before there was widespread analysis about the economic or emotional impact of COVID-19 on women (nonbinary people were rarely ever mentioned), the gendered impact of COVID-19 was mostly told through warnings about gendered violence. Advocates were quick to argue that lockdown measures could make an already dangerous situation explosive. On the same day the Abacus poll revealed that men were less concerned about the pandemic, journalists at many Canadian news outlets examined the impact the pandemic would have on domestic violence. In many articles across dozens of platforms, advocates from organizations and shelters all across Canada argued that the combination of layoffs, financial and health stresses and isolation could be a dangerous combination. On April 16, 2020, *iPolitics* reported that federal Women and Gender Equality Minister Maryam Monsef was committed to funding shelters as a primary intervention into the gendered impact of COVID-19. But they would only receive $40 million during the first wave of the pandemic, an amount that paled in comparison to the $1 billion government had promised to support students during summer 2020.[19]

The desperation and fear of gendered violence triggered by the pandemic was brought into sharp focus thanks to Canada's most deadly single-event mass shooting ever. On the night of April 18, 2020, a white man went on a shooting rampage that covered nearly 100 kilometres in Nova Scotia and left 22 people and himself dead. The RCMP was roundly criticized for how they managed the situation, possibly allowing the shooter to have killed more people as he moved through the night and into the morning. The shooter's first target was his partner, who managed to escape and survived by hiding in a forest.[20] In a statement from Nova Scotian feminists in reaction to the mass murder, a murder that was not at first understood as an act of misogyny, advocates called for an inquiry to examine what happened and insisted the inquiry include an explicitly feminist lens. "It is often wives, partners and children of men who kill who are their first victims," the letter read. "The sustained abuse and assaults they face are often the most obvious signs of the murderer's future mass violence."[21] While not specifically linked to the pandemic, the Nova Scotia mass murder put femicide and gendered violence into the national public spotlight and fuelled a general discussion about these topics in Canada. That this happened during the time of the pandemic tied this discussion to the gendered impact of the pandemic.

In the background of the gendered response to the pandemic, behind the bluster and benevolence of male politicians, there was very little being done to address the so-called shadow pandemic of domestic violence. Rates of domestic violence were on the rise even before March 2020, and COVID-19 exacerbated it.[22] Lockdowns were imposed at two speeds, either complete or partial, and both spelled danger for women already living in dangerous and violent situations. Domestic violence increased by double-digit percentages over the course of the pandemic and police reported an increase in responding to domestic violence calls.[23] So many low-income and no-income people being shut out of pandemic measures made it even more difficult for them to have the financial resources to be able to leave — if someone relied on their partner for all of their income, they would have been ineligible to receive CERB, for example. While shelters reported seeing a drop in clients during the first wave, numbers surged during the second.[24] Workers at gendered violence shelters and transition houses reported an overall increase in all forms of abuse, but especially violence.[25] In Québec, in the first six months of 2021 alone, there were 13 femicides. Feminists mobilized across the province demanding that more support and funding be flowed to give women the resources they need to escape violence.[26]

Marginalized women still experience higher rates of violence than white women, a key point that was usually written out of stories about gendered violence. Trans men, trans women and nonbinary people, especially if they are racialized, experience gendered violence at rates higher than cis women, data that was reinforced by a TransPulse Canada survey. The report, published in November 2020 using data from before the pandemic, concluded, "Overwhelmingly, racialized respondents reported high levels of discrimination, violence and assault, as well as anticipated and actual negative experiences with police and the legal system," a fact that made Québec's pandemic curfew and Ontario's stay-at-home orders even more dangerous for them.[27] And yet, journalists never teased out statistics, anecdotes or stories about trans or gender non-conforming people as they survived through the pandemic in stories about gendered violence. There were important regional differences that journalists rarely explicitly mentioned either. Rates of domestic violence in northern communities across the territories for both men and women were higher than in the South, while women were three times more likely to have experienced sexual violence.[28]

Shelters and transition houses had to manage servicing clients while also keeping everyone safe from COVID-19. As residential facilities, COVID-19 was most dangerous to them than any other kind of support service. A majority of these facilities reported having to reduce their services to meet public health protocols. This meant there was a reduction in available beds and shelters and transition houses had to seek units off-site to keep up with demand. In a survey conducted by Shelters Canada, 64% of the shelters and transition houses that responded used motel or hotel units for isolation, and 17% used off-site units that weren't in motels or hotels. The triple impact of increased costs, a lack of donations and reduced staffing due to child care and other pandemic-related needs of staff meant these facilities needed financial help to be able to manage the influx of users. The pandemic also reinforced the need for shelters and transition houses to have more private spaces for families even outside the pandemic — a need that comes with significant capital costs.[29] *Bay Today* reported that Suzanne Smoke, a counsellor for Indigenous women fleeing violence around the Parry Sound region of Ontario, said that she was seeing an increase in difficulty faced by Indigenous women, thanks both to the threat of losing their children if they report domestic violence and because shelters were overloaded during the pandemic. After being turned away from one shelter, a woman Smoke was assisting went to another one that denied care because she didn't live in the area. "Even though that's her homeland, that's her territory, that's where she comes from, because she was moved out of the area seeking safety, she no longer qualifies for services," Smoke said.[30]

The pervasiveness of gendered violence helped the issue receive high-profile media coverage throughout the pandemic, but this coverage didn't lead to enough increased supports for individuals in violent circumstances. Helping people flee gendered violence is expensive, and during the pandemic there should have been a blank cheque written to support services and survivors themselves. But the federal government only made $100 million available to fight gendered violence in 2020, including the $40 million first announced in 2020.[31] Gender Equality Minister Maryam Monsef said 1500 organizations received this money, which, if distributed equally, would only be about $66,666 per group. That would go very quickly for any organization with increased pandemic-related costs, paying for external spaces for clients to quarantine and a drop in fundraising or donations — to say nothing about necessary infrastructure repairs.[32] A majority of shelters built before 2012 — 193 in total — were in need of "major" repairs in 2019, according to the report.[33] Angela Marie MacDougall from the Battered Women's Support Services in Vancouver told *Global News* the funding has been insufficient, and "Canada has not prioritized the impact on women as part of the COVID-19 strategy."[34] To compare, groups representing women's shelters in Québec called for $77 million for Québec shelters alone to enable them to continue to serve clients at the start of March 2020, before it was clear that COVID-19 would exacerbate poverty and violence against women.[35]

Not only was the overall funding inadequate, there was also not enough critical attention from journalists on how it was doled out. Of the $100 million promised, only $1.1 million had been distributed to organizations in Yukon, Nunavut and the Northwest Territories, despite having higher rates of gendered violence than the rest of Canada.[36] Did shelters located in COVID-19 hotspots receive more money? And as the pandemic evolved, why was only intervention to combat gendered violence a meagre financial sum? What about changes in policies that could make it easier for someone to flee gendered violence, like breaks on rent, more personal income supplements or adding mandatory paid gendered violence leave into the Canadian Labour Code? After all, unions have been fighting this campaign for years. Why didn't journalists explore what it would take for governments to mandate food companies to donate food, products and personal protective equipment, or better yet, force them to hand over some of their profits to local initiatives to keep people safe as they escaped gendered violence?

In addition to the government inaction on gendered violence, the federal government also enacted policies that put women directly into harm's way. At the start of the pandemic, sex workers saw their incomes drop as a result of the fear of COVID-19 spread and lockdown measures in most of Canada. When the federal government excluded people who made less than $5000 in 2019 from CERB, it forced many sex workers to keep working as many could not apply for benefits. Jelena Vermilion from Hamilton's Sex Workers Action Program told CTV News that she feared increased violence and harassment toward sex workers forced to continue working because police powers had been heightened: "What's going to happen is they're going to be policed even more and liable to the new fines and potential jail time with the social distancing guidelines." When asked why her ministry had not provided direct aid to sex workers, a spokesperson for Monsef simply repeated the news of the $40 million they had committed to shelters, saying sex workers could access this money like everyone else.[37] None of it was directly targeted to sex workers' needs or safety.

Sex workers were clearly not a priority for government or for media. Even though sex work was a higher-risk profession during a pandemic, it was barely mentioned by politicians, and journalists rarely made a point of challenging them to do anything for sex workers. No governments made improvements to sex workers' material conditions after the first wave, even though it was clear the second wave was coming. When Québec imposed a near province-wide curfew in January 2021, anyone who worked in unofficial or underground work became the target of police harassment if they were caught on the street between 8:00 p.m. and 5:00 a.m. This put sex workers into an extremely precarious place, exposing many to increased gendered violence. In January 2021, sex workers and their advocates in Montréal reported seeing increased violence toward sex workers, including women who had gone missing and reports about sketchy individuals seemingly stalking sex workers. With police able to ticket anyone who was out at night, Jessica Quijano, coordinator of the Iskweu Project, told Ricochet, "Some of the women I work with, because of the curfew, are trading sex for a place to stay overnight." The Iskweu Project is a program of the Native Women's Shelter of Montréal that aims to intervene immediately when an Indigenous woman or girl goes missing.[38]

Rather than flowing resources directly to sex workers or pouring money into services and supports, sex workers were ignored — if mentioned at all, they were mostly relegated to stories about CERB.

The same forces that exacerbated other forms of inequality during the pandemic made it so much more difficult for women and nonbinary individuals as well: low-waged, precarious work and job loss both plunged families into untenable situations. Disabled people were ignored and forced to survive with very limited resources. Migrant workers were under incredible amounts of stress. Indigenous women living on reserves were contending with infection rates that were 40% higher than off reserves. The women and nonbinary individuals who found themselves in the crosshairs of this pandemic where often there due to their social location, their work, their ethnicity or their income. There should have been no surprise that the pandemic would have made worse all the ways in which women and nonbinary people are harmed in society. And yet, there was barely anything promised to help women exit dangerous situations, or even more importantly, avoid them altogether.

GOVERNMENT FAILURES

If women were struggling financially, economically and socially the most, then there should have been gendered measures implemented. But nowhere in Canada did that happen. The biggest aid programs did nothing to tackle systemic sexism and in fact exacerbated it. When the Canada Emergency Response Benefit (CERB) was announced, it was a universal amount for all people whose income fell within a particular range: not below $5000 in 2019 and not above $1000 per month. This disqualified the lowest-income Canadians, who were most likely to be women. While men's participation rate in the labour force is 91%, women's is 82%, meaning that CERB's requirement that individuals had worked in 2019 skewed toward benefiting men more than women.[39] Women at the head of single-parent households were particularly harmed. In 2009, Statistics Canada placed the net assets divide between single-parent households at a whopping $63,000 — women who were single parents had median net assets of $17,000 while single-parent men had net assets of $80,000. CERB was therefore a lifeline especially for single mothers, but also impossible to get if these people didn't make enough money in 2019 to qualify.[40]

For workers whose bosses decided to lay them off and pay them through CEWS, they would receive more money based on how much they made, thereby entrenching salary inequities. CEWS was intended to subsidize 75% of a workers' salary. If a man was paid more, the business would receive more money from government and the worker more aid. CEWS was a more generous funding program than CERB, and yet, it tethered aid to an employer's whim: aid was paid out as long as the employer kept applying for CEWS, which I explain in more detail in the chapter covering August 2020. It left workers in a tremendously precarious situation, and this precarity was especially bad for women workers.

When the CERB and CEWS were announced, journalists failed to explore the gendered impact of these programs. Journalists reported on what politicians had promised and did not examine either program through a gendered lens. Instead, women were relegated to two locations: either the victims of job losses or mothers who were struggling to get by. Stories about job losses rarely mentioned federal programs — if women were leaving the job market, were they also relying more on CERB? Instead, they focused on more rhetorical or moral arguments about why it was important for women to stay in the labour market, or fears that women's advancement was being set back a generation. Without tying job losses directly to the immediate support available, journalists were then also able to report on CERB without mentioning the disproportionate need that recently unemployed women had for CERB. The lack of pressure let the feminist government of Justin Trudeau off the hook.

Child care took centre stage during 2020 and 2021, though when journalists wrote about women through the frame of motherhood, it flattened the experience of being a parent into being a woman and took the place that journalists could have used to write about particular experiences of women who do not have children. To be sure, there was a lot to say about being a parent during the pandemic. Where single people had to navigate social isolation alone, parents had to navigate social isolation with one or several kids, a challenge that intensified with the number of kids, the lower in age the kids were, and how solid or shaky relationships were. The family stress of the pandemic was very well documented and widely reported. Journalists, many of whom had to continue their work from an ad hoc home office while also caring for children, had the issue front-of-mind. There were also important logistical challenges, like navigating the role of schools in perpetuating the spread of the virus, and how society should balance COVID-19 protections and school openings. But the problem with this singular frame is that women were reduced to mothers, even though a majority of women are not actively caring for children; it let politicians off the hook to develop a pandemic plan that specifically targeted the ways in which women were differently impacted by the pandemic, from higher rates of infection among racialized and/ or low-income women to supports that would help this group who had faced the worst of job losses.

At the beginning of the pandemic, when schools and daycares were shut down as part of lockdown measures, governments had to find a way to ensure some frontline workers could continue to work while their children were watched. Early emergency child-care measures created the instant public perception that the primary impact of the pandemic on women was lacking child care. When the Liberal government prorogued parliament in August 2020 to avoid criticism related to the WE Charity scandal, they knew they had to start the next parliamentary session with a big announcement that would curry favour with most voters. Despite rumours that it would be some kind of universal basic income, they settled on child care. Very quickly, the issue took off as the primary way to help women re-enter the workforce, aided by reports, such as the one from the Royal Bank mentioned earlier, that showed how job losses women experienced during the first wave had not been corrected as they had been for men. Child care did manage to turn media attention on the Throne Speech away from the inadequate measures the Liberals had promised for individuals — the most notable being their proposed changes to CERB — but it also allowed the Liberals to control the message: every future comment made about child care was a ready-to-publish story.

Child care was, of course, critical. But as a longer-term goal, it was hardly the most pressing way that the Liberals could have helped women. For one, struggling parents needed immediate support, and many who should have been able to access the federal benefits couldn't. Parents who had to transition either to parental benefits, or transition off parental benefits and onto CERB found themselves waiting for months before they got a single payment. In April 2020, the *Canadian Press* interviewed several expecting parents who had lost their jobs in March, applied for EI or CERB as they were told to, and then found they were ineligible because they also had to apply for parental benefits to be ready for the moment they gave birth, even if months away. Saying you were pregnant on the EI application was enough to disqualify many from accessing emergency benefits. Officials insisted this was just a bug related to how fast CERB was rolled out. The article goes on to say another bug, the one that required people to work a certain number of hours before receiving parental benefits, had also stopped some people from being able to access their full benefits due to having been laid off in March.[41] When the problem was still happening in June, government officials told the *Canadian Press* there was no simple fix, and Canadians would have to deal with the program hole a little longer.[42] By July, *Global News* reported that expecting parents were still struggling to make the threshold of hours and were subsequently being denied parental leave benefits as a result.[43] The problem was complicated only insofar as the government created a program that was unnecessarily restrictive: the interplay between benefit regimes was creating other problems, impacting expecting parents. Rather than making those parents the priority and flowing money to them, even if it meant some might receive an overpayment, it was more important for the government to ensure no one could receive aid from two government programs at the same time and no one would receive maternity benefits if they didn't work. This marginalizes poor women at the best of times, who are not eligible for parental benefits if their income or work hours are too low. But during the pandemic, parents who were already in a difficult situation would find themselves new mothers with no income to cover their basic needs.

These problems weren't resolved quickly. On September 27, more than six months into the pandemic, the government announced it would reduce the requisite hours to access EI parental benefits from 600 to 120, with the remaining 480 hours given to Canadians as a "one-time credit."[44] But for folks already stuck in the system, it was cold comfort. Three days later, CBC profiled two women who had still not received parental benefits, despite having given birth months earlier. Delays and complications with the program were blamed on CERB and the surge of work that government employees had faced.[45] The November economic update didn't promise to fix any of these issues. There was no new money to give to parents who were caught up in the bureaucratic mess of pre-pandemic programs colliding with pandemic programs. And while the financial update was supposed to be the moment the Liberals unveiled their spending plans for a new national child-care system, all they announced was the creation of an advisory committee. During 2021, the Liberals started to enter into some provincial agreements to start laying the foundation of a national system, but a federal election loomed large over the promise for national child care.

There is, of course, a direct line between the gendered impact of the pandemic and government refusal to enact gendered measures to mitigate these impacts. The child-care discussion took over the limited space available to talk about the gendered impact and politicians were simply not challenged to do more for women, especially women working as caregivers, healthcare workers, or in long-term care facilities. In the broad survey of media that I undertook to write this chapter, it was rare for journalists to bring racism into the question of the gendered impact in any meaningful way. But advocates were vocal. In May 2020, feminists in St. John's made five immediate demands to help ensure that a reopening plan for Newfoundland and Labrador could be equitable through a gendered lens. One of the calls included the need for a higher minimum wage, a demand that governments consistently resist.[46] In their report, *A Feminist Economic Recovery Plan for Canada*, the YWCA and researchers at the University of Toronto argued, "a truly feminist recovery will require tackling systemic racism, which results in Indigenous and Black communities being shuffled into low-income gigs and experiencing high poverty rates, and — in some cases — struggling to have even their most basic housing and clean water needs met." Released on July 28, 2020, the report featured 27 recommendations divided into eight categories, including implementing the recommendations from both the Truth and Reconciliation Commission and the Inquiry into Murdered and Missing Indigenous Women and Girls, changing the labour code and investing in good jobs.[47] Still, one *Global News* article on the report ignored all recommendations other than the ones related to child care, making the report look as if its principle recommendation was to support child care. Boiling down a systemic call for intersectional gender policies into child care was done consistently during the pandemic, erasing the diversity of demands coming from feminist advocates, and, again, essentializing womanhood as being solely in the service of parenthood.[48]

A Feminist Economic Recovery's recommendations should have informed government responses to the pandemic across Canada in the fall. But they didn't. They were barely mentioned in articles about the so-called she-covery or the gendered impact of the pandemic. In an op-ed written for Toronto's *Now Magazine*, NDP Member of Provincial Parliament Jill Andrew insisted the document should underpin the Ontario government's plan not just for recovery but also to mitigate what she guessed would be a serious second wave. Published on August 18, 2020, Andrew wrote,

Ontario needs an urgent intersectional feminist response from all governments to ensure our recovery centres the most marginalized. We must address systemic anti-Black and anti-Indigenous racism and make justice and equity a top priority for Ontario's post-pandemic recovery. We must strengthen our social safety net and recognize the gendered, racialized and classed impact COVID-19 has had on families first.[49]

Yet, just weeks after Andrew's article appeared, the second wave of COVID-19 ravaged Black and low-income communities in Toronto and was exacerbating the many inequalities that plague life in Canada. Governments had not listened.

The intersection of race and gender, the disproportionate impact of the pandemic on disabled women, the specific impact on racialized caregivers, especially Black caregivers — these are all obscured by turning the gendered impact into a story about motherhood and child care. COVID-19 was most deadly to Black women care workers of all workers who died. COVID-19 was most deadly to racialized workers who worked in precarious employment. Government responses to the clear gendered impact didn't attempt to remedy these structural inequities; rather, they adhered closely to the logic of woman as mother and woman as victim of a cruel job market, all while erasing, obscuring or downplaying the differential impacts that COVID had on different kinds of women.

THE DAD-PREMIER PHENOMENON

It's perhaps not surprising that government leaders didn't listen to the demands of feminist advocates. Feminism as a concept has had political currency, but it doesn't mix very well with the strongman approach to leadership that marked 2020 and 2021. All provincial premiers and the prime minister crafted a version of themselves as their own kind of strongman, rooted in one of two father archetypes. Both archetypes were premised on the belief that a strong pandemic response required a steady hand from a patriarch who was either kind and caring or a patriarch who was boisterous and angry. Caring dad and angry dad were not too different, always reminding us to follow public health orders to keep ourselves and others safe, while at the same time deflecting his own responsibility for not doing enough to contain the spread of COVID-19.

From the start of the pandemic, Québec Premier François Legault has been the best example of the calm, reassuring father. For most of 2020, when he hosted daily briefings, they always started with offering his condolences to the family members of people who had died, and he reassured Quebecers that as long as we obeyed the rules, we could get out of this pandemic together. His persona was that of *un bon père de famille,* an old legal term that refers to a steady and fair family head. Legault rarely lashed out at people, giving space for more flamboyant replies to journalists' questions to Québec's Director of Public Health Horacio Arruda. Legault's calm demeanour was a critical strategy: as Québec's deaths skyrocketed, Quebecers could be reassured they still had a steady, capable leader. His popularity even reached a record high: 51% of Quebecers said that they would vote for the CAQ in June 2020, even in the middle of confinement — a popularity number that had not been seen since Québec's political landscape only had two parties in it. That percentage had only dropped one point by the end of October.[50] His steady hand and tone didn't make up for criticisms of his style, though. *Journal Métro* asked several epidemiologists what they thought about how Legault handled the crisis, who gave him top marks for taking swift and decisive action in March at the start of the lockdown but then an average of 17.5 out of 25 points for his efficacy.[51]

Prime Minister Justin Trudeau and British Columbia Premier John Horgan took a similar track as Legault. In Trudeau's characteristically slow lilt, he constantly reminded Canadians that he would support and help them. His reassuring tones were most useful during the first weeks of the pandemic, when media outlets gave Trudeau full and uninterrupted live coverage, then dissected his comments immediately thereafter. When Sophie Gregoire Trudeau was diagnosed with COVID-19, it gave Trudeau the early opportunity to speak as a concerned husband and father. He understood this illness because it had struck so close to home. A CTV *News* article from March 12 about Sophie's positive COVID-19 result quoted Chrystia Freeland assuring Canadians that Trudeau was doing very well. They reported that she had spoken to Trudeau several times the night before and, "he sounded 'energetic as usual … he sounded fantastic. He is very much in charge'"[52] — again playing up the assuring and calming dad for a worried population. Horgan's approach was to also be a calm and reassuring father. His government put Health Minister Adrian Dix front-and-centre alongside their public health director Bonnie Henry for regular briefings. Henry became one of the few women heroes of the pandemic, inspiring memes and even a new line of shoes. On May 12, 2020, John Horgan told journalists he had been described as the province's dad, which prompted Richard Zussman from *Global News* to ask on Twitter if that then means Bonnie Henry is British Columbia's mom.[53]

The calm and reasoned *bon père de famille* approach of some leaders was one side of the patriarchy coin. Patriarchy relies on strong father figures to reassure a population that they're doing their best given the circumstances. Male politicians were able to take on these roles very easily, and while relying on advice from high-profile and colourful public health officers, they could calmly and firmly steer their populations through this storm. But there are two ways to be a premier-dad. The *bon père de famille* approach was not adopted by all premiers. On the other side of the coin were the leaders whose tough-talking approach to pandemic management came across more like angry dad than loving and worried dad. Nova Scotia Premier Stephen McNeil encapsulated this archetype well, when, as explained CTV *National News*' Lisa LaFlamme "the so-called covidiots made Nova Scotia's premier so angry, he said something, and it caught fire." When McNeil told Nova Scotians to "stay the blazes home," CTV journalist Todd Battis said, "to outsiders it must have sounded quaint, even corny like some type of rebuke from a 1950s TV dad. But Maritimers would understand the weight beyond those words."[54] Battis' description, a rebuke from an angry dad, perfectly captured McNeil's approach. McNeil told Nova Scotians to stay the blazes home on April 3, a time when the province had 207 confirmed COVID-19 cases. During the same press conference, he said, "I'm not trying to scare you, but part of me wishes you were scared," pleading with people to stay indoors. He complained that grocery stores, Walmarts and Tim Hortonses were full of people — a phenomenon that he could have put an end to by mandating capacity limits. But instead, he lectured Nova Scotians to stay home, as if work and other responsibilities would vanish thanks to a father's stern lecture.[55] When things started to improve for Nova Scotians in June, McNeil annoyingly told everyone to "get the blazes out there," as if COVID-19 could be controlled by individuals deciding to stay home or to go out alone.[56] If McNeil could have made COVID-19 go away by forcing you to smoke an entire pack to get the message, he would have done it.

Manitoba's Brian Pallister and Ontario's Doug Ford both took the same approach as McNeil, using bluster and angry comments directed at their populations as a key rhetorical tool to get people to comply with public health directives. Pallister routinely scolded Manitobans. On April 1, 2020, he called people who disobey rules "disrespectful," and then in a classic grandfatherly way brought up World War I and II:

> Understand that previous generations fought and gave up their lives to protect their fellow citizens ... Manitoba led the way in people volunteering for service in both the First (World) War and Second (World) War, young people did their part, they stood up and they did their part and you have the chance to do your part now.[57]

While the war metaphor was used a lot to describe the pandemic in 2020, Pallister took it up a notch, appealing to a spirit of responsibility that might lead someone to war. Such a patriarchal approach could only be authentically pulled off by an older white man who is appealing to a population's sense of soldier-esque duty. Ontario Premier Doug Ford played angry dad right out the gate of the pandemic too, responding to various public health challenges with anger rather than defending public health workers or promising to make things better. When asked about why Ontario was failing to meet its testing targets, Ford told journalists "my patience has run thin," as if he wasn't ultimately in charge of creating systems that would ensure Ontario could meet its testing capacity.[58] Ford called COVID-19 deniers "a bunch of yahoos," and he routinely admonished businesses who flouted public health orders.[59] He called the pandemic "a crappy situation," then immediately apologized but continued, "I think I've come up here a hundred times and said it's gunna bite us back in the butt if we don't tighten things up, so I just ask people, let's tighten it up."[60] He could have taken his own advice and tightened up emergency mandates in Ontario. But rather than tightening up his pandemic response, Ford appealed to individuals take personal responsibility to stop the spread of COVID-19.

In a feature on one of the American Sign Language interpreters who had been interpreting Ford's press conferences, Christopher Deslodges explained how he tried to convey the emotion in Ford's presentations through signing. He told the *Globe and Mail*, "Doug Ford over the last few days has been kind of ... taking the angry dad approach ... He held back, and then he let out. And to me that was the feeling that I was trying to capture to someone who can't hear."[61] Ford's body expression, his tone and his vernacular told Ontarians he's just like them: nervous parents, frustrated with the people who aren't following the rules, wishing this could end — all in a PR exercise to obscure that he had the power to do much more than he did throughout 2020 to stem the spread of COVID-19, including sitting on $9 billion in federal aid money that was intended to be spent on COVID-19 mitigation measures.

In a public health emergency that has had such an intense gendered and racialized impact, it is not a coincidence that white male premiers took on the dad persona to try and individualize how people responded to public health orders. Outbreaks within residential care and congregant settings could not be scolded back: scolding only served to place the blame on an individual who irresponsibly spread the infection, which then sadly made its way into a long-term care facility. Rather than pouring money into these facilities and forcing them to be more accountable, Ford actually limited facility owners' liability from impending lawsuits related to negligence in long-term care.[62] Brian Pallister was roundly criticized for not having done enough to stem the crisis, waiting until hospitalizations and ICU admissions reached record highs and positivity rates from testing surpassed 10% before banning social gatherings and restricting travel.[63] Scolding was not just inappropriate though; it actively made things worse. By blaming the spread of COVID-19 on a failure of personal responsibility, Pallister was off the hook to take his own personal responsibility seriously and enact measures that would have slowed the spread of COVID-19 in a more systemic way. CBC News talked to several experts in political science and communications who all thought Pallister's tone was not going to work. Kelly Saunders, a political science professor at Brandon University, said, "Instead of showing us the leadership that we need to see, he's instead turning to shaming Manitobans ... [it's] highly disappointing and I think very irresponsible.[64]

The angry dad approach harkened to another male archetype that dominated the world of pandemic management: the hypermasculine strongman. While few of the provincial premiers stylized themselves as hypermasculine strongmen, it was a motif that was never far from the surface. Writing for the London School of Economics blog, professor Georgina Waylen argued that the strongman approach shunned public health mitigation measures and capitalized on bluster and rhetoric to will the population to avoid COVID-19, and it had disastrous effects. While her article focused on U.K. prime minister Boris Johnson, she identified that Johnson was hardly alone in his approach: "[Johnson] shares characteristics with other right-wing populist leaders, including Narendra Modi in

India, Donald Trump in the United States, and Jair Bolsonaro in Brazil. Johnson's populist nativism is a white English nationalism, evoking a glorious Imperial past."[65] In Waylen's writing, there are echoes of Pallister's war nostalgia, Canada's version of its own 'white English nationalism, evoking a glorious Imperial past.' But there were material results from this hypermasculine bluster as well: people needlessly died. Waylen wrote,

> All these right-wing populist hypermasculine leaders performed poorly in their efforts to deal with the pandemic by refusing to take it seriously, continuing risk-taking behaviour, and delaying and undermining mitigation measures. Understanding what went wrong with the pandemic responses of leaders like Boris Johnson, with hypermasculine leadership styles, is an important part of avoiding similar disastrous mistakes in the future.[66]

Waylen's comments could be directly applied to the pandemic management styles of Alberta's Jason Kenney or Saskatchewan's Scott Moe, men who didn't exactly follow the premier-dad paradigm but who were indeed slow to enact measures when cases accelerated and quick to move away from COVID-19 mitigation policies, including mask wearing and confinement after a positive COVID-19 case. In the case of Saskatchewan, dropping these measures in July 2021 happened at the same time that Canada's worst COVID-19 outbreak was in northern Saskatchewan, a region that had been plagued with high case counts throughout the pandemic. The Athabasca Health Authority saw a 360% rise in COVID-19 cases from July 1 to July 31 2021 and the region was struggling with a healthcare worker shortage, low vaccination rates (almost a third of the population were too young to be vaccinated) and a lack of support from Regina.[67] Eighty percent of the authority's population's mother tongue is an Indigenous language, the vast majority of which is Dene. Whether a father figure or a strongman, the performance and the governance was always rooted in white supremacy.[68]

Just as women were often essentialized into the role of mother, the dad rhetoric, both angry and benevolent, painted the pandemic with a family brush where family members who break the rules need tough love, even scolding, to correct their behaviour. Hypermasculine responses around the world were replicated in Canada too. While the majority of us were doing our best, the father's role was to gently or angrily call out those flouting the rules so that together, we would get through this (and spare a thought for the dearly departed). This obscured that white male leadership was overseeing a crisis harming racialized communities the most, and their inaction effectively signalled their comfort with this pattern. Politicians knew journalists would mostly fail to compare this white-hetero-patriarchal governing style with the gendered and racialized impact of their inadequate policies. Missing this crucial lens was another media failure in translating the real story to Canadians: this rhetoric served to make things worse for most, reassuring only those who could reasonably imagine Ford, Legault, McNeil, Pallister and the rest as patriarchs in our own family. Angry or benevolent dad rhetoric was an insidious way in which the pandemic was able to get worse for some while getting better for others.

Many said the pandemic would set women's advancement back decades; the multiple forces that caused economic, social or physical harm to women and nonbinary people would undo years of feminist advances. But this kind of comment betrayed an incorrect assumption: COVID-19 wasn't a patriarchal force seeking to re-oppress the world's women. The pandemic simply operated within the same logic society did. It exposed cracks, heightened inequality and deepened marginalization. Politicians had the power to stop it and journalists had the responsibility to challenge them, but sadly, neither met these tasks. Politicians did the bare minimum for women, putting small amounts of money into shelters but refusing to give the poorest women any direct financial help. They did this by hiding behind an angrily or calmly disappointed father persona intended to shift blame onto the population: failing to stop the pandemic was ultimately our fault, not theirs. And by directing blame to us individually, politicians gave journalists the space to craft a narrative about how, ultimately, we are all responsible for our own health and well-being, regardless of how our identities intersect with political or economic oppression.

The pandemic should have been a moment not just for radical discussion about how to break from the status quo, but for politicians to finally take action to do so. But media did not lean on politicians to do this. Journalists individualized coverage about gender by highlighting an individual's plight, asking for comment from a feminist organization and maybe explaining how government had failed parents. With this being the dominant way that gendered issues were told by journalists, the cadre of premier-dads in charge of Canada would never budge on these issues in any meaningful way. But in the large mass of "woman" — the differentiations within which were rarely interrogated by journalists — disabled women, especially racialized disabled women, found themselves with the least support and the least attention. Disability was probably the most important frame through which to see the pandemic, as disabled people were more likely to get COVID-19 and die. Yet, contrary to the significant attention that journalists paid to select gendered issues during the pandemic, disabled people of all genders bore the brunt of the pandemic's violence.

January 2021
DISABILITY ERASED AND DISTORTED

Cases: 586,425
Deaths: 15,714[1]

There was little question that the pandemic would impact women, but politicians and journalists collapsed women into a single identity, rarely mentioned in relation to their economic location or ability. This hid the fact that disabled women were made to be more vulnerable in so many different ways. Just as disability was erased from the discussion about the gendered impact of COVID-19, disability was consistently erased and ignored by politicians and journalists alike. Politicians ignored disabled people's demands for COVID-19 protections and financial supports, and journalists rarely covered stories that explicitly examined disability and how it interacted with poverty, COVID-19 infection rates, job losses, gender, race or anything else.

Erasing disabled people didn't make sense from a moral perspective, but it made even less sense from a practical perspective. Nearly one-quarter of Canadians have a disability. Among disabled people were folks who had the most experience with infection control, with what works and what is broken within the medical system and how to survive a major event that changes life dramatically. By January 2021, Canadians were starting a new year with the same problems. Pandemic fatigue had firmly set it. When the ball dropped on New Years Eve, our passage from one year to the next was more meaningless than usual. The pandemic was still there.

Holly Witteman, a disabled professor at Université Laval, tweeted about pandemic fatigue just as the second wave was starting. She wrote,

> I am hearing talk of "pandemic fatigue" in media pieces and I wonder if it might be helpful for such discussion to include people with chronic illnesses and disabilities. Decades of chronic illness or disability provides expertise in dealing with similar kinds of

fatigue. I see parallels in having to do special things to function or stay alive, wanting a break but never getting one, etc.[2]

Her wisdom felt especially necessary staring down a new year with the same old pandemic. But by January 2021, it was still very rare to hear disabled voices in media. Their expertise would never get top billing by any media outlet, and no government created a disability support program the likes of which had been called for by disability activists.

Politicians had ignored calls from disability activists to help disabled people get through the pandemic and media's complete lack of analysis through a disability lens or featuring disabled people meant the people who were most at risk of dying from COVID-19 would also be heard from the least. In fact, disability was erased from the conversation. Instead, age became the factor most journalists focused on when it came to reporting on COVID-19 death and infection rates. When "comorbidity" appeared as a popular term, it was rare that journalists or politicians would explain what a comorbidity meant from a disability perspective, instead allowing it to transform into a vague explanation or even justification for someone's death. Disabled people were not represented in discussions about the pandemic, despite the fact that, as Witteman tweeted, they could offer some of the most incisive and compelling instruction for how to live through the pandemic. In the lack of representation, there was little attempt to explain or call out the ways in which jurisdictional issues often left disabled people out of the little amounts of aid that did exist. One kind of disability did get a lot of coverage — mental disability — through constant media attention that individualized and isolated issues related to mental health during the pandemic, rarely advocating for or demanding fundamental changes that would have improved access to services.

JONATHAN

In a makeshift cage at the National Assembly in Quebec City, Jonathan Marchand called on the Québec government to finally do something about inadequate living conditions within Québec's long-term care facilities, Centre d'hébergement et de soins de longue durée (CHSLD). It was August 2020, and Québec's deadly first wave had come and gone. Marchand, 43, lives with muscular dystrophy and was demanding a meeting with Premier François Legault. He lived at CHSLD Sainte-Anne-de-Beaupré and was one of about 3000 Quebecers under the age of 65 who live in these assisted living residences, mostly associated with elderly disabled people.[3] By the time Marchard spent August 12, his first night of many, in his makeshift shelter, the Institut national de santé publique du Québec (INSPQ) estimated that 3937 people had already died in Québec's CHSLDs.[4] Flanked by signs that said "imprisoned in a CHSLD" and "rights, not charity," Marchand's message was simple: stop warehousing people with disabilities in CHSLDs and give us access to what we need to survive at home.[5]

Marchand's protest didn't end with meeting Legault. Government officials that oversee Québec's system of CHSLDs agreed to create a group to study Marchand's concerns, a concession that Marchand characterized as leaving the door open to more changes rather than actually making changes. But as the second wave picked up in Québec, the plight of disabled Quebecers was swept aside for stories about public health directives and COVID-19 spread in schools and workplaces. Upon his return to CHSLD Sainte-Anne-de-Beaupré, Marchand told *Radio-Canada* he would not give up his fight to have access to services that would allow him to return home and live with his family. "I spent five days outside. Five nights too. I was in the community. I had the feeling of really living," he told journalist Alexandre Duval. This was just a few days after his protest and his sights were set on having the resources to be able to leave the CHSLD before Christmas.[6]

By December 8, Duval reported that Marchand was losing hope. The local health authority could not meet his demands: the pandemic had caused a staffing crisis that made it impossible for them to be able to meet his needs in a home-care setting, they said. They had offered to move him to another a CHSLD downtown. He refused, saying the only option was to give him more power over his own life.[7] The barriers to being able to live at home, from financial to legal, had created a system where institutionalization is one of the only options for adults with complex disabilities. While the unacceptable living conditions in these facilities pre-date the pandemic, this health crisis exposed just how dangerous these congregant living situations can be. Marchand was not alone in his struggle. The Disability Justice Network of Ontario condemned the inadequate living conditions of residential care facilities. In February 2021, they called on politicians and journalists to pay attention to the unacceptable living conditions so common for adults living in assisted living facilities:

> While fires, rats, financial abuse, resident deaths, and neglect
> have run rampant in these institutions for years, municipal and

provincial governments have ignored the pleading of city councillors, ministerial committees and coroners inquests ... Under
these conditions it is difficult to control the spread of COVID-
19, yet disabled people confined within these institutions were
exempt from priority vaccination status. This recent outbreak
at the Edgewood Care Centre is evidence of this — it is a 130
person privately operated institution, wherein 27% of residents
contracted COVID-19 and 1 person died.[8]

The death at Edgewood in Ottawa wasn't the only case of a disabled adult
dying from COVID-19 from an infection acquired within a residential
care facility, but there were no national statistics maintained publicly that
showed how many had died. In Ontario, at least 70 residents of facilities
for disabled adults died from March 2020 to June 2021. Among the 53
residents of the Northwood facility in Halifax, the site of that province's
worst outbreak, was 37-year-old Derrick Carvery. The next youngest
victim of the outbreak was 66.[9] Researcher Megan Linton uncovered that
18 disabled adults died in Manitoba as a result of COVID-19 they acquired
either in a day program or a residential facility. All that was known about
how disabled adults managed within residential care facilities was what
journalists could glean from bits of information here and there. Thanks to
research done by Linton, I could track the 70 residents with information
from three Ontario ministries and the City of Toronto, obtained through
questions asked by the opposition NDP and media inquiries to double
check and then update the information given in the Legislative Assembly.[10]

Disabled people living in residential care had to loudly assert their
voices to pierce mainstream discussions about the pandemic, despite being
the people most impacted by COVID-19. Marchand needed to move into a
cage for five days to get journalists to talk about life within a CHSLD from
the perspective of a young person who potentially faces decades of living within the public care home network. Amid the fog of the pandemic,
journalists and politicians ignored disabled people, despite this group
being most impacted by COVID-19 as well as the population with the most
experience and expertise in how to survive a devastating and life-altering
medical event. Ableism, compounded by racism, marginalized disabled
voices even more, and it put their lives in extreme danger.

IGNORING DISABILITY

In a major global crisis that impacted disabled people far more than it impacted anyone else, disabled people should have been front-and-centre: from job supports to housing, from essential work to income supplements, from vaccines to food security, from analysis to advocacy, there was no group more impacted than disabled people. And as such, there should have been no other group that got as much attention as disabled people during the pandemic. But this was the greatest failure of both politicians and journalists as they explained the pandemic in their respective ways: disabled people were almost entirely absent from every political discussion. This absence wasn't merely a lack of attention or resources. It was intentional; a cruel, glaring example of how ableism in Canadian society works. Even if they were more impacted by COVID-19 than anyone, there was no attempt from any politician to place disabled people at the centre of their COVID-19 response. Neither was there any attempt to place disabled people at the centre of media stories. They were silenced, obscured, ignored and intentionally forgotten.

In one of the few articles from the early days of the pandemic that centred disabled Canadians, Michelle McQuigge from the *Canadian Press* examined how disabled Canadians were experiencing the pandemic, emergency measures and lockdown. It was March 18, 2020; the economy was gradually closing down and Canadians everywhere were reading what they could find to learn about this new virus. That is, if it was available in a format that they could read. The format of documents or presentations provided by governments were not always accessible. McQuigge wrote that a consortium of deaf and hard-of-hearing Canadians had been lobbying to ensure that live briefings from the federal government be simultaneously interpreted in American Sign Language and Québec Sign Language. By that point, their briefings were not interpreted live and neither were many provincial or local government briefings, leaving 365,000 Canadians without the opportunity to understand the daily government briefings that came to define daily life under the first lockdown. For example, Karen McCall, who is blind, could not read the advice published by the Ontario Ministry of Health to avoid COVID-19, as it was not in a format that was compatible with her screen-reading technology.[11] Access to information at a time when the news was changing so quickly became a barrier for people who could not access information that wasn't put out in accessible formats — threatening to further marginalize many Canadians.

There were so many ways in which disabled people faced the worst of isolation during the first lockdown. From programs being cancelled to widespread masking that made it impossible to read lips, the rapid and blanket economic shutdown did not consider the needs of disabled people. And no governments made any significant effort to try and protect the locations offering community supports, which might have been able to continue. The combination of lack of information, data and political will to truly close things down in a way that could help create some locations where people could still access day programming or other services, meant that disabled people lost activities or services they relied on.

For some people, services were cut or strained due to changes within hospital systems that prioritized clearing space for COVID-19 patients. An already overburdened healthcare system, plus widespread anxiety about going to the hospital in case there was COVID-19 circulating, meant routine healthcare for many Canadians was no longer possible. At Participation House in Markham, an outbreak tore through the facility and infected 40 of 42 residents and dozens of staff. Seven residents died.[12] Residents of Participation House live in individual rooms grouped into pods, each with a common space. During March 2020, personal care workers were not limited to a single pod: over the course of a shift, they would move through various pods giving care to residents. It was a set up that was dictated by a lack of funding: Participation House didn't have enough money to hire enough personal support workers (PSWs) to work in a team and stay with a single pod of residents. As a result, workers had close contact with multiple residences in different pods, thereby allowing infection to spread more easily.[13]

After COVID-19 was detected within a facility, the most common, immediate action taken by staff within residential care was to isolate residents. This created confusion and made isolation even worse for the residents of these facilities. Disabled children and adults living in congregate care settings were ignored completely, plunging families into despair and forcing facilities to interpret policy directives without extra funding.[14] Pamela Libralesso's son, a bright and active 14-year-old who lives in a group home in Barrie, Ontario, couldn't see his parents for a staggering six months because of the Ontario government's group home COVID-19 policies. Even once he had been vaccinated against COVID-19, the restrictions that remained in place were more severe than elderly residents of long-term care. Her son wasn't even vaccinated as part of a congregant care home strategy: Libralesso had to arrange for him to have his vaccine herself. She challenged the parental visits rule at the Ontario Human Rights Tribunal and won her right to see her son.

With no plan to help combat the situation of isolation in which many disabled people found themselves, isolation wasn't relegated solely to people who lived in residential care. People who relied on day programs to socialize and keep active were isolated too. On April 6, 2020, CBC *News* featured Cameron and Cindy Ramage. Cameron was 22, living with cerebral palsy and unable to go to the day program he would typically attend. COVID-19 restrictions also meant that respite care was reduced, so Cindy became Cameron's primary aide. Cindy said Cameron's mood had changed when the program ended, and it made him very sad to have lost it because of the pandemic. Could this have been avoided, or was it unavoidable considering the multiple risk factors? In the same article, Krista Carr from the Canadian Association for Community Living said she knew of some cases where support workers didn't have adequate PPE, and families were removing their loved ones from these programs for fear of infections.[15] Protecting and supporting disabled people and their families might not have made it possible for programs to have run completely as usual, but extra funding and supports could certainly have helped improve some of the most isolating and marginalizing experiences of the first part of the pandemic.

Not only were many disabled people excluded from accessing information, their families or their regular supports, they were also shut out of most of the federal government's massive aid package. Canada's principle financial benefit, the Canada Emergency Response Benefit (CERB), was only available to individuals who had made more than $5000 in 2019. There was a special allowance given to students with disabilities or dependents, which increased the four-week student sum from $1250 to $2000. But otherwise, there was no aid for disabled people who were not working or whose income was too low or too high. On October 30, 2020, the government disbursed a one-time $600 payment to disabled Canadians who were eligible, an amount so low that it was an insult.

Even though journalists and politicians ignored disability, disability was talked about a lot. It was just couched in different terms. The way in which the disease was described was deeply ableist and journalists and politicians regularly indicated that people should be more or less concerned about COVID-19 depending on how far from "healthy" they found themselves.

Rather than discussing disability directly, the word comorbidity stood in as a descriptor, an explainer and even a justification for why some people died from COVID-19 and some did not. And then, when people who were "healthy" died from COVID-19, journalists paid special attention to their cases, signalling to the population that on the hierarchy of who was most at risk, the folks who had more comorbidities should have taken more care. Except there was no special care given to these individuals, and so as medical terms swirled above the discussion, disabled people who had comorbidities had the lion's share of the responsibility to keep themselves safe from COVID-19 with few to no resources to be able to actually do this.

TURNING DISABILITY INTO COMORBIDITY

COVID-19 was disproportionately impacting disabled elderly people, but disability itself was rarely mentioned. Instead, public health officials, politicians and journalists alike focused on age or if they were residents of long-term care facilities. There was no coordinated effort to protect disabled people, to flow more money, PPE or resources toward them. From early on, journalists and politicians knew COVID-19 was more deadly for people who had "comorbidities." The medical term comorbidity became popularly used and in so being used, immediately injected into the conversation an ableist frame that implied people who didn't have one or more underlying health conditions had little to worry about from the virus. This created two classes of people: those who could be less worried about COVID-19 and those who needed to be extremely worried about it. As stories emerged of people who didn't have any underlying health issues being walloped by COVID-19, journalists would tell their story through the lens of surprise. There were hundreds of examples of this happening, like this headline from CBC: "45-year-old Ontario farmer is among the young and healthy being devastated by COVID-19,"[16] or "B.C. family still searching for answers to how healthy 46-year-old dad died of COVID-19."[17] Despite the fact that it was clear by 2021 that some people died from COVID-19 who did not have comorbidities, journalists still framed stories of "healthy" individuals getting COVID-19 as if there was an answer to "search" for to explain how the virus ended up taking their loved one's life. Journalists didn't report a similar search undertaken by family of the tens of thousands who died and who did have a comorbidity.

Before March 2020, the word *comorbidity* was mostly used by journalists as medical jargon. A comorbidity is an underlying health issue that might become relevant when another circumstance arises: a new injury, a new medical treatment, a new diagnosis and so on. Depending on who is using it, it could mean anything from smoking to having had a stroke. With so much of COVID-19 messaging driven by public health officials who were doctors, it was not too surprising that by March, the word was creeping into more mainstream use.

While not everyone who has a comorbidity is disabled, there is significant overlap of individuals who are disabled and individuals who have one or many comorbidities. Canada didn't collect information specifically on disabled people, but comorbidity announcements became more and more common as the pandemic went on. Alberta was the only province that announced whether or not someone had comorbidities with every single death. Over the first 18 months of the pandemic, Alberta reported that 76.6% of those who died had three or more comorbidities, a proxy measure of disability. Of the Albertans with three or more chronic health issues who caught COVID-19 and who did not die, just 4.6% experienced non-severe symptoms. Of the conditions tracked by the Alberta government, hypertension was most common, with 84.3% of people who died from COVID-19 having it. Cardiovascular diseases and dementia were both just over and under 50%, followed by renal diseases, diabetes, respiratory diseases, cancer, stroke, liver diseases and immune-deficiency diseases.[18]

While many of these comorbidities are linked to age, they are linked to other characteristics too. For example, the Canadian Cardiovascular Society's guidelines for heart failure risk among different populations warns that South Asians have a higher risk of early death from coronary heart disease. They write that Black Americans have higher rates of heart failure than any other group — Black Americans develop symptoms of heart failure at an average age of 39, and at 20 times the rate of white people. Indigenous people have a higher frequency of cardiovascular disease than do European-descended white Canadians.[19] These facts demonstrate that targeted, race-based interventions through a disability lens were critical. Poverty is also positively associated with poorer health outcomes, making the stat that 70% of adults with intellectual disabilities live in poverty absolutely scandalous.[20] By ignoring disability and remixing it into comorbidity, journalists hid the fact that illness and disability have a very close relationship to white supremacy and colonization. Just as racism was a deciding factor in how COVID-19 spread and who was infected, there was no opening to have this discussion publicly, or force politicians to engage with it either. The ways in which social factors exacerbate illness and disability should have been at the fore of how governments managed the pandemic and how journalists wrote about the pandemic. The fault here was shared: public health officials should have talked far more about disability rather than relying on comorbidity as a descriptor, politicians should have stopped ignoring disabled people and journalists should have explained the connection between these terms.

The silence around targeted interventions for anyone with a comorbidity was absolutely indefensible. It was clear from the beginning that COVID-19 hit people with comorbidities harder than people without them. In early March 2020, Diagnostic and Interventional Cardiology published a feature on what was known about COVID-19 based on China's experience. They wrote,

> Published case reports from the Chinese Centers for Disease Control indicate patients with underlying comorbid conditions have a heightened risk for contracting COVID-19 and a worse prognosis; depending on the report, between 25% and 50% of COVID-19 patients present with underlying conditions.[21]

The figures from the Chinese Center for Disease Control and Prevention in March provided a useful guide for doctors around the world about what to expect and, critically, how to prepare to keep individuals safe. One year after this article was published, in Alberta, the number of people who had at least one comorbidity and who died was a stunning 95.4%.[22]

This information should have immediately oriented Canada's COVID-19 response to protect anyone with an underlying health condition. And yet, there was nothing done specifically to help these people. Even worse, by this time politicians and journalists were engaged in debates about who deserved to access a vaccine first, and it was only thanks to disability advocates that disabled people were even kind of considered as part of these plans. Krista Carr told CBC News Network that one study showed that people with intellectual disabilities were four times more likely to be hospitalized with COVID-19 and ten times more likely to die, a statistic that never was referenced in the daily death total updates from anywhere in Canada. Carr was relying on international data because Canada didn't pay attention to the connection between disability and severe COVID-19 outcomes beyond comorbidities.[23] Because comorbidity took the place of disability but wasn't a perfect proxy, Canadians had to look abroad get the best idea of how COVID-19 was impacting disabled people. In the U.K., by February 2021, data was indicating that disabled people were being killed by COVID-19 at alarming rates, and death rates were higher the more serious a disability was. The Office for National Statistics had showed that in 2020, disabled people accounted for six out of every ten deaths from COVID-19.[24]

Knowing that people who had comorbidities were at higher risk of severe outcomes if they caught COVID-19 should have triggered politicians and journalists to pay close attention to Canadians who have underlying medical conditions. Except they often had the least control over their own health. People living in residences were at the whim of the people who managed the facility: they were sometimes wholly dependent on them to make the best decisions possible. But with no national standards, no real provincial effort to intervene in residential care, hundreds of thousands of people were abandoned, either confined to a residence room or left without services or support during this uncertain time.

Comorbidity had a very important rhetorical impact: to a lay audience, it sounded like morbidity — death. It didn't matter that this was not what the term meant; it packed a silent punch that primed people to accept death as an inevitable outcome, which in turn allowed politicians off the hook for their inadequate policies. Politicians and journalists always targeted this messaging toward white, middle class, able-bodied cis people who were more likely to have the kind of power over their own lives to stay safe. Even though they did not have as much power as Canada's wealthy elite, this population segment had a significant amount of political power to punish or reward politicians, especially if they had loved ones who lived in residential care. In Québec, no one could adequately explain why, in the province with the highest number of deaths, Premier François Legault remained Canada's most popular premier by far. After years of stories of horrific conditions within CHSLDs, death was the assumed outcome. Dying from COVID-19 simply changed the cause of an inevitable death, and because of this, Legault's policies were insulated from criticism.

Disabled activists across North America challenged these narratives, though. While their voices were ignored or overlooked by journalists, through podcasts, social media and independent media, they sounded the alarm every time a conversation happened that suggested healthcare be doled out differently if someone had an underlying medical condition. And as data emerged that people dying from COVID-19 overwhelmingly had comorbidities, no government took specific action to intervene to give people with comorbidities more supports and resources. In an essay for the series *Dispatches from the Pandemic*, Faye Ginsburg, Mara Mills and Rayna Rapp argued,

> At the onset of the pandemic, disability activists challenged the flawed logic of mainstream pundits who proclaimed that only older and disabled people would die from COVID-19, suggesting that younger and non-disabled people need not fear, or contribute to general social precautions. Sunaura Taylor, for one, argues:
> "The conditions that make someone more vulnerable to COVID-19 are of course intimately tied up with poverty, environmental racism, and inadequate healthcare. Thus while such a sentiment is unabashedly ableist — should we mourn the lives of the healthy and robust more than the lives of the ill and disabled? — it is also deeply racialized, a message to America's white middle class that they have no need to panic."[25]

The same message existed in Canada too. In a Twitter thread that connected comorbidity to disability, activist Gabrielle Peters called *CTV News* out for not once using the word "disability" in an article titled "Dementia, Alzheimer's most common comorbidities associated with COVID-19 deaths: StatCan." She tweeted, "I'll just be over here in a permanent state of rage remembering all the ways the municipal, provincial and federal governments talked about just about every other possible demographic BUT disabled people."[26] Both Taylor and Peters argued that not only was it ableist to ignore the message but it was also racist, underlining the ways in which disability, illness, colonization and racism intersect in Canada with explosive violence.

Social and structural factors related to systemic racism play a big role in comorbidities. Food insecurity, for example, leads to higher rates of chronic illness, including hypertension, heart disease and diabetes, and the higher likelihood of having multiple chronic health issues, all comorbidities listed by the government of Alberta. People who are food insecure also have shorter life expectancies. With all the talk of comorbidities, why didn't media and politicians examine the cause of so many of the comorbidities and offer Canadians what they needed to keep themselves healthy during a health crisis? For example, they could have provided free food for anyone who was food insecure and isolating at home, especially since almost 20% of people who are the most food insecure are people whose incomes are less than $10,000 annually. In that group, people were unable to qualify for CERB because their income was too low. So government policy intended to help lower-income people get through the pandemic actively refused to help people who had chronic health issues related to food insecurity by giving them direct access to free, healthy food.[27] It would have lessened the impact of the pandemic to address these social and structural forces and individual need for services and aid. But how easy was it to get healthy food within a public retirement residence in Québec? How expensive was rent in a for-profit facility in Saskatchewan? For people living with illness and/or disability who did not live in a residential facility, what did they need? Did anyone care about these questions? Was anyone even listening to their demands? Why were their voices relegated to blogs and social media rather than directly quoted and influencing how the pandemic was covered? The voices of disabled people were rarely highlighted by politicians or journalists, who for much of the pandemic were driven by the daily statistics of who was sick, who was in the ICU, who was dying — always talking about them and rarely hearing their voices directly.

REPRESENTATION

On March 16, 2020, the CBC podcast *Front Burner* interviewed Andrew Gurza, a disability advocate and podcaster. The episode looked at social distancing — at that time a concept that was still new and bizarre — and how people with disabilities were navigating the pandemic. Gurza has cerebral palsy and told host Jayme Poisson about how afraid he was: the CDC had listed cerebral palsy as a condition that could result in a more severe COVID-19 infection. Gurza told Poisson that in many ways, he felt safer at home. "Many people who go into the hospital who are disabled don't receive the best care because many healthcare systems don't know how to navigate disability," he said. Gurza was far more concerned about going to the hospital and dealing with an overloaded system that would be even less likely able to care for someone with complex disabilities than he was of dying from a COVID-19 infection. He argued that Prime Minister Trudeau needed to talk far more about people who were most at risk: the elderly and people who are immunocompromised and/or disabled. While Gurza was worried for himself, he hoped the pandemic would be a moment where all Canadians could see what disabled people had been demanding for a long time: accommodations and barrier-free access, from using more accessible technology or formats to identifying systemic problems within all systems, including healthcare.[28]

But interviews like the one with Gurza were rare in mainstream media during the pandemic. And rarer still were policies that came from these kinds of discussions that could have made improvements to services or the quality of life for disabled people in Canada. When CBC *News Network*'s Natasha Fatah asked Krista Carr why disability had been so ignored, Carr, whose organization works with people labelled with intellectual disabilities, was frank. "People with disabilities are never prioritized. They are 22 percent of the Canadian population and they seem to be at the bottom of the list for everything."[29]

Alice Wong was one high-profile disabled writer, whose writing online and on social media continuously reminded readers to listen to disabled people. Not doing so, she argued in one piece for *Vox*, could end up becoming a modern eugenics program. Wong took aim at the early discussions happening across the U.S. about how to judge whose life was worth more if a strained healthcare system meant stretched resources. Wong uses a ventilator to help her breathe and is the editor of *Disability Visibility: First-Person Stories from the Twenty-First Century*. She wrote,

> Were I to contract coronavirus, I imagine a doctor might read my chart, look at me, and think I'm a waste of their efforts and precious resources that never should have been in shortage to begin with. He might even take my ventilator for other patients who have a better shot at survival than me. All of these hard choices doctors have to make primarily hurt those hit hardest, not the people who present as worthy investments of scarce resources. Who gets to make these hard choices and who bears the brunt of them is a matter of inequality and discrimination toward protected classes.[30]

Underpinning Wong's writing was the fact that disabled people were experts in many of the issues that society at large were now grappling with. The experts who navigated insufficient systems and kept one another safe knew what needed to be fixed. The experts who provided mutual aid to care for one another, sheltered from the daily harms and indignities that an ableist system routinely delivers. The experts who knew how to do these things and still find joy, solidarity and community. Wong continued,

Vulnerable "high-risk" people are some of the strongest, most interdependent, and most resilient people around. We may still face significant disparities in political power, which results in being left out of policymaking, but we know how to show up for each other. Disabled communities, queer communities, and communities of color have been hustling and providing mutual aid since time began. Many of us know the safety net has gaping holes and the state will not save us, so we're going to save ourselves with abundance, wisdom, joy, and love.[31]

Imagine how different Canada's pandemic response would have been if disabled people and people with chronic health issues were seen as experts and given access to resources to implement the changes they knew were necessary? How many lives would have been saved?

A few days after the *Front Burner* interview with Gurza, *Sins Invalid* published a list of ways disabled people were managing the pandemic. The disability justice performance project introduced the list like this:

In some ways, it isn't so different from how many of us live our lives every day as crips, with long stretches of time at home, limited access to community or touch or social engagement, engaging in mutual aid, sharing meds & home remedies. Many of us who are immunocompromised/suppressed or chemically injured have had to think about how many people we will encounter on any given day, what that will expose us to, and how it could impact our health. It's an irony that the whole world is talking about and problem solving with us now. It's painful that able bodied/minded people evidence their ableist privilege with frustration that air travel is inaccessible, that their schedules are impacted by others' schedules, that they can't do their normal social routines … Welcome to our world![32]

That comment — welcome to our world — had a very wise underlying message: if you want to know how to survive (and even thrive) during this moment, you'd better listen to disabled people and, more importantly, give them the power to implement programs and services.

Yet, politicians did not seek out the opinions of disability activists with the intention of implementing bold and life-saving policy. Residential facilities were mostly left alone to manage the pandemic themselves, resulting in nearly 18,000 dead. Rather than listening to disability groups the way the federal government did to the Canadian Federation of Independent Business (CFIB) — for example, where CFIB demands were regularly adopted by government — the federal government created their own committee of disability representatives to offer advice to the government. On April 10, 2020, Disability Inclusion Minister Carla Qualtrough announced she had formed a disability committee to, "ensure they're included in national efforts to respond to the crisis."[33] The committee met several times from April to August 2020 and developed 21 recommendations for the Government of Canada. They included calls for more income supports, to establish accessible communications guidelines across federal departments, ensure access to PPE (including transparent masks) and develop public health guidelines for congregant living settings similar to what already existed for long-term care. There was also a recommendation for the government to re-examine Bill C-7, changes to Medical Assistance in Dying legislation, "in light of strong evidence of medical ableism that has come to light during the pandemic."[34] By February 2021, no new financial supports had been promised and most of the recommendations were unfulfilled. The recommendation to re-examine Bill C-7 didn't seem to reach the government, who was committed to rushing through an amended Bill C-7 that had been fundamentally expanded by the Senate to allow for medical assistance in death even when death was not imminently foreseeable and where the only underlying health condition was mental illness. Disability justice groups panned this draft legislation, which still passed its final House of Commons vote the night of March 11, 2021. Qualtrough voted in favour.[35] Aside a $600 cheque sent to Canadians who received the Disability Tax Credit, the Veteran Affairs Disability Benefit or disability payments under either the Canada or Québec pension plans, the rest of the federal government's aid went to agencies who support people with disabilities.[36] Most notably, disabled people who did not make $5000 in 2019 received nothing from CERB. The Canadian Association for Community Living called on the government to eliminate the minimum so anyone could have been eligible for CERB.[37]

Qualtrough's disability advisory committee summary mentioned a consistent problem: federalism. Many of the issues they identified as important, like hospital visitation, were outside of the scope of the federal government.[38] This meant two things: one, the responsibility the federal government had to give disabled people money directly, as one of the ways it could help people within its scope, was even more important. Its refusal to give money to disabled people beyond a single $600 cheque was a massive failure. Two, the ability of the committee to make radical recommendations that the federal government could implement was limited from the start. In a *Canadian Press* article from April 2020 when the committee was established, David Lepovsky, a well-known disability rights activist, warned that this would be the limit of the federal committee's work:

> Only provincial governments can take 95 per cent of the action people with disabilities desperately need to avert the disproportionate hardships that the COVID-19 crisis inflicts on them, including the horrifying risk that their disability could be used as a reason to deny them medical services during rationing ... We're disproportionately vulnerable to get this disease, to suffer its harshest impacts and then to slam into serious barriers in our healthcare system.[39]

Aside from Michelle McQuigge's reporting for the *Canadian Press*, there was very little written about this committee or their recommendations. That meant there were very few locations for journalists to examine the interplay between jurisdictions and whether these issues caused even more harm to individuals. There was more coverage about how much the one-time disability payment would cost the federal government than there was about the struggles faced by people with disabilities living through a pandemic, for whom there was no more direct aid than just $600. One *Canadian Press* story in December 2020 about the one-time payment, which ran across multiple news organization platforms, included the $792 million expense in its headline and the first sentence, focusing solely on the parliamentary budgetary officer's report rather than examining how little help disabled Canadians had received.[40] In November 2020, *iPolitics'* Jolson Lim reported that Qualtrough was frustrated by her government's inability to get money to disabled people, and felt that "too few" Canadians with disabilities actually received the benefit. While flowing money to the provinces to give money directly to people receiving disability benefits was an option, Krista Carr from Inclusion Canada worried that money would just be clawed back from provincial program, leaving disabled Canadians no better off.[41]

The constitution got in the way of a lot during the pandemic. It was used as the Liberal excuse for not creating a national pharmacare program despite having promised to create one years earlier; in matters of healthcare, provinces and the federal government used the constitution as an excuse for inaction. With few journalists paying attention to this, most Canadians likely had no idea that the disability committee's work was quietly happening on the government's videoconferencing line. Lepovsky's warning — that 95% of the issues that disabled people face ultimately fall on the shoulders of provincial governments — should have meant that provincial politicians and journalists were talking about these issues, even if the federal government's aid for disabled people was so pathetically little.

PROVINCIAL PROBLEMS

Canada's constitution grants power over healthcare mostly to the provinces, except it also gives the federal government the power to raise the kind of money required to operate health systems. Federal programs can negatively or positively interact with provincial programs. Federal money intended to be spent on something in particular can be diverted elsewhere. Federal politicians can express their desire for something to change, and provincial politicians can ignore them. This dance is at the heart of how politics in Canada operates, and during the pandemic, the constitution became a favoured justification by both politicians and journalists for why the pandemic response was so weak. For disabled people who receive public assistance, federal-provincial wrangling meant they mostly ignored, and they also had to contend with two separate bureaucracies that often negatively interacted, thereby reducing how much support was available.

This was particularly acute in how assistance programs were managed. In Ontario, anyone who was receiving money from the Ontario Disability Support Program (ODSP) or Ontario Works (OW) were partly disqualified from being able to access CERB. *Kitchener Today* spoke with Cait Glasson, who pays 90% of what she receives from ODSP on rent, saying "[It] Just seems (sighs) odd to me that the government found all kinds of money for helping every adult in Canada, except those who happen to be on ODSP or OW, or the equivalent in other provinces."[42] Anyone who received CERB but who also received Ontario social assistance had their monthly amount reduced by $900, leaving them with $1100 rather than the $2000 that everyone else received. Over the course of the pandemic, there was a sharp drop in how many people received social assistance, a fact that worried many social policy analysts. This drop, combined with the money that was clawed back from CERB, amounted to Ontario spending less on social assistance during the pandemic than it had the year before.[43] In so doing, they put their boots on the necks of low income and/or disabled Ontarians, who were most at risk of illness and death from COVID-19, during the worst economic and social crisis in a century. By May 2020, it was reported that landlords in some geared-to-income rental units were planning to hike rents. Even with $900 kept by the province, ODSP supports were so low that renters would still end up with more income than usual. But only if they qualified for CERB.

Ontario wasn't alone in clawing back CERB. Even though the federal government had asked that governments not claw back CERB amounts from people receiving provincial social assistance money, most did. Only B.C., the Northwest Territories and Yukon planned not to claw back the benefit either in whole or in part. Saskatchewan and provinces in Atlantic Canada planned to claw it all back. In B.C., Social Development and Poverty Reduction Minister Shane Simpson estimated that of the 10,000 people receiving social assistance who also received CERB, the majority were disabled people who had lost jobs due to the pandemic. Simpson told the *National Post* they weren't going to claw this money back because, "We made the decision that we would not treat them differently than any others who lost income."[44]

Like Ontario, Alberta also saw a drop in social assistance caseloads during the pandemic. Rajan Sawhney, minister of community and social services told CBC *Calgary* that the drop was due to CERB. Thousands of people had the amounts totally clawed back. Anyone who received CERB had to re-apply for provincial benefits when CERB ended or they stopped being eligible for it.[45] Alberta's assistance program for people with complex disabilities, called Assured Income for the Severely Handicapped (AISH), only offered a maximum $1685 per month, an amount that was untied from inflation in 2019 by the United Conservative Party government. This amount stayed the same despite the pandemic increasing costs for cleaning, PPE and food. The Alberta government had signalled its desire to cut the program: professional Alberta government Twitter troll Matt Wolf, executive director of issues management for Jason Kenney, had tweeted that it wasn't "unrealistic" to look at whether or not all AISH recipients were actually disabled enough to receive the money, implying that program regulations may be further restricted. Despite the rumours, in 2021 the Alberta government did not slash the program.[46]

In the rare instances that politicians actually spoke about disabled people, it was usually with suspicion, making references or innuendo to double dipping or accessing money they didn't have the right to access. When Saskatchewan's social services minister Paul Merriman explained that CERB was only for income loss to CBC *Saskatchewan*, he made it sound as if disabled people couldn't receive disability assistance while also losing a job that paid them more than $5000 per year. And when asked about whether or not they would supplement incomes for increased pandemic costs, he said they wouldn't claw back the federal government's grant (of $600), and they too gave people a grant to pay for increased costs ... of $50. Where B.C.'s Simpson made the perfectly reasonable argument that disabled people shouldn't be treated differently when it comes to income loss and CERB, politicians like Merriman spoke as if there is a wall between who can work and who cannot, telegraphing to his supporters that there are people who are worthy of having more money and others who are not. Merriman said, as if this would have somehow been bad, that some people who received CERB because of income loss and disability assistance would have received $3600 per month.[47] Never mind that someone who has a complex disability and who requires home-care services might also work a regularly paying job, these state-imposed poverty programs had been decried by disabled people for years.[48] During the pandemic, there was a particular cruelty in hearing from politicians about how impossible or irresponsible it would be to give people more money to help them keep themselves as safe as possible.

Journalists didn't do enough to challenge these narratives. There was never any effort to report these numbers with any humanity. They focused on hot topics, like in April 2020 when a wave of stories from all across Canada were written about the American Sign Language interpreters who became common, popular faces at daily COVID-19 news briefs. When disabled voices did break into media coverage, it was due to the concerted efforts of activists from groups like Dignity Denied or the Disability Justice Network of Ontario, when they took aim at the proposed changes to Medical Assistance in Dying legislation. Or, it was when individuals could stage protests, like the one that Jonathan Marchand set up in August 2020. Otherwise, disabled people were absent from media, ignored by politicians and journalists alike. And the consequences were deadly: tens of thousands of disabled Canadians died preventable deaths from 2020 to 2021.

MENTAL HEALTH

One kind of disability did get a lot of media attention, however. Stories that expressed concern for people's mental health were the most common story about disability that was told during the pandemic. While rarely discussed in the frame of disability, the endemic impact of widespread and increasingly poor mental health appeared in articles and features, even acknowledged as a concern by politicians. Governments took out newspaper and bus ads reminding people to take care of their mental health. There was reporting on children's mental health, teen mental health, parent or caregiver mental health, men's mental health, the mental health of people living in assisted living and healthcare worker mental health. Mental health stood in direct contrast to other disabilities in how widespread the conversations were about it. However, for all the attention on mental health, there were precious few resources distributed to actually help people get through whatever mental health struggles they had.

An Ipsos survey released in February 2021 found that 44% of Canadians, and a majority of younger Canadians, had said the second lockdown impacted their mental health more than the first had. Twenty-eight percent of respondents said their mental health was worse in winter 2021 than it had been the previous fall. Almost one-quarter of respondents aged 18–34 said they struggle with addiction.[49] Unlike other kinds of disability, mental health became the argument that many people used to reduce the safety measures in society and allow people to "go back to normal." This was a special kind of ableist frame, where poor mental health was posited as being the result of pandemic suffering, not related to fixable or changeable forces that would have enabled people to live better, even under lockdown. By opening the economy, people who were suffering from poor mental health would be immediately helped. Mental health was even used as an excuse by some who escaped the pandemic to warmer climates, like former Saint John City Councillor Sean Casey, who used his poor mental health as a justification for leaving Canada for a vacation in Mexico.[50] This framing ignored the myriad ways in which social forces exacerbated poor mental health, as well as the crucial intersection of mental health with other issues, like trauma, poverty, physical disability, isolation, systemic racism and/or illness. By ignoring these other issues, politicians could wax on about mental health being important but never plan to do anything to fix people's material conditions. Journalists could have written about the systemic issues that surrounded the phenomenon of worsening mental health, but mostly, they didn't.

On February 10, 2021, *Global News* examined how a COVID-19 diagnosis alone can cause depression, stress and anxiety, and that it has negatively impacted many people's mental health. Journalists Dave McIvor and Sam Thompson referenced a study from the *Lancet* that found a strong connection between COVID-19 infection and the appearance of a new mental illness: 18% of patients developed depression, anxiety, dementia or other issues. But their article stopped short of explaining what supports actually existed to help people who were managing poor mental health as a result of a COVID-19 diagnosis. The only advice was to "stay connected to what you're feeling" and then to "reach out to other people."[51] Another *Global News* article from February 2021 interviewed Angie Daigle, a Moncton-based salon owner who found the pandemic had made her post-traumatic stress disorder (PTSD) and anxiety worse. The article then quoted Julie Allain from the Canadian Mental Health Association of New Brunswick who reminded people, "there is help for people that need it," after suggesting people do small things that bring them joy.[52] For anyone struggling with a serious and debilitating mental illness, this kind of advice was useless, as help was often not available when people sought it. Accessing mental health supports are difficult at the best of times. During the pandemic, with medical facilities strained and more people in need, it became even harder to access a system that was already stretched way too thin.

Mental health was particularly urgent for youth. Media paid close attention to school closures and made a direct link between online school and declining mental health, but this story was usually told in the context of the tug-of-war between voices who wanted schools to stay open and voices who wanted schools to close down. There were stories of worrisome trends, like a spike of youth with eating disorders at the Children's Hospital of Eastern Ontario. The youth who arrived at the hospital sick from disordered eating were "sicker than ever," and requests to the hospital were up 50%. In-patient admissions were up 63% over the same period in 2019.[53] There was a crisis in youth mental health, as whether or not someone had access to immediate services depended on whether the services were available, or even existed, in their communities. Mental health services were inadequate before the pandemic, so they were even more stretched during the pandemic, and the fixes required were bold and radical.

In a piece for *The Conversation*, Ranmalle Jayasinha and Patricia Conrod from the Université de Montréal argued that youth mental health services were so critical because 70% of mental health issues first appear when someone is young. They wrote that affordability and accessibility of mental health services posed huge problems, as waiting lists were so long, and for young people, "such delays can make the difference between the need for preventive services versus treatment." School-based programs rarely went beyond academic concerns, and the ratio between students and psychologists was far higher than recommended by the Canadian Psychological Association. New programs that were developed in collaboration with youth were necessary, as well as politicians making these issues a priority and funding them, they argued.[54] Their recommendations were thorough and systemic, which was quite different from the kind of advice that was most common. For example, just like the aforementioned *Global News* article, one CTV News article featured five ways to handle mental health during the second wave, and each recommendation was isolated and individualized — nothing that could help someone whose mental health was spinning out of control and who needed to see a doctor immediately. It recommended that people practice self-care like sleeping well and exercising, "practice and master coping skills," be proactive based on what you learned about yourself during the first wave, "honour your unique mental health needs," and to watch out how much time you spend online.[55] While the recommendations made for okay wellness advice, they would do nothing to help someone who was experiencing mental illness, triggered by the pandemic or not. Mainstream media refused to make connections between structural issues and poor mental health. So rather than exploring paid time off or free food programs as possible ways to improve mental health, Canadians were given individualized wellness advice. By separating mental health from these broader forces, journalists never made critical connections between a widespread mental health crisis and public policy decisions that were actively exacerbating poor mental health.

Despite the abundance of reporting on mental health, the reporting always turned mental illness into a story of individual struggle. This gave politicians cover to do the absolute minimum to help people's mental health improve. For example, most of the federal government's support for mental health went into research or into an online portal called Wellness Together, where Canadians could track their mental health by answering online questions through their online portal and see what kind of services they might be able to access. The federal government paid $46 million to set the portal up. But federal programs also directly caused a rise in calls to distress and anxiety support agencies, specifically when it was announced in August 2020 that CERB would be discontinued.[56]

Provincially, very little was committed to funding services for people's mental health. Québec Premier François Legault promised to hire more mental health professionals. Ontario Premier Doug Ford committed $19.25 million to improve mental health supports at Ontario's colleges and universities, which wasn't likely to make improvements that students could access for months at least.[57] The British Columbia government committed $3.75 million to "promote mental wellness and provide additional support for students, families and educators."[58] And New Brunswick expanded the mobile crisis response unit pilot project, which paired nurses with police when doing wellness checks. N.B. Health Minister Dorothy Shephard promised to build on a new walk-in mental health clinic that had opened in December 2020 in Cambellton and develop 13 located all over the province.[59] The same day as Shephard's announcement, 16-year-old Lexi Dakan committed suicide not long after she had waited for eight hours in the emergency room of Everett Chalmers Hospital and left without seeing a psychiatrist.[60] The tragic story was a reminder that every delay in improving mental health services in Canada puts someone's life at risk. The pandemic exacerbated an already inadequate system and people struggling with mental illness were the victims.

If one reason for why the gendered impact of COVID-19 received so much coverage was because of how many journalists were working and living the gendered impact of the pandemic directly, the widespread experiences of poor mental health impacting a population that had otherwise not experienced poor mental health in their lives may also explain why mental health received so much attention. However, despite the visibility of mental illness versus physical disability, there were still very few changes imposed anywhere in Canada that would immediately provide support and relief to Canadians struggling with mental health. Where physical disability was nearly entirely hidden from discussion, mental disability was on full display but repackaged to become an isolated, individual struggle that staying in touch with others or a good night's sleep alone could improve. It put tremendous strain on Canadians and their families who, regardless of if they had experience with the mental health medical system before, had to navigate it as it was even more overwhelmed. The victims of this system were barely accounted for, with suicide rates released well after the time that they happened. And the survivors, who would live with the mental scars for years from the isolation, loneliness or COVID-19–triggered mental illness — would they have the help they needed? Or would journalists and politicians continue to torque the story from one that required radical and fundamental systemic change, to one that could be solved through therapist TikToks and self-care? Despite the attention these issues did receive, the ableism that is built into Canadian society ensured that unless people organized and forced systemic change, politicians would get by doing as little possible.

Ableism, along with racism and colonialism, dictated the ways in which COVID-19 would impact Canada from the start. In a society that is racist, ableist and colonial, the structures that have been in action since the founding of Canada itself would continue to endure during the pandemic, unless there was a powerful moment where politicians broke with the status quo. Disabled people, especially non-white disabled people, were at most risk of severe illness or death. While it wasn't surprising that politicians continued in their status quo fashion, journalists had an added responsibility to reframe these issues and question how COVID-19 was differently impacting people with disabilities. Disabled people needed journalists to hold politicians to account, not simply report on what politicians said, often uncritically. The failure to centre disability was not just a failure of justice; it was also a failure of prudence: no other population was so keenly aware of the cracks within the system that COVID-19 was going to ravage. Why did it take until April 2020 for a federal advisory committee to be established — one that was limited by the constitution from the start? Why wasn't it obvious from the moment that COVID-19 was circulating in North America that disabled people needed to be brought into positions of power to help drive Canada's pandemic response? Why wasn't there more attention on people who had been disabled by a COVID-19 infection, and who were dealing with a new chronic illness with very few supports? Disability was either ignored, repackaged to appease and relieve a non-disabled audience or individualized such that the systemic causes of oppression would never be adequately addressed.

Where awareness related to disability would never get better, in 2021, there was finally more awareness about the role that congregant settings played in propagating COVID-19. There was little doubt that residential care, including adult assisted living, was more dangerous than living within the community. But the role that work played — in large congregant settings especially — would ensure that COVID-19 continued to infect people, both inside congregant work settings but also the community at large. And disabled people, who had worked so hard to stay safe during the pandemic, especially with so few resources keeping them afloat, were given nothing. Canadians were forced to live in a world where the largest corporations were given money and supports to continue to operate as usual, while their workplaces became COVID-19 factories, pumping out the virus to people within their communities.

February 2021
WORKPLACE SPREAD

Cases: 786,417
Deaths: 20,213[1]

The thread that connected every single outbreak in Canada was work. Just as Canadians who didn't work were seen as disposable or ignored, as was the case for disabled people, the state considered one's proximity to work as the most important part of someone's identity. Even though the risk of in-home transmission was highest, the workplace was where COVID-19 moved from household to household. It was never far away from any infection, any transmission or any amount of community spread. Residential care facilities, schools, hospitals, fitness studios, concert halls, banks, grocery stores, mines: all these important sites of COVID-19 transmission and abatement were places of work. But it was rare that the world of work was written about through the lens of collective labour.

The systems and communities in which people were located were key to understanding how COVID-19 infected individuals. Work was the location where individuals spent the most of their waking hours. Groups of individuals became more susceptible to COVID-19 due to many different factors: workers' statuses, the precarity of the work, the physical space and location of the job, transportation to and from work and the ability of a worker to refuse to come into work. And yet, journalists favoured the individualized, personal responsibility narrative far more than one that examined workplace outbreaks and their impact. For example, a search of the CBC News website on December 15, 2020, for the keywords *"workplace outbreak"* over the course of the pandemic only netted 66 results, while *"personal responsibility"* covid netted 93 articles. *"Private gatherings"* netted 329 results. Compare that with a search of CERB, which netted 1685 articles, and it was obvious that the CBC in general deprioritized coverage of workplace outbreaks. A similar ratio is found at CTV News, where *"workplace outbreak"* netted just 38 articles, while *"personal responsibility"* covid netted 57. *"Private gatherings"* netted 189 articles and CERB pulled up 573 articles.[2] However, every single story was related in some way to work.

Constructing a narrative that elevated personal responsibility over collective workplace failures required that workplaces be hidden, obscured or ignored, and politicians were deft in how they did this. Workplaces were locations where individuals could not respect public health guidelines, and yet, politicians allowed them to mostly govern themselves. Journalists were not critical enough about this, and for months, COVID-19 spread within workplaces with very little attention, with the exception of some headline-grabbing outbreaks. This was made possible because when journalists and politicians did talk about "the economy," they focused on small businesses in place of large businesses. The emphasis on small businesses allowed governments to quietly allow business to continue as usual while Canadians were told that business was shutting down. All of these tricks hid one industry in particular that proved to be the most deadly from the statistics that were readily available: transit, rendered invisible thanks to racism against its mostly racialized workforce.

DAVID

Every time a safety officer came around, David Parrott said that management seemed to take COVID-19 safety measures a bit more seriously. While there had been plexiglass dividers installed in the lunchroom, daily temperature checks and masks given to workers, he said that normally, the second the pace of work sped up social distancing measures were forgotten as workers scrambled to fulfill a rush of orders. Safety was more of a priority when it needed to be, like if someone was watching. Otherwise, workers were expected to work, regardless of whether or not distance could be maintained. David worked at the Amazon Fulfillment Centre in Bolton, Ontario, north of Brampton. There, he and hundreds of other workers dispatched Amazon products to get them ready to be shipped to wherever they needed to go.

David started working there in November 2020, just as the holiday rush started. With Canadians unable to see family members for the end of 2020, many turned to online retailers like Amazon to send their loved ones gifts — the only practical sign of love in a consumerist society where people were told to stay locked down. While Amazon didn't report what it made specifically in Canada, the global retail giant made $125.56 billion in the fourth quarter of 2020 alone,[3] and Amazon Canada reported a record-breaking holiday season on December 28.[4] Amazon needed workers to help manage the influx of holiday orders and David needed a job. The pay was decent and it came with consistent hours, so he applied. He started with a three-month contract and eventually became full time.

Warehousing and shipping were regular COVID-19 workplace hotspots, and not too surprisingly either: workers were sometimes in close contact with one another, and if safety wasn't privileged over efficiency, COVID-19 spread easily. Even if company policy was to limit the spread, contradictory incentives made it easy to spread the virus. For example, workers who wanted to fulfill their tasks as quickly as possible or who were afraid of discipline (or both), could inadvertently spread the virus. Gagandeep Kaur, an organizer with the Canadian Union of Postal Workers told CBC Radio's *As It Happens* that the increase of employees during the holiday rush packed more employees into warehouses, making it even harder for them to socially distance at work.[5]

David caught COVID-19. While he couldn't be 100% sure that it was from his workplace, the only other option was that his father, who he lived with, got it while shopping. Shopping was a much lower-risk activity than working in a large, congregant setting, so it's highly probable that David's infection happened at work. When David told his employer about his infection, he found that Amazon had little set up for adequate contact tracing. They didn't shut a facility down or provide rapid tests. They relied on employee information to contain possible exposures. The problem for David was that he was new; he didn't even know all of the names of the people he worked with, let alone recall which masked coworker he had been working alongside when he was asymptomatic. When he was in touch with human resources, they couldn't say who he had been working around either, and therefore, they didn't know who should be sent home to self-isolate for potential exposure. Amazon offered two weeks of paid time off for its employees who caught COVID-19, and because of the fatigue that comes after the worst of the symptoms pass, David took an extra week off, which he had to make multiple calls and leave multiple messages to confirm he'd be able to do.

Amazon was notoriously mum on outbreaks within their facilities, leaving workers to rely on the grapevine to know if they came into contact with COVID-19 or worse, find out after they had been infected and likely worked alongside others. With nothing compelling Amazon's management to go beyond the most basic measures, workers had very little power to protect themselves. All of the personal responsibility messaging in the world from politicians and public health officials could not combat a workplace-acquired illness.

During the pandemic, workplaces were a key node of transmission of the virus. But politicians suppressed the role they played, instead focusing on other kinds of transmission, like the random kind you might pick up while shopping. In 2020, journalists mostly ignored the role these large, congregant workplaces played too, focusing instead on small businesses, schools or entertainment. By the time workplaces did get the attention they deserved, the third wave was ravaging much of Canada, only to be stopped by mass vaccination. While able to meet some basic protocols, corporations were rarely forced to do anything drastic, like shut down, even when COVID-19 was tearing through their facilities. As David told me, Amazon seemed to understand what it should do (they sent home the one person he was able to name that he had been in close contact with), but they weren't compelled to do anything further. It meant that as orders picked up, employees could easily find themselves in unsafe circumstances as they just tried to do their jobs. Despite the individual intentions or desires of workers to stay healthy, their lives were in the hands of their bosses.

OBSCURING WORKPLACE OUTBREAKS

In December 2020, results were released from a study conducted by the B.C. Centre for Disease Control (BCCDC). They surveyed 400,000 participants from May 12 to May 31 about how they were following public health orders. The survey found only 1% reported that they had taken no health precautions. Ninety percent of people reported washing their hands regularly and 93% reported they were physically distancing. Eighty-nine percent reported they had avoided gatherings. By all measures, British Columbians were following public health orders to the extent that they could in the areas of their lives they had control over. They had taken personal responsibility in the way that public health officials and politicians had hoped.

But the percentages dropped when people were asked about following public health orders at work. One-third of respondents reported they could not stay home when they were sick, 45% could not work remotely and only 50% were able to socially distance while at work.[6] If 45% of British Columbians reported they could not follow public health orders while at work, it meant that no public health measure that targeted personal responsibility alone would be enough to allow almost half of British Columbians to follow public health directives. Public health directives that didn't demand employers go as far as they could to protect workers would not be enough.

In Québec, workplaces were a key driver of the second wave. As it crested over the province, Public Health Director Horacio Arruda admitted that 46% of all outbreaks in the province involved a workplace.[7] At the start of Québec's second wave, retail stores accounted for the majority of Montréal's workplace outbreaks — 98 employees at 38 workplaces — compared to 27 outbreaks within schools and nine within residential facilities and healthcare. It wasn't hard to see that workplace outbreaks would find themselves into other parts of society, especially if people were asymptomatic or pre-symptomatic but also contagious.[8] By October 23, 2020, the wheels were in motion for COVID-19 to become an emergency like it had been in the spring, but this time outside of the hotspots of the first wave when COVID-19 infections were highly concentrated in Montréal. The virus sent an early-warning signal through day-shift workers at the Olymel plant at Vallée-Jonction south of Quebec City. Within a couple of days and after hundreds of tests, at least 60 workers tested positive. One week later, the entire region of Chaudière-Appalaches in Québec was officially designated a red zone, with a majority of cases linked to two outbreaks: the Olymel plant outbreak and a private long-term care facility called CHSLD de Cap-St-Ignace, where 18 people died. Fifty percent of outbreaks in Québec by November 1, 2020, were in workplaces.[9] Workers at the Vallée-Jonction Olymel plant went on strike on April 28, 2021. Well into September 2021, the strike was still ongoing.

Finding information about outbreaks was not easy. Each public health unit had its own way of reporting outbreaks: some listed workplace outbreaks, others did not, and many changed their reporting systems over the course of the pandemic both for better and worse. Alberta was the only province that consistently posted names of workplaces where there were outbreaks. Everywhere else, it took more work to get an idea of where outbreaks were happening. During British Columbia's second wave, there was no consistent, central location to see outbreak information. The BCCDC regularly posted flight exposure information, but the section of their website for workplace exposures was limited; by mid-December, it had zero workplace outbreaks reported, and the archived list of worksite outbreaks had not been updated since October 16, 2020.[10] Even then, the list was incomplete because all of the workplace outbreak sites listed occurred in Alberta, where workers from B.C. worked, and cruise ship exposures from March. The regional health websites weren't much better. Interior Health's website said there were no active outbreaks in their region, even though their list of recent news releases mentioned active outbreaks at Teck Resources and the Big White Ski Resort. In the wake of the Big White outbreak in December 2020, several workers were fired by the resort for "breaching Big White's Social Responsibility Contract." Many of the staff lived in shared accommodations, and while it wasn't illegal to gather with the people you live with, there was a party of 20 to 25 people that led to Big White firing these staff. Interior Health blamed gatherings and "large households," a feature of how Big White managed it staff accommodations.[11] Dormitory residences for workers, whether in agriculture or tourism, became super-spreader locations, and employers were not forced to give their employees private quarters as a pandemic mitigation strategy.

The lack of data in B.C. frustrated journalists, academics and other public officials. On November 19, 2020, mayors of five municipalities in the Fraser Health region formally asked the province for "more granular and frequent data." B.C. Premier John Horgan responded to say that the data wasn't necessary and (incorrectly) that B.C. is as transparent as any other jurisdiction in Canada. He then used the request to insist it was private gatherings, not workplaces, that were driving the pandemic. Workplace outbreaks, he argued, were triggered by private gatherings, which then brought COVID-19 to work. He responded to the request for more data by saying, "My message to the mayors is the same as my message to the citizens in [Fraser Health] — you need to amend your behaviour, you need to reduce your social gatherings."[12] At the same time, one workplace outbreak spread from a single person to 80 infections in the Fraser Health region. On November 27, 2020, the same day public health warned that COVID-19 spread among workers was "a major prob-lem," 25 workers at the Surrey courthouse tested positive for COVID-19. Public health wouldn't call it an outbreak and the B.C. Government and Service Employees Union deplored the lax public health measures at the courthouse.[13] If only one person could create a workplace outbreak, it showed the need for all workplaces to prepare for the likelihood that at least one worker may come to work contagious. Large congregant work settings were spaces where individuals would come into contact with far more people than they would in private settings. Yet, politicians like Horgan blamed individual behaviour rather than going after employers and forcing them to ensure their employees be kept safe.

By December 8 in Québec, the Institut national de santé publique (INSPQ) found there were 470 workplace outbreaks across the province with manufacturing, meatpacking, construction, trucking and warehouses being hardest hit, just like in Ontario and Alberta. And even then, the *Montreal Gazette* quoted Richard Martin, a scientific adviser to INSPQ who mostly laid the blame at employees' feet for being too lax with following the rules:

> He believes some of the outbreaks seen during the second wave have been the result of bad habits that took hold during the summer. When the virus was less present in Québec, some workplaces let up on measures and never re-implemented them in the fall. But even those putting every possible measure in place aren't immune. Employees will often follow measures while working, Martin said, but it's in the little moments in between — during breaks or informal meetings — that people let their guard down. Part of the issue, he believes, comes from the misplaced sense of safety many feel around the coworkers they see every day.[14]

Rather than examining how much freedom workers have on the job to respect the rules, the frame offered by Martin and highlighted by the *Gazette*, was one that blamed COVID-19 spread on human nature and pandemic fatigue rather than asking whether or not these industries should be operating at the same capacity as before the pandemic.

Between March 13, 2020, and March 1, 2021, there were 10,843 COVID-19 cases reported by the Public Health Agency of Canada connected to industrial settings, all untouched by enhanced COVID-19 safety measures. This was likely an undercount and also didn't include later numbers from Amazon's Brampton outbreak that would have almost doubled the number of warehouse worker cases, which had been at 620.[15] The vast majority of these cases were within meat production at 4750 cases, followed by agricultural workers at 2190 cases. Knowing this should have meant these workers were given more supports, including temporary lodging and other help to stop the spread within their households. And employers should have been sanctioned, as many of these infections were the result of lax safety protocols that had been decried by workers for months.

Understanding which outbreaks were the most common in which regions should have driven public health authorities to make specific interventions. For example, by March 2021, in Toronto, offices and warehouses accounted for 253 of all reported workplace outbreaks, outnumbering all other workplace kinds combined; food processing was the second highest location at 51 outbreaks.[16] Yet, there were no supports given to workers who worked in offices and warehouses in Toronto. Toronto was not an outlier: ensuring that the work environment was safe for employees was left up to company owners. By focusing on gyms, bars and small businesses, journalists reformulated the economy into something that erased large congregant settings from the popular conversation entirely, for most of 2020.

THE SMALL BUSINESS MOTIF

Closing large congregate work environments, especially if there had been an outbreak, would have done far more to stop the spread of COVID-19 than simply sending sick workers home to isolate. But for most of 2020, there was very little attention paid to the role that these workplaces played in driving community spread. Instead, there was a generalized sense that every public health measure for businesses had been tried and nothing could work with this stubborn virus. Politicians personalized the pandemic not only through appealing to individual measures and actions to keep people safe, but also by personifying individuals in a corporate homologue: small businesses. This obscured the differential impacts on communities — either by hiding the way in which white and wealthier people were kept safer during the pandemic than poorer, racialized communities, or by zooming in so closely on how a particular issue impacted someone, like a healthcare worker who died, that broader connections to community were impossible to see.

The lack of attention on workers' issues as they were tied to systemic forces kneecapped the depth of analysis, thereby obscuring possible solutions. Politicians needed more than simply blaming youth and youthful activities on spreading COVID-19. They needed to manufacture an image of the corporate world that didn't look like it was made of the ones making the most money during the pandemic — Enbridge, TD, RBC, TC Energy and Scotia Bank to be specific, who collectively made more than $2.6 billion in the third quarter of 2020 alone. It needed to be an image that fit perfectly with the individualized narrative of our lives: the small business on the corner, operated by a married couple who poured their lives into it and who lost it all because of government lockdown measures. Small businesses were lionized as the backbone of Canada's economy while larger businesses who were benefiting off loose COVID-19 measures to keep plant operations running as usual received little to no coverage, unless their facility experienced a massive outbreak.

Small businesses were the perfect tool to personify the economy. The owners and workers were not anonymous in the same way that warehouse or logistics workers are — journalists would tell us that we actually knew them (and sometimes, we did), and the pandemic was causing tremendous harm to their livelihoods. Small businesses form a significant part of the employer base in Canada: according to Statistics Canada, small businesses make up 98% of all employer businesses in Canada, employing 68.8% of Canadians. Politicians and journalists rarely talked about the diversity of workforces among small businesses and instead, lumped them into a rhetorical group of people who all needed to be saved from the pandemic. But the differences between small businesses were really important. The mom and pop shop on the corner was suffering in a way that a company with 100+ employees was not. Statistics Canada found that the smaller the business, the more worried the employers were about losing money: while 30.4% of small businesses with one to four employees were worried that they'd see a decrease in sales in 2021, that number dropped to 19.2% for businesses with 100 or more employees. A similar pattern could be seen with which businesses lost money in 2020: 32.7% of the smallest businesses reported that their sales were down by at least 30% while just 17.5% of businesses with more than 100 employees saw a similar revenue drop. But there were also some businesses who reported increased revenue, again tied to business size: 15.7% of businesses with fewer than four employees reported revenue increases, while 35.8% of businesses with 100 or more employees reported revenue increases.[17] The Canada Emergency Wage Subsidy (CEWS) was designed specifically with these losses in mind, and gave emergency funding to all businesses who had a 30% or more drop in their income, regardless of their size, as I explore in the August 2020 chapter. The companies with more employees both made it through 2020 with the highest profits and were the locations that were more likely to have higher COVID-19 spread. But in the popular conception of "small business," journalists and politicians alike talked about small businesses as the group with the fewest employees and the biggest pandemic-related losses.

Small businesses have always been an important rhetorical category for politicians, and that was even more true during the pandemic. Both the Conservatives and the NDP regularly referred to small businesses as "the backbone of the economy." The backbone analogy wasn't just to liken small businesses to a critical piece of anatomy that holds up a body. It also personified the economy, giving the economy human-like features. Therefore, politicians and business lobbyists could talk about the economy as a living entity that needed to be saved from death, with a spine formed out of small businesses. By personifying the economy in this way, the death of the economy held equal weight as the death of a human, and therefore, it was politically possible to choose to 'save the life' of the economy, even if it cost human lives. Conservative leader Erin O'Toole claimed to be the preferred political leader of small businesses. On August 26, 2020, when Cormack Builders in Cape Breton posted a congratulatory sign for his successful election, he tweeted the image saying "small business is the backbone of the Canadian economy — and I'll never forget them."[18] A few months later in November, the Conservatives moved a motion that they said demonstrated their support for small businesses that paused CRA audits for any small business that received the CEWS, even though it was not reported that any audits had actually happened, aside from 90 small business audits that were part of a pilot project of the 352,000 companies that had applied to CEWS.[19] Their motion passed thanks in part to the full support of the NDP, a party that also exploited the small business motif. On March 3, 2021, when the NDP revealed three demands related to small businesses, the party tweeted, "Small businesses are the backbone of our economy,"[20] and on their website, "Small businesses are the engine of job creation in Canada, and an important part of every community across the country."[21] Politicians on either side of the Liberals knew there was political currency in the small business motif, even if it didn't make any objective sense to stop them from being scrutinized for how they used public grants to subsidize their wages during the pandemic.

Creating the identity of what a small business *is* was key to formulating an image of the economy that could suffer like a human and therefore needed to be saved like an unemployed worker. And media was key to creating this formulation. After five weeks of lockdown during the first wave, entrepreneur and writer of entrepreneurialism David Sax wrote an ode of over 2700 words to small businesses in the *Globe and Mail* where he explained the virtues of small businesses through the idyllic Ontario town of Thornbury:

> Even the largest businesses up here [sic] — such as the apple farm and processing facility owned by the Botden family, who I wrote about in one of my previous books — employ just a few dozen people. But when you add up these farms, feed businesses, small manufacturing companies, restaurants and bars, shops and galleries, gas stations, dental and veterinary offices, massage therapists and personal trainers, plumbers and carpenters, butchers, bakers, and grocery stores, you have the foundation of a robust middle-class economy, where opportunity is within the grasp of most residents and becoming an entrepreneur is something anyone can do.[22]

This kind of great equalizer narrative was critical to laundering the impact of the pandemic, as it erased the impact that colonialism, racism and misogyny had both on success in Canada and on the differential experience of COVID-19. There was no need to talk about systemic racism and COVID-19 when "becoming an entrepreneur is something anyone can do," even though by the time that Sax wrote this piece, it was clear that COVID-19 was disproportionately injuring Black people. But it wasn't just *Globe and Mail* opinion features that pushed this narrative. The "backbone" spirit of Canada's middle-class narrative took up a lot of airtime, with journalists dispatched to cover every hiccup that small business owners made either in defiance of public health orders — like Nobletoyz in Caledon, Ontario, whose owner defied public health orders by staying open and providing the essential service of toys to local Caledonians[23] — or in support of them, like Catherine Choi's three Hanji Gift shops in Toronto, who argued it was unfair that the largest box retailers were allowed to stay open because many sold some items that were considered essential, like groceries. Choi was regularly asked for comment by the *Toronto Star*. The article then quoted CFIB's Dan Kelly in a press release asking, "If it is dangerous to buy a book at an independent bookseller, why isn't it dangerous at Costco?"[24] Kelly was key in the process that transformed popular understanding of Canada's economy to be small- and medium-sized businesses.

The small business motif was useful because it could be warped to make any argument. Journalists routinely prioritized stories about small businesses as a way to provide a sympathetic face to the pandemic. They became the excuse for why public health measures needed to be relaxed. The most effective lobby organization that pushed this message was the CFIB. Kelly said they had been referenced in media more than 50,000 times by October 30, 2020.[25] It was hard to find a single small business–related story in the Canadian media that didn't quote Kelly. One of the ways in which the CFIB garnered so much media attention was that they published regular surveys from their members. The results from the first big survey, on March 17, 2020, was broadcast across news agencies across Canada. Kelly warned,

> we must recognize that calls for self-isolation have massive economic consequences for many Canadian small businesses, especially as close to two-thirds of small firms would not be able to quickly shift more than 10 percent of sales to online or telephone options.[26]

That was the first of 24 surveys that the CFIB ran between March and October 2020, and every time they released new results, journalists covered them.[27] Their intense lobby efforts, aided by the attention that journalists paid them, had deep influence on government policy.

Politicians needed to spin the definition of "essential" to ensure that as much of the economy could stay open as possible. Because the largest retailers were more likely to have goods that could be considered essential, it was more likely they would be allowed to operate as usual. There were legitimate complaints that small businesses had — to see the largest retailers, already a threat to the smallest businesses, stay open while smaller retail locations were forced to shutter their stores all in the name of public health signalled to the population that the largest stores were safer to open, even though they were open not because they were safer but because their goods fit into what the government considered to be essential. There was no jurisdiction that allowed businesses with fewer than some number of workers stay open, even though smaller commercial enterprises were less likely to have large outbreaks that would quickly spread. In Ontario, as of December 15, 2020, there were 810 active outbreaks at 44 retail workplaces, an average of 18 outbreaks per location. Compare that to the Ontario government's "Workplace-Other" category, which included offices, warehouses, logistics, manufacturing, construction and shipping, in which 44 worksites had 6433 active outbreaks for an average of 146 infections per workplace.[28]

Clearly, small retail businesses were not driving COVID-19 spread the way that large businesses were. But the fact that the Workplace-Other data wasn't even teased out, while short-term accommodations, food processing, retail and others were, demonstrated the lack of attention that these industries got from journalists and politicians. Brampton mayor Patrick Brown told the *National Post* in mid-December,

> [Large, congregant work spaces have] been overlooked, and intentionally so ... I've been told by senior officials in the federal government and the provincial government "Oh, we could never shut down those sectors. There wouldn't be food in the grocery stores across Canada, or there wouldn't be medical supplies that come in from the U.S."[29]

Suppressing the data about outbreaks within large congregant settings was a tactic intended to lead Canadians away from pinning the blame for outbreaks on the very locations, outside of healthcare, where they were most serious. When this was no longer possible, aided by the narrative shift offered by the COVID-19 variants of concern, the role of large congregant workplaces became undeniable. Journalists could no longer ignore the Amazons of the world by focusing on the local tattoo shop.

The same week in Alberta, outbreaks were very concentrated around schools, residential care and acute care. By December 15, 2020, 292 schools were listed as having at least two cases, and 353 outbreaks on the Alberta Health Services school database (the remainder were schools classified as "open" where "parents may have received an alert from their school");[30] a combined 178 outbreaks in acute, long-term, supportive services and retirement residence care; and 64 in all other locations, including shelters, correctional facilities, warehouses and energy industry camps.[31] At the time, Alberta had the most per capita infections in all of Canada at 11,299 and was speeding toward a crisis that would not easily be solved with limited lockdown measures.[32] Contract tracing had completely broken down near the end of November, as public health agents stopped notifying anyone who had been in close contact with someone who was COVID-19 positive unless the contact happened in a hospital, school or care facility.[33] Because of this, it was impossible to know how much of the pandemic was circulating within a community, though it would show up most obviously within the school data. While the highest non-health-related number of outbreaks were in service organizations where people would have prolonged indoor contact together, like shelters, the thread that connected Alberta's outbreak locations wasn't the type of business; it was how much people congregated within them — workplaces where many workers worked closely together, like the 13 outbreaks in food processing, manufacturing and warehouses, and the 12 outbreaks in tar sands labour camps or related businesses.[34]

Alberta's most aggressive public health measures exempted certain businesses from the orders — notably the businesses with the highest number of workplace outbreaks. Of the 64 outbreak locations where there were outbreaks one week after the more restrictive measures were introduced in December 2020, only four would be impacted by the new measures: Earl's restaurant in Edmonton, a sport cohort and two private, personal gatherings. The rest were all businesses exempted in some way from the rules, even though they had the most outbreaks.[35] Because journalists had been obsessively covering small businesses whenever they wrote about the economy, the role that large, congregate setting workplaces played in spreading COVID-19 was very difficult for the average person to see. Canadians were left imagining the pandemic as an endless tug-of-war between public health and small businesses in a futile attempt to stop the spread. Near the end of 2020, no province had plans to shut down manufacturing or construction, even as many faced record-high COVID-19 cases and increasingly strict public health measures.[36]

Ontario's government announced the province would go into a province-wide lockdown starting on December 26, 2020. At the time, almost one-quarter of Ontario's active outbreaks were at warehouses, food processing plants and manufacturing facilities. Just like Alberta, these facilities were exempt from the lockdown measures, ensuring that COVID-19 could still circulate there while most of the rest of the province was locked down.[37] On February 2, 2021, Sara Mojtehedzadeh and Andrew Bailey at the *Toronto Star* found that 65% of workers in the Greater Toronto Area worked in sectors that were allowed to maintain some level of in-person staffing. They also found a deep income divide among those workers who could work from home and those who worked in the service industry:

> grocery store workers, for example, earn half the median hourly wage of employees who can work from home. Almost three-quarters of workers in food manufacturing are immigrants to Canada, compared to less than half of those who can work from

home. Food manufacturing is also one of the lowest-paid jobs in the GTA's manufacturing industry, the Star's analysis shows.[38]

By allowing Canadians to think first of the small businesses they frequent and not the hidden, usually large facilities that had been exempted from lockdowns, politicians could avoid needing to justify the large net cast by the word "essential businesses." But instead, it hived off people from one another by income: the lowest-income workers had to put themselves at risk while middle-income workers could find safer ways to undertake their work.

GOVERNMENT INACTION

It was almost the end of 2020 when workplace outbreaks started to get the attention they warranted from journalists. Even though there was no question that workplaces, just like long-term care facilities and schools, were a principal driver of outbreaks, they were rarely written about in such terms. Instead, workplace outbreaks were confined to longform investigations, often coming out long after the last case was officially recovered. This made it easy for politicians to skirt responsibility, as there was always doubt about just how much workplace spread caused COVID-19. Two analyses that did zero in on workplace outbreaks and spread focused on a cluster of workplaces in Ontario's Peel Region — the logistics and shipping capital of Canada. Eighty-two percent of warehouse workers who work in the GTA live in Peel.[39] Reporting by Stefanie Marotta for the *Globe and Mail* and Sara Mojtehedzadeh for the *Toronto Star* showed not only how widespread the problems of large workplace outbreaks are but, importantly, what kind of public policy interventions would have made an important difference in slowing the spread of COVID-19.

When Marotta's piece was published on November 17, 2020, there were 116 workplaces with an outbreak, and Peel Region had the highest cumulative rate of cases in Ontario. Peel Region Public Health had determined that 34% of workplace outbreaks were in manufacturing and industrial facilities, 14% were in food processing and 10% were in retail. Marotta wrote, "Details about the workplace outbreaks are few," and quoted mayors of both Brampton and Mississauga, frustrated that workplace outbreak locations were not being published.[40] There was one outbreak in Mississauga in September where 61 workers had acquired COVID-19 and public health didn't release any information about where or in which facility it occurred. Peel Region Public Health said that employers were getting laxer as the pandemic rolled on, and it was creating conditions where the virus could spread:

> A lack of physical distancing in lunch rooms and other common areas, improper mask use, carpooling with other employees and failure to conduct an on-site screening process to prevent symptomatic workers from entering a facility are the leading causes of infection in workplaces.[41]

Mojtehedzadeh looked specifically at Amazon facilities and the impact on its mostly racialized workers. While American COVID-19 rates among Amazon workers had been made public in October 2020 — 20,000 workers had caught COVID-19 — no similar disclosure was made in Canada.[42] By December 10, 2020, the *Toronto Star* could only confirm 25 COVID-19 cases at a Brampton warehouse alone, but the company would not say how many cases there have been in their facilities across Canada. During the first wave of the pandemic, workers told the *Star* that 200-plus person meetings continued, and employers couldn't socially distance either in the workplace or the lunchroom. Ontario's WSIB contacted Amazon in May 2020 after complaints were made that Amazon wasn't enforcing public health orders. WSIB concluded that during "the outreach" Amazon was in compliance with orders.[43] Later in December, the *National Post*'s Tom Blackwell confirmed at least 400 COVID-19 cases at Peel Region Amazon facilities.[44] An outbreak at Amazon's Brampton facility in March 2021 infected more than 600 workers, and public health closed the facility down for several days.[45]

Advocates pointed to the obsession that Amazon has with speed and how, combined with precarious work, it reduced resistance to a COVID-19 outbreak. Mojtehedzadeh quoted Mandeep Singh, a seasonal hire who quit after he realized that working up to 60 hours per week during the busiest times would be, "impossible to juggle with his other job." Mojtehedzadeh doesn't tease this out further, but this piece of information pointed to one of the most efficient ways that COVID-19 spread, and therefore the most effective way in which it could have been slowed: employee movement was one of the most rapid and dangerous forms of COVID-19 transmission. Workers who weren't paid enough to hold only one job and who then must cobble together a living working in multiple workplaces expand their social bubble by necessity. Outside healthcare, there was no discussion at all among politicians, public health officials or journalists about the role this kind of necessary mobility played in spreading COVID-19, even though it was known to be dangerous in healthcare.

Rather than close down manufacturing and parts of construction, as was done during Québec's first wave, the Québec government said in early December that it had no plans to do it again during the second wave, despite COVID-19 spreading more than it had been during the spring.[46] Instead, the government promised to increase inspections from the Commission des normes, de l'équité, de la santé et de la sécurité du travail (CNESST). The organization focused more on awareness and education than handing out fines, according to Nicolas Bégin from the CNESST, and only handed out 35 fines: 11 in food industries, 11 in construction, five in health, five in commerce and three listed as "other." In the region Montérégie-Est, most complaints were related to workplace sanitary measures: social distancing, physical barriers, air quality and masks.[47] When the province imposed its curfew in January 2021, it again exempted manufacturing, business services companies and construction, despite these being the workplace industries with the highest number of outbreaks.

Mining and energy work camps were also a source of major outbreaks and COVID-19 spread. And, as workers flew into these locations from all over Canada, they were important nodes of virus spread into communities all across the country. Worksites were very rarely shut down, despite public health measures that were inadequate. In Alberta, tar sands camps were the sites of Canada's biggest outbreaks.[48] More than 1400 workers got COVID-19 at Canadian Natural Resources Limited's (CNRL) Horizon site. More than 1100 workers at the Syncrude Mildred Lake site caught COVID-19, 750 at Suncor base plant and 16 at other tar sands operations across the province. One worker at the CNRL Horizon site told CBC *Edmonton*, "I am sharing my washroom and shower with someone who has COVID every week ... I have been in a lunchroom with 36 people and 34 of them had tested positive for COVID." Even though in these locations some work had been scaled back, there were still an estimated 10,000 workers at sites across the province; they were never shut down.[49] On May 5, 2021, the Alberta government announced new restrictions to try and get COVID-19 spread under control. The announcement closed restaurants and moved all schools online, but exempted tar sands work camps. The government made it clear that it believed vaccines were the only way to stop transmission and worked with companies to set up vaccination sites.[50] From March 2020 to July 2021, at least 14 workers died from COVID-19 they contracted working either in mines, forestry or energy.[51]

There was very little information anywhere in Canada about who was dying from COVID-19 they had obtained on the job, outside of healthcare settings. I tracked 167 deaths related to a workplace outbreak from March 2020 to July 2021, including healthcare settings, but this number was undoubtedly low. While there were some regional public health agencies that reported this information, and some information that was available through workplace health and safety organizations like the CNESST, WSIB or WorkSafeBC, the data was hard to obtain, rarely named which employer a worker worked for and didn't provide dates of deaths. The numbers that I had compiled came from a combination of GoFundMe information, media reports and announcements made by a worker's union. Canada's lack of data stood in direct contrast with how the United Kingdom's Office for National Statistics (ONS) reported deaths from among its working-age population. In a report that covered March 9 to December 28, 2020, the ONS reported that 7961 people in England and Wales died from COVID-19 between the ages of 20 and 64. While the data didn't specifically connect deaths to workplace outbreaks, they connected the deaths to the person's place of work. They found that men working "elementary occupations" which are characterized as being jobs performing mostly routine tasks and often requiring physical labour and little education, and caring, leisure and service occupations had the highest rates of death. For women, the highest rate of death occurred among workers from caring, leisure, service occupations and process, plant and machine operatives. Almost three-quarters of deaths in the social care occupations happened among care workers. It also found that deaths among teachers were not statistically significant when compared with death in the general population.[52] This data is similar to the data that I collected for Canada, but we had no way of knowing just how similar the two countries' death patterns are because of how poor Canada's data collection and reporting mechanisms are.

Even though there was such little data related to workplace deaths, workers dying from COVID-19 preoccupied journalists. As such, there was a lot of attention on the movement that was calling for mandatory paid sick days. But paying workers to stay home was the kind of radical idea that not one single government seriously considered, aside from the fact that a CEWS payment for a laid-off worker was effectively paying someone to stay home. The most basic version of this was paid sick leave. By the end of 2020, this key struggle emerged as a key demand. One of the organizations fighting hardest for this was Toronto's Workers' Action Centre, who argued again and again that workers needed the ability to skip work for any hope to slow the spread of COVID-19:

> Since the onset of the pandemic, medical experts have repeatedly called on government officials to bring in paid sick leave measures, which have been proven to be an effective tool in curbing infection rates and saving lives. As Dr. Lawrence Loh, Peel's Medical Officer of Health recently observed: "It's time for employers who choose not to pay employees when they are sick to put people over profit. The cost of COVID-19 spreading across our community is far greater than the price of a few sick days."[53]

Paid sick days and other workplace measures were all necessary to help slow the spread of COVID-19. As the BCCDC survey mentioned earlier showed, workplace accommodations were necessary for nearly half of British Columbians to be able to respect social distancing orders. Statistics Canada found that among small businesses, the businesses with the most workers were least likely to provide their employees with time off: where more than 40% of businesses with fewer than 19 employees provided staff with paid or unpaid time off, that number dropped to just 24% of businesses with 100 employees or more. That's despite the relatively higher revenues these businesses reported than smaller businesses. Governments needed to mandate that workers be given paid time off for it to have happened, and without it, COVID-19 would, of course, continue to spread within workplaces.[54]

The advocacy group Warehouse Workers Centre called for more rapid testing of warehouse workers, a solution that would have caught at least some infections from workers who are asymptomatic. Rapid tests did eventually become part of Ontario's pandemic measures, but when they were announced on February 12, 2021, the government gave essential businesses six times the number of rapid tests than they gave schools. Large congregant workplaces were not being required to pay for tests and use them. But still, they received more help than other large congregant settings like schools that were under the direct control of the province. In Doug Ford's Ontario, all pandemic measures were undertaken to ensure business as usual in the pursuit of profit, at the expense of everyone on whose backs those profits were made possible.

There were many ways that large congregant workplaces could have been made safer, but journalists rarely engaged with ideas to make these spaces safer, and politicians didn't feel the pressure to impose more regulations on them. CUPW's Kaur mentioned to CBC Radio's *As It Happens* that Amazon should have rented another warehouse facility to allow workers to spread out more, an option that made a lot of sense considering the internal pressures on social distancing. But where was this suggestion in all the other coverage on Amazon or large warehouse outbreaks? In Tom Blackwell's article about Amazon, he wrote, "And no one suggests the industrial plants be shut down entirely," an unattributed claim that sounded like there were no options between doing nothing and shutting down industry entirely. Indeed, during a holiday rush where Canadians were shipping items more than usual, to close down Amazon entirely would have caused a lot of headache. But while Blackwell's article featured several suggestions to make these workplaces safer, the question of an industry slowdown couldn't be entertained, brushed off instead as something that "no one" would think of. Why couldn't something like construction be paused for a few weeks? Or labour camps for mining or tar sands projects? Were they so essential to Canadians that we simply had to live with the outbreaks they caused, while Canadians were told that seeing a loved one was absolutely too risky and they would have to abstain for a few weeks, a few months or even a year? Why did factories in outbreak stay open, while tens of thousands of people missed out on the final days of a loved one's life, told that their presence was simply too dangerous? The clear contradiction exposed governments of all stripes' priorities: profits are more important than everything else, even worker health.

TRANSIT

By the end of 2020, the role that workplaces played in perpetuating the pandemic was, finally, undeniable. In December, media started to pay closer attention to outbreaks at large congregant worksites, reported more and more by journalists who weren't normally on the workplace beat. It shouldn't have taken so long to hear the calls of worker advocacy organizations for paid sick leave, more profound workplace inspections and workplace closures. During 2021, as attention increased on these workplaces, politicians finally moved to shut some of them down due to COVID-19 outbreaks, in very limited circumstances. The impact workplaces had on workers' health was obvious during the first wave, and the information about who was dying from COVID-19 should have brought intense focus to the safety of workers, especially in transit. But it didn't, barely warranting more than a mention here and there as outbreaks arose or as a worker's death was announced. By the end of 2020, even though transit was not the site of the most workplace outbreaks, the majority of workers who had died from COVID-19 worked in transit.

The first cluster of transit-industry deaths occurred among Aerofleet airport limousine drivers based at Toronto's Pearson Airport. On May 6, 2020, the union representing these workers, the Airport Taxi Association, revealed that at least ten airport taxi and limo drivers had died from COVID-19, though that number was likely far higher. The story appeared quietly each time the union announced a new death toll — first four, then five and then finally, ten.[55] Two more deaths related to Pearson Airport limo drivers would be announced in passing in a feature from *Toronto Life* magazine. After that, journalists stopped covering it as a story in and of itself, only appearing from time to time as taxi drivers raised concerns about their safety and security. The employee fleet comprised of mostly racialized and immigrant men surely played into the lack of attention that journalists paid this crisis. In Montréal, the Regroupement des propriétaires de Taxi de Montréal reported that by June 5, at least two drivers who regularly serviced Trudeau Airport had died.[56] Despite these stories, there was hardly any follow-up about the deceased, taxi safety, what Canada might learn from other countries' taxi industries and what travellers' options are if they arrive in Canada and don't have a ride from the airport. And unlike other stories of worker death, journalists rarely looked at the personal lives or featured grieving family members the way they did for other COVID-19 victims.

At least 12 deaths in a single industry in just a few months should have changed how journalists wrote about transit workers, but it didn't. There were no other reports in large international hubs like Vancouver or Calgary of taxi driver deaths, or follow-ups in Montréal and Toronto. While the taxi fleet that services Pearson Airport was diminished by the pandemic, it still remained necessary work, as flights continued to arrive in and depart from Toronto. But it wasn't until June 24, 2020, that the Greater Toronto Airport Authority (GTAA) promised to give plastic dividers to drivers to install in their cars — a critical health and safety improvement for taxis.[57] Drivers were also still expected to pay at least some of their airport fees, regardless of how much less they were driving due to decreased flight activity. The GTAA had waived the fee for April to June but still wanted drivers to pay 50% of their fees for the rest of the year — a ridiculous thing to ask of drivers, some of whom had stopped working completely because of the pandemic.[58] But aside from a few articles related to these negotiations, there was no more media attention paid to taxi drivers who worked at Canada's largest transportation hub where flights were routinely landing with COVID-19 positive passengers on board.[59]

Stories about transit workers and COVID-19 were few and far between, mostly clustered in December 2020. Taxi drivers were often lumped in a general category of workers who were essential, frontline or taking tremendous risks, but journalists didn't examine how government policy was failing them by allowing COVID-19 to spread within their industry. *CTV News Windsor* talked with Bogand Herbetko, a taxi driver who got COVID-19 and who had regularly driven people to and from the local hospital at a moment where COVID-19 cases were surging. "My job is not very safe, but you know, everybody has gotta bring food to the family," he said.[60] Soner Yasa told *Global News Edmonton* that he had been following all safety protocols he could, and yet when a passenger asked him to take her to get a COVID-19 test, he worried that he was not adequately protected to drive someone who thought they might have COVID-19. The *Winnipeg Free Press* interviewed drivers who made the same points, adding that the lack of places to use a bathroom was a particularly vicious change to their jobs, in addition to seeing their salaries plummet. Malkeet Makkar said, "It's not safe, but we have no choice ... It's our duty. We are also front-liners."[61] Fadel Al-Othman told the *Regina Leader-Post* in January 2021 he also didn't feel safe driving a cab as cases were growing in Prince Albert. The former Syrian refugee had been tested for COVID-19 several times.[62] Journalists chose to tell these stories as a narrative that focused tightly on the subject, rather than trying to understand the social forces that combined to make driving a cab so dangerous. Canada's pandemic mitigation strategy relied heavily on low-income workers doing dangerous work to keep others safe, and yet taxi drivers were rarely part of that conversation, even though they were part of the transportation strategy for potentially infected individuals in towns and cities all across Canada. And because they were rarely a part of the conversation, there was no pressure placed on politicians to force them to improve taxi drivers' safety and security.

When journalists covered drivers' complaints as individualized, personal struggles, they created a narrative that was absent of broader connections to public policy that placed taxi drivers in danger. On December 14, when a journalist asked about the possibility of Edmonton helping to better equip taxi drivers to transport people who have COVID-19, Edmonton Mayor Don Iveson said that this kind of request had never been made. The city told people to use a taxi if they needed to get a COVID-19 test and didn't have access to a car, and yet Iveson had no plans to make taxis safer.[63]

As a key part of transportation networks, taxis should have been seen as a service that government had a responsibility to make safer. In Toronto, the operations manager of Beck Taxi told CBC News that Beck drivers were routinely asked to transport people with probable or confirmed cases of COVID-19, including by Toronto Public Health agents. Still, the city made no effort to equip drivers with adequate PPE, train them to reduce their risk with passengers, or pay them better for their necessary services. Driver Jafar Mirsalari said,

> When people call 911 now, the ambulance people, they show up, fully equipped and fully covered … Now I heard that the city wants us, knowingly, to take the risk without any protection. I don't know if they want us to do the essential work, but who wants to be [responsible] for my loss — not only for my business, but for my health?[64]

Mirsalari spoke to CBC News in November 2020, seven months after Beck Taxi had found out that City of Toronto officials had told people to take a cab home after their COVID-19 tests. In May 2020, Beck spokesperson Kristine Hubbard told CTV News they were angry with the city for potentially putting their workers' lives at risk. In response, Toronto Mayor John Tory promised to develop a plan with taxi companies to ensure that people who had COVID-19 could be transported safely. Fast-forward to the fall when the second wave was picking up, and still, nothing Tory had promised had been done for the taxi industry.[65] In the intervening seven months, the City of Toronto had not made arrangements with the taxi companies to ensure that this could be done safely.

Taxis were integrated into city transportation networks, relied on by city services and public health to transport people, and necessary for people who are most at risk of COVID-19, yet the plight of cab drivers was ignored. Drivers, as individual operators, may not have even been represented in official workplace outbreak counts because if a driver was infected on the job, it was unlikely that they were infected by a coworker. There's no question that this industry, already battered by new rideshare apps driving down the price of rides, was hit hard. This is directly related to its workers — mostly racialized men, many recent immigrants and people who make a modest living — who don't have the political capital necessary to force journalists to write about their stories more than a few times or to force politicians to actually do something to make their jobs safer. And journalists, hearing daily pleas from officials for people to get tested, didn't dig into this problem of how people are expected to do this if they can't access a testing centre without relying on a taxi to get them there. Taxi drivers were dying, in plain sight.

It wasn't just taxi drivers who were catching COVID-19 and dying; other transport workers faced the same dangerous contexts of mobility, contact with many different people over the course of a day's work and being deemed an essential service. Public transit employees were particularly at risk: at least eight died from March 2020 to June 30, 2021. Drivers with public transport agencies in Brampton, Calgary, Montréal and Toronto died, as did a bus driver who worked transporting Cargill employees to work at their Guelph, Ontario, plant.[66] Bus drivers got more coverage than taxi drivers, but not as much as other kinds of employees, even though outbreaks within transit company ranks were rampant. Coverage was mostly tied to exposure alerts: telling passengers they may have been exposed to COVID-19 on a particular route and time of day. Some of the coverage focused on whether masks should be made mandatory for drivers, many of whom were working behind a plexiglass barrier that didn't seal the driver away from passengers.[67] School bus drivers received more media coverage than city bus drivers as parents were a more profitable target audience than bus riders. There were also reports of violence faced by bus drivers who tried to enforce public health orders like mask wearing among their passengers, including one London bus driver who was shoved by a passenger when he asked her to put a mask on.[68] News reported about hundreds of public transit employees being laid off as ridership dropped and anxiety was "through the roof" — a sentiment from Ken Wilson, president of the Amalgamated Transit Union Local 508 in Halifax, and echoed across transit authorities. But it was rare to find a news report or analysis that explored what made public transit so dangerous for drivers; if the question was explored at all, the story focused on users, not workers. In the black hole of information, there was very little discussion about necessary public health or public policy interventions beyond the plexiglass and mask.[69]

If Canada's largest workplace death cluster was known by May 2020, it should have triggered Canadian journalists to dig into what was known about air circulation and virus propagation within vehicles, and they could have posed broader societal questions about transportation during a crisis. Stories about the danger faced by public transportation drivers in the U.S., or Uber and Lyft drivers in the United Kingdom circulated widely during spring 2020. On May 8, NBC reported that almost 100 public transit operators in New York City had died from COVID-19, as did workers in New Orleans, Boston, Seattle and Chicago. In the U.S., more than half of all transit operators are racialized.[70] These stories about American transit operator deaths sparked workers at dozens of Canadian transit authorities to refuse to accept fares during spring 2020 to avoid interacting directly with passengers, insisting they could instead hop on and off from the back door without needing to show proof of payment or deposit a fare. By summer 2020, drivers were mostly behind plexiglass, and fare collection resumed. But during the second wave in fall 2020, there were no new measures in place to protect drivers thereafter, and none of the measures that had been in place, like free fares, were re-imposed.

Vehicles were obviously a COVID-19 hazard, as none of the most important social distancing measures could be implemented inside a tiny space. Bus drivers could rely on their unions and collective power to simply not collect fares in the early stages of the pandemic; cab drivers didn't have any similar options. Taxis were unsafe for similar reasons that buses were unsafe: lots of contact with many different people throughout a day spent in an enclosed space. But where buses had more square footage, cars were far more dangerous. This was suggested early on in the pandemic, and one study released in January 2021, which simulated airflow within a car modelled on a Toyota Prius, confirmed what made general sense. Risk of COVID-19 transmission was higher in a car with all windows rolled up and air conditioning on than it was with a car with all of its windows rolled down. Interestingly, they found that rolling only the windows down of occupants (if the car had two individuals inside) was less effective than if the windows adjacent to the driver and passenger was open. And, when cars were driving slowly, there was a higher chance of pathogen spread than when they were driving fast.[71]

The erasure of the transit industry from the discussions about safety and COVID-19 cannot be untied from the fact that transit is an industry full of racialized workers, especially among cab drivers. When the Pearson Airport drivers died, that should have triggered a wave of coverage that focused on how safe driving is, because driving with people you don't live with is ubiquitous even if you are not a cab or bus driver. But, for politicians and journalists, it just didn't warrant attention beyond a passing reference to 12 dead drivers. How many drivers could have avoided getting sick if, in May 2020, journalists explored ways in which drivers could be kept safer, and politicians were called on to implement these changes? Just as with other workplace outbreaks, the risks were clear and the impact of the virus was sometimes deadly, yet the stories were obscured, relegated to a simple passing reference, or ignored entirely.

Every time it appeared that lockdown measures were doing little to stop the spread of COVID-19, a new round of hand wringing started. Politicians made it sound as if they were doing everything they possibly could, and journalists were not challenging them enough on their talking points. When increasing lockdown measures did little to stop the spread, it should have been a national scandal that the worksites with the largest outbreaks were also the ones mostly exempt from the same rules making so many Canadians miserable. It caused extreme cognitive dissonance to hear a public health official like Alberta's Chief Medical Officer of Health Deena Hinshaw telling young people to do more to stop the spread of COVID-19 while labour camps, food processing facilities and manufacturing facilities were unaffected by new, stricter public health measures.

But perhaps journalists could have been forgiven for missing this story for most of the pandemic. Maybe it wasn't fair to expect so much from a group of people who had lost so much themselves. As Canada faced year two of pandemic measures in March 2021, the journalism industry was hobbling across the first anniversary of pandemic reporting. Battered, bruised and far lighter than it was one year earlier, the very industry Canadians needed to tell them the story of COVID-19 had barely made it through.

March 2021
ONE YEAR IN MEDIA CUTS

Cases: 817,591
Deaths: 22,017[1]

In each chapter of this book, I've explored how journalists' lack of critical reporting on the pandemic enabled politicians to get away with doing the bare minimum to help Canadians. But while politicians had an interest in supressing information, confusing the population and using the pandemic in various ways to boost their popularity, journalists did not have such an obvious reason for going along with this rhetoric. And indeed, dozens of journalists refused to go along with it. But the default coverage was uncritical. It didn't give Canadians the tools they needed to be able to effectively call out their politicians. It didn't challenge politicians enough. There are many reasons for why this was the case, and it wasn't as simple as pleasing a corporate ownership structure that had an interest in maintaining the status quo, though there was certainly a lot of that. During 2020, Canada's media industry went through changes like never before and journalists were caught in a difficult situation: not enough resources, not enough time, not enough colleagues to be able to effectively challenge political rhetoric and give Canadians the kind of reporting we so desperately needed. Structural problems within journalism added to the problems: an overwhelmingly white establishment with too many white, able-bodied journalists writing about a pandemic that disproportionately impacted and caused harm to non-white, disabled individuals meant that the coverage was always going to fall short of what the moment demanded.

Staying on top of workplace outbreaks was labour intensive. Sometimes, knowing about them required that journalists were in steady contact with workers and could bypass a company's corporate communications office. Or, sometimes a reporter might learn about an outbreak in a small community through personal connections, which could then be reported earlier than even public health was willing to confirm. Reporting during a pandemic required a well-funded, well-connected and diverse media industry, with enough resources to maintain smaller community newspapers as well as beat reporters who could watch industries closely. As it was, there were very few journalists who were able to immediately see what COVID-19 would do to communities generally and workers specifically. With politicians guided by their own agendas, journalism that was proactive, critical and local was absolutely necessary. And yet by March 2021, the industry had been battered, with thousands fewer jobs remaining after year one of the pandemic than there had ever been in the modern era of Canada's mass communications industry.

With the obvious exception of travel, few industries were hit as hard by the pandemic as journalism was. Almost overnight, many journalists worked under double pressure: the pressure from the pandemic that forced them to stay home, both away from their desks and away from covering stories on the ground, but also the pressure of trying to write about a global and historical phenomenon with fewer colleagues to pick up other stories and angles. Journalists found themselves laid off or politely told there was just no money to be able to pay for their freelance pieces. Downsizing had a particular impact on local news, where stories about the pandemic were close to home and where citizens needed to hear, more than ever, a local perspective on what was happening.

While many journalists did excellent reporting during the pandemic, daily reports from large news agencies were not much more than stenography, repeating the messages of politicians and public health officials without adding important details like who owned what facility, what owners were doing to reduce the spread of COVID-19 and how political directives were or were not being followed. And because the national networks and chains influence local coverage, it meant that this stenography filtered down into smaller outlets too. The pandemic was a disaster for journalism at the exact time that Canadians needed journalists more than ever to stand up to power, challenge rhetoric and, critically, offer Canadians a vision of Canada that could grow from the disastrous impacts of the pandemic.

MEDIA LAYOFFS

During the pandemic, journalism became many things for Canadians. It was an emergency alert broadcast system that could carry live political and public health messages to people immediately. It was a public education tool, explaining to individuals how they could keep themselves safe during the pandemic, what to do if they thought they had COVID-19 and where they could go or call to get a test. It broadcast daily changes about the spread of COVID-19, from new COVID-19 cases to ICU bed counts or COVID-19 recoveries. It also tracked trends: from emerging variants to emerging outbreaks. Journalism was a contradictory location of power: both power that upheld and maintained the status quo, and power that could confront the status quo. Through investigations and analysis, journalists could influence public policies, generate favour or opposition for public health measures, and try to hold politicians to account for their actions, be they a trip to Hawaii for Christmas while everyone was locked down, or a decision to purchase millions of certain vaccines rather than others. The role of journalism was so broad and so important, that it was clear by the first weeks of March that Canada's media establishment would not be up to the challenge of doing all of these tasks, even in spite of the herculean efforts of hundreds of individual journalists.

It certainly didn't help that many of the cuts were self-imposed, usually owing to a culture of cuts and downsizing that predated the pandemic. On March 18, 2020, CBC News announced that all local dinnertime and late-night news broadcasts in English would be cancelled, and news would be broadcast centrally out of Toronto. Brodie Fenlon, editor-in-chief and executive director for daily news for CBC News argued that the move was necessary, due to a lack of skills required to pull off local TV with people isolating at home. In a post from his editors' blog, he wrote,

> A story of this magnitude — one that changes by the hour — places incredible demands on our staff and our infrastructure in order to get the most accurate and up-to-date information to audiences. Television is especially resource-intensive, and many jobs are difficult to do at home. Our systems are overtaxed, and we had to make adjustments as a result.[2]

Decentralized versus centralized news would be the struggle at the heart of how the pandemic was covered, moving from reporting that understood a certain flow and culture of a community to reporting that glossed over regional differences and gave Canadians something that was supposed to be one-size-fits-all. The organization Friends of Canadian Broadcasting argued the decision was only inevitable thanks to the multi-year squeeze on CBC News' operating budget: "It is the result of chronic underfunding and generations of CBC management teams that regard local news as expendable."[3] Steve Faguy, journalist and imitable media watcher similarly argued it was the CBC's previous decisions to centralize that likely created the crisis in the first place:

> This wouldn't be an issue if CBC hadn't centralized so much of its technical operations. If local stations truly controlled their own broadcasts, they wouldn't need Toronto. Under normal circumstances, centralization saves money and staff and works well enough. But when a crisis happens, this system has a huge vulnerability.[4]

On the first day of this new media landscape, Faguy noted that due to the content of the new, centrally coordinated line-up, "Montréal viewers tuning into their 6pm local newscast got a total of 90 seconds of local news. And Ottawa viewers got a grand total of zero."[5] It wasn't until April 15 that all local news broadcasts were restored.[6]

Faguy argued that local newsrooms could have been able to manage their own pandemic reporting from March until April 2020 if they had been properly resourced and given the opportunity. The pandemic made local coverage absolutely critical: journalists who knew their communities would be able to spot infection patterns far faster than someone who was located in Toronto. They would also be able to follow public health decisions, local outbreaks and COVID-19 spread more efficiently than a news service located hundreds or thousands of kilometres away. While there were roles for both national and local news to play, COVID-19 put tremendous strain on both, and centralization often won out in the tug-of-war.

The first six weeks of the pandemic were especially brutal for Canadian media. *J-Source's* COVID-19 Media Impact Map tracked layoffs and closures from March 11 to April 29, 2020, and found that 129 media outlets across Canada had experienced some kind of COVID-19-related impact. Fifty outlets closed, either temporarily or permanently, 19 cancelled some or all of their print editions, 16 cut back on broadcasts and four reduced coverage. There were 78 outlets where people had lost jobs and 53 where workers had their pay or hours reduced. Of these were outlets owned by Atlantic Canada–based Saltwire Network (25) and Postmedia (15). The overwhelming majority of cuts occurred in English-language media (107). Eighteen outlets were French-language, two were Chinese, two were Russian and one was Inuktitut.[7] The Saltwire layoffs represented 40% of its staff.[8]

On April 6, 2020, Torstar announced that it would eliminate 85 jobs and reduce executive pay as the pandemic ravaged their income. But in an article tucked behind a paywall, it was reported that Torstar CEO John Boynton said while advertising revenue was down (because people were not shopping), subscription revenues and web traffic increased.[9] On August 5, 2020, Torstar was acquired by NordStar Capital LP, a private equity firm.[10] Some of these jobs were saved, like 24 positions at the *Hamilton Spectator*, thanks to negotiations with the union, Unifor Local 87-M.[11] Québecor also announced temporary layoffs of 1150 employees and Black Press Media and Glacier Media cut pay and reduced hours. Journalism professor April Lindgren noted that the exact number of how many was not released.[12]

Layoffs only got worse from there. In June 2020, *Vice* laid off 19 people.[13] In July, it was *Global*'s turn, laying off 70 people according to the Canadian Association of Journalists, though the corporation refused to clarify how many people would be impacted. These layoffs decimated their lifestyle, entertainment and social media divisions, and surprisingly cut one of Canada's most popular daily news podcasts, *Wait, There's More*.[14] *Global* also laid off Jamie Orchard, the anchor of their daily Montréal news broadcast, and replaced her with Tracy Tong who broadcasted out of Toronto. This was part of a broader shift, which started years ago, to centralize news operations in Toronto and fill in the content of the broadcasts with local content: in 2015, *Global* shifted all local news shows to be centrally hosted in Toronto, with the exception of Vancouver, Edmonton and Calgary.[15]

By September, Friends of Canadian Broadcasting estimated that there had been 2096 layoffs in media so far in 2020. That same month, *Le Journal de Québec* announced 14 layoffs[16] and Postmedia announced a third round of layoffs in 2020 alone.[17] In October, the Weather Network eliminated 14 positions,[18] Groupe TVA and TVA Sports Québec cut 37 positions combined.[19]

October was also when the CBC announced that it would cut 130 positions across Canada, mostly in Toronto — the location where staff shortages in March forced the corporation to centralize all television evening and nighttime news. Management blamed the cuts on a loss of revenue from COVID-19 and a $21 million deficit left over from 2019. The corporation did not receive COVID-19 aid money from the federal government. While private telecommunication companies received more than $240 million from Canada Emergency Wage Subsidy (CEWS) between March 2020 and February 2021, and still paid out shareholders, as I explain below, the CBC was given nothing: no help through the CEWS and no additional funding to help make up for the drop in advertising.[20] In December, management announced that Radio-Canada International would be cut to just nine employees, from "several hundred years earlier" as explained by the organization Friends of Canadian Broadcasting.[21] The cuts were a devastating example of where management's priorities were: there was no attempt to restructure to save local news, no large campaign for federal money to help them weather the storm. With $1.2 billion in operating funding from the federal government and an employee base of 7400 before the 2020 layoffs, the CBC should have been a central part of COVID-19 relief measures.[22] The federal government could have flowed millions to the CBC to give newsrooms across Canada more resources to support crucial local news during a global health crisis. Instead, more than 100 workers were laid off while remaining staff were expected to maintain a level of news quality under the pressure of shrinking revenues and the generalized stress of the pandemic.

It didn't take too long into 2021 for another massive round of layoffs to be announced. Just days after Bell's annual mental health fundraising day, the corporation announced hundreds of layoffs across multiple platforms. There were 210 layoffs in Toronto alone, and TSN-branded radio stations in Vancouver, Winnipeg and Hamilton would be commuted to BNN Bloomberg stations no longer covering only sports. Management announced that channels in Vancouver and Winnipeg would be now following a "funny format, which has already proven highly successful in markets like Hamilton and Calgary with its stand-up comedy content."[23] All newsroom staff at Montréal's CJAD, including one of only three English-language reporters at the National Assembly in Quebec City, were laid off.[24] Not only had Bell received more than $100 million in federal wage subsidy support, the corporation made a sizable profit during the pandemic. With so many people stuck at home needing both better Internet access and electronic diversions, it wasn't surprising that the corporation ended 2020 solidly in the black. Their dividends increased by 5.1% and while their net profit over 2019 was down, Bell Canada Enterprises (BCE) still made $2.699 billion.[25] In the context of both a massive dip into the federal wage subsidy (which was a perfectly legal thing to do: they could demonstrate a drop in revenue from 2019, and certainly if they teased their media properties out from their holdings) and massive profits, laying off hundreds of media workers was a bad look. After Bell, it was *Huffington Post Canada*, which was closed completely by its U.S.-based parent company *Buzzfeed*.

Clearly, media owned and operated in the pursuit of profit didn't actually care if local journalists were overworked or only able to republish or broadcast a press release. It's in this context that the CBC, Canada's national public broadcaster, should have been seen as the antidote to for-profit media corporations and in the service of creating content in the public's interest. But managers are managers, and CBC management, even if some of them spent months of the pandemic managing the corporation from outside of Canada, are subject to same obsession to reduce costs at the expense of quality news.[26]

Canadian media corporations saw their workers, the ones who gather, report and analyze the news, as expendable. Sometimes, it was justified in the face of shrinking revenues. Sometimes, it was explained with buzzwords like "streamlining" or "efficiencies." But regardless of why, in the wake of these decisions was a crisis in reporting as historic as the pandemic itself. Pandemic reporting tended to be so rote that there was little difference between copy from corporation A and corporation B in daily reporting. The overall result was that Canadians were missing credible analysis that could help explain what the public health officers meant to say or what the impact of a political decision might mean based on the evidence available. This was especially a problem for local news, both in small parts of Canada and its largest cities, where a lack of bodies at desks meant that daily COVID-19 coverage was disjointed, ahistorical and very often, not much deeper than the daily report that a local public health officer had delivered.

THE DEMISE OF LOCAL NEWS

At the start of the pandemic, when everything shut down quickly, people were told to stay at home if they could. I had been laid off. I had kids home for the next foreseeable months, and I was obsessed with what has happening in the world around me that I could no longer access. I needed to hear voices explain how the latest updates affected my family, so I turned to local news. Local news is powerful because you come to know the voices who explain your community to you. You might know what they normally think about politics. Your kids might be in the same class. You might know the story behind some salacious report about a driveway dispute. Local news allowed me to ground myself in the disorienting early days of the pandemic. I read my local newspaper, *le Soleil*, aloud to my kids each morning.

It wasn't too long after lockdown started when the cooperative that owns *le Soleil*, the Coopérative nationale de l'information indépendante announced it would be cancelling daily newspaper delivery to make up for revenue shortfalls. The cooperative had only just formed at the end of 2019, after a judge approved the plan to buy out six local newspapers previously owned by Groupe Capitales Médias and for the employees to run it.[27] The daily newspapers *le Soleil* in Quebec City, *Le Nouvelliste* in Trois-Rivières, *La Trubune* in Sherbrooke, *La Voix de l'Est* in Granby and Ottawa's *Le Droit* decided that ending daily circulation while maintaining a weekend newspaper was their best option. There I was, after seven years of receiving a daily newspaper that I never had time to read, finally in the rhythm of reading every word on the page, losing my newest daily routine. At least I still had CBC Radio, which broadcast to all of Québec in English until 8:37 each morning. But it was barely local either: at 8:37 a.m. it switched to Toronto, and then Ottawa for the live coverage of Justin Trudeau's daily outdoor briefing at 11:00 a.m. until noon. My airwaves would then be occupied by Montréal until 2:00 p.m., and then back to Toronto until the province-wide drive-home show at 4:00 p.m. I wasn't alone in my desire for more local news or my reliance on the CBC. One survey found that 51.3% of Canadians relied on news outlets for their main source of news (rather than social media or public health officers or politicians directly). When split among age groups, Canadians aged 50 and over were more likely to get their information from news, though 47.1% of Canadians under 50 also said they get their information from news sources.[28] By April 2021, I would also lose my weekend routine of reading the Saturday *Globe and Mail*, as circulation was cut east of Montréal.

I consumed a lot of not-local news. The daily din of doctors, epidemiologists, politicians, public health officers, the CFIB and other voices that Toronto, mostly, decided Canada should hear didn't tell me what was happening in my neighbourhood or my city. I heard reports from Montréal about an outbreak just past my kids' school, and only when the outbreak had grown large enough to merit out-of-Québec-City, English-language coverage. My kids' school was never in the news — we were at the whim of the grapevine to find out what was going on. Stories of COVID-19 exposures in restaurants and bar kitchens passed through text messages or Facebook. It wasn't until November 2020 that public health issued a list of ongoing outbreaks in the Quebec City region. They stopped reporting outbreaks publicly at the end of June 2021. I may have been up-to-date with every announcement made by Canadian politicians while writing this book, but almost everything I knew about COVID-19 in my community came from word-of-mouth.

The lack of local news created a pernicious problem. Stories about COVID-19 were told in proximity to where they were written rather than from the perspectives of people living within an area. The Local News Research Project found that during the first months of the pandemic, Canada lost 50 community newspapers (both temporarily and permanently) and 18 cancelled some or all print editions and three reduced coverage. There were 59 layoffs associated with these news organizations and 33 reduced their workers' pay or hours. Community news organizations were hit hardest by these financial compressions. University X School of Journalism Professor April Lindgren, founder of the Local News Research Project, argued that the loss of local news has complex and far-reaching consequences:

> Researchers have argued that local journalism in particular is as important to the functioning and vibrancy of local communities as clean drinking water, safe streets and good schools. Scholars have linked loss of access to local news to increased political polarization, reduced public input into municipal decision-making, drops in voter turnout, better re-election prospects for incumbents, and the emergence of hyper-partisan websites masquerading as straight news. Local reporting is also integral to democracy because it holds power accountable and builds a sense of community by providing residents with shared knowledge, which fosters empathy and understanding of other perspectives.[29]

While bad enough in normal times, losing local information during a pandemic was catastrophic. If local news can help individuals feel rooted to their communities in a formal and networked way, losing it explains part of why thinking collectively or from a community perspective through the pandemic was difficult, especially when politicians and national news agencies emphasized individual responsibility. Politicians could announce they had tried everything when, in fact, they had tried very little. Individuals who did not hear local issues broadcast back to them, who did not have access to what their local politicians were or were not doing in relation to COVID-19 aid or who did not hear any connection from the news to their real-life circumstances, experienced an information deficit.

Local news has been in crisis in Canada for years and politicians have debated what they think is the best way forward to fund local news. In 2018, the federal government decided to flow money directly to news organizations to fund new reporter positions. The one-year, renewable grants funded more than 160 reporting positions across Canada and reporters funded through the Local Journalism Initiative (LJI) became key voices from the front lines of the pandemic. LJI journalists in smaller markets were often the only reporters who did daily COVID-19 reporting. Positions funded through the LJI were indicated as such, so it became obvious as I scoured daily news summaries just how many print organizations relied on this envelope of money to fund local news.

The federal money was controversial. Many argued government should not be in the business of funding news at all, or that the program developed in 2018 privileged the largest corporations and a dying news model over newer media organizations. In a *Nieman Lab* article, Jeremy Klaszus from Calgary's *The Sprawl* is quoted from Twitter, where he decries the expectations tied to the funding: LJI -funded journalists must publish at least five stories per week and they must be regularly employed journalists. This automatically disqualified news organizations like *The Sprawl* while providing for the largest media corporations, who were struggling because they were loyal to an old journalism model where subscriptions and advertising generate profits, some of which could be used to create more daily journalism. It also disqualified freelancers from being able to access jobs funded through the LJI. In 2019, the government established a system to decide which news organizations got the LJI money to ensure that industry representatives, not government, handed the money out. This was also criticized, as the newspaper industry group News Media Canada was chosen to dole out this money, indicating latent support for legacy media organizations. Christian Dognon from News Media Canada replied to criticism that the initiative squeezed out new initiatives:

> By nature, pop-up journalism organizations do not have an ongoing presence in the communities they cover and therefore are not engaged in ongoing service to the community ... The civic journalism created under the LJI is meant for the residents of the community, but if the pop-up journalism organization does not

have a relationship with those residents, we cannot be certain that their stories will reach them.[30]

Dognon's defence sounded like the money indeed sought to protect legacy media organizations by ensuring they could access aid while keeping smaller or newer organizations out, rather than for a local community to receive quality, local news. After all, what kind of journalist is able to take a single-year contract in a small community? It isn't likely that someone can put roots down into this community through a journalism career, if their job isn't guaranteed beyond one year.

Criticisms aside, the LJI was probably the most important boost to local news in a generation. Large dailies were able to hire reporters specifically dedicated to rural coverage, like the two Saskatchewan Postmedia dailies *Regina Leader-Post* and *Saskatoon StarPhoenix*. Positions were earmarked for Indigenous reporting all over Canada, from Delaware First Nation in southwestern Ontario to Kitikmeot in Nunavut, and from Osoyoos to Northern and Western Québec. The list of approved positions placed local reporters at small news organizations across Canada. And while not all of these positions were specifically focused on COVID-19 coverage — indeed, the program started before the pandemic — they certainly helped share the load of reporting during the pandemic. This was critical especially in regions of Canada where local public health unit information was confusing, insufficient or not available.

Local news should have played a critical role in watching local outbreaks, uncovering how they were managed and examining where COVID-19 had come from. In some cases, especially where there was a higher population density with small community newspapers like in the Greater Toronto Area, it did play this role. But in others, there were simply not enough resources to fully tell this story. When Saskatchewan's first major outbreak hit La Loche, a community of 2800 located 600 kilometres northeast from Saskatoon, most of the news about the outbreak came from outside the community. On April 30, 2020, just as news about La Loche had started circulating, CTV *Saskatoon's* Jonathan Charlton wrote an email Q&A with Toronto-based epidemiology professor David Fisman called "La Loche the most concerning COVID-19 outbreak in Canada, epidemiologist says." Fisman became a high-profile go-to thanks to his daily Twitter posts with analysis of the evolution of the virus across Canada. But when Charlton asked Fisman about how the Saskatchewan government has been managing COVID-19, Fisman had to admit that he didn't know the details of the Saskatchewan approach. Not exactly useful information for readers in Saskatoon and even less helpful for the people of La Loche who were living through the outbreak.[31]

Because journalists were located far outside the community, they had to rely on secondary sources to tell stories. One television piece about one of the community's first deaths was constructed using a mix of video and images taken from Facebook, B-roll that mixed spring and winter seasons together and recordings from a distance. The story featured the words of Suzanne Sylvestre, the granddaughter of Joseph Sylvestre who was one of two people who died from COVID-19 at the La Loche Health Centre, and a phone interview with Rick Laliberte, one of the individuals who had been coordinating lockdown responses. The story doesn't mention where Sylvestre lived when he passed away. The journalist, Roberta Bell, didn't sign off the report with her location, but she was a Regina-based reporter for *Global News*. Regina is 850 kilometres from La Loche.[32]

Online, the video report was paired with an in-depth *Canadian Press* article from Kelly Geraldine Malone, a Winnipeg-based reporter. On May 9, 2020, Malone interviewed many people connected to La Loche, both residents and family members who live in larger city centres. She situated the physical location of the community and explained the importance of La Loche for services for surrounding communities and reserves, so readers could understand the community better. Her article was informative, explaining how a winter road usually connects La Loche to Alberta, where many residents go to work at the Kearl Lake tar sands site. Public health said this connection was likely how COVID-19 came to the community. As a *Canadian Press* story, it was written to be re-published anywhere in Canada and a reader could understand why the outbreak there was so worrisome.[33] The Kearl Lake outbreak spread quickly beyond the worksite, and it wasn't just La Loche that was impacted. Calgary-based reporter Emma Graney reported for the *Globe and Mail* that by May 8, the outbreak had surpassed 100 people across B.C., Alberta, Saskatchewan and Nova Scotia.[34] In total, 220 people in La Loche and 62 people in Clearwater River Dene Nation caught COVID-19 from this outbreak. By the time it was over on July 16, 2020, of a total of 4066 residents in the two communities combined, the community had an infection rate of an astounding 6936 cases per 100,000 residents.[35] That's higher than Regina's 5263 total cases per 100,000 residents or Vancouver Coastal Health region's 2839 total cases per 100,000 residents, with both tallies spread out over 18 months.

But where were the local voices telling the story from the perspective of the community itself? Was Facebook really the only option?

Reporting this story from afar, whether from within Saskatchewan or outside the province would be fine, even necessary considering the distance that the Kearl Lake outbreak travelled, if there were also reporters in the community who had similar resources to tell local stories. But there isn't much local news in La Loche. They are served by conglomerates that broadcast across northern Saskatchewan, like the Jim Pattison broadcast group and Glacier Media news websites. CHPN 89.9 FM, part of the northern Saskatchewan radio network MBC, bills itself as the sole provider of local news in the community and broadcasts in multiple languages, including Michif, Diné, Cree and English. MBC is based in La Ronge, about 500 kilometres to the east from La Loche. Had there been local reporters in La Loche, there would have been better and more consistent information about what spread was looking like, especially as it related to worksites located outside the community, and the rest of Canada would have had local experts to better guide provincial or national coverage.

La Loche is hardly unique in Canada. When an outbreak hit Extendicare Kapuskasking in northeastern Ontario, most of the news about the outbreak came out of larger centres, like Timmins, which is about two hours south of the community, or from broadcasting centres in Toronto. The community of just over 8000 people is underserved by news agencies as well. *My Kapuskasing Now*, which feeds news to 100.9 Moose FM, mostly features updates from the Porcupine Health Unit, which stretches from Timmins to James Bay. Sixteen people died at the outbreak at Extendicare Kapuskasing but the stories about what may have led to such a high death toll were rare. Whether due to distance or a lack of resources, there were few to no articles that held Extendicare to account for why this outbreak happened. CTV's Northern Ontario video journalist Sergio Arangio, reporting from Timmins, featured comments that Melissa Caron made during a virtual town hall. Her grandfather was among the victims. Her grandmother and other grandfather had COVID-19 as well, and the one who died had previously lost his brother and roommate to COVID-19. She said it was Extendicare's management and political inaction that led to such a deadly outbreak in the tiny community.[36] CBC Radio's *Morning North*, which broadcast out of Sudbury, about a five-hour drive from Kapuskasing, talked with Pierre Dorval who lost his father and uncle in the outbreak.[37] In small communities, an outbreak didn't just mean disaster for an individual family the way that it might in a larger centre. When COVID-19 spread in a community like La Loche or Kapuskasing, the likelihood that multiple relatives would get sick and even die is far higher, making the impact on the community that much more important.

Coverage of the outbreaks in La Loche and Kapuskasing were important but stopped short of asking: Whose responsibility was it to keep these residents safe? How was Kearl Lake controlling for infection of workers? Should that site have even been open? Was COVID-19 in Kapuskasing simply inevitable or were there ways in which transmission could have been stopped before it started? What about the owners or operators of care facilities? Were there lapses in protocol or was COVID-19 unavoidable? In the case of Kapuskasing — where the outbreak didn't hit until 2021 and when it did it was at a private, for-profit care facility owned by Canada's largest network of for-profit providers — how could the families at the Kapuskasing site reach owners and shareholders who have likely never even heard of their community? Across Canada, local news was mostly unable to dig deeper than a few personal stories. There was already far too much to write from following the daily or weekly briefs of local public health units. This meant residents in smaller communities or regions underserved by news had to rely on larger news organizations to do the necessary investigative work to understand where systems failed and allowed COVID-19 to spread. But even national news outlets — under similar pressure as local news with job cuts and advertising revenue that nearly dried up as people bought less — weren't able to produce the kind of consistent investigative reporting required to give Canadians a sense of the scale or depth of the problems that allowed COVID-19 to spread so quickly and be so deadly. Like so many local news outlets, larger, national chains often produced abridged news reports, leaving so many questions unclear or unanswered.

NATIONAL NEWS AND DATA

Local news was under tremendous strain but so too was province-wide and national news. National news had to broadcast epidemiological forecasts and modelling, cover daily briefings, sort through or simply publish a barrage of data, produce coverage for vast and diverse regions and diffuse public health information. Delivering public health information was a very difficult task to do well given that broadcast ranges spread across public health units, various jurisdictions and importantly, across infection rates.

Information about what to do if you were living in a green zone was not very helpful if your zone was actually red. And in large urban centres, where the level of COVID-19 spread changed from neighbourhood to neighbourhood, the information became even more confused.

Most national media organizations are structured to reflect Canadian federalism. National chains have primary broadcast centres and political coverage is divided by where journalists are based. Ottawa journalists cover Ottawa: Prime Minister Justin Trudeau and Chief Medical Officer of Health Theresa Tam. The provincial capital journalists who still exist cover provincial leaders and one or several public health unit offices. This division of labour makes a lot of sense considering how Canada is structured.

But federalism is not the best way to organize a country to fight a pandemic. COVID-19 doesn't care about the imaginary line between Saskatchewan and Alberta just like it doesn't care about the imaginary line that separates Canada and the United States. This rigid silo system meant the news Canadians got was broadcast through a tunnel: either federal information with very little or no provincial or local context, or local news with no mention of the federal government. This created national news with two speeds: it was either focused on the federal government, political debates among federal parties and issues that fell upon federal jurisdiction, or it was investigative or narrative, looking at regions outside of the rigid structures of Canada and drawing together stories that better reflected similarities outside of the federal arrangement. This allowed for stories about communities like fly-in workers who experienced the pandemic differently as people who had to travel great distances to get to work, seasonal migrant workers regardless of which province they lived or worked, or Indigenous communities that saw parallels even if they were separated by thousands of kilometres. Shockingly, there was no national news outlet that made it a priority to track COVID-19 comparatively: no weekly reporting about national hotspots, no calculations to give Canadians an idea about how bad an outbreak on one side of the country was compared to another. Reporting on an outbreak never considered comparing the outbreak to other communities where there were also outbreaks, which made it impossible to get a constant national map of how COVID-19 was spreading. There weren't even regular hot-spot/cold-spot reporting figures from any national news agencies.

Even though there was no national reporting that compared and contrasted communities as cases rose and fell, the vast majority of national reporting was chasing the day's numbers: national figures released by PHAC, national vaccination figures and the announcement of the day made by Justin Trudeau. Sometimes opposition leaders stole a headline from Trudeau, but mostly, the lens was firmly on his rapidly aging mug. This was especially the case in the early days of the pandemic, where Trudeau masterfully led journalists from one announcement to another, not giving anyone enough time to pause and ask if the tail was wagging the dog. But this was a very big problem: what became normal allowed journalists to gloss over the fact that Canada suffers from an incredible lack of national information. The vast majority of daily reporting, whether from national, provincial or local news was reporting publicly available numbers from health units, but far less attention was paid to the figures where there was no national information. For example, most networks had some kind of national set of COVID-19 data embedded in their articles. These summaries changed over the course of the pandemic but gave Canadians a snapshot of provincial COVID-19 totals, death totals and testing rates. If a data set wasn't released by PHAC, national outlets really struggled to cover the issue. This was especially a problem for the three major kinds of pandemic deaths: the number of deaths in residential facilities, the number of deaths among healthcare workers and the number of deaths that could be attributed to a workplace outbreak. No journalist was consistently gathering these national outbreak deaths, except for me.

The first problem was also the most difficult to sort through: deaths in residential facilities were not tracked at the federal level. This meant national journalists had to build their own lists to have a clear picture of who was dying where or rely on the work of others. At different points during the pandemic, these deaths were tracked provincially by a few news organizations, like *Toronto Star, CP24,* and *Global News B.C.,* but none of the lists were national. On December 31, 2020, the image on the front page of the *Toronto Star* looked like a stylized skyscraper. The rectangle, which ran the length of the paper's front page, consisted of tiny people icons standing tall beside an editorial written by Jordan Bitove and Paul Rivett, the two men who had acquired Torstar earlier in 2020. The icons represented 2721 residents and eight staff from Ontario long-term care facilities who had died. This was supposed to be the *Star's* year-end *crie de coeur*: enough is enough with deaths in long-term care. But the *Toronto Star* didn't have their own database to track these deaths. They used provincial data for long-term care alone while ignoring the people who died in retirement residences, which to average people looked and operated an awful lot like long-term care facilities.[38] Through my own research, my estimate of deaths by December 30 (the day the *Star* collected the data) was 504 deaths higher.[39] Even though the newspaper had journalists closely tracking these deaths, they defaulted to an official, lower number that excluded everyone who had died from COVID-19 as a result of a hospital outbreak or anyone who had died in a retirement residence, assisted living or shelter outbreak. Why would the *Toronto Star* have chosen a lower number that didn't offer its readers a full picture?

The argument was likely that they were focusing specifically on long-term care. But with so many of Ontario's worst long-term care operators also in the business of retirement residences, and with outbreaks that had resulted in hundreds of deaths in these facilities too, the decision of the *Star* to narrowly reflect the amount of COVID-19 deaths was a curious one. It was certainly much harder to use a number that wasn't updated daily at Ontario's Ministry of Health website: many public health units didn't publicly give information about deaths in retirement residences. So even though 16 people died at The Village of Humber Heights Retirement Home and 23 people died at The Village of Humber Heights Long-term Care — facilities both owned and operated by Schlegel Villages — the *Toronto Star* used a figure that didn't include the retirement home deaths. In so doing, they erased hundreds of deaths that happened by similar living conditions and owned and operated by many of the same players. Similar decisions were made all the time, where journalists left out data or didn't mention important things like how many people had died across an entire chain of residences. In fact, not one article that was written about deaths at a specific location owned by a national or provincial chain mentioned the global death toll of the company's facilities.

It was rare to see deaths in long-term care tied directly to the owners or boards of directors of corporations at all, especially when an owner had multiple outbreak sites. This was unless it was tied to another story, like news that Chartwell gave out massive executive bonuses. If there had ever been a time for anti-capitalist analyses to go mainstream, it was during 2020 where a direct line from profits to death could be easily traced, even in a 600-word article. Instead, journalists continued to focus on the personal angle of stories, like workers living through an outbreak, or a family who lost a loved one, erasing the broader forces that created the crisis in the first place.

This lack of national, official data caused a lot of problems. Not only was it difficult to get a truly national picture of how badly COVID-19 was tearing through residential facility care (and depending on where you lived, a provincial picture was sometimes also impossible to have), but it also left gaps in the data that were easy to exploit by far-right voices who wanted to underplay the danger posed by COVID-19 and push for fewer public health measures. On November 15, 2020, CTV *National News'* nightly national broadcast reported on long-term care across Canada and how advocates and resident family members were calling for national standards to be imposed to help improve care. To set the segment up, CTV ran two images: one that said 10,946 people in Canada had died from COVID-19, and another that said 10,781 people had died in long-term care homes. It ran at 3:55 minutes into the broadcast, and when the two numbers were subtracted from each other, it showed that 166 people had died in Canada from COVID-19 who were not living in long-term care. .[40] That same night, my research had placed the figure of people who had died in residential care at 8668 — and that included retirement residences and other non-long-term-care residential facilities, so the number of people living in long-term care alone, as CTV *News* reported, was even lower.[41]

Even though the figure was squeezed between segments in a national news line-up, it made a small sensation online among people who were outraged that their lives were inconvenienced because of, as many argued on social media channels, "only" 166 people dying. If nearly all the deaths had occurred in long-term care, then why should everyone be impacted by such strict social distancing measures? In the *Calgary Herald*, Canada's hardest working anti-lockdown columnist Licia Corbella relied on CTV's bunk figure to argue, "lockdowns do more harm than good."[42] When it was clear that CTV's figure was off by several thousand, Postmedia quietly removed it from Corbella's article, with a cryptic and unclear correction: "A previous version of this column contained a paragraph referring to figures from another news organization. Those figures are incorrect and have been removed." "Those figures," central to Corbella's argument, probably merited a mention.[43] But it didn't matter. Corbella's article was shared by many right-wing social media accounts insisting that COVID-19 deaths were overhyped. Ten days after Corbella's article, a memo was sent to doctors in Calgary requesting they avoid wasting oxygen as COVID-19 hospitalizations were climbing so fast that there were fears they would run out of it.[44]

CTV never explained where they got the number and there didn't seem to be a correction for their incorrect information. The online video of that broadcast that was archived had the images cut: the original video running for 23:06 minutes, while the version that remained archived online runs for 22:41 with no mention of the edit.[45] This was just one error that didn't go too much further than a few weeks of disinformation and a *Calgary Herald* column. But it revealed a far bigger issue: at least one national news agency wasn't collecting its own numbers internally. By November 15, anyone who had been reporting on COVID-19 should absolutely have known that a claim placing 98.4% of all of Canada's COVID-19 deaths in long-term care was impossible. Was it an overburdened newsroom? Overreliance on insufficient public agency data leading to back-of-the-napkin math to come up with a national picture? Whatever the cause, it was an example of where national media failed to adequately contend with the scale and scope of the crisis.

It wasn't just with the deaths in residential care, though. It was also in reporting on deaths from workers, both from within healthcare and from other kinds of workplaces. When healthcare workers died, it was extremely rare for a journalist to situate their death in a broader context. If there was context provided, it was usually provincial or local. *Global News* reported that Antonio Gaerlan, a hospital worker in Etobicoke, was the 19th health worker to die, even though he was the 37th. The report didn't say but intended to mean 19th in Ontario, and they didn't attribute that estimate to the Ontario Council of Hospital Unions.[46] The day after, on January 15, 2021, Rose Vandelannoite died in Edmonton. CBC *Edmonton* reported that she was Alberta's fourth healthcare worker to die and didn't mention anything about the worker who had just died in Ontario, but did mention the circumstances known about the previous three Alberta deaths. Tom Thomas was the first healthcare worker in Saskatchewan to die, but journalists didn't mention that he was, at least, Canada's 27th racialized healthcare worker to die, or that he was, at least, the 47th healthcare worker to die.[47] Nearly every report about the death of every healthcare worker followed a very similar pattern: explain the immense loss experienced by the individual's family, ask people close to them about what they were like and absolutely do not draw any broader connections to political or systemic failures that resulted in their death. Journalists took an individualized approach to memorialize people who had died rather than examining broader forces so a reader could decide to demand change. While the obituary style of reporting was important to humanize and pay homage to someone, it alone was not enough. Canadians needed something to connect these deaths to why they were happening.

This was where independent media played such an important role. It was independent journalists who were able to step back and make these broader connections, whether for progressive outlets like *Passage, Canadian Dimension, rabble, Ricochet, Spring, Briarpatch* or others, or through personal social media channels and email newsletters. Independent magazine *The Local* broke news related to vaccine inequity and virus spread across the Greater Toronto Area, including creating a "hotspot tracker" that offered weekly vaccination updates in high-risk neighbourhoods. The *Halifax Examiner* posted daily updates with mapped-out exposure notices and provincial vaccination progress and made all of its COVID-19 coverage free. Calgary-based *The Sprawl* uncovered that Alberta's government was well aware that the pandemic would have differential impacts on women and racialized Albertans as early as mid-March 2020.[48] Independent media did an incredible amount of heavy lifting during the pandemic, critically helping to fill in the gaps left by mainstream coverage.

TACTICS TO NARROW COVERAGE

Individualizing the pandemic was a key way in which journalists absolved people and systems of their culpability, whether directly or indirectly. When Judy Hawkins, an activity assistant at a retirement residence from Windsor, Ontario, died from COVID-19, CBC *News Windsor* reported that she was "warm, steadfast and present."[49] Those words were attributed to Tigrena Domi, the general manager of the facility, and presumably, Hawkins' boss. What the story does not ask is how implicated Domi was in Hawkins' death. Were there management lapses that put Hawkins into contact with COVID-19, or was this just a sad and unfortunate situation management was powerless to stop? The story also didn't mention that the facility, Shoreview at Riverside Retirement Residence, is a private, for-profit facility run by Oxford Living, an affiliate of Oxford Capital Group LLC. The story didn't seem to attempt to find out if any residents of Shoreview had died, information that a journalist would have to press someone like Domi to say, as it was not reported publicly by the local public health unit. Oxford Living is a private, for-profit retirement residence operator that, "acquires, manages and develops seniors housing properties throughout North America."[50] What was the role that profit played in cutting corners within the facility's COVID-19 safety protocols? How many deaths had happened among Oxford Living's 15 Ontario-based facilities? Like at Shoreview, most of the public health units in which they operated facilities did not report retirement resident deaths. But one Oxford Living facility, Lundy Manor in Niagara Falls, experienced one of Ontario's earliest outbreaks. Nineteen people died. One lawsuit alleged that the facility didn't take adequate precautions, including continuing social events like a pub night and bingo. The lawsuit alleged that Lundy Manor had, for lengthy periods of time,

> expected a single nurse, lacking adequate training, to care for the entirety of its residents without providing any established or proper protocols. A single nurse had to administer routine medications to all residents, which are critical for those residents who require cardiac medication or similar essential medications.[51]

After the outbreak at Lundy Manor during the first pandemic wave, the residence was inspected three times on July 8, October 11 and February 2, 2021, and it was found in non-compliance related to food safety twice.[52]

There are so many possible threads to follow in the news about Hawkins's death. But CTV Windsor and the Windsor Star had essentially the same stories as CBC News Windsor: they were obituaries, not reporting. This pattern was replicated over and over again, in news about new outbreaks, new resident deaths or new worker deaths. From time to time, there were articles that looked a bit deeper, like one CTV News feature that interviewed Floyd Ambersley, the son of Maureen Ambersley, another worker who died from COVID-19. She had worked at Extendicare Mississauga and had told her son conditions were difficult:

> He said sometimes his mother would be so pressed for time due to staff shortages that she would have to go directly from moving one patient to another, and wouldn't have time to fully change her PPE to prevent cross-contamination.
>
> "You have to rush and sometimes you might leave her gloves on, it might be like the same mask," he said.[53]

Yet still, there was no part of the article that tried to explain why Extendicare was allowed to create such a dangerous environment for staff and residents alike. The frame was simply: *this is tragic, they shouldn't*

have to put their lives on the line but, in the end, what are you going to do?
Journalism was overwhelmed with this kind of reporting, and it served
a very pernicious purpose: it didn't show Canadians who is to blame and
why. In avoiding that conversation, the audience would come to understand healthcare deaths as sad but inevitable, and they would not have a
coherent direction to organize around for change.

If journalism is supposed to 'afflict the comfortable and comfort the
afflicted,' Canadian media maybe scored 30% during the pandemic. The
features on people who died were often touching and comforting. But
the afflicting the comfortable bit was so often insufficient. It wasn't just
by zeroing in on individual stories that media managed to consistently
avoid talking about broader issues; there were many different ways that
journalists spun a narrative that would keep politicians mostly unharmed,
even vaulted, especially during the first wave of the pandemic when the
missteps of politicians were harder to see and understand. Shrinking newsrooms played a big role in having the resources available to write more
thorough stories (although it took me literally 30 minutes to research and
write the paragraph about Oxford Living), but of far greater significance
was that some of the people who played the biggest role in making the
pandemic worse were well-connected, wealthy Canadians who Canadian
journalism has a hard time going after even when there isn't a pandemic.
Canada's media establishment is conservative at the best of times. It accepts
political talking points as truth-y enough and rarely challenges the basis
on which the entire economy is premised: profits above all else, even
people's lives. When the pandemic took this logic and launched it into
overdrive, it was not surprising that mainstream media was ill equipped
to challenge corporate power.

Media also over-relied on doctors and epidemiologists to explain the
pandemic to Canadians at the expense of highlighting the voices of the
people most at risk of severe outcomes of COVID-19 infection. Personal
care workers died in numbers that far surpassed other healthcare workers,
like doctors and nurses, yet they were rarely interviewed about what their
working conditions were like.[54] Most of the stories that looked closely at
the lives of personal care workers were obituaries. CBC Radio's national
current affairs program *The Current* was obsessed with doctors and professors providing expert opinions on all manners of the pandemic; in 33
segments from December 1, 2020, to February 1, 2021, that were about
COVID-19, they featured 51 doctors and 13 professors. Over the same

time period, they interviewed one paramedic, one patient, one social worker, and three nurses. It's not surprising: there is a gender, race and class dynamic to this phenomenon. Doctors are more likely to be wealthy white men, so the more often a media outlet quotes a doctor, the more likely it will be the case that they quote a wealthy, white male. And the inverse is true: personal care workers tend to be low-income, feminized and racialized, so when they're shut out of explaining the pandemic from their perspective, there will be fewer racialized, feminized and/or low-income voices. Informed Opinions' Gender Gap Tracker showed that during the first 11 months of the pandemic, males were interviewed 69% more often than females. CBC News led the pack with a gender balance of 65% to 35%. For the rest, the numbers are abysmal: women were quoted just 33% of the time at CTV News, 32% at *Global News*, 29% in *Huffington Post*, 27% in the *Toronto Star*, 25% in the *Globe and Mail* and 23% in the *National Post*. While the Gender Gap Tracker doesn't also collect racial data, it follows that this would be similarly abysmal.[55] Informed Opinions' Shari Graydon wrote,

> The disproportionate social and economic impacts of COVID-19 on women — Black, Indigenous and women of colour, as well as those living in poverty, with a disability, or with an abuser — have been well-documented and extensively lamented.
>
> In the process, many have called for greater attention to the voices of those least well-represented in the corridors of power. Clearly, we can't fix the problems in long-term care homes that imperil the elderly and their minimum-wage-earning caregivers who are often working multiple jobs in order to survive, without hearing from the people directly affected. That we haven't previously paid heed to their realities is in no small part due to the fact that most of those residents are female, and most of their caregivers are women of colour.[56]

The pandemic had an intense impact on women (as I explore in the December 2020 chapter), so journalists systemically privileging men's voices meant that coverage about the problems, and therefore solutions, were often bandied about by individuals who were not experiencing these issues directly — if they were discussed at all.

There was also the issue of paywalls: they forced people to be a paid subscriber to a news organization before they could access coverage. This meant that news coverage was more likely geared toward people who had enough disposable income to be able to pay for a subscription than it was toward the most impacted by the pandemic. At the start of the pandemic, many news organizations promised to drop their paywall to allow Canadians access to their reporting. The *Globe and Mail* announced on March 14, 2020, that COVID-19 coverage would be free. The *Hamilton Spectator*, the *Logic*, the *National Observer*, the *Pointer*, the *Toronto Star*, the *Waterloo Region Record*, the *Winnipeg Free Press* and Postmedia all announced they would not paywall COVID-19 stories, as the information was just too important for people to not be able to access because of cost.[57] The *Toronto Star*'s editor Irene Gentle wrote,

> As coronavirus continues to spread, we know you have questions about how it impacts you, what you can do and what it might mean. We want the most people possible to have access to those answers so we're removing our paywall from the stories that aim to answer them.[58]

This promise wouldn't last, however. Torstar papers the *Toronto Star*, the *Hamilton Spectator* and the *Waterloo Region Record*, reinitiated their paywalls soon after, even for articles written by their reporters paid through the Local Journalism Initiative. It created the perverse situation where an investigation into a COVID-19 outbreak in a workplace, which would have relied on the free labour and even risk of employees to be written, wouldn't be easily accessible to these same workers unless they had paid for a subscription to the *Toronto Star*, or had the patience and library card necessary to navigate through their local library's website. The *National Post*'s paywall was dropped for all content, including at its daily city newspapers, thanks to funding from the fast-food company Mary Brown's Chicken & Taters.[59]

Paywalls made it harder for Canadians to get journalism in Canada, especially in-depth investigative research. Every one of the investigations done by the *Toronto Star*, from examining the racialized impact of the virus to COVID-19 outbreaks at locations like Amazon or food processing facilities, were paywalled. This meant that access to news became a matter of personal wealth: if you could afford a subscription, you had more access to pandemic-related news. But by locking this information away from many, important information about the pandemic didn't reach everyone equally. Just as the sources chosen impact the kind of opinions reflected in the daily news, so too did paywalls impact who could access the daily news.

Paywalling pandemic information was not a great idea, especially as disinformation spread rapidly. If people are hungry for news and analysis and they can't easily access something that's behind a paywall, they will move toward other kinds of news. That's something Nathan Robinson argued in an article he wrote for *Current Affairs* in August 2020 called "The Truth is Paywalled but the Lies are Free." He pointed to a stark divide between news organizations who offer paid news that is fair, fact-checked and balanced, like the *New York Times*, the *Washington Post, Harper's,* the *Financial Times* and the London *Times.* But the most popular far-right sources of disinformation — *Brietbart, Fox News* and *InfoWars* — are all freely available. Robinson also pointed to academic articles as the extreme version of paywalls in publishing, noting that bunk science is free and easily accessible, but peer-reviewed articles in reputable journals are out of reach for most people. The damage caused by this divide between freely available academic information is especially important to consider when public health and safety relies on people reading good science. Robinson wrote,

> At *Current Affairs* we have no paywall, even though this might cost us some money, because we are trying to make it as easy as possible to hear what we have to say. This is what the right does. They tell people what to think, offer them books and pamphlets and handy five-minute YouTube videos. On the left we are not nearly as slick.[60]

It's necessary advice as so many people ponder the future of news and how to pay for it. And it's hard to see the decision to paywall COVID-19 news specifically as anything other than stopping good information from going as far as it can.

Of course, not all media organizations use paywalls. Television news had advertising built into it and so *Global News* and CTV *News* were never paywalled. And programs from CBC/Radio-Canada, as Canada's national public broadcaster, were available to anyone for free online or over the radio. CBC/Radio-Canada's multiplatform national reach and easy access placed the public broadcaster into an even more important role to push out critical and accurate reporting that an audience could share. This made the October 2020 cuts of 130 staff even more unacceptable.

THE DOOM MACHINE

One defining feature of the pandemic was doom. There was doomscrolling, doomposting and a generalized sense of doom everywhere. This included how media reported the pandemic. The pandemic was scary, and journalists were the ones that you could trust to give you the facts, even if they were depressing or sad. A new kind of social media influencer was born, usually out of posting daily updates related to some aspect of the pandemic that ended with a warning that things could always get worse. That idea that things could always get worse was key to ensuring that audiences stayed glued to wall-to-wall COVID-19 coverage. In a study of English-language media coverage on COVID-19, three American researchers found that the majority of it was negative in tone: in COVID-19 coverage related to school reopening, the researchers found that coverage was 56% negative. In the U.S. alone, that shot up to 90%. U.S. coverage of the Pfizer-BioNTech vaccine was also more generally negative, both in the lead-up to the vaccine's approval and after. They categorized more than 9.4 million published news stories from 2020 and then drilled into about 20,000 COVID-19 news stories to analyze their level of negativity. They found that the more popular stories from the *New York Times* had "high levels of negativity, particularly for COVID-19-related articles." Of the 40 Anglophone international media outlets they analyzed articles from, three were Canadian: *CTV News*, the *Globe and Mail* and the *Toronto Star*.[61]

Whether or not the negativity itself played a role in boosting viewership is impossible to say, but there's no doubt that Canadians consumed more news media than they had in years during 2020. Three-quarters of adults read newspapers each week, on various platforms. And in daily news consumption, that number increased too, with more than one-third of adults saying they consumed more media than they had a year prior. Whether or not it was thanks to negativity hardly mattered: there was a new kind of journalism emerging and people were paying attention.

Negativity certainly turned heads, and there was more than enough to be negative about. For example, Aaron Derfel from the *Montreal Gazette* broke the first story of horror and depravity within long-term care when he reported about the mass deaths at Dorval's The Herron CHSLD. His COVID-19 reporting earned him more awards than most other journalists in Canada. He tweeted daily threads that drilled into local Montréal COVID-19 spread, and the threads were relentlessly negative in tone — not just because of the topics that he was covering. Québec Premier François

Legault blamed Derfel on scaring Québec Anglophones through his reporting, and argued that his reporting, "was intended to systemically discredit his government."[62] Many saw Legault's comments as an attack on the press — he had certainly had an easier time with French-language journalists than he had had with Derfel and turning the journalist into the object of a story was Legault's way of intimidating Derfel. The accusations were levelled early on in the pandemic, when there was still a kind of honeymoon period with the Québec government's handling the issue. Derfel continued to do his nightly Twitter threads and became a relied upon source both within Québec and outside.

But his writing did tango with extreme negativity. His Twitter threads almost always ended with a warning that things would get worse, even if the thread was about things getting better, and his analysis articles for the *Gazette* were consistently negative. In an article titled "Experts blast Legault for saying Québec is 'resisting' third wave," Derfel cited two people who were sure that the government's approach in March 2021 would lead to a third wave, which in most parts of the province including Montréal, didn't come to pass. In the article, there's no counter-balance voice to the experts that he chose, and both were regulars in his columns: Simona Bignami, a demographer from the Université de Montréal, and Matthew Oughton, a medicine professor at McGill and whose image illustrated the article.[63] One week later in another analysis article, Derfel warned that COVID-19 outbreaks in Montréal could jump by 50%, and quoted Bignami and Oughton again. He wrote that Bignami "cautioned that the picture might not be as stable in the city as the premier suggested."[64] Two weeks after that, Derfel asked, "Why hasn't COVID's third wave flared up yet in Montréal?" where he quoted Oughton again saying that it's still coming: "It's that Montréal is on a slower burn, but it's still heating up." Oughton argued that schools and non-essential businesses needed to close down in Montréal. Derfel concluded, "Yet so far, the premier has not seen the need to do so."[65] The way in which Derfel asked why the third wave hasn't come for Montréal, rather than focusing on why Gatineau and Quebec City had experienced a third wave, was a way of telling Montrealers that they needed to worry about the worst that would be coming, instead of identifying what caused the flare-ups in the other regions. Legault would be proven correct: the third wave didn't come for Montréal or most of Québec like it came for other parts of Canada. There was never an attempt to understand who was really making the decisions — Legault, or public health representatives. So blaming Legault became rote, even lazy, rather than questioning what was the basis or data assumptions for the decisions that Legault was making and going deeper than his talking points that everything was ok. Instead, Derfel posted publicly available charts and graphs from public health agencies to show where spread was. On June 5, Derfel wrote "Super contagious delta variant has public health experts worried" even though Québec had only sequenced 16 cases total of the variant. He quoted Michel Roger, a doctor: "We don't have to panic yet with the Indian variant in Québec," and then quoted Oughten again, who likened Québec's vaccination campaign to being a race against the spread of delta. He concluded, "it's fair to assume more cases of delta will be sequenced in Québec," as if that would even be a debatable question.[66] And then on July 14, 2021, as cases were the lowest they had been since July 2020 and were on a downward trend, Derfel's analysis was doom-y again: "COVID-19 outbreaks down to 15 in Montréal, but threats remain." Oughten was again featured in the photo of the article as he warned that the delta variant, even though it had not hit Québec in the same way that it hit other provinces, was a threat to Quebecers.[67] While of course variants remained a threat, the reality in Québec was that the delta variant was not an immediate threat. The state of Montréal's COVID-19 spread was trending positively, especially in relation to the previous year, and there was no need to continuously go to the same sources to offer readers the same level of doom they had endured for the year previous. And worse, the only solutions ever proposed where to appeal to government to lock down again or move faster with vaccination. His analyses rarely delved into the broader structural issues at play and how to address rising cases in a way that appreciated disability, race and income.

Derfel stood out not because he was more consistently doom-y than other journalists, but because he was a rare and persistent health reporter from a city daily newspaper, though he was hardly unique in focusing on the doom. The constant message of doom that came from so much of Canadian journalism had a very deep anxiety-inducing effect. The *Canadian Medical Association Journal* published an article in March 2021 about the link between a constant barrage of bad news and someone's levels of anxiety. Robin Blades wrote,

> This negative spiral — lately dubbed "doomscrolling" — can take a toll on mental health. Studies have linked the consumption of bad news to increased distress, anxiety and depression, even

when the news in question is relatively mundane. According to Graham Davey, professor emeritus of psychology at the University of Sussex, exposure to bad news can make personal worries seem worse and even cause "acute stress reactions and some symptoms of post-traumatic stress disorder that can be quite long-lasting."[68]

The constant barrage of negative news had an impact on average people's mental health and worse, took space from other possible ways of telling the story of the pandemic that, yes, focused on how bad things were, but also gave the audience some ideas for what they could do to address whatever issue it was, like how to keep family safe or even participate in a campaign calling for more healthcare workers. But with none of those action items built into the narrative of doom, COVID-19 journalism was more likely to leave readers in the fetal position on the floor than it was to launch us into a demonstration outside of a politician's office, or even better, the doors that boards of directors from national residential care chains were hiding behind.

COVID-19 tore open already frail systems in every aspect of Canada's economy and society. The media industry had the unique position of being one that had to not only operate firing on full cylinders during pandemic — like food processing or long-term care — it also had the incredible task of explaining the pandemic, too. That was just too much for an industry that had been financially battered both before the pandemic and during. So, many journalists relied on tropes, stayed too close to the official line or zoomed in too closely on an individual subject, robbing the audience of the connections embedded within a story that could have made everything make more sense. Questions about who to blame, who to question and who needed to be held to account were often sidelined or outright ignored. When articles that asked such questions were published, they were often placed behind paywalls, preventing equal access to that information for all.

Accountability relies on figuring out who is at fault. Without knowing who was to blame, Canadians would never be able to determine how to demand justice for a broken system. Every chapter in this book examines how a set of problems related to an industry or an issue were exacerbated by COVID-19, but none of the problems were caused by COVID-19. This means "going back to normal" will not fix anything that COVID-19 revealed to be broken. During the pandemic, Canadians needed unflinching investigations as well as daily reports that mentioned things like how many residents were sharing rooms together in an outbreak or how much money a company stood to lose if they were forced to shut down during an outbreak. This information could have shown people, for example, why there was such resistance to closing down large, congregant work settings, even though the evidence was overwhelming that that was one critical measure for pandemic mitigation. But most news stayed close to the official line, rarely straying from the expectations and limits imposed on them by corporate media, whose owners preferred to fire people in the middle of a pandemic to boost their bottom line than endure a year of lower profits or debt in the service of providing information for the common good.

Conclusion

CANADA AFTER COVID-19?

On July 1, 2021, Prime Minister Justin Trudeau appeared in front of a camera to wish Canadians a happy Canada Day. His face and head were liberated from the extra hair he had been carrying around since March 2020. The beard he grew was gone. His flowing locks, coiffed. He was set to have his second COVID-19 vaccine dose on July 2. In just a few months, he would call an election and bring an end to the 43rd Parliament, which oversaw the bulk of Canada's pandemic response. As if he were an NHL player growing a playoff beard, Trudeau's image throughout the first, second and third waves — tired, grizzled and unkempt — was intended to signal to Canadians that he too was struggling through this pandemic. And on July 1, it was gone. The pandemic, announced Trudeau's new look, was over.

Just two days earlier, a report was released by the Royal Society of Canada that estimated that Canada's official death toll from COVID-19 was likely double what had been officially announced. The report was coauthored by Tara Moriarty, Janet McElhaney, Anna Boczula, Eemaan Thind, and me. Our analysis demonstrated that through various measures — excess death calculations, comparisons to peer countries, cremation data in Ontario, case-fatality ratios, seroprevalence research and data collection related to cause of death — it was reasonable to assume that Canada's real death toll was closer to 52,000 than it was to 26,274, which was Canada's official death toll the day the report was released. The most important finding was that Canada was not keeping up-to-date death data, so there was no way to confirm this number immediately. The same day our report came out, Ontario dumped an additional, previously unreported 90 deaths from 2020 into its death reporting system. Canada's death reporting systems were so old that it would be long after the last COVID-19 death before Canadians would have the official word on how many died from COVID-19 — before we could see how closely our estimate aligned with what the official reporting would say.

Trudeau may have felt confident on July 1 that he could telegraph to Canadians through his image that the pandemic was over, but it was far from it. By June 30, 2021, there were COVID-19 surges in Yukon, cases in Québec had gone up for the first time in months and it was becoming clear that COVID-19 spread among unvaccinated individuals was a serious concern. By that date, Canada had led most of the world in vaccination: 65.89% of Canadians had received at least one dose (75.33% if children under 12 were removed). The numbers were very positive and daily cases were low relative to the early spring, but there was still a sizable unvaccinated population at risk of catching the virus and evidence was emerging that breakthrough COVID-19 cases, though rare, could still propagate the virus. Because it would take a long time to learn the full extent of the damage from the previous 18 months, even after vaccination reached its highest level and cases either vanished, mutated into something else or became part of the regular seasonal illness cycle, there would still be news of horrors missed in the preceding months. The pandemic would continue to rage in locations around the world too, made worse by vaccine-hoarding countries like Canada, who also blocked attempts made at the World Trade Organization to release intellectual property information about the vaccines so countries could manufacture them themselves. Our own selfishness to get vaccinated first helped to create the global conditions where new variants could emerge and come back to Canada to bite us all in the back of the lung.

Despite the pockets of COVID-19 outbreaks in Canada, a peer-reviewed scientific analysis about how Canada had likely undercounted its COVID-19 deaths by half, and a global pandemic that was far from over, Justin Trudeau's image tacitly welcomed Canada to its two-dose summer. Journalism shifted gears into summer mode and Canadians started to emerge into a changed world. While Trudeau was wrong to telegraph that we were finally back to normal, it seemed the era of COVID-19 mass deaths was over.

Everything that went wrong in Canada during the COVID-19 pandemic was due to factors that had long been established as problems. From systemic racism to structural inequality, from an overburdened healthcare system to crowded classrooms, from a broken and exploitative residential care system to a broken and exploitative food services industry, all of the problems that made COVID-19 worse were well known. These problems, combined with ableism and racism woven into every aspect of Canada's economy and society, meant that the individuals most impacted by COVID-19 were the ones who were made to be most disposable: low-income, racialized workers; disabled adults and children; and Indigenous communities who for generations had been starved of adequate social and health services within their communities.

On March 10, 2020, writing for the *Washington Post*, I argued that while Canada's public system of healthcare had set Canada up to be in a better situation to manage the pandemic than the United States, gaps in Canada's healthcare system would threaten Canadians too. And, critically, "Canadians also need paid workplace leave provisions."[1] Paid sick leave would become a national rallying cry, uniting people of all partisan stripes as an urgent and obvious demand. Canada has managed the pandemic far better than the United States, thanks in large part to the fact that Canadian politicians have more or less followed the same kind of advice from public health officials. But paid sick leave was a basic demand that was too much to ask for from Canadian politicians.

Politicians had two options before them for how they would manage the pandemic: they could have oriented policies toward helping people avoid getting COVID-19, or they could have oriented policies toward defending the status quo: helping businesses pull through the pandemic with as little damage as possible and protecting profits at all costs. They enthusiastically chose the latter, and journalists rarely questioned this logic. That status quo assumes economic growth must continue at all costs; workers' wages and working conditions should not be too much of a threat to bosses' bottom lines; and individuals should be valued based solely on their economic location in society, their racial identity and personal capacity. To protect the status quo, politicians needed to spin the pandemic to make it sound as if they were actually doing everything possible to protect Canadians given the information they had. They clearly were not.

Media companies' business operations rely on maintaining the status quo, and their journalists were ill equipped to all of a sudden be able to challenge politician logic. Canada's media establishment is a key cheerleader of this status quo logic, breaking with it from time to time only to report on an outrageous story here and there. And so, faced with this historic crisis that both put new demands on journalists to report the news differently and undercut their resources to even be able to report the news at all, journalists did what they have always done in Canada: there were few journalists who challenged power. They wrote about daily COVID-19 death totals, relied heavily on the opinions of people who are called "doctor" and were late in covering the biggest crises of the pandemic. Unless they had the help of advocacy organizations to compel them to understand the impact of the pandemic on a certain group of people, reporting tended to uncritically repeat politician talking points, which were drafted by spin doctors who had their bosses' political futures in their minds above all else.

The pages of this book describe all the ways in which Canadian politicians failed to contain COVID-19 and protect people, despite always having the option to do better. The stories of these decisions were told by hundreds of journalists, many of whom perhaps for the first time realized that there are some fundamental cracks at the foundation of our society. At the start of the pandemic, journalists were obsessed with China, thereby letting Canadian failures slide out of public sight. Had there been more critical reporting then — had politicians' and public health agents' words been taken with more skepticism — Canada's response to COVID-19 could have started earlier, and with more significant steps taken, like ensuring better personal protections through offering resources to high-risk locations. Grant Robertson's investigation into the Global Public Health Intelligence Network (GPHIN) demonstrated that Liberal mismanagement effectively killed the world's best early-warning system to identify pandemics, putting scientists and doctors around the world far behind where they might have been had the system been working. While the government has said that it intends to restore GPHIN, one year since Grant Robertson's investigation that had not yet happened.

In residential care, the problems were profound and widespread. Breaking with status quo logic would have required politicians to nationalize private, for-profit long-term care facilities and promise to pour a lot of money into the system. Instead, the federal government gave billions to bail out Air Canada, and jurisdictional wrangling became the justification why nothing too drastic could be done in residential care. No jurisdiction had announced any significant changes to long-term care. Collective bargaining at Nova Scotia's worst outbreak location, Northwood, stalled at the end of June 2021 because the government didn't want to agree to workers' demand for higher wages and better working conditions as it would set a precedent with other healthcare unions.[2]

There have not been any changes made to working conditions within food processing and agriculture industries either. No governments have implemented fundamental changes to help the mostly racialized, low-income workers within industrial agri-food operations. In fact, outbreaks were still ongoing at several facilities across Canada at the end of June 2021. At the Exceldor poultry plant in Blumenort, Manitoba, where earlier outbreaks resulted in two worker deaths, nearly two dozen workers had contracted COVID-19 at the end of June 2021. Public health refused to declare an outbreak, claiming that workers all caught COVID-19 from outside the plant. The rhetoric, as reported by the *Winnipeg Free Press*, sounded as if it could have been said more than a year earlier. The article about the outbreak even quotes "a provincial spokesperson" saying "the most common type of transmission is outside the workplace." The journalist does not quote any research that challenges this line.[3] Exceldor was in bargaining at the same moment with their workers in Québec. Workers went on strike demanding a very small increase to their wages. Because Exceldor refused their demands, the strike was prolonged and one million chickens were euthanized because the slaughterhouse wasn't operating.[4] The problems that plagued this industry before the pandemic had not been changed over the course of the first 18 months of the pandemic.

While the obsession with race-based data has evaporated and it's generally accepted that racism played a fundamental role in spreading COVID-19, governments have done nothing significant to reduce the structural and systemic ways in which racism continues to cause harm within Canadian society. The racial reckoning that journalism was supposed to have had in the summer of 2020 didn't result in material changes to the industry, though racialized journalists have found ways to increasingly call out white supremacy in their industry. In 2021, hate-based incidents in London and Edmonton brought national attention to Islamophobia and anti-Black racism. But racism within policing and healthcare remained firmly in place after 18 months of the pandemic, despite all the documented ways in which racism caused harm and killed so many Canadians.

There was also never a serious shift in how politicians and journalists talked about personal responsibility versus community protection. From the start of the pandemic until the summer of 2021, pandemic mitigation measures remained firmly personal: be careful, wash your hands, stay home if you're feeling sick. The Liberals significantly cut back the Canada Response Benefit (what became of CERB after September 2020), forcing many people into even more difficult situations and parents looked forward to another school year in September 2021 with the same problems that had plagued September 2020: large classes, no improvements to air quality and unvaccinated children. In fact, the obsession with getting everyone vaccinated was an outgrowth of this personal responsibility narrative, and it left behind everyone who couldn't get vaccinated, including children who were too young to be vaccinated before September 2021.

Despite the government rhetoric about helping women, there were no significant changes made in this area of policy. Child care remained an elusive promise and was set up to become a major political bargaining chip for the September 2021 federal election. Far worse, there was still no mainstream discussion about ableism and how the worst of the pandemic was rooted in ableist attitudes and public policies. Politicians and journalists alike mostly ignored disabled people, especially people living in congregant care facilities. There were no promises made to de-institutionalize care for disabled people or significantly increase funding. Ableism embedded across the entire medial establishment was barely written about and, in remaining hidden, it was hard for activists to be heard by journalists or politicians.

And finally, journalism mostly got worse over the pandemic. The industry continued to shed jobs and journalists who managed to score a full-time journalism job were on edge because they could lose their jobs in a flash. There was no evolution in reporting and no *mea culpas* related to stoking the fires of racist hatred toward Asians. There was one positive advancement, which grew in opposition to media managers who ensured that the status quo was protected through reporting that was only lightly critical, if at all: there was an explosion of new media endeavours. Independent media punched far above its weight covering the pandemic in Canada and so much of what is known about the failures was thanks to independent and freelance journalists working for little to no money.

The impact of the pandemic will define the next era. How we understood what happened will play a very big role in that. Will this era be erased and forgotten like the influenza epidemic of 1918–19? Or will we be able to grab back the narrative of this moment and unwind the talking points we have been bombarded with for 18 months? If we have any hope at all to protect us from the ravages of privatized public services and the militarized protection of private profits, let alone to save us from the next pandemic, we have to understand what really happened: politicians chose to save profits over lives. They oriented public policies toward protecting capitalism at all costs and allowed COVID-19 to infect and kill as many people as it did. Journalism did not challenge this enough, nor did it give Canadians the information we needed to be able to effectively challenge our politicians' deadly decisions. It's critical that we unspin the narrative that politicians did everything they could to try and stop the spread of COVID-19 and reject attempts to confuse and confound the history of what has happened here. Looking ahead to the next crisis — and there will surely be one because the unsustainable and unjust global system of racial capitalism is hurtling toward a violent demise — how can we prepare better?

The 18 months that this book covers are just a beginning. Many of us said that the pandemic would usher in a new world, and that world could go either of two ways: it could be more cruel, more barbaric and more deadly, or, it could be a world where the status quo is radically upended. The pandemic also coincided with new, record-breaking weather events, making the end of the world feel like it is just around the corner. But then again, every generation believes that it's the earth's last. As I write these words in July 2021, the B.C. coroner's office is sorting through hundreds of heat-related deaths. The people of Lytton, B.C., are combing through the rubble of their town, recently incinerated by fires triggered by either world-record-setting temperatures or by negligence from one of Canada's railway companies. Researchers have just estimated that one billion creatures died in this recent heatwave. New Yorkers are literally swimming in some subway stations to get to their trains after another "once-in-a-lifetime storm." And global COVID-19 deaths surpassed four million. COVID-19 may have been the spark, but it's global capitalism that has been the pile of extremely flammable garbage.

You know how this turns out. You know whether the delta or lambda variants trigger a fall wave in Canada. You know if the omega variant ever comes to pass. You know what October 2021 looked like. You know if COVID-19 sticks around until 2022, if the global death toll hits ten million or if COVID-19 dies out. If you're reading these words, it means you're still alive and there's still enough hope for you to spend any time at all reading books. Your time is precious. Your time is needed. Your time is now.

NOTES

Introduction

1. *Buffalo News*. 2021. "Covid-19 in Western New York: The latest statistics." March 23, 2021. <web.archive.org/web/20210323211607/www.buffalonews.com/news/local/covid-19-in-western-new-york-the-latest-map-and-statistics/article_261f0820-dcb5-11ea-9ade-d3e35b30860b.html>.
2. Andrews, Luke, and Joe Davies. 2021. "Britain's daily Covid cases spike 68% in a week to 27,989 but hospital rates are running at one TENTH of level at start of second wave with 259 new admissions as Boris hails vaccines for 'breaking the link.'" *Daily Mail*, July 1. <dailymail.co.uk/news/article-9745925/Covid-cases-surging-area-England-one-doubled-fifth-local-authorities.html>.
3. Pan American Health Organization. 2021. "Region of the Americas Update." July 1. <iris.paho.org/bitstream/handle/10665.2/54480/COVID-19DailyUpdate1July2021_eng.pdf?sequence=1&isAllowed=y>.
4. Ortaliza, Jared, Kendal Orgera, Krutika Amin, and Cynthia Cox. 2021. "COVID-19 continues to be a leading cause of death in the U.S. in June 2021." Peterson-KFF Health System Tracker. July 1. <healthsystemtracker.org/brief/covid-19-continues-to-be-a-leading-cause-of-death-in-the-u-s-in-june-2021/>.
5. Public Health Agency of Canada. 2021 "COVID-19 daily epidemiology update." July 1. <health-infobase.canada.ca/covid-19/epidemiological-summary-covid-19-cases.html>.
6. Ibid.
7. Tuchman, Gaye. 1978. "News as the Reproduction of the Status Quo: A Summary." In Robert McChesney and Ben Scott (eds.), *Our Unfree Press, 100 Years of Radical Media Criticism*. New York Press: 2004, p. 399.

March 2020

1. *CTV News*. 2020. "Novel coronavirus in Canada: Here's a timeline of COVID-19 cases across the country." March 3. <ctvnews.ca/canada/novel-coronavirus-in-canada-here-s-a-timeline-of-covid-19-cases-across-the-country-1.4829917>.
2. Princess Cruises. 2020. "Diamond Princess Updates." February 27. <princess.com/news/notices_and_advisories/notices/diamond-princess-update.html>.
3. Stroh, Perlita. 2020. "'There was no normal to come back to': Former Diamond Princess cruise passengers struggle with long isolation." *CBC News*, April 4. <CBC.ca/news/canada/diamond-princes-cruise-passenger-continued-isolation-1.5516101>.
4. Hutchins, Aaron, and Marie-Danielle Smith. 2020. "The coronavirus can't be contained. Are you ready?" *Maclean's*, February 28. <macleans.ca/society/health/the-coronavirus-cant-be-contained-are-you-ready/>.
5. Andone, Dakin, Jamie Grumbrecht, and Michael Nedelman. 2020. "First death from coronavirus in the United States confirmed in Washington state." *CNN*, February 29. <cnn.com/2020/02/29/health/us-coronavirus-saturday/index.html>.
6. *CBC News*. 2020. "B.C.'s 6th presumptive COVID-19 case flew from Montreal to Vancouver on Feb. 14." February 23. <cbc.ca/news/canada/british-columbia/

bc-coronavirus-flight-montreal-vancouver-1.5473283>.

7. *Le Journal de Montréal*. 2020. "Une femme de la région de Montréal: un premier cas probable de COVID-19 au Québec." February 27. <journaldemontreal. com/2020/02/27/un-premier-cas-de-coronavirus-au-Québec-1>.

8. Lawler, Dave. 2020. "Timeline: How Italy's coronavirus crisis became the world's deadliest." *Axios,* March 24. <axios.com/italy-coronavirus-timeline-lockdown-deaths-cases-2adb0fc7-6ab5-4b7c-9a55-bc6897494dc6.html>.

9. Leung, Kathy, Joseph T. Wu, Di Liu, and Gabriel Leung. 2020. "First-wave COVID-19 transmissibility and severity in China outside Hubei after control measures, and second-wave scenario planning: a modelling impact assessment." *The Lancet,* 395, 10233. <thelancet.com/journals/lancet/article/PIIS0140-6736%2820%2930746-7/fulltext>.

10. Blewett, Taylor. 2020. "Tracking the coronavirus, from Wuhan, China to Canada's capital: A COVID-19 timeline." *Ottawa Citizen,* March 17. <ottawacitizen.com/news/local-news/tracking-the-coronavirus-from-wuhan-china-to-canadas-capital-a-covid-19-timeline>.

11. Sharp, Morgan. 2020. "Ontario's first presumptive COVID-19 death reported in Muskoka." *National Observer,* March 17. <nationalobserver.com/2020/03/17/news/unconfirmed-covid-19-death-reported-ontarios-muskoka>.

12. Cruz, Araceli. 2020. "A Latina Was the First U.S. Citizen to Die of COVID-19." *HipLatina,* April 28. <hiplatina.com/california-woman-is-one-of-the-first-known-people-to-die-of-covid-19/>.

13. Galloway, Matt. 2020. "The Current for Feb. 6, 2020." *CBC Radio,* February 6. <cbc.ca/radio/thecurrent/the-current-for-feb-6-2020-1.5454037>.

14. Schumaker, Erin. 2020. "Timeline: How coronavirus got started." *ABC News,* September 22. <abcnews.go.com/Health/timeline-coronavirus-started/story?id=69435165>.

15. Little, Simon. 2020. "B.C. identifies 8 new COVID-19 cases, one through community contact." *Global News,* March 5. <globalnews.ca/news/6638081/bc-eight-new-covid-cases-1-community/>.

16. Ibid.

17. Bochove, Danielle. 2020. "Canada sees first COVID-19-related death as man dies in BC." *Bloomberg,* March 9. <bnnbloomberg.ca/canada-sees-first-covid-19-related-death-as-man-dies-in-b-c-care-centre-1.1402793>.

18. Schumaker, Erin. 2020. "Timeline: How coronavirus got started." *ABC News,* September 22. <abcnews.go.com/Health/timeline-coronavirus-started/story?id=69435165>.

19. CBC News. 2020. "B.C.'s 6th presumptive COVID-19 case flew from Montreal to Vancouver on Feb. 14." February 23. <cbc.ca/news/canada/british-columbia/bc-coronavirus-flight-montreal-vancouver-1.5473283>.

20. Ali, Zulfiqar. 2020. "Coronavirus: How Iran is battling a surge in cases." *BBC News,* August 20. <bbc.com/news/52959756>.

21. Little, Simon. 2020. "B.C. identifies 8 new COVID-19 cases, one through community contact." *Global News,* March 5. <globalnews.ca/news/6638081/bc-eight-new-covid-cases-1-community/>.

22. Hager, Mike, and Andrea Woo. 2020. "How the coronavirus took North Vancouver's Lynn Valley Care Centre." *Globe and Mail,* March 21. <theglobeandmail.com/canada/article-how-the-coronavirus-took-north-vancouvers-lynn-valley-care-centre/>.

23. Seyd, Jane. 2020. "COVID-19 outbreak declared over at Lynn Valley Care Centre." *North Shore News,* May 5. <nsnews.com/news/covid-19-outbreak-declared-over-at-lynn-valley-care-centre-1.24129982>.

24. Little, Simon, and Jon Azpiri. 2020. "COVID-19: B.C. announces Canada's first coronavirus death." *Global News*, March 9. <globalnews.ca/news/6650774/bc-covid-coronavirus-update-monday/>.

25. *Bloomberg.* 2021. "Third wave of COVID-19 reignites debate over paid sick days in Canada." April 8. <bnnbloomberg.ca/third-wave-of-covid-19-reignites-debate-over-paid-sick-days-in-canada-1.1587887>.

26. Miller, Adam. 2020. "Canada's first COVID-19 death is not cause for panic — but shows need to protect most vulnerable." CBC *News*, March 10. <cbc.ca/news/health/coronavirus-canada-death-1.5491907>.

27. Lang, Amanda. 2020. "Canada sees first COVID-19-related death as man dies in B.C." [Video.] *Bloomberg*, March 9. <bnnbloomberg.ca/canada-sees-first-covid-19-related-death-as-man-dies-in-b-c-care-centre-1.1402793>.

28. Ibid.

29. CBC *News.* 2021. "Coronavirus: What's happening in Canada and around the world on Sunday." March 21. <cbc.ca/news/world/coronavirus-covid19-canada-world-march21-2021-1.5958212>.

30. Miller, Adam. 2020. "Canada's first COVID-19 death is not cause for panic — but shows need to protect most vulnerable." CBC *News*, March 10. <cbc.ca/news/health/coronavirus-canada-death-1.5491907>.

31. D'Amore, Rachael. 2020. "Study sheds light on coronavirus 'long-haulers,' but experts still lack clear picture." *Global News*, September 16. <globalnews.ca/news/7335744/coronavirus-long-hauler-study/>.

32. Ibid.

33. Favaro, Avis, Elizabeth St. Philip, and Brooklyn Neustaeter. 2020. "'There's a lot of confusion inside of me': COVID-19 'long-haulers' suffering from neurological symptoms months later." CTV *News*, August 29. <ctvnews.ca/health/coronavirus/there-s-a-lot-of-confusion-inside-of-me-covid-19-long-haulers-suffering-from-neurological-symptoms-months-later-1.5084869>.

34. Office of the Prime Minister. 2020. "Prime Minister Trudeau updates Canadians on COVID-19." March 13. <pm.gc.ca/en/videos/2020/03/13/prime-minister-trudeau-updates-canadians-covid-19?p=1>.

35. Ibid.

36. Tasker, John Paul. 2020. "Sophie Grégoire Trudeau's coronavirus infection comes after attending U.K. event." CBC *News*, March 12. <cbc.ca/news/politics/gr%C3%A9goire-trudeau-self-isolating-1.5495419>.

37. Syed, Fatima, Zane Schwartz, Murad Hemmadi, and Jordan Timm. 2020. "COVID-19 roundup: Morneau commits $10 billion to Canada's coronavirus response." *The Logic*, March 13. <thelogic.co/news/whatever-is-necessary/>.

38. Wherry, Aaron. 2020. "Everything happens at once: how one week of the COVID-19 crisis went for the Trudeau government." CBC *News*, March 14. <cbc.ca/news/politics/covid-19-trudeau-coronavirus-hajdu-morneau-1.5497674>.

39. Ibid.

40. Ibid.

41. Yang, Jennifer (@jyangstar). 2020. "This #covid19 graphic is gutting." Twitter, August 2, 2020. <twitter.com/jyangstar/status/1289940943462895616>.

42. Robertson, Grant. 2020. "'Without early warning you can't have early response': How Canada's world-class pandemic alert system failed." *Globe and Mail*, July 25. <theglobeandmail.com/canada/article-without-early-warning-you-cant-have-early-response-how-canadas/>.

43. Ibid.

44. Government of Canada. 2017. "About GPHIN." March 15. <gphin.canada.ca/cepr/

aboutgphin-rmispenbref.jsp?language=en_CA>.

45. Robertson, Grant. 2020. "'Without early warning you can't have early response': How Canada's world-class pandemic alert system failed." *Globe and Mail*, July 25. <theglobeandmail.com/canada/article-without-early-warning-you-cant-have-early-response-how-canadas/>.

46. Brewster, Murray. 2020. "Canadian military intelligence unit issued warning about Wuhan outbreak back in January." CBC *News*, April 10. <cbc.ca/news/politics/coronavirus-pandemic-covid-canadian-military-intelligence-wuhan-1.5528381>.

47. Bronskill, Jim. "COVID-19 a 'failure of early warning' for Canada, intelligence expert says." *Toronto Star*, April 12. <thestar.com/news/canada/2020/04/12/covid-19-a-failure-of-early-warning-for-canada-intelligence-expert-says.html>.

48. Mykhalovskiy, Eric, and Lorna Weir. 2006. "The Global Public Health Intelligence Network and Early Warning Outbreak Detection: A Canadian Contribution to Global Public Health." *Canadian Journal of Public Health*, 97, 1. <ncbi.nlm.nih.gov/pmc/articles/PMC6976220/pdf/41997_2006_Article_BF03405213.pdf>.

49. Robertson, Grant. 2020. "'Without early warning you can't have early response': How Canada's world-class pandemic alert system failed." *Globe and Mail*, July 25. <theglobeandmail.com/canada/article-without-early-warning-you-cant-have-early-response-how-canadas/>.

50. Ibid.

51. Ibid.

52. Brewster, Murray. 2020. "Inside Canada's frayed pandemic early warning system and its COVID-19 response." CBC *News*, April 22. <cbc.ca/news/politics/covid19-pandemic-early-warning-1.5537925>.

53. Robertson, Grant. 2020. "'Without early warning you can't have early response': How Canada's world-class pandemic alert system failed." *Globe and Mail*, July 25. <theglobeandmail.com/canada/article-without-early-warning-you-cant-have-early-response-how-canadas/>.

54. Robertson, Grant. 2020. "Canada's international pandemic alert back in operation, more than 400 days after falling silent." *Globe and Mail*, August 13. <theglobeandmail.com/canada/article-canadas-international-pandemic-alert-back-in-action-more-than-40/>.

55. Turnbull, Sarah. 2020. "Canada's pandemic alert system will be reviewed in wake of concerns: health minister." CTV *News*, September 8. <ctvnews.ca/politics/canada-s-pandemic-alert-system-will-be-reviewed-in-wake-of-concerns-health-minister-1.5096298>.

56. Government of Canada. 2021. "Interim report for the review of the Global Public Health Intelligence Network." Independent review of the Global Public Health Intelligence Network (GHPIN). February 26. <canada.ca/en/public-health/corporate/mandate/about-agency/external-advisory-bodies/list/independent-review-global-public-health-intelligence-network/interim-report.html>.

57. Aiello, Rachel. 2021. "Key fixes needed to Canada's early-warning system before next pandemic: review." CTV *News*, July 12. <ctvnews.ca/politics/key-fixes-needed-to-canada-s-early-warning-system-before-next-pandemic-review-1.5505849>.

58. Hudson, Greg. 2020. "How social media is tracking the coronavirus epidemic in real time." *The Hill*, February 6. <thehill.com/changing-america/well-being/prevention-cures/481687-how-health-experts-are-using-social-media-to>.

April 2020

1. *CP24.* 2020. "The latest numbers on COVID-19 in Canada: April 1." April 1. <cp24. com/news/the-latest-numbers-on-covid-19-in-canada-april-1-1.4878746>.
2. Simpson, James. 2020. "Simpson: Ontario hospitals are not prepared for coronavirus." *Ottawa Citizen,* February 13. <ottawacitizen.com/health/family-child/ simpson-ontario-hospitals-are-not-prepared-for-coronavirus>.
3. Crawford, Blair. 2020. "Son angry after Ottawa care home locks door on aged mother, refuses to let her back from hospital." *Ottawa Citizen,* February 10. <ottawacitizen. com/news/local-news/children-anguish-after-dying-mother-refused-entry-to-hillel-lodge>.
4. Hutchins, Aaron, and Marie-Danielle Smith. 2020. "The coronavirus can't be contained. Are you ready?" *Maclean's,* February 28. <macleans.ca/society/health/ the-coronavirus-cant-be-contained-are-you-ready/>.
5. Snan, Nebal. 2020. "COVID-19 could hit Nova Scotia's aging population hard." *Cape Breton Post,* February 27. <capebretonpost.com/news/provincial/ covid-19-could-hit-nova-scotias-aging-population-hard-416478/>.
6. Forest, P.G., and Jason Sutherland. 2020. "Opinion: Canada must prepare its hospitals for COVID-19. And do it quickly." *National Post,* March 5. <nationalpost.com/opinion/ opinion-canada-must-prepare-its-hospitals-for-covid-19-and-do-it-quickly>.
7. World Trade Organization. 2020. "Report of the WHO-China Joint Mission on Coronavirus Disease 2019 (COVID-19)." February 16–24. <who.int/docs/default-source/coronaviruse/who-china-joint-mission-on-covid-19-final-report.pdf>.
8. Russell, Andrew. 2020. "'Pre-pandemic mode': How Canadian long-term care homes are preparing for coronavirus." *Global News,* March 4. <globalnews.ca/news/6630232/ coronavirus-covid-19-seniors-homes-canada/>.
9. Zafar, Amina. 2020. "Long-term care homes in Canada step up pandemic plans for COVID-19." *CBC News,* March 4. <cbc.ca/news/health/covid-19-nursing-homes-seniors-1.5484196>.
10. Loreto, Nora. 2021. "Deaths: long-term care." Google Spreadsheets. <https://docs.google. com/spreadsheets/d/1M_RzojK0vwF9nAozI7aoyLpPU8EA1JEqO6rq0g1iebU/ edit#gid=0>.
11. Gentile, Davide, and Daniel Boily. 2020. "Québec limite les transports de malades des CHSLD vers les hôpitaux." *Radio-Canada,* April 2. <ici.radio-canada.ca/ nouvelle/1690688/coronavirus-transports-chsld-aines-hopitaux-covid-19>.
12. Weeks, Carly, and Tu Thanh Ha. 2020. "Québec hospitals struggling with influx of COVID-19 patients even as province moves to reopen." *Globe and Mail,* April 29. <theglobeandmail.com/canada/article-Québec-hospitals-struggling-with-influx-of-covid-19-patients-even-as/>.
13. McKenna, Kate, Sarah Leavitt, and Benjamin Shingler. 2020. "'They said, try and keep the patients alive': Nurses overwhelmed by outbreak at Laval long-term care home." *CBC News Montreal,* April 8. <cbc.ca/news/canada/montreal/laval-chsld-covid19-ste-dorothe-1.5525872>.
14. Descurninges, Clara. 2021. "Des symptômes, mais pas de tests avant l'éclosion de COVID-19." *La Presse Canadienne,* June 16. <lapresse.ca/covid-19/2021-06-16/ enquete-sur-le-chsld-sainte-dorothee/des-symptomes-mais-pas-de-tests-avant-l-eclosion-de-covid-19.php>.
15. Montpetit, Jonathan. 2021. "How François Legault has avoided blame for Québec's heavy COVID-19 death toll." *CBC News Montreal,* March 11. <cbc.ca/news/canada/ montreal/Québec-pandemic-anniversary-legault-accountability-1.5944982>.
16. Loreto, Nora. 2021. "Canadians have been in the dark about covid-19 deaths in hospitals. We need more transparency." *Washington Post,* August 3. <washingtonpost.

com/opinions/2021/08/03/canada-hospital-deaths-covid-19-transparency>.

17. Ministry of Long-Term Care. 2020. "Memorandum — COVID-19 Updates." March 9. <health.gov.on.ca/en/pro/programs/publichealth/coronavirus/docs/memos/MLTC_ADM_Memo_COVID19_Updates_March_9_2020.pdf>.

18. Brown, Desmond. 2020. "Ontario building 'iron ring' around long-term care homes after 71 deaths this week, health minister says." *CBC News Toronto*, November 13. <cbc.ca/news/canada/toronto/long-term-care-home-deaths-covid-19-second-wave-1.5801804>.

19. Picard, André. 2021. *Neglected No More*. Random House Canada, p. 89.

20. Ritts, Madeleine. 2020. "The crisis of privatized care in Ontario." *Healthy Debate*, December 4. <healthydebate.ca/2020/12/topic/crisis-privatized-care-in-ontario>.

21. Ibid.

22. Loreto, Nora. 2018. "Vulnerable patients were easy prey for Ontario serial killer." *National Observer*, July 4. <nationalobserver.com/2018/07/04/opinion/vulnerable-patients-were-easy-prey-ontario-serial-killer>.

23. Gillese, Eileen E. 2019. "Public Inquiry into the Safety and Security of Residents in the Long-Term Care Homes System." July 31. <longtermcareinquiry.ca/wp-content/uploads/LTCI_Final_Report_Volume1_e.pdf>.

24. Noorsumar, Zaid. 2020. "Ontario PC donor and nursing home CEO appointed to Ford's long-term care panel." *Rank and File*, March 3. <rankandfile.ca/schlegel-villages-long-term-care/>.

25. Loreto, Nora. 2021. "Deaths: workplace outbreaks." Google Spreadsheets. <https://docs.google.com/spreadsheets/d/1M_RzojK0vwF9nAozI7aoyLpPU8EA1JEqO6rq0g1iebU/edit#gid=404463485>.

26. Picard, André. 2021. *Neglected No More*. Random House Canada, p. 42.

27. Noorsumar, Zaid. 2020. "Taking profits out of long-term care: a conversation with Albert Banerjee." *rabble.ca*, January 3. <rabble.ca/news/2020/01/taking-profits-out-long-term-care-conversation-albert-banerjee>.

28. Sinha, Samir. 2020. "Commission Interview of Dr. Sinha on 9/2/2020." Long-Term Care COVID-19 Commission Meeting. September 2. <ltccommission-commissionsld.ca/transcripts/pdf/Dr_Sinha_Transcript_Final_September_2_2020.pdf>.

29. College of Physiotherapists of Ontario. n.d. "Long-Term Care and Retirement Homes: Information and Resources." Accessed March 15, 2021. <collegept.org/coronavirus/long-term-care-and-retirement-homes>.

30. Lacoursière, Ariane. 2020. "Quel est le secret de la Colombie-Britannique?" *La Presse*, October 10. <lapresse.ca/covid-19/2020-10-10/interdiction-de-la-mobilite-du-personnel/quel-est-le-secret-de-la-colombie-britannique.php>.

31. Giesbrecht, Lynn. 2021. "Take Care: COVID-19 pushes long-term care issues into the spotlight." *Regina Leader-Post*, March 6. <leaderpost.com/news/saskatchewan/take-care-covid-19-pushes-long-term-care-issues-into-the-spotlight>.

32. *CBC News*. 2020. "Ottawa, provinces and territories reach $4B deal to boost essential workers' pay." May 7. <cbc.ca/news/politics/essential-worker-pay-boost-1.5559332>.

33. Johnson, Lisa. 2021. "Alberta frontline workers to receive one-time $1,200 payment from government." *Edmonton Journal*, February 11. <edmontonjournal.com/news/politics/alberta-workers-covid-kenney-copping>.

34. Herhalt, Chris. 2021. "'This has to be the variant,' Barrie, Ont. long-term care home saw 55 COVID-19 cases in 2 days." *CP24*, January 21. <cp24.com/news/this-has-to-be-the-variant-barrie-ont-long-term-care-home-saw-55-covid-19-cases-in-2-days-1.5276460?cache=wfwhhfmnihogp>.

35. CBC *News Toronto*. 2021. "COVID-19 variant detected at Ontario long-term care home very concerning, public health officials say." January 21. <cbc.ca/news/canada/toronto/covid19-barrie-roberta-place-1.5883298>.

36. Herhalt, Chris. 2021. "'This has to be the variant,' Barrie, Ont. long-term care home saw 55 COVID-19 cases in 2 days." *CP24*, January 21. <cp24.com/news/this-has-to-be-the-variant-barrie-ont-long-term-care-home-saw-55-covid-19-cases-in-2-days-1.5276460?cache=wfwhhfmnihogp>.

37. Tendercare Living Centre. n.d. "Home Report Years 2010-2021." *Reports on Long-Term Care Homes*. <publicreporting.ltchomes.net/en-ca/homeprofile.aspx?Home=2649&tab=1>.

38. CBC *News Toronto*. 2021. "COVID-19 variant detected at Ontario long-term care home very concerning, public health officials say." January 21. <cbc.ca/news/canada/toronto/covid19-barrie-roberta-place-1.5883298>.

39. Simon, Chris. 2021. "Inspection of Barrie's Roberta Place, done during outbreak, witnessed residents intermingling, lack of staff cohorting." *The Barrie Advance*, January 25. <simcoe.com/news-story/10316697-inspection-of-barrie-s-roberta-place-done-during-outbreak-witnessed-residents-intermingling-lack-of-staff-cohorting/>.

40. Galloway, Matt. 2021. "The Current aired January 27, 2021." *The Current*, January 27. <cbc.ca/listen/live-radio/1-63-the-current/clip/15821112-what-coronavirus-variants-mean-trajectory-pandemic-canada-patricia>.

41. Howlett, Karen, and Tu Thanh Ha. 2021. "COVID-19 hit long-term care homes harder in second wave." *Globe and Mail*, March 3. <theglobeandmail.com/canada/article-covid-19-hit-long-term-care-homes-harder-in-second-wave/>.

42. Sinha, Samir. 2020. "Commission Interview of Dr. Sinha on 9/2/2020." Long-Term Care COVID-19 Commission Meeting. September 2. <ltccommission-commissionsld.ca/transcripts/pdf/Dr_Sinha_Transcript_Final_September_2_2020.pdf>.

43. Boily, Daniel, and Davide Gentile. 2020. "«Je n'ai jamais eu un emploi aussi gratifiant»: 7115 préposés arrivent en CHSLD au Québec." *Radio-Canada*, September 8, 2020. <ici.radio-canada.ca/nouvelle/1732110/hebergement-beneficiaires-retraites-soins-residents>.

44. Loriggio, Paola. 2021. "Ontario rejected proposals to protect LTC residents, deeming them 'too expensive': documents." CBC *News Toronto*, March 9. <cbc.ca/news/canada/toronto/covid-ont-ltc-commission-1.5942776>.

45. Ibid.

46. Perkel, Colin. 2021. "Ontario lacked updated pandemic response plan before COVID-19 hit, public commission told." CBC *News Toronto*, February 25. <cbc.ca/news/canada/toronto/ontario-long-term-care-public-commission-1.5928892>.

47. Howlett, Karen, and Tu Thanh Ha. 2021. "COVID-19 hit long-term care homes harder in second wave." *Globe and Mail*, March 3. <theglobeandmail.com/canada/article-covid-19-hit-long-term-care-homes-harder-in-second-wave/>.

48. Rayside, Ron. 2020. "Pour des chambres individuelles dans les CHSLD." *Le Devoir*, May 26. <ledevoir.com/opinion/idees/579590/pour-des-chambres-individuelles-dans-les-chsld>.

49. Sinha, Samir. 2020. "Commission Interview of Dr. Sinha on 9/2/2020." Long-Term Care COVID-19 Commission Meeting. September 2. <ltccommission-commissionsld.ca/transcripts/pdf/Dr_Sinha_Transcript_Final_September_2_2020.pdf>.

50. Luck, Shaina. 2020. "What the design of long-term care homes can and can't do." CBC *News Nova Scotia*, June 16. <cbc.ca/news/canada/nova-scotia/design-long-term-care-homes-1.5606576>.

51. White-Crummey, Arthur. 2021. "Take Care: Sask. LTC homes raised warning signals long before outbreaks." *Regina Leader-Post*, March

4. <leaderpost.com/news/saskatchewan/take-care-sask-ltc-homes-raised-warning-signals-long-before-outbreaks>.

52. Pedersen, Katie, Melissa Mancini, and William Wolfe-Wylie. 2020. "Ont. nursing homes have had 22 years to do safety upgrades. COVID-19 reveals deadly cost of delay." CBC *Marketplace,* June 9. <cbc.ca/news/health/covid-19-coronavirus-long-term-care-homes-ontario-1.5604009>.

53. Brown, Desmond. 2020. "Ontario building 'iron ring' around long-term care homes after 71 deaths this week, health minister says." CBC *News Toronto,* November 13. <cbc.ca/news/canada/toronto/long-term-care-home-deaths-covid-19-second-wave-1.5801804>.

54. Loreto, Nora (@nolore). 2021. "Media are reporting deaths in Halton related to outbreaks in relation to when their outbreak started, rather than being cumulative." Twitter, January 27. <twitter.com/NoLore/status/1354635800772751361?s=20>.

55. Noorsumar, Zaid. 2020. "Party of Profits: Ontario Tories and the profit motive in long-term care." *Rank and File,* April 1. <rankandfile.ca/party-of-profits-ontario-tories-and-the-profit-motive-in-long-term-care/>.

56. Ministry of Long-Term Care. 2020. "Amendments to Emergency Order O. Reg. 95/20, under the Emergency Management and Civil Protection Act." July 17. <health.gov.on.ca/en/pro/programs/ltc/memo_20200717.aspx>.

57. Welsh, Moira. 2020. "Province suspends rules protecting vulnerable, long-term care resident." *Toronto Star,* March 28. <thestar.com/news/canada/2020/03/28/province-suspends-rules-protecting-vulnerable-long-term-care-residents.html>.

58. Loreto, Nora. 2021. "Deaths: long-term care." Google Spreadsheets. <https://docs.google.com/spreadsheets/d/1M_RzojK0vwF9nAozI7aoyLp PU8EA1JEqO6rq0g1iebU/edit#gid=0>.

59. Noorsumar, Zaid. 2020. "Party of Profits: Ontario Tories and the profit motive in long-term care." *Rank and File,* April 1. <rankandfile.ca/party-of-profits-ontario-tories-and-the-profit-motive-in-long-term-care/>.

60. StrategyCorp. n.d. "Leslie Noble." Accessed March 23, 2021. <strategycorp.com/people/noble-leslie/>.

61. Office of the Integrity Commissioner of Ontario. n.d. "Jenni Byrne" and "Simon Jeffries." Accessed July 20, 2021. <http://lobbyist.oico.on.ca/Pages/Public/PublicSearch/Default.aspx>.

62. Leslie, Keith. 2020. "Real long-term care reform demands more than finger-pointing and spin." *Hamilton Spectator,* July 19. <thespec.com/opinion/contributors/2020/07/19/real-long-term-care-reform-demands-more-than-finger-pointing-and-spin.html>.

63. Milstead, David. 2021. "Golden years, golden boards: Mike Harris's post-politics career." *Globe and Mail,* January 20. <theglobeandmail.com/business/commentary/article-a-look-at-mike-harriss-post-politics-career/>.

64. Milstead, David. 2021. "Chartwell hikes executive bonuses, gives high marks for pandemic response." *Globe and Mail,* April 16. <theglobeandmail.com/business/article-chartwell-hikes-executive-bonuses-gives-high-marks-for-pandemic/>.

65. Loreto, Nora. 2021. "Deaths: residential care." Google Spreadsheets. <https://docs.google.com/spreadsheets/d/1M_RzojK0vwF9nAozI7aoyLp PU8EA1JEqO6rq0g1iebU/edit#gid=0>.

66. Revera. 2017. "Real Talk with Hazel McCallion." January 20. <reveraliving.com/en/think-with-us/blog/real-talk-with-hazel-mccallion>.

67. Ontario Lobbyist Registry. n.d. "In-house Organization Lobbyist Registration - active - Ontario Long Term Care Association." Accessed July 5, 2021. <lobbyist.oico.on.ca/Pages/Public/PublicSearch/OrganizationPreview.aspx>.

68. Lobbyist Registry. 2021. "Chartwell Retirement Residences / Conal

Slobodin, Consultant." <https://lobbycanada.gc.ca/app/secure/ocl/lrs/do/vwRg?cno=366191&regId=898068>.

69. Noorsumar, Zaid. 2021. "Record of long-term care coverage shows failure to challenge power structures." *J-Source,* May 5. <j-source.ca/record-of-long-term-care-coverage-shows-failure-to-challenge-power-structures/>.

70. Rivett, Paul, and Jordan Bitove. 2020. "Enough is enough: We demand change to the inhumane tragedy playing out in Ontario's long-term care homes." *Toronto Star,* December 31. <thestar.com/opinion/editorials/2020/12/30/enough-is-enough-we-demand-change-to-the-inhumane-tragedy-playing-out-in-ontarios-long-term-care-homes.html>.

71. Rivett, Paul, and Jordan Bitove. 2021. "Sign this open letter calling for urgent action to fix our failing long-term care system." *Toronto Star,* January 9. <web.archive.org/web/20210110163908/https://act.newmode.net/action/torstar-corporation/sign-open-letter-calling-urgent-action-fix-our-failing-long-term-care>.

72. Wherry, Aaron. 2021. "'The story is … still being written': A pandemic Q&A with Health Minister Patty Hajdu." *CBC News,* March 13. <cbc.ca/news/politics/patty-hajdu-coronavirus-pandemic-1.5948112>.

73. Chartwell. 2021. "Chartwell Announces Fourth Quarter and Year End 2020 Results." March 4. <investors.chartwell.com/English/press-market-information/press-releases/news-details/2021/Chartwell-Announces-Fourth-Quarter-and-Year-End-2020-Results/default.aspx>.

May 2020

1. *CP24.* 2020. "The latest numbers on COVID-19 in Canada: May 1, 2020." May 1. <cp24.com/news/the-latest-numbers-on-covid-19-in-canada-may-1-2020-1.4921887>.

2. UFCW Local 401. 2020. "RELEASE: 'A quiet, gentle, and humble man:' UFCW Local 401 grieves the loss of union leader amid Cargill High River COVID-19 outbreak." May 12. <gounion.ca/news/release-a-quiet-gentle-and-humble-man-ufcw-local-401-grieves-the-loss-of-union-leader-amid-cargill-high-river-covid-19-outbreak/>.

3. Gofundme. "Quesada Family." Accessed October 7, 2020. <ca.gofundme.com/f/quesada-family>.

4. Croteau, Jill. 2020. "Widow and children of Cargill worker who died from COVID-19 share heartbreak." *Global News,* May 26. <globalnews.ca/news/6987049/coronavirus-cargill-worker-died-family/>.

5. Loreto, Nora. 2021. "Deaths: workplace outbreaks." Google Spreadsheets. <https://docs.google.com/spreadsheets/d/1M_RzojK0vwF9nAozI7aoyLpPU8EA1JEqO6rq0g1iebU/edit#gid=404463485>.

6. Croteau, Jill. 2020. "Widow and children of Cargill worker who died from COVID-19 share heartbreak." *Global News,* May 26. <globalnews.ca/news/6987049/coronavirus-cargill-worker-died-family/>.

7. "Statement on Safety in Cargill's North American Protein Facilities." 2020. Cargill, July 15. <cargill.com/story/statement-on-safety-in-cargill-north-american-protein-facilities?k_cca=cargill_search_intent_all+traffic&gclid=CjwKCAjwzvX7BRAeEiwAsXExo93hyZZbepto43B5giu8dyXJ-OtKNrPy_AcxFB-8_OZDgUK8MgZc4hoCaGAQAvD_BwE>.

8. Loreto, Nora. 2021. "Deaths: workplace outbreaks." 2021. Google Spreadsheets. <https://docs.google.com/spreadsheets/d/1M_RzojK0vwF9nAozI7aoyLpPU8EA1JEqO6rq0g1iebU/edit#gid=404463485>.

9. Lanese, Nicoletta. 2020. "'Superspreader' in South Korea infects nearly 40 people with coronavirus." *Live Science,* February 23. <livescience.com/

coronavirus-superspreader-south-korea-church.html>.

10. Davidson, Sean. 2020. "Grocery store worker who died of COVID-19 fought virus until 'last breath.'" *CTV News Toronto,* March 27. <toronto.ctvnews.ca/grocery-store-worker-who-died-of-covid-19-fought-virus-until-last-breath-1.4871097#_gus&_gucid=&_gup=twitter&_gsc=EonAjFh>.

11. Yun, Tom. 2020. "Second employee at Oshawa Real Canadian Superstore tests positive for coronavirus." *Hamilton Spectator,* March 29. <thespec.com/news/ontario/2020/03/29/second-employee-at-oshawa-real-canadian-superstore-tests-positive-for-coronavirus.html>.

12. Bowden, Olivia. 2020. "Loblaws employees say stores are handling COVID-19 unsafely, putting them at risk." *Global News,* July 2. <globalnews.ca/news/7131861/loblaws-employees-stores-handling-covid-19-coronavirus/>.

13. Ibid.

14. Ibid.

15. Dryden, Joel. 2020. "What led to Alberta's biggest outbreak? Cargill meat plant's hundreds of COVID-19 cases." *CBC News,* April 19. <cbc.ca/news/canada/calgary/cargill-alberta-covid-19-deena-hinshaw-1.5537377>.

16. Ibid.

17. Ibid.

18. Bain, Beverly, Nora Loreto, and Harsha Walia. 2020. "Gendering the political landscape." Ryerson Social Justice Week, October 29. <ryerson.ca/socialjustice/social-justice-week/2020/10/gendering-the-political-landscape-feminist-activism-now/?>.

19. Ibid.

20. Loblaw Inc. 2021. "Loblaw Companies Limited 2020 Annual Report – Financial Review." <dis-prod.assetful.loblaw.ca/content/dam/loblaw-companies-limited/creative-assets/loblaw-ca/investor-relations-reports/annual/2020/LCL_2020%20AR.PDF>.

21. *CTV News.* 2021. "Loblaw reports Q4 profit up from year earlier, but falls short of expectations." February 20. <ctvnews.ca/business/loblaw-reports-q4-profit-up-from-year-earlier-but-falls-short-of-expectations-1.4820084>.

22. Metro Inc. 2020. "Interim Report 12-week period ended September 26, 2020 4th Quarter and Fiscal 2020." <corpo.metro.ca/userfiles/file/PDF/Rapport-trimestriel/2020/Rapport_intermediaire_2020_Q4_EN_(r74).pdf>.

23. JBS. 2020. "JBS Earnings Release Third Quarter 2020." November 11. <api.mziq.com/mzfilemanager/v2/d/043a77e1-0127-4502-BC5b-21427b991b22/9077303c-b25f-6724-8ab5-b839ac5b6eb2?origin=2>.

24. *Reuters.* 2020. "Cargill fiscal 2020 revenue rises 1% to $114.6 billion." July 16. <reuters.com/article/us-cargill-results/cargill-fiscal-2020-revenue-rises-1-to-114-6-billion-idUSKCN24H2L9>.

25. Bundale, Brett. 2021. "All the jobs lost in 2020 among workers with wages below Canadian average: report." *CTV News,* February 20. <ctvnews.ca/business/all-the-jobs-lost-in-2020-among-workers-with-wages-below-canadian-average-report-1.5317194>.

26. Mojtehedzadeh, Sarah, and Jennifer Yang. 2020. "More than 180 workers at this Toronto bakery got COVID-19 — but the public wasn't informed. Why aren't we being told about workplace outbreaks?" *Toronto Star,* August 10. <thestar.com/business/2020/08/10/more-than-180-workers-at-this-toronto-bakery-got-covid-19-but-the-public-wasnt-informed-why-arent-we-being-told-about-workplace-outbreaks.html>.

27. Ibid.

28. Ibid.

29. UFCW Local 401. n.d. "COVID-19 Action." Last accessed October 16, 2020. <gounion.ca/covidaction/>.

30. De Souza, Mike, and Andrew Russell. 2020. "1 dead, 24 Maple Leaf Foods employees infected with COVID-19 at Montreal plant." *Global News,* May 15. <globalnews.ca/news/6948106/maple-leaf-foods-montreal-covid-19/>.

31. Migrante Manitoba. 2020. "Open Letter from workers at Maple Leaf Foods." August 24. <facebook.com/115246555302759/posts/open-letter-from-workers-at-maple-leaf-foods-brandonaugust-24-2020workers-at-map/1652730404887692/>.

32. Ibid.

33. Maclean, Cameron. 2020. "Brandon dealing with 'fairly large outbreak' as more cases linked to cluster: chief public health officer." *CBC News Manitoba,* August 7. <cbc.ca/news/canada/manitoba/brandon-meat-processing-plant-covid-cluster-update-1.5678161>.

34. Thompson, Sam. 2020. "Migrant workers at Brandon Maple Leaf plant seek shutdown, increased health measures." *Global News,* August 24. <globalnews.ca/news/7295412/maple-leaf-foods-brandon-covid-19-outbreak/>.

35. Ibid.

36. Weber, Tara. 2020. "More COVID-19 cases at Maple Leaf Foods plant." *Bloomberg.* <bnnbloomberg.ca/company-news/video/more-covid-19-cases-at-maple-leaf-foods-plant~2012046>.

37. Klatt, Emily. 2020. "Province downgrades Prairie Mountain Health to level yellow: caution." *Brandon Sun,* September 18. <brandonsun.com/local/province-downgradesprairie-mountain-healthto-level-yellow-caution-572448622.html>.

38. Dorning, Mike. 2020. "Meatpacking link found in up to 8% of early U.S. Covid Cases." *Bloomberg,* November 23. <bloomberg.com/news/articles/2020-11-23/study-ties-6-to-8-of-u-s-covid-cases-to-meatpacking-plants>.

39. Agriculture and Agri-Food Canada. 2021. "Workplace guidance for agriculture and agri-food sector employers and employees." June 25. <agriculture.canada.ca/en/covid-19-information-agriculture-and-agri-food-industry/workplace-guidance>.

40. Ibid.

41. Ibid.

42. Tunney, Joseph. 2020. "PM calls grocery store employees 'heroes' after grocery chains cancel pay bump." *CBC News,* June 19. <cbc.ca/news/politics/grocery-store-workers-pandemic-covid-coronavirus-1.5619715>.

43. Ibid.

44. Mojtehedzadeh, Sara. 2020. "Public health won't tell us which employers have COVID-19 outbreaks. But we obtained WSIB data to help paint a picture." *Toronto Star,* October 11. <thestar.com/news/gta/2020/10/11/public-health-wont-tell-us-which-employers-have-covid-19-outbreaks-but-we-obtained-wsib-data-to-help-paint-a-picture.html>.

45. *Radio Canada International.* 2021. "How Montreal, not long ago the epicenter of the pandemic in Canada, avoided a disastrous 3rd wave." April 29. <ici.radio-canada.ca/rci/en/news/1788888/montreal-epicentre-pandemic-canada-disastrous-3rd-wave>.

46. Syed, Fatima. 2021. "You can't stop the spread of the virus if you don't stop it in Peel." *The Local,* April 22. <thelocal.to/you-cant-stop-the-spread-of-the-virus-if-you-dont-stop-it-in-peel/>.

47. Glauser, Wendy. 2021. "Changing the minds of the vaccine hesitant requires actually listening to them." *Maclean's,* June 28. <macleans.ca/news/vaccine-hesitancy-canada>.

48. Loreto, Nora. 2021. "Deaths: workplace outbreaks." Google Spreadsheets. <https://docs.google.com/spreadsheets/d/1M_RzojK0vwF9nAozI7aoyLpPU8EA1JEqO6rq0g1iebU/edit#gid=404463485>.

June 2020

1. Boynton, Sean. 2020. "Canada sees lowest daily coronavirus death toll in 2 months, 759 new cases." *Global News,* June 1. <globalnews.ca/news/7014211/canada-coronavirus-cases-june-1/>.

2. Boisvert, Yves. 2020. "Il s'appelait Marcelin François." *La Presse,* May 8. <lapresse.ca/covid-19/2020-05-08/il-s-appelait-marcelin-francois>.

3. Boisvert, Yves. 2020. "Pour des motifs humanitaires." *La Presse,* April 29. <lapresse.ca/covid-19/2020-04-29/pour-des-motifs-humanitaires>.

4. Samual, Sigal. 2020. "'There's a Perception That Canada Is Being Invaded.'" *The Atlantic,* May 26. <theatlantic.com/international/archive/2018/05/theres-a-perception-that-canada-is-being-invaded/561032/>.

5. Teisceira-Lessard, Philippe, and Caroline Touzin. 2020. "Une manne pour des agences aux pratiques douteuses." *La Presse,* October 1. <lapresse.ca/covid-19/2020-10-01/pandemie/une-manne-pour-des-agences-aux-pratiques-douteuses.php>.

6. Pilon-Larose, Hugo. 2020. "L'opposition réclame un moratoire." *La Presse,* October 1. <lapresse.ca/covid-19/2020-10-01/agences-de-placement-en-sante/l-opposition-reclame-un-moratoire.php>.

7. Bain, Beverly, OmiSoore Dryden, and Rinaldo Walcott. 2020. "Coronavirus discriminates against Black lives through surveillance, policing and the absence of health data." *The Conversation,* April 20. <theconversation.com/coronavirus-discriminates-against-black-lives-through-surveillance-policing-and-the-absence-of-health-data-135906>.

8. Ibid.

9. Timothy, Roberta K. 2020. "Coronavirus is not the great equalizer — race matters." *The Conversation,* April 6. <theconversation.com/coronavirus-is-not-the-great-equalizer-race-matters-133867>.

10. Nasser, Shanifa. 2020. "Early signs suggest race matters when it comes to COVID-19. So why isn't Canada collecting race-based data?" *CBC News,* April 17. <cbc.ca/news/canada/toronto/race-coronavirus-canada-1.5536168>.

11. Flanagan, Ryan. 2020. "Does COVID-19 discriminate? This is how some Canadians are harder-hit." *CTV News,* April 15. <ctvnews.ca/health/coronavirus/does-covid-19-discriminate-this-is-how-some-canadians-are-harder-hit-1.4897298>.

12. Fletcher, Robson. 2020. "Alberta is now collecting race-based COVID-19 data but won't publish it yet." *CBC News Calgary,* December 1. <cbc.ca/news/canada/calgary/alberta-race-based-data-collection-but-no-publishing-1.5822148>.

13. Loreto, Nora. 2021. "Deaths: workplace outbreaks." Google Spreadsheets. <https://docs.google.com/spreadsheets/d/1M_RzojK0vwF9nAozI7aoyLpPU8EA1JEqO6rq0g1iebU/edit#gid=404463485>.

14. Okwuosa, Ashley. 2021. "'They're at risk': How COVID-19 is affecting health-care workers of colour." *TVO,* February 1. <tvo.org/article/theyre-at-risk-how-covid-19-is-affecting-health-care-workers-of-colour>.

15. Loreto, Nora. 2021. "Deaths: workplace outbreaks." Google Spreadsheets. <https://docs.google.com/spreadsheets/d/1M_RzojK0vwF9nAozI7aoyLpPU8EA1JEqO6rq0g1iebU/edit#gid=404463485>.

16. Loreto, Nora (@nolore). 2020. "COVID-19 has hit poorest and Black communities in Toronto hardest. Here are three maps that help you see the connection (thanks to a twitter friend)." Twitter, May 29. <twitter.com/NoLore/status/1266559315621576705>.

17. Abboud, Elias. 2020. "A virus that discriminates between rich and poor: Why the data collected matters in the fight against COVID-19." *CBC News,* April 30. <cbc.ca/news/canada/montreal/montreal-discrimination-covid-19-rich-poor-1.5551622>.

18. McKie, David. 2020. "Poverty and COVID-19: More data would help explain the

connection." *National Observer*, May 12. <nationalobserver.com/2020/05/12/analysis/poverty-and-covid-19-more-data-would-help-explain-connection>.

19. Zimonjic, Peter. 2020. "Trudeau, Ontario health minister say they're looking at collecting race-based pandemic data." CBC *News*, June 5. <cbc.ca/news/politics/trudeau-elliott-covid-19-race-based-data-1.5600824>.

20. Amin, Faiza, and Meredith Bond. 2020. "COVID-19 disproportionally impacting Black communities, people of colour in Toronto." *City News Toronto*, July 9. <toronto.citynews.ca/2020/07/09/race-data-covid-toronto/>.

21. Indigenous Services Canada. 2021. "Confirmed cases of COVID-19." June 22. <sac-isc.gc.ca/eng/1598625105013/1598625167707>.

22. Moriarty, Tara, Anna Boczula, Eemaan Kaur Thind, Nora Loreto, and Jane McElhaney. 2021. "Excess All-Cause Mortality During the COVID-19 Epidemic in Canada." Royal Society of Canada. <rsc-src.ca/sites/default/files/EM PB_EN.pdf>.

23. Wong, Nicole. 2021. "Study finds Indigenous people twice more likely to struggle due to COVID crisis." *Winnipeg Sun*, March 7. <winnipegsun.com/news/news-news/study-finds-indigenous-people-twice-more-likely-to-struggle-due-to-covid-crisis>.

24. Aiello, Rachel. 2020. "Canada's top doctor calls for 'structural change' to address COVID-19 inequities." CTV *News*, October 28. <ctvnews.ca/health/coronavirus/canada-s-top-doctor-calls-for-structural-change-to-address-covid-19-inequities-1.5164415>.

25. *City News 1130*. 2020. "Better Data needed to address inequalities exposed by COVID-19: Njoo." October 14. <citynews1130.com/2020/10/14/better-data-needed-to-address-inequalities-exposed-by-covid-19-njoo/>.

26. Yang, Jennifer (@jyangstar). 2020. "This #covid19 graphic is gutting." Twitter, August 2. <twitter.com/jyangstar/status/1289940943462895616>.

27. Aiello, Rachel. 2020. "Canada's top doctor calls for 'structural change' to address COVID-19 inequities." CTV *News*, October 28. <ctvnews.ca/health/coronavirus/canada-s-top-doctor-calls-for-structural-change-to-address-covid-19-inequities-1.5164415>.

28. Hune-Brown, Nicholas. 2021. "The Vaccine Rollout is Leaving Toronto's Hardest-Hit Postal Codes Behind." *The Local*, April 6. <thelocal.to/the-vaccine-rollout-is-leaving-torontos-hardest-hit-postal-codes-behind/>.

29. Loreto, Nora. 2021. "Ontario Government press releases." August 1.

30. Office of the Premier. 2020. "Ontario supporting high priority communities: Backgrounder." December 21. <news.ontario.ca/en/backgrounder/59793/ontario-supporting-high-priority-communities>.

31. Timothy, Roberta K. 2020. "Coronavirus is not the great equalizer — race matters." *The Conversation*, April 6. <theconversation.com/coronavirus-is-not-the-great-equalizer-race-matters-133867>.

32. Statistics Canada. 2020. "Police-reported crime incidents down during the early months of the pandemic, while domestic disturbance calls increase." September 1. <www150.statcan.gc.ca/n1/daily-quotidien/200901/dq200901a-eng.htm>.

33. Statistics Canada. 2020. "Selected police-reported crime and calls for service during the COVID-19 pandemic, March to October 2020." January 27. <www150.statcan.gc.ca/n1/daily-quotidien/210127/dq210127c-eng.htm>.

34. *Sault Online*. 2020. "OPP: How Police Enforcement will Help Limit the Spread of COVID-19." March 20. <saultonline.com/2020/03/opp-how-police-enforcement-will-help-limit-the-spread-of-covid-19/>.

35. Dryden, OmiSoore. 2020. "OMISOORE DRYDEN: Racist responses to COVID-19 place us all at greater risk." *Halifax Chronicle Herald*, September 2. <thechronicleherald.ca/opinion/local-perspectives/

omisoore-dryden-racist-responses-to-covid-19-place-us-all-at-greater-risk-492256/>.

36. *CBC News.* 2021. "Couple who snuck into Yukon community for vaccine pleads guilty to breaking pandemic rules." June 16. <cbc.ca/news/canada/north/bakers-beaver-creek-vaccine-plea-1.6031121>.

37. McClelland, Alexander, and Alex Luscombe. 2020. "Policing the Pandemic: Tracking the Policing of COVID-19 Across Canada." *Scholars Portal Database,* July 12. <policingthepandemic.ca/>.

38. Bain, Beverly, OmiSoore Dryden, and Rinaldo Walcott. 2020. "Coronavirus discriminates against Black lives through surveillance, policing and the absence of health data." *The Conversation,* April 20. <theconversation.com/coronavirus-discriminates-against-black-lives-through-surveillance-policing-and-the-absence-of-health-data-135906>.

39. Glowacki, Laura. 2020. "Bylaw, police to crack down on 'idiotic' behaviour, mayor warns." *CBC News Ottawa,* March 30. <cbc.ca/news/canada/ottawa/ottawa-enforcement-covid-19-1.5515329>.

40. Jones, Ryan Patrick. 2020. "People of colour make up 66% of Ottawa's COVID-19 cases." *CBC News Ottawa,* September 21. <cbc.ca/news/canada/ottawa/covid-19-strategy-racialized-communities-1.5730934>.

41. Ho, Solarina. 2020. "Millions of dollars in COVID-19 fines disproportionately hurting Black, Indigenous, marginalized groups: report." *CTV News,* June 24. <ctvnews.ca/health/coronavirus/millions-of-dollars-in-covid-19-fines-disproportionately-hurting-black-indigenous-marginalized-groups-report-1.4999052>.

42. *Washington Post.* 2021. "Fatal Force - police shooting database." Accessed February 12, 2021. <washingtonpost.com/graphics/investigations/police-shootings-database/>.

43. Statistics Canada. 2020. "Police-reported crime incidents down during the early months of the pandemic, while domestic disturbance calls increase." September 1. <www150.statcan.gc.ca/n1/daily-quotidien/200901/dq200901a-eng.htm>.

44. Kerr, Jason. 2020. "Mayor warns residents of potential rise in petty crime." *Prince Albert Daily Herald,* October 23. <paherald.sk.ca/2020/10/23/mayor-warns-residents-of-potential-rise-in-petty-crime/>.

45. Blair, Alexandra, Abtin Parnia, and Arjumand Siddiqi. 2021. "A time-series analysis of testing and COVID-19 outbreaks in Canadian federal prisons to inform prevention and surveillance efforts." Public Health Agency of Canada. January 2021. <canada.ca/en/public-health/services/reports-publications/canada-communicable-disease-report-ccdr/monthly-issue/2021-47/issue-1-january-2021/covid-19-federal-prisons.html>.

46. Pauls, Karen. 2021. "Inside Canada's largest COVID-19 outbreak in a federal prison." *CBC News Manitoba,* January 26. <cbc.ca/news/canada/manitoba/covid-coronavirus-outbreak-prison-class-action-lawsuit-1.5886561>.

47. Loreto, Nora. 2021. "Deaths: residential care." Google Spreadsheets. <https://docs.google.com/spreadsheets/d/1M_RzojK0vwF9nAozI7aoyLpPU8EA1JEqO6rq0g1iebU/edit#gid=0>.

48. Statistics Canada. 2020. "Average daily counts of adults in correctional services, by type of supervision and jurisdiction, 2018/2019." December 21. <www150.statcan.gc.ca/n1/pub/85-002-x/2020001/article/00016/tbl/tbl01-eng.htm>.

49. Walby, Kevin, and Justin Piché. 2021. "Tracking the Politics of Criminalizaton and Punishment in Canada." Criminalization and Punishment Education Project, July 2. <http://tpcp-canada.blogspot.com/2021/06/>.

50. Owusu-Bempah, Akwasi, Maria Jung, Firdaous Sbaï, Andrew S. Wilton, and Fiona Kouyoumdjian. 2021. "Race and Incarceration: The Representation and

Characteristics of Black People in Provincial Correctional Facilities in Ontario, Canada." *Race and Justice.* <journals.sagepub.com/doi/full/10.1177/215336872110 06461>.

51. Malahieh, Jamil. 2020. "Adult and youth correctional statistics in Canada, 2018/2019." *Canadian Centre for Justice and Community Safety Statistics,* December 21. <www150. statcan.gc.ca/n1/pub/85-002-x/2020001/article/00016-eng.htm>.

52. Rowe, Daniel. 2020. "Anti-Asian racism on the rise in Canada's biggest cities amid COVID-19 crisis: poll." *CTV News Montreal,* April 27. <montreal.ctvnews.ca/ anti-asian-racism-on-the-rise-in-canada-s-biggest-cities-amid-covid-19-crisis-poll-1.4913957>.

53. Raymond, Ted. 2021. "Reports of anti-Asian racism spike in Ottawa in 2020." *CTV News Ottawa,* January 5. <ottawa.ctvnews.ca/reports-of-anti-asian-racism-spike-in-ottawa-in-2020-1.5254558>.

54. Chung, Amy. 2021. "In 2021, Asian Canadians Document Hate Crimes To Be Believed." *Huffington Post,* March 1. <huffingtonpost.ca/entry/ anti-asian-racism-canada_ca_603d08cdc5b682971502118f>.

55. Ibid.

56. Arthur, Bruce. 2020. "Conservative MP's ugly smear against Theresa Tam comes from an infection in Canadian politics." *Toronto Star,* April 23. <thestar.com/opinion/ star-columnists/2020/04/23/conservative-mps-ugly-smear-against-theresa-tam-comes-from-an-infection-in-canadian-politics.html>.

57. Abdel-Nabi, Hadeel. 2020. "The Systemic Racism of Canadian Journalism." *Sprawl Calgary,* June 23. <sprawlcalgary.com/bipoc-representation-in-local-newsrooms>.

58. Malik, Asmaa, and Sonya Fatah. 2019. "Newsrooms not keeping up with changing demographics, study suggests." *The Conversation,* November 11. <theconversation.com/ newsrooms-not-keeping-up-with-changing-demographics-study-suggests-125368>.

59. Cohn, Martin Regg. 2020. "If you're powerless or homeless, COVID-19 has you in its sights." *Toronto Star,* October 19. <thestar.com/politics/political-opinion/2020/10/19/ if-youre-powerless-or-homeless-covid-19-has-you-in-its-sights.html>.

60. Cohn, Martin Regg. 2020. "Canada has a racism problem, and it's uniquely ours." *Toronto Star,* June 5. <thestar.com/politics/political-opinion/2020/06/05/canada-has-a-racism-problem-and-its-uniquely-ours.html>.

61. Cohn, Martin Regg. "When white Canadians think of racism, they think of America. These Black MPPs know better." *Toronto Star,* October 4. <thestar.com/politics/ political-opinion/2020/10/04/a-black-caucus-at-queens-park-is-an-idea-whose-time-has-come.html>.

62. Delacourt, Susan. 2020. "Donald Trump lost, but Trumpism is still thriving. Could it take hold in Canada, too?" *Toronto Star,* November 8. <thestar.com/opinion/ star-columnists/2020/11/08/donald-trump-lost-but-trumpism-is-still-thriving-could-it-take-hold-in-canada-too.html>.

63. Delacourt, Susan. 2020. "Female politicians endure misogyny, racism and hurtful comments. It's time for them to talk about that." *Toronto Star,* October 15. <thestar. com/politics/political-opinion/2020/10/15/female-politicians-endure-misogyny-racism-and-hurtful-comments-its-time-for-them-to-talk-about-that.html>.

64. Delacourt, Susan. 2020. "Susan Delacourt: Black Lives Matter made a big impact and Trump-style populism is on the slide in Canada and U.S., says poll." Orangeville.com, October 9. <orangeville.com/opinion-story/10220363-susan-delacourt-black-lives-matter-made-a-big-impact-and-trump-style-populism-is-on-the-slide-in-canada-and-u-s-says-poll/>.

65. Ibid.

66. Gee, Marcus. 2020. "Toronto's progress against COVID-19 justifies easing the

lockdown." *Globe and Mail,* August 1. <theglobeandmail.com/canada/toronto/article-torontos-progress-against-covid-19-justifies-easing-the-lockdown/>.

67. Ibid.

68. Gee, Marcus. 2020. "Jagmeet Singh showed an appalling lack of judgment in tweet about Korchinski-Paquet death." *Globe and Mail,* September 4. <theglobeandmail.com/canada/toronto/article-jagmeet-singh-showed-an-appalling-lack-of-judgment-in-tweet-about/>.

69. Goldstein, Lorrie. 2020. "Our leaders fretted about racism more than COVID-19." *Toronto Sun,* May 9. <torontosun.com/opinion/columnists/goldstein-our-leaders-fretted-about-racism-more-than-covid-19>.

70. Paradkar, Shree. 2020. "'Why am I being treated this way?' Between the pandemic and city bylaws, massage parlour workers are struggling." *Toronto Star,* July 9. <thestar.com/opinion/star-columnists/2020/07/09/why-am-i-being-treated-this-way-between-the-pandemic-and-city-bylaws-massage-parlour-workers-are-struggling.html>.

71. Sinclair, Niigaan. 2020. "Simple remedy for racism in health-care system." *Winnipeg Free Press,* October 17. <winnipegfreepress.com/local/simple-remedy-for-racism-in-health-care-system-572779771.html>.

July 2020

1. *City News Ottawa.* 2020. "The latest numbers on COVID-19 in Canada." July 1. <ottawa.citynews.ca/national-news/the-latest-numbers-on-covid-19-in-canada-2532823>.

2. Turnbull, Jeff. 2020. "Long Term Care Covid-19 Commission Mtg." December 16. <ltccommission-commissionsld.ca/transcripts/pdf/Dr._Turnbull_Transcript_December_16_2020.pdf>.

3. Ibid.

4. Bologna, Caroline. "How To Stop Touching Your Face." *Huffington Post,* March 10. <huffingtonpost.ca/entry/how-to-stop-touching-your-face_l_5e59555ac5b6010221103ad0>.

5. *Google Trends.* December 10, 2020.

6. Aiello, Rachel. 2020. "PM Trudeau: Feds will soon 'strongly' recommend contact tracing app." *CTV News,* May 22. <ctvnews.ca/canada/pm-trudeau-feds-will-soon-strongly-recommend-contact-tracing-app-1.4949895>.

7. Statistics Canada. 2020. "Statistics Canada and contact tracing." December 30. <statcan.gc.ca/eng/transparency-accountability/contact-tracing>.

8. Dangerfield, Katie. 2020. "Why contact tracing becomes 'impossible' as coronavirus cases surge." *Global News,* October 9. <globalnews.ca/news/7388215/contact-tracing-becomes-impossible-coronavirus-surge/>.

9. Ruths, Derek. 2020. "Canada's proposed contact-tracing app takes the right approach on privacy." *Globe and Mail,* June 18. <theglobeandmail.com/opinion/article-canadas-proposed-contact-tracing-app-takes-the-right-approach-on/>.

10. Ibid.

11. *CBC News North.* 2020. "Federal COVID-19 contact tracing app now being rolled out in N.W.T." November 26. <cbc.ca/news/canada/north/federal-covid-19-contact-tracing-app-now-being-rolled-out-in-n-w-t-1.5817300>.

12. Tomesco, Frédéric. 2020. "A COVID-19 exposure notification app won't work if people aren't motivated to use it: AI expert." *Montreal Gazette,* September 25. <montrealgazette.com/health/a-contact-tracing-app-wont-work-if-people-arent-motivated-to-use-it-ai-expert>.

13. Turnbull, Sarah. 2020. "COVID Alert app nears 3 million users, but only 514 positive

test reports." *CTV News,* September 29. <ctvnews.ca/health/coronavirus/covid-alert-app-nears-3-million-users-but-only-514-positive-test-reports-1.5125256>.

14. Canadian Digital Service (@CDS_GC). 2020. "How it started. How it's going." Twitter, December 18. <twitter.com/CDS_GC/status/1339979660143243264>.

15. Daigle, Thomas. 2021. "Federal COVID Alert app to collect more data to gauge effectiveness." *CBC News,* February 9. <cbc.ca/news/technology/covid-alert-app-data-collection-1.5907307>.

16. Lévesque, Catherine. 2021. "Seulement 20 000 personnes ont signalé leur infection." *La Presse,* March 17. <lapresse.ca/covid-19/2021-03-17/application-alerte-covid/seulement-20-000-personnes-ont-signale-leur-infection.php>.

17. D'Amore, Rachael. 2020. "As coronavirus resurges, 'now is the time' to push COVID Alert app: experts." *Global News,* September 24. <globalnews.ca/news/7352806/coronavirus-covid-19-second-wave-covid-alert-app/>.

18. Ibid.

19. *City News.* 2020. "Health Canada's COVID-19 contact tracing app a help even if it works only on newer phones: Tam." August 4. <toronto.citynews.ca/2020/08/04/covid-alert-app-tam/>.

20. Frketich, Joanna. 2020. "COVID-19 spiking among young adults disregarding physical distancing, says Hamilton's top doctor." *Hamilton Spectator,* June 5. <thespec.com/news/hamilton-region/2020/06/05/covid-19-spreading-in-hamilton-among-young-adults-disregarding-distancing.html>.

21. Ibid.

22. Ibid.

23. Ho, Solarina. 2020. "'Be a lifesaver': Tam tells young adults to stop spreading COVID-19." *CTV News,* July 24. <ctvnews.ca/health/coronavirus/be-a-lifesaver-tam-tells-young-adults-to-stop-spreading-covid-19-1.5038531>.

24. Wan, William, and Moriah Balingit. 2020. "WHO warns young people are emerging as main spreaders of the coronavirus." *Washington Post,* August 18. <washingtonpost.com/health/who-warns-young-people-are-emerging-as-main-spreaders-of-the-coronavirus/2020/08/18/1822ee92-e18f-11ea-b69b-64f7b0477ed4_story.html>.

25. Pelley, Lauren. 2020. "It's easy to point the finger at parties — but younger Canadians spread COVID-19 in all kinds of settings." *CBC News Toronto,* September 16. <cbc.ca/news/canada/toronto/young-canadians-covid-parties-1.5724789>.

26. Campbell, Taylor. "Family parties, card games, sleepover linked to 31 COVID-19 cases." *Windsor Star,* September 2. <windsorstar.com/news/local-news/family-parties-card-games-sleepover-linked-to-31-covid-19-cases>.

27. Pelley, Lauren. 2020. "It's easy to point the finger at parties — but younger Canadians spread COVID-19 in all kinds of settings." *CBC News Toronto,* September 16. <cbc.ca/news/canada/toronto/young-canadians-covid-parties-1.5724789>.

28. Ibid.

29. *CBC Radio.* 2020. "Sept. 15, 2020 episode transcript." *The Current.* <cbc.ca/radio/thecurrent/the-current-for-sept-15-2020-1.5724417/sept-15-2020-episode-transcript-1.5725150>.

30. Ibid.

31. Paikin, Steve (@spaikin). 2021. "Can I gently push back by saying I know plenty of 9-13 year olds who are certainly NOT at the mercy of their parents' decisions." Twitter, January 12. <twitter.com/spaikin/status/1349044855096401920>.

32. Bench, Allison. 2020. "1,270 new cases of COVID-19 confirmed Wednesday as Hinshaw pushes for Albertans to accept vaccine." *Global News,* December 16. <globalnews.ca/news/7526008/covid-19-update-alberta-dec-16/>.

33. Macdonell, Beth. 2021. "Ontario college student who died of COVID-19 had concerns

over parties at residence." *CTV News Toronto,* March 17. <toronto.ctvnews.ca/
ontario-college-student-who-died-of-covid-19-had-concerns-over-parties-at-
residence-1.5351829>.

34. Bergen, Rachel. 2020. "'Easy to feel paranoid' living in an apartment building with
    positive coronavirus case." *CBC Manitoba,* April 4. <cbc.ca/news/canada/manitoba/
    apartments-pandemic-covid-19-1.5518061>.

35. Bascaramurty, Dakshana. 2020. "High anxiety: In Toronto's immigrant-
    rich apartment towers, elevators and density keep many students
    at home." *Globe and Mail,* October 15. <theglobeandmail.com/canada/
    article-high-anxiety-in-torontos-immigrant-rich-apartment-towers-elevators/>.

36. Franklin, Michael. 2020. "More than 50 cases of COVID-19 connected to
    Calgary condo building." *CTV News Calgary.* July 2. <calgary.ctvnews.ca/
    more-than-50-cases-of-covid-19-connected-to-calgary-condo-building-1.5008655>.

37. Leal, Jenine, and Heather Gagnon. 2020. "COVID-19 Scientific Advisory Group Rapid
    Evidence Brief." *Alberta Health Services,* July 16. <albertahealthservices.ca/assets/
    info/ppih/if-ppih-covid-19-sag-transmission-in-condo-or-apartment-buildings-
    rapid-review.pdf>.

38. CBC News. 2020. "Alberta to send COVID-19 teams to hard-hit areas in Edmonton,
    Calgary." *CBC News Edmonton,* December 15. <cbc.ca/news/canada/edmonton/
    jason-kenney-deena-hinshaw-alberta-covid-19-coronavirus-1.5842142>.

39. Statistics Canada. 2017. "Dwellings in Canada." May 3. <www12.statcan.gc.ca/census-
    recensement/2016/as-sa/98-200-x/2016005/98-200-x2016005-eng.cfm>.

40. Emmanuel, Rachel. 2020. "COVID response must adjust to social inequalities,
    say health experts." *iPolitics,* October 15. <ipolitics.ca/2020/10/15/
    covid-response-must-adjust-to-social-inequalities-say-health-experts/>.

41. Rocha, Roberto, Benjamin Shingler, and Jonathan Montpetit. 2020. "Montreal's
    poorest and most racially diverse neighbourhoods hit hardest by COVID-19, data
    analysis shows." *CBC News Montreal,* June 11. <cbc.ca/news/canada/montreal/
    race-covid-19-montreal-data-census-1.5607123>.

42. Bieman, Jennifer. 2020. "Health unit caught off-guard by cluster of COVID-19 cases at
    apartment: deputy." *London Free Press,* December 30. <lfpress.com/news/local-news/
    health-unit-caught-off-guard-by-cluster-of-covid-19-cases-at-london-apartment-
    deputy>.

43. White, Erik. 2021. "'You feel like you're one swab away from a disaster'— battling
    COVID variants in North Bay." *CBC News Sudbury,* February 24. <cbc.ca/news/canada/
    sudbury/north-bay-parry-sound-lockdown-covid-variants-1.5924106>.

44. Taekema, Dan, and Justin Mowat. 2021. "Rebecca Towers outbreak declared over as
    Hamilton reports 77 new COVID-19 cases, 2 deaths." *CBC News Hamilton,* May 28.
    <cbc.ca/news/canada/hamilton/rebecca-towers-outbreak-over-covid-1.6044168>.

45. Dingman, Shane. 2020. "Housing advocates push for eviction ban in response to
    coronavirus pandemic." *Globe and Mail,* March 16. <theglobeandmail.com/canada/
    article-housing-advocates-push-for-eviction-ban-in-response-to-coronavirus/>.

46. CMHC. 2020. "COVID-19: eviction bans and suspensions to support
    renters." March 25. <cmhc-schl.gc.ca/en/consumers/renting-a-home/
    covid-19-eviction-bans-and-suspensions-to-support-renters>.

47. CBC News Sudbury. 2021. "Tenants in 'nerve-wracking' game with landlords despite
    Ontario's moratorium on evictions." April 9. <cbc.ca/news/canada/sudbury/
    provincial-eviction-notice-moratorium-1.5979705>.

48. Gawley, Kelvin. 2020. "Housing activists call for rent strike in B.C. during
    COVID-19 pandemic." *News 1130,* March 31. <citynews1130.com/2020/03/31/
    housing-activists-call-for-rent-strike-in-b-c-during-covid-19-pandemic/>.

49. Ibid.
50. BC Housing. 2020. "COVID-19." <bchousing.org/COVID-19>.
51. Ministry of Municipal Affairs and Housing. 2020. "Framework gives renters until July 2021 to repay arrears." August 14. <news.gov.bc.ca/releases/2020MAH0094-001527>.
52. 2021. "Programme d'aide financière aux locataires pour le paiement de leur loyer dans le cadre de la pandémie de COVID-19." *Société d'habitation*, June 23. <shq.gouv. qc.ca/programme/programme/programme_daide_financiere_aux_locataires_pour_ le_paiement_de_leur_loyer_dans_le_cadre_de_la_pandem.html>.
53. Chang, Arturo. 2021. "Impossible to tell why applicants for COVID support programs were rejected, AG says." *CBC News PEI*, August 10. <cbc.ca/news/canada/ prince-edward-island/pei-auditor-general-covid-report-hearing-1.6136705>.
54. Gawley, Kelvin. 2020. "Housing activists call for rent strike in B.C. during COVID-19 pandemic." *News 1130*, March 31. <citynews1130.com/2020/03/31/ housing-activists-call-for-rent-strike-in-b-c-during-covid-19-pandemic/>.
55. McCarthy Tetrault. 2020. "COVID-19: Economic relief measures announced to date." August 28. <mccarthy.ca/en/insights/articles/covid-19-economic-relief- measures-announced-date>.
56. Hersh, Sam. 2021. "Ottawa needs to put an end to cruel winter evictions." *Ottawa Citizen*, January 6. <ottawacitizen.com/opinion/hersh-ottawa-needs-to-put-an- end-to-cruel-winter-evictions>.
57. Cook, Dustin. 2020. "Capacity slashed at Edmonton Convention Centre shelter after COVID-19 cases double in a day." *Edmonton Journal*, November 28. <edmontonjournal.com/news/local-news/covid-19-outbreak-declared- at-edmonton-convention-centre-24-7-shelter>.
58. Ross, Selena. 2020. "First major outbreaks among homeless Montrealers lead to expanded red zone, new hotel-shelter." *CTV News Montreal*, December 29. <montreal. ctvnews.ca/first-major-outbreaks-among-homeless-montrealers-lead-to-expanded- red-zone-new-hotel-shelter-1.5247962>.
59. Ibid.
60. Loreto, Nora. 2021. "Deaths: workplace outbreaks." Google Spreadsheets. <https://docs.google.com/spreadsheets/d/1M_RzojK0vwF9nAozI7aoyLp PU8EA1JEqO6rq0g1iebU/edit#gid=404463485>.
61. Loreto, Nora. 2021. "The COVID outbreaks that Ontario wasn't counting." *Maclean's*, July 1. <macleans.ca/news/canada/the-covid-outbreaks-that-ontario-wasnt-counting/>.
62. MacCharles, Tonda. 2020. "How many COVID-19 deaths has Ottawa counted among homeless people? Would you believe four?" *Toronto Star*, November 27. <thestar. com/politics/federal/2020/11/26/how-many-covid-19-deaths-has-ottawa-counted- among-homeless-people-would-you-believe-four.html>.
63. Ibid.
64. Draaisma, Muriel. 2021. "Security fence in Trinity Bellwoods to stay for weeks so grass can grow back, city says." *CBC News Toronto*, July 5. <cbc.ca/news/canada/toronto/ blue-security-fence-trinity-bellwoods-park-encampment-clearing-1.6091144>.
65. Press, Jordan. 2020. "Delay in pandemic-related rise in homelessness gives feds time to prevent it: report." *CP24*, December 10. <cp24.com/news/delay-in-pandemic- related-rise-in-homelessness-gives-feds-time-to-prevent-it-report-1.5225281>.

August 2020

1. Breen, Kerri. 2020. "Canada adds 285 new coronavirus cases on Saturday, most in Ontario and Québec." *Global News*, August 1. <globalnews.ca/news/7244534/ coronavirus-canada-new-cases-aug-1/>.

2. Department of Finance Canada. 2020. "Government introduces Canada Emergency Response Benefit to help workers and businesses." March 25. <canada.ca/en/department-finance/news/2020/03/introduces-canada-emergency-response-benefit-to-help-workers-and-businesses.html>.

3. Pazzano, Sam. 2020. "Gangsters using CERB to buy guns, protect turf: Sources." *Toronto Sun,* October 19. <torontosun.com/news/local-news/gangsters-using-cerb-to-buy-guns-protect-turf-sources>.

4. Ibid.

5. Ibid.

6. *RD News Now.* 2020. "UCP MLA suggests CERB funds used for Cheezies, cartoons and illegal drugs." September 30. <rdnewsnow.com/2020/09/30/ucp-mla-suggests-cerb-funds-used-for-cheezies-cartoons-and-illegal-drugs/>.

7. Ibid.

8. Botner, Cory. 2020. "LETTER: Glad to say goodbye to CERB for local drug users." *BC Local News,* September 28. <bclocalnews.com/opinion/letter-glad-to-say-goodbye-to-cerb-for-local-drug-users/>.

9. Morgan, Geoffrey. 2020. "Nearly half of Canadians say they can't afford to miss work as coronavirus cases escalate." *Financial Post,* March 22. <financialpost.com/news/nearly-half-of-canadians-say-they-cant-afford-to-miss-work-as-coronavirus-cases-escalate>.

10. CBC *News.* 2020. "Canada lost nearly 2 million jobs in April amid COVID-19 crisis: Statistics Canada." May 8. <cbc.ca/news/business/canada-jobs-april-1.5561001>.

11. Government of Canada. n.d. "Questions and Answers on the Canada Emergency Response Benefit." <canada.ca/en/services/benefits/ei/cerb-application/questions.html>.

12. Lewis, Michael. 2020. "One third of Canadian workers won't be able to access government aid, economist says." *Toronto Star,* April 2. <thestar.com/business/2020/04/02/covid-19-job-loss-fund-will-let-many-down-analysis-finds.html>.

13. Morgan, Geoffrey. 2020. "Nearly half of Canadians say they can't afford to miss work as coronavirus cases escalate." *Financial Post,* March 22. <financialpost.com/news/nearly-half-of-canadians-say-they-cant-afford-to-miss-work-as-coronavirus-cases-escalate>.

14. CBC *News.* 2020. "Household debt ratio rises to 176.9%, Statistics Canada says." June 12. <cbc.ca/news/business/statistics-canada-debt-1.5609510>.

15. Harris, Kathleen. 2020. "CERB payments to be extended for 2 more months." CBC *News,* June 16. <cbc.ca/news/politics/cerb-extended-trudeau-1.5613782>.

16. Ibid.

17. Ibid.

18. Wilson, Jim. "Is the CERB making people lazy?" *Canadian HR Reporter,* April 17. <hrreporter.com/focus-areas/payroll/is-the-cerb-making-people-lazy/332400>.

19. Employment and Social Development Canada. 2020. "Government of Canada announces plan to help support Canadians through the next phase of the recovery." Government of Canada, August 20. <canada.ca/en/employment-social-development/news/2020/08/government-of-canada-announces-plan-to-help-support-canadians-through-the-next-phase-of-the-recovery.html>.

20. Tumilty, Ryan. 2020. "Liberals boost proposed pandemic benefits to $500 per week, a move that should gain them NDP support." *National Post,* September 25. <nationalpost.com/news/politics/liberals-propose-to-boost-pandemic-benefits-to-500-per-week-up-from-400>.

21. Government of Canada. 2021. "Canada Recovery Benefit (CRB)." January 11. <canada.

ca/en/revenue-agency/services/benefits/recovery-benefit/crb-who-apply.html>.

22. Saba, Rosa. 2020. "Confusion is spreading across Canada as the emergency benefit payments begin." *Toronto.com*, April 9. <toronto.com/news-story/9938299-confusion-is-spreading-across-canada-as-the-emergency-benefit-payments-begin/>.

23. Gallant, Collin. 2020. "CERB repayment leaves Hatters broke." *Medicine Hat News*, June 23. <medicinehatnews.com/news/local-news/2020/06/23/cerb-repayment-leaves-hatters-broke/>.

24. *Campbell River Mirror*. 2020. "CERB payments docked to account for April advance." June 19. <campbellrivermirror.com/news/cerb-payments-docked-to-account-for-april-advance/>.

25. Almazora, Leo. 2020. "Documents reveal CERB double payments of nearly $443 million." *Wealth Professional*, July 28. <wealthprofessional.ca/news/industry-news/documents-reveal-cerb-double-payments-of-nearly-443-million/331882>.

26. Cullen, Catherine. 2020. "Canadians applying for new pandemic benefit report confusion, frustration." *CBC News*, October 16. <cbc.ca/news/politics/canada-recovery-benefit-crb-cerb-pandemic-covid-1.5764377>.

27. Bensadoun, Emerald. 2020. "Did you receive double CERB payments? The CRA wants its money back." *Global News*, October 27. <globalnews.ca/news/7424806/cra-double-payments-cerb/>.

28. Racine, Francis. 2020. "Disability recipients get less than CERB; inequality persists." *Cornwall Standard-Freeholder*, August 27. <standard-freeholder.com/news/local-news/disability-recipients-get-less-than-cerb-inequality-persists>.

29. Nunavut Tunngavik Incorporated. 2020. "Impacts of COVID-19, resolution RSA-20-10-13." October 20–22. <tunngavik.com/files/2020/10/RSA-20-10-13-COVID-19-Impacts-eng.pdf>.

30. Ibid.

31. George, Jane. 2020. "Inuit who collected CERB despite being ineligible shouldn't have to repay, says NTI." *Nunatsiaq News*, October 23. <nunatsiaq.com/stories/article/inuit-who-collected-cerb-despite-being-ineligible-shouldnt-have-to-repay-says-nti/>.

32. Golombek, Jamie. 2021."Ottawa changed the rules on CERB repayments — here's what it means for taxpayers." *Financial Post*, February 12. <financialpost.com/personal-finance/taxes/ottawa-changed-the-rules-on-cerb-repayments-and-heres-what-it-means-for-taxpayers>.

33. Gagnon, Raina. 2020. "Gagnon: Drug use in Ottawa, aided by the CERB subsidy, has skyrocketed." *Ottawa Citizen*, May 29. <ottawacitizen.com/opinion/gagnon-drug-use-in-ottawa-aided-by-the-cerb-subsidy-has-skyrocketed>.

34. Overdose Prevention Ottawa. 2020. "Listen to Drug Users and Advocates, the CERB is Harm Reduction." June 7. <overdosepreventionottawa.wordpress.com/2020/06/07/listen-to-drug-users-and-advocates-the-cerb-is-harm-reduction/>.

35. Steeves, Shelley. 2020. "Harvest House says CERB payments fueling illicit drug market in Moncton." *Global News*, September 1. <globalnews.ca/news/7309965/cerb-drugs-moncton/>.

36. Peterson, Julia. 2020. "For Canadian sex workers, CERB was a lifeline — if they could get it." *CBC News Saskatchewan*, October 25. <cbc.ca/news/canada/saskatchewan/cerb-sex-worker-access-1.5769650>.

37. Curtis, Christopher. 2021. "Pandemic creating 'endless crisis' for sex workers." *Ricochet*, January 14. <ricochet.media/en/3437/pandemic-creating-endless-crisis-for-sex-workers>.

38. Press, Jordan. 2021. "Where did CERB go? Data shows disparities between Canada's urban and rural areas." *Global News*, February 15. <globalnews.ca/news/7641184/covid-cerb-money-federal-data/>.

39. Tasker, John Paul. 2020. "What you need to know about the new COVID-19 emergency wage subsidy." CBC News, April 1. <cbc.ca/news/politics/canadian-emergency-wage-subsidy-explainer-1.5518180/>.

40. Ibid.

41. Forani, Jonathan. 2020. "CRA snitch line now open to report fraudulent CERB claims." CTV News, June 2. <ctvnews.ca/health/coronavirus/cra-snitch-line-now-open-to-report-fraudulent-cerb-claims-1.4965033>.

42. Reynolds, Christopher. 2020. "Air Canada to rehire workers laid off due to COVID-19." CTV News, April 8. <ctvnews.ca/business/air-canada-to-rehire-workers-laid-off-due-to-covid-19-1.4887925>.

43. Kelly, Dan. 2020. "CEBA, CEWS and rent assistance changes — everything you need to know." CFIB, October 30. YouTube Video. <youtu.be/YgmfxxWzZdY>.

44. Antunes, Pedro. 2020. "Extend wage subsidy program, not individual response benefits." *Globe and Mail,* July 9. <theglobeandmail.com/business/commentary/article-extend-wage-subsidy-program-not-individual-response-benefits/>.

45. Retail Council of Canada. 2020. "Minimum hourly wage rates as of October 1 2020." October 1. <web.archive.org/web/20200717010042/https://www.retailcouncil.org/resources/quick-facts/minimum-wage-by-province/>.

46. Antunes, Pedro. 2020. "Extend wage subsidy program, not individual response benefits." *Globe and Mail,* July 9. <theglobeandmail.com/business/commentary/article-extend-wage-subsidy-program-not-individual-response-benefits/>.

47. CBC News Hamilton. 2020. "'White nationalist' Paul Fromm received federal COVID-19 relief money to fund his groups." December 23. <cbc.ca/news/canada/hamilton/paul-fromm-white-nationalist-covid-19-relief-funds-1.5852700>.

48. Air Canada. 2020. "Air Canada Announces Intention to Adopt the Canada Emergency Wage Subsidy for the Benefit of its 36,000 Canadian-based Employee Workforce." April 8. <aircanada.mediaroom.com/2020-04-08-Air-Canada-Announces-Intention-to-Adopt-the-Canada-Emergency-Wage-Subsidy-for-the-Benefit-of-its-36-000-Canadian-based-Employee-Workforce>.

49. Jones, Ryan Patrick. 2021. "Federal government, Air Canada reach deal on relief package that includes customer refunds." CBC News, April 12. <cbc.ca/news/politics/air-canada-financial-relief-1.5984543>.

50. Rubin, Josh, and Robert Williams. 2020. "Air Canada to immediately rehire more than 16,000 workers." *Toronto Star,* April 8. <thestar.com/business/2020/04/07/air-canada-to-immediately-rehire-more-than-16000-workers.html>.

51. Ibid.

52. Government of Canada. 2021. "Claims to date — Canada emergency wage subsidy (CEWS)." June 27. <canada.ca/en/revenue-agency/services/subsidy/emergency-wage-subsidy/cews-statistics.html>.

53. Lanthier, Allan. 2020. "The wage subsidy: A windfall for Canadian corporation." *Globe and Mail,* August 9. <theglobeandmail.com/business/commentary/article-the-wage-subsidy-a-windfall-for-canadian-corporations/>.

54. Rogers Communications Inc. 2021. "Rogers Communications reports fourth quarter and full-year 2020 results." <1vjoxz2ghhkclty8c1wjich1-wpengine.netdna-ssl.com/wp-content/uploads/2020/01/Rogers-Q4-2020-Press-Release-1.pdf>.

55. Nowak, Peter. 2021. "Bell blasted for taking $122M labour subsidy while boosting dividends." *TekSavvy,* January 29. <blogs.teksavvy.com/bell-blasted-for-cews-subsidy-dividends>.

56. *Financial Post.* 2020. "Canadian companies that received CEWS and kept paying a dividend." December 7. <financialpost.com/investing/canadian-companies-that-received-cews-and-kept-paying-a-dividend>.

57. Ibid.
58. Welsh, Moira, and Jesse McLean. 2020. "Extendicare subsidiary gets taxpayer-funded wage subsidy while dividends paid to shareholders." *Toronto Star,* August 15. <thestar.com/news/canada/2020/08/15/extendicare-subsidiary-gets-taxpayer-funded-wage-subsidy-while-dividends-paid-to-shareholders.html>.
59. Department of Finance Canada. 2020. "Extending the Canada Emergency Wage Subsidy." October 14. <canada.ca/en/department-finance/news/2020/10/extending-the-canada-emergency-wage-subsidy.html>.
60. CBC News Calgary. 2020. "WestJet workers demand clarity from Ottawa on wage subsidy changes amid pay cut." September 25. <cbc.ca/news/canada/calgary/westjet-wage-subsidy-confusion-1.5739561>.
61. Thurton, David. 2020. "Government's effort to publicize Big 3 cell service prices isn't driving them down, advocates say." CBC News, July 29. <cbc.ca/news/politics/rogers-telus-bell-cellphone-wireless-bain-1.5667824>.
62. Currie, Brooklyn. 2020. "No more free transit in Halifax starting Aug. 1." CBC News Nova Scotia, July 21. <cbc.ca/news/canada/nova-scotia/no-more-free-transit-halifax-covid-19-masks-1.5657987>.
63. Turner, Logan. 2020. "Could free public transit be in Thunder Bay's future? That's what a local anti-poverty group is calling for." CBC News Thunder Bay, October 20. <cbc.ca/news/canada/thunder-bay/free-transit-tbay-survey-1.5768474>.
64. Newport, Ashley. "Mississauga considering raising transit fares and other fees to cope with COVID-19 downturn." *InSauga,* October 9. <insauga.com/mississauga-considering-raising-transit-fares-and-other-fees-to-cope-with-covid-19-downturn>.
65. D'Sa, Premila. 2020. "As CERB winds down, calls for universal basic income intensify." *National Observer,* September 15. <nationalobserver.com/2020/09/15/news/cerb-winds-down-calls-universal-basic-income-intensify>.
66. Romaniuk, Colleen. 2020. "Sudbury health board backs guaranteed basic income." *Sudbury Star,* September 19. <thesudburystar.com/news/local-news/sudbury-health-board-backs-guaranteed-basic-income>.
67. Coteau, Michael. "The post-pandemic future: A basic income will bring millions of people out of poverty." *Toronto Life,* August 19. <torontolife.com/city/the-post-pandemic-future-a-basic-income-will-bring-millions-of-people-out-of-poverty/>.
68. Baldwin, Derek. 2020. "MP Ellis pushing Bay of Quinte as pilot riding for guaranteed basic income." *Belleville Intelligencer,* September 18. <intelligencer.ca/news/local-news/mp-ellis-pushing-bay-of-quinte-as-pilot-riding-for-guaranteed-basic-income>.
69. Bush, David. "Basic Income and the Left: The Political and Economic Problems." *The Bullet,* April 26. <socialistproject.ca/2017/04/b1402/>.

September 2020

1. *City News Toronto.* 2020. "The latest numbers on COVID-19 in Canada for Sept. 1." September 1. <toronto.citynews.ca/2020/09/01/the-latest-numbers-on-covid-19-in-canada-for-sept-1/>.
2. Néron, Jean-François. 2020. "Confiner ou déconfiner, là est la question." *Le Soleil,* May 1. <lesoleil.com/actualite/covid-19/confiner-ou-deconfiner-la-est-la-question-6eab83636933be52b6865ccd4fbfbecc>.
3. Ibid.
4. Campbell, Susan. 2020. "Québec's partial reopening of schools this spring gets passing grade." CBC News Québec, June 27. <cbc.ca/news/canada/montreal/schools-reopen-Québec-lessons-fall-1.5628936>.
5. Ibid.

6. Hutchins, Aaron, and Marie-Danielle Smith. 2020. "The coronavirus can't be contained. Are you ready?" *Maclean's*, February 28. <macleans.ca/society/health/the-coronavirus-cant-be-contained-are-you-ready/>.

7. Lemay, Éric Yvan, and Andrea Valeria. 2020 "COVID-19: 2 semaines qui ont marqué le Québec." *Journal de Montréal*, March 21. <https://www.journaldemontreal.com/2020/03/21/2-semaines-qui-ont-marque-le-quebec>.

8. Lecavalier, Charles. 2020. "Le Québec, la province la plus touchée avec 628 personnes infectées." *Journal de Québec*, March 23. <journaldeQuébec.com/2020/03/23/le-Québec-la-province-la-plus-touchee-avec-628-personnes-infectees>.

9. Tumilty, Ryan. 2020. "Canada's early COVID-19 cases came from the U.S. not China, provincial data shows." *National Post*, April 30. <nationalpost.com/news/politics/canadas-early-covid-19-cases-came-from-the-u-s-not-china-provincial-data-shows>.

10. Goldenberg, Susan. 2018. "Killer Flu." *Canada's History*, September 11. <canadashistory.ca/explore/arts-culture-society/killer-flu>.

11. Public Health Agency of Canada. 2021. "Coronavirus disease 2019 (COVID-19): Epidemiology update." February 3. <health-infobase.canada.ca/covid-19/epidemiological-summary-covid-19-cases.html>.

12. Statistics Canada. 2021. "Population estimates on July 1st, by age and sex." February 4. <www150.statcan.gc.ca/t1/tbl1/en/cv.action?pid=1710000501>.

13. Loreto, Nora. 2021. "Deaths: healthcare worker outbreaks." Google Spreadsheets. <https://docs.google.com/spreadsheets/d/1M_RzojK0vwF9nAozI7aoyLpPU8EA1JEqO6rq0g1iebU/edit#gid=404463485>.

14. Public Health Agency of Canada. 2021. "Coronavirus disease 2019 (COVID-19): Epidemiology update." June 29. <health-infobase.canada.ca/covid-19/epidemiological-summary-covid-19-cases.html>.

15. Banerjee, Sidhartha. 2020. "La réouverture des écoles s'est plutôt bien déroulée." *Le Soleil*, June 21. <lesoleil.com/actualite/covid-19/la-reouverture-des-ecoles-sest-plutot-bien-deroulee-c7f813970dc2d8866a26ecade54f39a1>.

16. *La Presse*. 2020. "Les garderies s'approchent d'un retour à la normale." June 28. <lapresse.ca/covid-19/2020-06-28/les-garderies-s-approchent-d-un-retour-a-la-normale.php>.

17. *La Presse*. 2020. "La CNESST dévoile un guide pour les écoles et les garderies." May 4. <lapresse.ca/covid-19/2020-05-04/la-cnesst-devoile-un-guide-pour-les-ecoles-et-les-garderies>.

18. Gibson, Shane. 2020. "No new COVID-19 cases reported Monday as Manitoba starts Phase 2 reopening." *Global News*, June 1. <globalnews.ca/news/7011282/manitoba-health-officials-to-give-coronavirus-update-monday/>.

19. CBC News British Columbia. 2020. "What you need to know about COVID-19 in B.C. for June 1, 2020." June 1. <cbc.ca/news/canada/british-columbia/coronavirus-update-bc-what-you-need-to-know-june-1-1.5592775>.

20. Zeidler, Maryse. "B.C. announces part-time, voluntary return to school June 1." *CBC News British Columbia*, May 15. <cbc.ca/news/canada/british-columbia/bc-education-update-1.5571175>.

21. *Global News*. 2020. "Here's how each province is preparing for back-to-school amid coronavirus." September 8. <globalnews.ca/news/7321061/coronavirus-back-to-school-canada/>.

22. Draaisma, Muriel, and Ali Chiasson. 2019. "Some classes at a Toronto high school have as many as 40 students each, principal says." *CBC News Toronto*, September 10. <cbc.ca/news/canada/toronto/

class-sizes-40-students-high-schools-ontario-toronto-principal-1.5278538>.

23. Jeffords, Shawn. 2020. "NDP calls for Ontario ombudsman to review province's back-to-school plan." *CP24*, September 2. <cp24.com/news/ndp-calls-for-ontario-ombudsman-to-review-province-s-back-to-school-plan-1.5089362>.

24. *Durham Radio News*. 2020. "Ontario's major teachers unions to file complaints with labour board over back to school plan." August 31. <durhamradionews.com/archives/128893>.

25. *CTV News*. 2020. "Thousands of students return to schools as new COVID-19 cases emerge." September 8. <ctvnews.ca/health/coronavirus/thousands-of-students-return-to-schools-as-new-covid-19-cases-emerge-1.5096374>.

26. Grant, Kelly. 2020. "These two northwest Toronto neighbourhoods have COVID-19 positivity rates above 10 per cent, newly released data show." *Globe and Mail*, October 19. <theglobeandmail.com/canada/article-toronto-reveals-rates-of-positive-covid-19-tests-by-neighbourhood/>.

27. Grant, Kelly, and Chen Wang. 2020. "How safe is school? It depends on your neighbourhood." *Globe and Mail*, August 28. <theglobeandmail.com/canada/article-how-safe-is-school-it-depends-on-your-neighbourhood/>.

28. Pringle, Josh. 2020. "Long lines for COVID-19 testing in Ottawa on Friday, with west-end care clinic at capacity by 9 a.m." *CTV News Ottawa*, September 18. <ottawa.ctvnews.ca/long-lines-for-covid-19-testing-in-ottawa-on-friday-with-west-end-care-clinic-at-capacity-by-9-a-m-1.5110456>.

29. Pringle, Josh. 2020. "COVID-19 in Ottawa: Fast facts for Sept. 18, 2020." *CTV News Ottawa*, September 18. <ottawa.ctvnews.ca/covid-19-in-ottawa-fast-facts-for-sept-18-2020-1.5109620>.

30. *CBC News*. 2020. "Ontario sees 409 new COVID-19 cases, rolls out $1B updated testing and contact-tracing plan." September 24. <https://www.cbc.ca/news/canada/toronto/covid-19-coronavirus-ontario-september-24-update-1.5736841>.

31. Ibid.

32. Wilson, Kerrisa. 2020. "COVID-19 testing could soon be done a Shoppers Drug Mart." *CTV News Toronto*, August 24. <toronto.ctvnews.ca/covid-19-testing-could-soon-be-done-at-shoppers-drug-mart-1.5077198>.

33. *CBC News Toronto*. 2020. "Ontario sees 409 new COVID-19 cases, rolls out $1B updated testing and contact-tracing plan." September 24. <cbc.ca/news/canada/toronto/covid-19-coronavirus-ontario-september-24-update-1.5736841>.

34. Ho, Solarina, and Sahima Singh. 2020. "These are the COVID-19 protocols in public schools across Canada." *CTV News*, September 25. <ctvnews.ca/health/coronavirus/these-are-the-covid-19-protocols-in-public-schools-across-canada-1.5121345>.

35. Ibid.

36. Perreaux, Les. 2020. "School COVID-19 cases consistent with community transmission, but Québec could be in trouble, data show." *Globe and Mail*, November 4. <theglobeandmail.com/canada/article-school-covid-19-cases-consistent-with-community-transmission-but/>.

37. Hristova, Bobby. 2020. "'High priority' schools in low-income neighbourhoods get extra help during COVID-19." *CBC News Hamilton*, September 18. <cbc.ca/news/canada/hamilton/high-priority-covid19-schools-1.5725039>.

38. *Collingwood Today*. 2020. "COVID-19: Nearly half of Canadians visited friends, family over holidays, new poll suggests." January 6. <collingwoodtoday.ca/local-news/covid-19-nearly-half-of-canadians-visited-friends-family-over-holidays-new-poll-suggests-3233854>.

39. Alam, Hina. 2020. "Shutting down schools early in pandemic 'probably a mistake,' B.C.'s education minister says." *CTV News Vancouver*, November 18. <bc.ctvnews.ca/

shutting-down-schools-early-in-pandemic-probably-a-mistake-b-c-s-education-minister-says-1.5193831>.

40. Mangione, Kendra. 2021. "Here's what Vancouver Coastal Health says about COVID-19 transmission at school." *CTV News Vancouver,* January 14. <bc.ctvnews.ca/here-s-what-vancouver-coastal-health-says-about-covid-19-transmission-at-school-1.5266955>.

41. Jones, Ryan Patrick. 2021. "Limited COVID-19 transmission in Ottawa schools: OPH report." *CBC News Ottawa,* February 2. <cbc.ca/news/canada/ottawa/oph-covid-19-transmission-schools-ottawa-1.5898221>.

42. Perreaux, Les. 2021. "All eyes on Québec and Alberta schools as Southern Ontario weighs return to in-person learning." *Globe and Mail,* January 31. <theglobeandmail.com/canada/article-all-eyes-on-Québec-and-alberta-schools-as-other-provinces-weigh-return/>.

43. Tait, Carrie. 2021. "Alberta completes COVID-19 vaccination of all long-term care residents, staff." *Globe and Mail,* January 18. <theglobeandmail.com/canada/alberta/article-alberta-completes-covid-19-vaccination-of-all-long-term-care-residents/>.

44. Bachand, Olivier. 2021. "95 % des résidents en CHSLD ont été vaccines." *Radio-Canada,* February 11. <ici.radio-canada.ca/nouvelle/1769283/covid-19-vaccinations-personnes-agees-deuxieme-dose>.

45. Perreaux, Les. 2021. "All eyes on Québec and Alberta schools as Southern Ontario weighs return to in-person learning." *Globe and Mail,* January 31. <theglobeandmail.com/canada/article-all-eyes-on-Québec-and-alberta-schools-as-other-provinces-weigh-return/>.

46. Mitchell, Don. 2021. "Asymptomatic testing, closing of learning gap key issues in students' return to Hamilton schools." *Global News,* February 7. <globalnews.ca/news/7622082/hamilton-return-to-school-monday-feb-08-2021/>.

47. Herhalt, Chris. 2021. "Ontario giving essential industries six times as many COVID-19 rapid tests than school system." *CTV News Toronto,* February 12. <toronto.ctvnews.ca/ontario-giving-essential-industries-six-times-as-many-covid-19-rapid-tests-than-school-system-1.5306778>.

48. Parrillo, Felicia. 2021. "In effort to curb spread of COVID-19, rapid tests coming to 2 Montreal high schools." *Global News,* January 19. <globalnews.ca/news/7586335/coronavirus-covid-19-rapid-tests-montreal-high-schools/>.

49. McDermott, Vince, and Ashley Joannou. 2021. "Suncor base plant included in rapid COVID-19 screening; one new case and recovery in Fort McMurray." *Fort McMurray Today,* February 10. <fortmcmurraytoday.com/news/suncor-site-included-in-rapid-covid-19-screening-one-new-case-and-recovery-in-fort-mcmurray>.

50. Al-Hakim, Aya. 2021. "COVID-19: N.S. education minister calls it a 'successful school year' despite pandemic." *Global News,* July 2. <globalnews.ca/news/7997675/covid-19-n-s-education-minister-calls-it-a-successful-school-year-despite-pandemic/>.

51. Bundale, Brett. 2021. "'Like a pregnancy test:' Rapid COVID-19 tests key tool to keep virus out of offices." *CTV News Atlantic,* June 23. <atlantic.ctvnews.ca/like-a-pregnancy-test-rapid-covid-19-tests-key-tool-to-keep-virus-out-of-offices-1.5482321>.

52. Favaro, Avis, St. Philip, Elizabeth, and Alexandra Mae Jones. 2021. "Schools don't pose higher COVID-19 risk than outside community: Canadian study." *CTV News,* June 22. <ctvnews.ca/health/coronavirus/schools-don-t-pose-higher-covid-19-risk-than-outside-community-canadian-study-1.5481731>.

53. Gallagher-Mackay, Kelly, Prachi Srivastava, Kathryn Underwood, Elizabeth Dhuey, et al. 2021. "COVID-19 and Education Disruption in Ontario: Emerging Evidence on Impacts." *Science Table*

– *COVID-19 Advisory for Ontario,* June 16. <covid19-sciencetable.ca/sciencebrief/covid-19-and-education-disruption-in-ontario-emerging-evidence-on-impacts/>.

54. *Vernon Morning Star.* 2021. "Canada's women, youth bear the brunt of January job losses as unemployment rate hits 9.4%." February 5. <vernonmorningstar.com/news/canadian-women-youth-bear-the-brunt-of-january-job-losses-as-unemployment-rate-hits-9-4/>.

October 2020

1. *City News Toronto.* 2020. "The latest numbers on COVID-19 in Canada for Oct. 1." October 1. <toronto.citynews.ca/2020/10/01/the-latest-numbers-on-covid-19-in-canada-for-oct-1/>.

2. Baxter, Mary. 2020. "'They all were labour abused': Demanding action on the exploitation of migrant workers." *TVO,* June 26. <tvo.org/article/they-all-were-labour-abused-demanding-action-on-the-exploitation-of-migrant-workers>.

3. Gatehouse, Jonathon. 2020. "How undocumented migrant workers are slipping through Ontario's COVID-19 net." *CBC News,* July 2. <cbc.ca/news/canada/leamington-migrant-workers-1.5633032>.

4. Baxter, Mary. 2020. "'They all were labour abused': Demanding action on the exploitation of migrant workers." *TVO,* June 26. <tvo.org/article/they-all-were-labour-abused-demanding-action-on-the-exploitation-of-migrant-workers>.

5. Gatehouse, Jonathon. 2020. "How undocumented migrant workers are slipping through Ontario's COVID-19 net." *CBC News,* July 2. <cbc.ca/news/canada/leamington-migrant-workers-1.5633032>.

6. Cocullo, Jenna. 2020. "Local likely caused Greenhill Produce outbreak." *Chatham Voice,* April 29. <chathamvoice.com/2020/04/29/local-likely-caused-greenhill-produce-outbreak/>.

7. Gatehouse, Jonathon. 2020. "How undocumented migrant workers are slipping through Ontario's COVID-19 net." *CBC News,* July 2. <cbc.ca/news/canada/leamington-migrant-workers-1.5633032>.

8. Cocullo, Jenna. 2020. "Another Greenhill employee sends letter raising COVID concerns." *Chatham Voice,* May 4. <chathamvoice.com/2020/05/04/another-greenhill-employee-sends-letter-raising-covid-concerns/>.

9. Ayres, Shelley. 2020. "Pandemic in the fields: The harsh realities temporary foreign workers face in Canada." *CTV W5,* September 26. <ctvnews.ca/w5/pandemic-in-the-fields-the-harsh-realities-temporary-foreign-workers-face-in-canada-1.5120806>.

10. Harris, Kathleen. 2020. "Canada to bar entry to travellers who are not citizens, permanent residents or Americans." *CBC News,* March 16. <cbc.ca/news/politics/cbsa-border-airports-screening-trudeau-covid19-coronavirus-1.5498866>.

11. Lupton, Andrew. 2020. "COVID-19 restrictions on migrant workers will be devastating, Ontario farmers warn." *CBC News London,* March 17. <cbc.ca/news/canada/london/covid-19-restrictions-on-migrant-workers-will-be-devastating-ontario-farmers-warn-1.5500269>.

12. Ibid.

13. Immigration, Refugees and Citizenship Canada. 2020. "Canada provides update on exemptions to travel restrictions to protect Canadians and support the economy." March 20. <canada.ca/en/immigration-refugees-citizenship/news/2020/03/canada-provides-update-on-exemptions-to-travel-restrictions-to-protect-canadians-and-support-the-economy.html>.

14. Migrant Rights Network. 2020. "63 migrant workers affected by COVID-19 due to government and employer negligence!" April 1. <migrantrights.

ca/63-migrant-workers-infected-by-covid-19-due-to-government-inaction/>.

15. Lale, Brent. 2020. "Balancing workers' safety and crop production amid COVID-19 crisis." *CTV News London,* March 29. <london.ctvnews.ca/balancing-workers-safety-and-crop-production-amid-covid-19-crisis-1.4873364>.

16. LaFleche, Grant. 2020. "EXCLUSIVE: Ottawa to ease COVID-19 travel restrictions on migrant farm workers." *St. Catharines Standard,* March 19. <stcatharinesstandard.ca//news/niagara-region/2020/03/19/exclusive-ottawa-to-ease-covid-19-travel-restrictions-on-migrant-farm-workers.html>.

17. Hristova, Bobby. 2020. "Hotline became lifeline for migrant workers secretly reporting poor conditions on Canadian farms." *CBC News Hamilton,* July 16. <cbc.ca/news/canada/hamilton/migrant-farm-workers-covid-19-1.5650437>.

18. Grant, Tavia, and Kathryn Blaze Baum. 2020. "Migrant workers on farms across Canada are being told they can't leave, raising rights concerns." *Globe and Mail,* August 3. <theglobeandmail.com/business/article-migrant-workers-on-farms-across-canada-are-being-told-they-cant-leave/>.

19. Employment and Social Development Canada. 2020. "Guidance for Employers of Temporary Foreign Workers Regarding COVID-19." March 27. <mcusercontent.com/f79d2a33b823f8c549069c39b/files/a7039f88-7b4b-4198-b433-3afc22121aa9/Guidance_for_Employers_of_TFWs_on_COVID_19_March_27_2020_FINAL_EN.pdf>.

20. Emmanuel, Rachel. 2020. "Federal guidelines for temporary foreign workers aren't enforceable, says advocate." *iPolitics,* April 9. <ipolitics.ca/2020/04/09/federal-guidelines-for-temporary-foreign-workers-arent-enforceable-says-advocate/>.

21. Migrant Rights Network. 2020. "63 Migrant Workers Affected by COVID-19 Due to Government & Employer Negligence!" April 1. <migrantrights.ca/63-migrant-workers-infected-by-covid-19-due-to-government-inaction>.

22. Wells, Nick. 2020. "Lack of protections for migrant workers could be a 'disaster' in the making: advocates." *CTV News,* April 5. <ctvnews.ca/health/coronavirus/lack-of-protections-for-migrant-workers-could-be-a-disaster-in-the-making-advocates-1.4883180>.

23. Grant, Tavia, and Kathryn Blaze Baum. 2020. "Ottawa didn't enforce rules for employers of migrant farm workers during pandemic." *Globe and Mail,* July 13. <theglobeandmail.com/canada/article-how-ottawas-enforcement-regime-failed-migrant-workers-during-the/>.

24. Ibid.

25. Employment and Social Development Canada. 2020. "Government of Canada invests in measures to boost protections for Temporary Foreign Workers and Address COVID-19 outbreaks on farms." July 31. <canada.ca/en/employment-social-development/news/2020/07/government-of-canada-invests-in-measures-to-boost-protections-for-temporary-foreign-workers-and-address-covid-19-outbreaks-on-farms.html>.

26. Wright Allen, Samantha. 2020. "Pace of virtual inspections on migrant worker conditions a concern, say critics, with half completed this summer." *The Hill Times,* October 28. <hilltimes.com/2020/10/28/pace-of-virtual-inspections-on-migrant-worker-conditions-a-concern-say-critics-with-half-completed-this-summer/269312>.

27. Hernandez, Maribel, and Reyna Alvarez. 2021. "Migrant workers: When we caught COVID on the job, we went from essential to expendable." *USA Today,* February 12. <usatoday.com/story/opinion/voices/2021/02/12/migrant-workers-covid-19-coronavirus-safety-osha-column/6719210002/>.

28. Dubinski, Kate. 2020. "40 workers at Elgin County orchard test positive for COVID-19." *CBC News London,* November 2. <cbc.ca/news/canada/london/elgin-farm-covid-1.5788053>.

29. Colgan, Greg. 2020. "Bayham farm now has 40 workers test positive for COVID-19." *Sudbury Star,* November 3. <thesudburystar.com/news/local-news/bayham-farm-has-31-workers-test-positive-for-covid-19/wcm/1d996f84-e55f-4e5c-acef-196263da3c82>.

30. Martin, Max. 2021. "Some COVID-stranded migrant workers finally flying home to Trinidad." *London Free Press,* January 19. <lfpress.com/news/local-news/some-covid-stranded-migrant-workers-finally-flying-home-to-trinidad>.

31. Health and Social Services, Haldimand and Norfolk. n.d. "Trends." <hnhu.org/additional-daily-statistics/>.

32. Martin, Max. 2021. "Some COVID-stranded migrant workers finally flying home to Trinidad." *London Free Press,* January 19. <lfpress.com/news/local-news/some-covid-stranded-migrant-workers-finally-flying-home-to-trinidad>.

33. Veneza, Ricardo. 2020. "Migrant advocacy group pushes for immigrant status following tribunal victory, rising COVID-19 cases." November 12. <windsor.ctvnews.ca/migrant-advocacy-group-pushes-for-immigrant-status-following-tribunal-victory-rising-covid-19-cases-1.5186830>.

34. Martin, Max. 2021. "Some COVID-stranded migrant workers finally flying home to Trinidad." *London Free Press,* January 19. <lfpress.com/news/local-news/some-covid-stranded-migrant-workers-finally-flying-home-to-trinidad>.

35. Faraday, Fay. 2021. "COVID-19's impact on migrant workers adds urgency to calls for permanent status." *The Conversation,* February 24. <theconversation.com/covid-19s-impact-on-migrant-workers-adds-urgency-to-calls-for-permanent-status-148237>.

36. Ibid.

37. McGregor, Janyce. 2020. "Not so ready-to-pick: Canadian growers left hanging by COVID-19." *CBC News,* May 17. <cbc.ca/news/politics/sunday-tfw-fruit-veg-1.5571508>.

38. Lupton, Andrew. 2020. "COVID-19 restrictions on migrant workers will be devastating, Ontario farmers warn." *CBC News London,* March 17. <cbc.ca/news/canada/london/covid-19-restrictions-on-migrant-workers-will-be-devastating-ontario-farmers-warn-1.5500269>.

39. Ibid.

40. Doyle, Sabrina. 2020. "Migrant workers falling through cracks in healthcare coverage." *Canadian Medical Association Journal,* July 13. <cmaj.ca/content/192/28/E819>.

41. Martin, Max. 2020. "I'm a local farmer who brought in migrant workers. Here's how the season went." *London Free Press,* November 1. <lfpress.com/news/local-news/i-am-a-local-farmer-who-brought-in-migrant-workers-this-is-how-the-season-went>.

42. Ibid.

43. Ibid.

44. Pazzano, Jasmine. 2020. "Coronavirus: Canada's migrant farm workers face fatal COVID-19 outbreaks, alleged mistreatment." *Global News,* August 28. <globalnews.ca/news/7301324/coronavirus-canadas-migrant-farm-workers-alleged-mistreatment/>.

45. Ibid.

46. Antonacci, J.P. 2020. "Dispute between Norfolk farmers and public health unit threatens food security." *Hamilton Spectator,* May 15. <thespec.com/news/hamilton-region/2020/05/11/dispute-between-norfolk-farmers-and-public-health-unit-threatens-food-security.html>.

47. Antonacci, J.P. 2020. "'Every day here is a little better than a good day home': Migrant farm workers lobby to work in Canada during COVID-19." *Hamilton Spectator,* July 31. <thespec.com/news/hamilton-region/2020/07/31/every-day-here-is-a-little-better-than-a-good-day-home-migrant-farm-workers-lobby-to-work-in-canada-during-covid-19.html>.

48. Ibid.

49. McGregor, Janyce. 2020. "Not so ready-to-pick: Canadian growers left hanging by COVID-19." *CBC News*, May 17. <cbc.ca/news/politics/sunday-tfw-fruit-veg-1.5571508>.

50. Ibid.

51. Grant, Tavia, and Kathryn Blaze Baum. 2020. "Migrant workers on farms across Canada are being told they can't leave, raising rights concerns." *Globe and Mail*, August 3. <theglobeandmail.com/business/article-migrant-workers-on-farms-across-canada-are-being-told-they-cant-leave/>.

52. Nash, Chelsea. 2020. "Migrant agricultural workers experiencing a food crisis." *rabble.ca*, July 23. <rabble.ca/news/2020/07/migrant-agricultural-workers-experiencing-food-crisis>.

53. Grant, Tavia, and Kathryn Blaze Baum. 2020. "Migrant workers on farms across Canada are being told they can't leave, raising rights concerns." *Globe and Mail*, August 3. <theglobeandmail.com/business/article-migrant-workers-on-farms-across-canada-are-being-told-they-cant-leave/>.

54. *CBC News Windsor*. 2020. "Migrant advocacy group demands Ontario shut down agricultural sector amid COVID-19 spike." June 29. <cbc.ca/news/canada/windsor/migrant-farm-workers-demand-sector-shut-down-1.5631324>.

55. Ayres, Shelley. 2020. "Pandemic in the fields: The harsh realities temporary foreign workers face in Canada." *CTV W5*, September 26. <ctvnews.ca/w5/pandemic-in-the-fields-the-harsh-realities-temporary-foreign-workers-face-in-canada-1.5120806>.

56. Dubinski, Kate. 2020. "Migrant worker wins labour board case after being fired for speaking out about unsafe conditions amid COVID-19." *CBC News London*, November 12. <cbc.ca/news/canada/london/migrant-worker-wins-labour-board-ruling-1.5799587>.

57. Flores, Luis Gabriel Flores. 2020. "Letter from Luis Gabriel Flores Flores." *Migrant Workers Alliance for Change*, July 30. <migrantworkersalliance.org/wp-content/uploads/2020/07/Letter-to-Immigration-Minister-English.pdf>.

58. Inclan, Isabel. 2020. "Farm Worker Sues Scotlynn Farms for Unlawful Reprisals." *New Canadian Media*, August 1. <newcanadianmedia.ca/farm-worker-sues-scotlynn-farms-for-unlawful-reprisals/>.

59. Dubinski, Kate. 2020. "Migrant worker wins labour board case after being fired for speaking out about unsafe conditions amid COVID-19." *CBC News London*, November 12. <cbc.ca/news/canada/london/migrant-worker-wins-labour-board-ruling-1.5799587>.

60. Ayres, Shelley. 2020. "Pandemic in the fields: The harsh realities temporary foreign workers face in Canada." *CTV W5*, September 26. <ctvnews.ca/w5/pandemic-in-the-fields-the-harsh-realities-temporary-foreign-workers-face-in-canada-1.5120806>.

61. Grant, Tavia, and Kathryn Blaze Baum. 2020. "Migrant workers on farms across Canada are being told they can't leave, raising rights concerns." *Globe and Mail*, August 3. <theglobeandmail.com/business/article-migrant-workers-on-farms-across-canada-are-being-told-they-cant-leave/>.

62. Cheung, Christopher. 2020. "For Overseas Filipinos Like Loida Ubay, Essential Work Feels Increasingly Sacrificial." *The Tyee*, June 8. <thetyee.ca/News/2020/06/08/Overseas-Filipinos-Essential-Work/>.

63. Szeto, Winston. 2020. "Over 40% of Filipino Canadians responding to StatsCan survey report job losses amid COVID-19." *CBC News British Columbia*, July 22. <cbc.ca/news/canada/british-columbia/filipino-canadian-job-losses-1.5658723>.

64. Donato, Al. "Filipino Front-Line Workers Risk Their Lives To Keep Canada Running." *Huffington Post*, May 21. <huffingtonpost.ca/entry/filipino-workers-canada-frontlines_ca_5ec3eb66c5b63e39157bef51>.

65. Curtis, Christopher. 2020. "Migrant workers detail COVID-19 outbreaks at warehouses, factories." *Montreal Gazette*, June 29. <healthing.ca/news/migrant-workers-detail-covid-19-outbreaks-at-warehouses-factories>.

66. Ibid.
67. Mojtehedzadeh, Sara. 2021. "'In almost all outbreaks we encounter agency staff.' How Peel – and the province – grappled with a quiet crisis: temp work." *Toronto Star,* July 20. <thestar.com/news/gta/2021/07/20/in-almost-all-outbreaks-we-encounter-agency-staff-how-peel-and-the-province-grappled-with-a-quiet-crisis-temp-work.html>.
68. Migrant Workers Alliance for Change. 2020. "Behind Closed Doors." October. <migrantrights.ca/wp-content/uploads/2020/10/Behind-Closed-Doors_Exposing-Migrant-Care-Worker-Exploitation-During-COVID19.pdf>.
69. Gatehouse, Jonathon. 2020. "How undocumented migrant workers are slipping through Ontario's COVID-19 net." *CBC News,* July 2. <cbc.ca/news/canada/leamington-migrant-workers-1.5633032>.
70. Ibid.

November 2020

1. *City News Toronto.* 2020. "The latest numbers on COVID-19 in Canada for Sunday Nov. 1, 2020." November 1. <toronto.citynews.ca/2020/11/01/the-latest-numbers-on-covid-19-in-canada-for-sunday-nov-1-2020/>.
2. Nadeau, Jean-François, and Audrey Paris. 2021. "Le préposé mort de la COVID au CHSLD Saint-Antoine "mérite qu'on ne l'oublie pas." *Radio-Canada Québec,* January 6. <ici.radio-canada.ca/nouvelle/1760920/chsld-saint-antoine-covid-mort-prepose-Québec>.
3. Desmeules, Judith. 2020. "Éclosion au CHSLD Saint-Antoine: pas de souci pour la vaccination." *Le Soleil,* December 11. <lesoleil.com/actualite/covid-19/eclosion-au-chsld-saint-antoine-pas-de-souci-pour-la-vaccination-69b540771c1ff3f2ec87340 70e469601>.
4. Nadeau, Jean-François. 2021. "La première vaccine du Canada a contracté la COVID-19." *Radio-Canada Québec,* January 14. <ici.radio-canada.ca/nouvelle/1763100/covid-gisele-levesque-chsld-st-antoine-Québec-ciusss-vaccination>.
5. Pelletier, Émilie. 2021. "Après 49 décès et 263 infectés, plus aucun cas de COVID-19 au CHSLD Saint-Antoine." *Le Soleil,* February 9. <lesoleil.com/actualite/covid-19/apres-49-deces-et-263-infectes-plus-aucun-cas-de-covid-19-au-chsld-saint-antoine-ae5f8c42580e9dbea9c6c78f8e5c675d>.
6. Samson, Fanny. 2020. "Vaccins dans un CHSLD en éclosion : « la réponse immunitaire n'est pas instantanée »." *Radio-Canada Québec,* December 30. <ici.radio-canada.ca/nouvelle/1760058/eclosion-covid-chsld-saint-antoine-Québec-vaccin>.
7. Russell, Andrew. 2020. "How long will coronavirus measures last in Canada? Experts say June or July." *Global News,* April 1. <globalnews.ca/news/6762854/coronavirus-how-long-will-social-distancing-last-in-canada/>.
8. Wherry, Aaron. 2020. "Canadians want to know how bad this could get. Is anyone ready to tell us?" *CBC News,* April 2. <cbc.ca/news/politics/trudeau-coronavirus-pandemic-covid-1.5518249>.
9. Bronskill, Jim. 2020. "Trudeau announces $1.1B to fund COVID-19 vaccine development, tracking of cases." *Global News,* April 23. <globalnews.ca/news/6857058/coronavirus-canada-science-vaccine-funding/>.
10. Aiello, Rachel. 2020. "PM Trudeau returns to the Hill, says 'normal' life still a ways off." *CTV News,* April 8. <ctvnews.ca/health/coronavirus/pm-trudeau-returns-to-the-hill-says-normal-life-still-a-ways-off-1.4888301>.
11. Government of Canada. 2020. "Authorization of Pfizer-BioNTech COVID-19 Vaccine with English-only Carton and Vial Labels." *Recalls and Safety Alerts,* December 12. <healthycanadians.gc.ca/recall-alert-rappel-avis/hc-sc/2020/74541a-eng.php>.
12. *CBC News.* 2020. "The latest on the coronavirus outbreak for Dec. 9." December 10.

<cbc.ca/news/canada/coronavirus-newsletter-dec-9-1.5834004>.

13. *City News Toronto.* 2020. "The latest numbers on COVID-19 in Canada for Wednesday, Dec. 9." December 9. <toronto.citynews.ca/2020/12/09/the-latest-numbers-on-covid-19-in-canada-for-wednesday-dec-9/>.

14. Thomson, Graham. 2020. "Kenney's optimistic vaccine announcement designed to placate disgruntled Albertans." *iPolitics,* December 13. <ipolitics.ca/2020/12/03/kenneys-optimistic-vaccine-announcement-designed-to-placate-disgruntled-albertans/>.

15. Rodrigues, Gabby. 2020. "Premier Doug Ford on hand for 1st shipment of COVID-19 vaccine in Ontario." *Global News,* December 14. <globalnews.ca/news/7520257/doug-ford-first-shipment-covid19-pfizer-vaccine-ontario/>.

16. CBC *News Toronto.* 2021. "Hospital figures reach pandemic highs as Ontario reveals more details about vaccine rollout." January 5. <cbc.ca/news/canada/toronto/covid-19-ontario-january-5-2021-vaccine-update-1.5861626>.

17. Thompson, Nicole. 2021. "Ontario could have moved faster on COVID-19 vaccine booking site, experts say." CTV *News Toronto,* February 25. <toronto.ctvnews.ca/ontario-could-have-moved-faster-on-covid-19-vaccine-booking-site-experts-say-1.5324783>.

18. Aiello, Rachel. 2020. "Feds outline plan to administer first COVID-19 vaccines, launching 'dry run' next week." CTV *News,* December 3. <ctvnews.ca/politics/feds-outline-plan-to-administer-first-covid-19-vaccines-launching-dry-run-next-week-1.5215641>.

19. Mathieu, E., H. Ritchie Ortiz-Ospina, E. et al. 2021. "Coronavirus (COVID-19) Vaccinations." *Our World in Data,* July 5. <ourworldindata.org/covid-vaccinations>.

20. Walters, Joanna. 2021. "US in 'another pivotal moment' as Delta variant drives surve in Covid cases." *The Guardian,* July 23. <theguardian.com/us-news/2021/jul/22/us-covid-cases-rise-delta-variant>.

21. Cortez, Michelle Fay, Soraya Permatasari, and Jinshan Hong. 2021. "With 50,000 cases a day, one country opens up as another suffers." *Bloomberg News,* July 22. <bnnbloomberg.ca/with-50-000-cases-a-day-one-country-opens-up-as-another-suffers-1.1632014>.

22. Galloway, Matt. 2020. "Feb. 3, 2020 episode transcript." *The Current.* <cbc.ca/radio/thecurrent/the-current-for-feb-3-2020-1.5449813/feb-3-2020-episode-transcript-1.5450516>.

23. Abedi, Maham. 2020. "Canada to spend $192M on developing COVID-19 vaccine." *Global News,* March 23. <globalnews.ca/news/6717883/coronavirus-canada-vaccine-spending/>.

24. Rody, Bree. 2020. "Lifestyle and entertainment affected by Global News layoffs." *Media in Canada,* June 24. <mediaincanada.com/2020/07/24/lifestyle-and-entertainment-journalists-affected-by-global-news-layoffs/>.

25. CTV *News Sports.* 2020. "Djokovic says he wouldn't take anti-coronavirus vaccination." April 20. <ctvnews.ca/sports/djokovic-says-he-wouldn-t-take-anti-coronavirus-vaccination-1.4903923>.

26. Gerster, Jane. 2020. "Vaccine hesitancy is a global threat. Experts say watch out for coronavirus misinformation." *Global News,* April 18. <globalnews.ca/news/6828787/coronavirus-anti-vaxxers/>.

27. Yoshida-Butryn, Carly. 2020. "Majority of Canadians would take a COVID-19 vaccine, survey suggests." CTV *News Vancouver,* April 21. <bc.ctvnews.ca/majority-of-canadians-would-take-a-covid-19-vaccine-survey-suggests-1.4905668>.

28. Berthiaume, Lee. 2020. "Canadians divided over making COVID-19 vaccine mandatory: poll." CTV *News,* April 28. <ctvnews.ca/health/coronavirus/canadians-divided-over-making-covid-19-vaccine-mandatory-poll-1.4914824>.

29. Ibid.
30. Veneza, Ricardo. 2021. "Three in four Canadians would take COVID-19 vaccine: survey." *CTV News Windsor,* September 2. <windsor.ctvnews.ca/three-in-four-canadians-would-take-covid-19-vaccine-survey-1.5090090>.
31. *CTV News.* 2020. "Safety won't be compromised for vaccine, Canada's top doctors say." August 11. <ctvnews.ca/health/coronavirus/safety-won-t-be-compromised-for-vaccine-canada-s-top-doctors-say-1.5060045>.
32. Ibid.
33. Veneza, Ricardo. 2021. "Three in four Canadians would take COVID-19 vaccine: survey." *CTV News Windsor,* September 2. <windsor.ctvnews.ca/three-in-four-canadians-would-take-covid-19-vaccine-survey-1.5090090>.
34. Ibid.
35. Christensen, Jen. 2020. "Past vaccine disasters show why rushing a coronavirus vaccine would be 'a prescription for disaster.'" *CTV News,* September 1. <ctvnews.ca/health/coronavirus/past-vaccine-disasters-show-why-rushing-a-coronavirus-vaccine-would-be-a-prescription-for-disaster-1.5087737>.
36. Bogart, Nicole. 2020. "Anti-mask rallies held across Canada despite increased support for mandatory masks." *CTV News,* July 20. <ctvnews.ca/health/coronavirus/anti-mask-rallies-held-across-canada-despite-increased-support-for-mandatory-masks-1.5031078>.
37. Gillis, Len. 2020. "Anti-mask 'freedom fighters' in Sudbury sharing tips in private Facebook group." *Sudbury.com,* July 28. <sudbury.com/local-news/anti-mask-freedom-fighters-in-sudbury-sharing-tips-in-private-facebook-group-2597880>.
38. *Ottawa Citizen.* 2020. "Parliament Hill protestors denounce 'tyranny,' demand end to COVID-19 restrictions." August 29. <ottawacitizen.com/news/local-news/parliament-hill-protestors-denounce-tyranny-demand-end-to-covid-19-restrictions>.
39. Shepert, Elana. 2020. "Video: Co-founder of 'anti-mask' movement speaks out after public backlash." *Richmond News,* August 31. <richmond-news.com/local-news/video-co-founder-of-anti-mask-movement-speaks-out-after-public-backlash-3126980>.
40. Lamoureux, Mack. 2021. "Canadian Anti-Mask Protesters Marched With Tiki Torches This Weekend." *Vice,* February 22. <vice.com/en/article/akd9yg/canadian-anti-mask-protestors-marched-with-tiki-torches-this-weekend>.
41. Potenteau, Doyle, and Darrian Matassa-Fung. 2021. "Massive crowd gathers in downtown Kelowna for 'freedom' protest rally." *Global News,* March 20. <globalnews.ca/news/7709485/massive-crowd-kelowna-protest-rally/>.
42. Champagne, Éric-Pierre. 2021. "Dépistage obligatoire pour les employés?" *La Presse,* March 19. <lapresse.ca/covid-19/2021-03-19/eclosion-au-chsld-lionel-emond/depistage-obligatoire-pour-les-employes.php>.
43. Ontario Ministry of Health. 2021. "COVID-19: Guidance for Prioritizing Health Care Workers for COVID-19 Vaccination." March 17. <health.gov.on.ca/en/pro/programs/publichealth/coronavirus/docs/Guidance_for_Prioritizing_HCW_covid19_vaccination_2020-01-08.pdf>.
44. Harris, Kathleen. 2021. "Conservatives slam vaccine rollout plan that prioritizes some federal prisoners." *CBC News,* January 6. <cbc.ca/news/politics/covid19-vaccine-rollout-csc-prisoners-1.5863435>.
45. Malakieh, Jamil. 2020. "Adult and youth correctional statistics in Canada, 2018/2019." Statistics Canada, December 21. <www150.statcan.gc.ca/n1/pub/85-002-x/2020001/article/00016-eng.htm>.
46. Harris, Kathleen. 2021. "Conservatives slam vaccine rollout plan that prioritizes some federal prisoners." *CBC News,* January 6. <cbc.ca/news/politics/

covid19-vaccine-rollout-csc-prisoners-1.5863435>.

47. Willcocks, Paul. 2021. "Opposing Prisoner Vaccination, Erin O'Toole Is Unmasked." *The Tyee,* January 6. <thetyee.ca/Analysis/2021/01/06/ Opposing-Prisoner-Vaccination-Erin-O-Toole-Unmasked/>.

48. Reynolds, Christopher. 2021. "COVID-19 cases more than double in federal prisons during second wave of pandemic." *CTV News,* February 23. <ctvnews.ca/health/ coronavirus/covid-19-cases-more-than-double-in-federal-prisons-during-second-wave-of-pandemic-1.5320846>.

49. Ontario Government. 2021. "Ontario's COVID-19 vaccination plan, Phase 1." <covid-19.ontario.ca/ontarios-covid-19-vaccination-plan#phase-1>.

50. Short, Dylan. 2021. "Older inmates at Alberta jails will be part of Phase 1B of vaccine rollout." *Edmonton Journal,* January 24. <edmontonjournal.com/news/local-news/ older-inmates-at-alberta-jails-will-be-part-of-phase-1b-of-vaccine-roll-out>.

51. Ouellet, Valérie, and Sylvène Gilchrist. 2021. "Some prisoners not offered COVID-19 shots until months after general public, CBC analysis finds." *CBC Investigates,* June 16. <cbc.ca/news/canada/covid-vaccinations-in-jails-1.6066293>.

52. Ibid.

53. NDP. 2021. "Jagmeet Singh introduces mass vaccination plan to get Canadians vaccinated." February 16. <ndp.ca/news/jagmeet-singh-introduces-mass-vaccination-plan-get-canadians-vaccinated>.

54. *National Post.* 2021. "A look at COVID-19 vaccinations in Canada on Wednesday, Feb. 10, 2021." February 10. <nationalpost.com/pmn/news-pmn/canada-news-pmn/a-look-at-covid-19-vaccinations-in-canada-on-wednesday-feb-10-2021-2>.

55. Hune-Brown, Nicholas. 2021. "The Vaccine Rollout Is Leaving Toronto's Hardest-Hit Postal Codes Behind." *The Local,* April 6. <thelocal.to/ the-vaccine-rollout-is-leaving-torontos-hardest-hit-postal-codes-behind/>.

56. Loreto, Nora. 2020. "Canada Is Robbing The Global South Of A Pandemic Recovery." *Passage,* December 16. <readpassage.com/ canada-is-robbing-the-global-south-of-a-pandemic-recovery/>.

57. Jones, Ryan Patrick. 2020. "Canada 'not at the back of the line' for COVID-19 vaccine, Moderna chairman says." *CBC News,* November 29. <cbc.ca/news/politics/ canada-vaccine-moderna-covid-19-hadju-health-1.5821166>.

58. Blanchfield, Mike. 2021. "Canada heralds first COVAX vaccine in Africa; NDP criticizes Canada for using program." *CTV News,* February 24. <ctvnews.ca/politics/ canada-heralds-first-covax-vaccine-in-africa-ndp-criticizes-canada-for-using-program-1.5322813>.

59. Holder, Josh. 2021. "Tracking Coronavirus Vaccinations Around the World." *New York Times,* March 22. <nytimes.com/interactive/2021/world/covid-vaccinations-tracker.html>.

60. National Union of Public and General Employees. 2021. "Canada must support global access to COVID-19 vaccines at WTO." March 10. <nupge.ca/content/ canada-must-support-global-access-covid-19-vaccines-wto>.

61. Holder, Josh. 2021. "Tracking Coronavirus Vaccinations Around the World." *New York Times,* March 22. <nytimes.com/interactive/2021/world/covid-vaccinations-tracker.html>.

62. National Union of Public and General Employees. 2021. "Canada must support global access to COVID-19 vaccines at WTO." March 10. <nupge.ca/content/ canada-must-support-global-access-covid-19-vaccines-wto>.

63. Alhmidi, Maan. 2021. "Canada expects major surge in COVID-19 vaccine deliveries this week." *Global News,* March 22. <globalnews.ca/news/7710846/ covid-vaccine-effort-canada-pfizer/>.

December 2020

1. *City News Toronto.* 2020. "The latest numbers on COVID-19 in Canada for Dec. 1, 2020." December 1. <toronto.citynews.ca/2020/12/01/the-latest-numbers-on-covid-19-in-canada-for-dec-1-2020/>.

2. Landsberg, Michele. 2020. "For 50 Years, Canadian Women Have Needed Child Care. Then Came COVID." *Chatelaine,* November 10. <chatelaine.com/living/politics/50-years-childcare/>.

3. Goldberg, Jennifer, and Nora Loreto. 2020. "3 Mothers On How COVID-19 Is Hurting Their Careers." *Chatelaine,* November 12. <chatelaine.com/living/mothers-how-covid-19-careers/>.

4. Anjum, Sultana, and Carmina Ravanera. 2020. "A feminist economic recovery plan for Canada." YWCA Canada and Gender and the Economy, July 28. <feministrecovery.ca/>.

5. Mooney, Chris. 2020. "Coronavirus: More men dying than women as they account for 70% of virus fatalities in Italy." *Independent,* March 10. <independent.co.uk/news/world/americas/coronavirus-death-toll-italy-south-korea-sex-update-cases-map-men-women-a9413271.html>.

6. Mae James, Alexandra. 2020. "National survey indicates men less concerned about COVID-19 than women." *CTV News,* March 24. <ctvnews.ca/health/coronavirus/national-survey-indicates-men-less-concerned-about-covid-19-than-women-1.4867023>.

7. Kennedy, Brendan. 2020. "Two million Canadians could soon be out of work — and women and low-wage workers will be hit the hardest." *Toronto Star,* March 25. <thestar.com/business/2020/03/25/two-million-canadians-could-soon-be-out-of-work-and-women-and-low-wage-workers-will-be-hit-the-hardest.html>.

8. Edwardson, Lucie. 2020. "U of C study finds women suffered more during first months of COVID isolation with anxiety, depression." *CBC News Calgary,* November 2. <cbc.ca/news/canada/calgary/u-of-c-study-finds-women-suffered-more-during-first-months-of-covid-isolation-with-anxiety-depression-1.5787068>.

9. Thibault, Alissa. 2020. "Report finds B.C. women are more impacted by the COVID-19 pandemic than men." *CTV News British Columbia,* November 25. <bc.ctvnews.ca/report-finds-b-c-women-are-more-impacted-by-the-covid-19-pandemic-than-men-1.5203370>.

10. *Global News.* 2020. "Mothers of kids under age 6 make up majority of workforce exodus amid coronavirus: RBC." November 20. <globalnews.ca/news/7474451/coronavirus-childcare-women-leaving-workforce/>.

11. Harley-McKeown, Lucy. 2020. "COVID-19 could set 'a generation of women' back in business." *Yahoo Finance,* November 24. <ca.style.yahoo.com/covid-19-could-set-a-generation-of-women-back-in-business-104126860.html>.

12. Lama, Amandine, and Etienne Mercier. 2020. "The pandemic risks significantly worsening gender equality – it is time to act!" *Ipsos,* November 24. <ipsos.com/en/pandemic-risks-significantly-worsening-gender-equality-it-time-act>.

13. Payne, Elizabeth. 2020. "Racialized people in Ottawa — especially Black — at greater risk for COVID-19, new data finds." *Ottawa Citizen,* November 25. <ottawacitizen.com/news/local-news/racialized-people-in-ottawa-especially-black-at-greater-risk-for-covid-19-new-data-finds>.

14. Ibid.

15. Daily Bread Food Bank. 2020. "Hunger Lives Here." July 12. <dailybread.ca/wp-content/uploads/2020/07/DB-COVID-Impact-Report-2020-Final-Web.pdf>.

16. Francis, Angelyn. 2020. "COVID-19 has slowed surgeries across Ontario. For some trans people that is particularly painful." *Toronto Star,* December 13. <thestar.com/

news/gta/2020/12/13/covid-19-has-slowed-surgeries-across-ontario-for-some-trans-people-that-is-particularly-painful.html>.

17. Prokopenko, Elena, and Christina Kevins. 2020. "Vulnerabilities related to COVID-19 among LGBTQ2+ Canadians." Statistics Canada, December 15. <www150.statcan.gc.ca/n1/pub/45-28-0001/2020001/article/00075-eng.htm>.

18. Paradis, Danielle. 2021. "The UCP knew the inequitable impacts of COVID-19 all along." *The Sprawl*, July 27. <sprawlalberta.com/ucp-knew-the-inequitable-impacts-of-covid-19-all-along>.

19. Gibson, Victoria. 2020. "Domestic violence organizations laud new funding, but call for more supports as COVID-19 escalates risk." *iPolitics*, April 16. <ipolitics.ca/2020/04/16/domestic-violence-organizations-laud-new-funding-but-call-for-more-supports-as-covid-19-escalates-risk/>.

20. Bensadoun, Emerald. 2020. "'Pandemic of violence': Calls mount for recognition of misogyny in Nova Scotia shooting." *Global News*, April 26. <globalnews.ca/news/6868709/nova-scotia-mass-shooting-femicide/>.

21. @comrade_jo_may. 2020. "Nova Scotian feminists fighting femicide statement on the mass shooting." Twitter, April 24. <twitter.com/comrade_jo_may/status/1253735799247572997/photo/1>.

22. Emmanuel, Rachel. 2020. "Pandemic has sparked more violence against women in Canada's North." *iPolitics*, December 2. <ipolitics.ca/2020/12/02/pandemic-has-sparked-more-violence-against-women-in-canadas-north/>.

23. Anjum, Sultana, and Carmina Ravanera. 2020. "A feminist economic recovery plan for Canada." YWCA Canada and Gender and the Economy, July 28. <feministrecovery.ca/>.

24. Amin, Faiza. 2020. "The double pandemic: COVID-19 and gender-based violence." *CityNews*, November 30. <toronto.citynews.ca/2020/11/30/the-double-pandemic-covid-19-and-gender-based-violence/>.

25. Hétu, Marie-Hélène. 2020. "Québec women's shelters call for increased funding ahead of budget." CBC *News Montreal*, March 6. <cbc.ca/news/canada/montreal/Québec-women-shelters-funding-1.5487758>.

26. Carpentier, Camille. 2021. "Une marche pour denouncer les féminicides à Québec." *Radio-Canada Québec*, June 17. <ici.radio-canada.ca/nouvelle/1802528/marche-contre-feminicides-Québec-denoncer-violence-femmes-meurtre-nathalie-piche>.

27. Chih, Caiden, Jia Qing Wilson-Yang, Kimberly Dhaliwal, Moomtaz Khatoon, et al. 2020. "Health and well-being among racialized trans and non-binary people." *Trans PULSE*, November. <transpulsecanada.ca/wp-content/uploads/2020/11/Health-and-well-being-among-racialized-trans-and-non-binary-people-FINAL-ua-1.pdf>.

28. Emmanuel, Rachel. 2020. "Pandemic has sparked more violence against women in Canada's North."*iPolitics*, December 2. <ipolitics.ca/2020/12/02/pandemic-has-sparked-more-violence-against-women-in-canadas-north/>.

29. Women's Shelters Canada. 2020. "Shelter Voices: 2020." November 1. <endvaw.ca/wp-content/uploads/2020/11/Shelter-Voices-2020-2.pdf>.

30. McFadden, John. 2021. "COVID-19 has been devastating for Indigenous women in Parry Sound-Muskoka area: counselor." *Bay Today*, March 17. <baytoday.ca/coronavirus-covid-19-local-news/covid-19-has-been-devastating-for-indigenous-women-in-parry-sound-muskoka-area-counsellor-3550003>.

31. Alhmidi, Maan. 2020. "Feds double COVID-19 fund for abused women to $100 million." CTV *News*, October 8. <ctvnews.ca/politics/feds-double-covid-19-fund-for-abused-women-to-100-million-1.5138332>.

32. Ibid.

33. Women's Shelters Canada. 2019. "More than a bed." May 1. <endvaw.ca/wp-content/

uploads/2019/04/More-Than-a-Bed-Final-Report.pdf>.

34. Aziz, Saba. 2020. "'Perfect storm': Growing calls to address domestic violence during coronavirus." *Global News*, November 25. <globalnews.ca/news/7483974/coronavirus-domestic-violence-covid-19/>.

35. Hétu, Marie-Hélène. 2020. "Québec women's shelters call for increased funding ahead of budget." *CBC News Montreal*, March 6. <cbc.ca/news/canada/montreal/Québec-women-shelters-funding-1.5487758>.

36. Emmanuel, Rachel. 2020. "Pandemic has sparked more violence against women in Canada's North." *iPolitics*, December 2. <ipolitics.ca/2020/12/02/pandemic-has-sparked-more-violence-against-women-in-canadas-north/>.

37. Wright, Teresa. 2020. "Sex workers say they have been left out of Canada's COVID-19 response." *CTV News*, April 19. <ctvnews.ca/health/coronavirus/sex-workers-say-they-have-been-left-out-of-canada-s-covid-19-response-1.4902772>.

38. Curtis, Christopher. 2021. "Pandemic creating 'endless crisis' for sex workers." *Ricochet*, January 14. <ricochet.media/en/3437/pandemic-creating-endless-crisis-for-sex-workers>.

39. Statistics Canada. 2018. "The surge of women in the workforce." May 17. <www150.statcan.gc.ca/n1/pub/11-630-x/11-630-x2015009-eng.htm>.

40. Statistics Canada. 2015. "Assets, debts and net worth, by family type, 2009." *Statistics Canada, Survey of Financial Capability, 2009*, November 30. <www150.statcan.gc.ca/n1/pub/89-503-x/2010001/article/11388/tbl/tbl014-eng.htm>.

41. Press, Jordan. 2020. "Canadian mothers-to-be feel forgotten by COVID-19 benefits." *Global News*, April 17. <globalnews.ca/news/6833119/coronavirus-canada-cerb-maternity-leave/>.

42. Press, Jordan. 2020. "New moms told go work to get EI parental benefits after jobs lost to COVID-19." *CTV News*, June 8. <ctvnews.ca/health/coronavirus/new-moms-told-go-work-to-get-ei-parental-benefits-after-jobs-lost-to-covid-19-1.4974673>.

43. Gregory, Laurel. 2020. "Pregnant Canadians worry they won't get parental leave benefits because work hours affected by COVID-19." *Global News*, July 9. <globalnews.ca/news/7154595/pregnant-canadians-maternity-leave-benefits-coronavirus/>.

44. Government of Canada. 2020. "Changes to support you during COVID-19." September 28. <canada.ca/en/services/benefits/ei/ei-maternity-parental/apply.html>.

45. Bergen, Rachel. 2020. "New parents waiting months for financial benefits amid surge in CERB claims." *CBC News Manitoba*, September 30. <cbc.ca/news/canada/manitoba/parental-benefits-delayed-1.5734454>.

46. Mercer, Juanita. 2020. "Panel urges a feminist approach to COVID-19 recovery plan in Newfoundland and Labrador." *The Telegram*, May 5. <thetelegram.com/news/local/panel-urges-a-feminist-approach-to-covid-19-recovery-plan-in-newfoundland-and-labrador-446138/>.

47. Anjum, Sultana, and Carmina Ravanera. 2020. "A feminist economic recovery plan for Canada." *YWCA Canada and Gender and the Economy*, July 28. <feministrecovery.ca/>.

48. Connolly, Amanda. 2020. "Want a full economic recovery? Childcare is critical, report says." *Global News*, July 30. <globalnews.ca/news/7230073/child-care-coronavirus-recovery-canada/>.

49. Andrew, Jill. 2020. "Ontario needs a feminist recovery plan from COVID-19." *Now Magazine*, August 18. <nowtoronto.com/news/ontario-feminist-recovery-plan-coronavirus>.

50. Bougault-Côté, Guillaume. 2020. "Sondage Léger-Le Devoir: la CAQ écrase la concurrence." *Le Devoir*, October 21. <ledevoir.com/politique/Québec/588183/Québec-la-caq-ecrase-la-concurrence>.

51. Carabin, François. 2020. "Legault et le coronavirus: un bilan de la gestion de

crise." *Journal Métro,* June 22. <journalmetro.com/actualites/national/2476508/legault-coronavirus-bilan-gestion-crise/>.

52. Slaughter, Graham, and Nicole Bogart. 2020. "Sophie Gregoire Trudeau tests positive for COVID-19; PM begins 14-day isolation." *CTV News,* March 12. <ctvnews.ca/health/coronavirus/sophie-gregoire-trudeau-tests-positive-for-covid-19-pm-begins-14-day-isolation-1.4850159>.

53. Zussman, Richard. 2020. "Premier John Horgan has been described as the province's dad. (Not by me, by others). Is Dr. Bonnie Henry now the province's mom." Twitter, May 12. <twitter.com/richardzussman/status/1260341989532332033>.

54. Battis, Todd. 2020. "How N.S. Premier McNeil's 'stay the blazes home' caught on." [Video.] *CTV News,* April 7. <youtube.com/watch?v=nENyhvqwhqI>.

55. Patil, Anjuli. 2020. "'Stay the blazes home,' premier warns as COVID-19 cases rise in Nova Scotia." *CBC News Nova Scotia,* April 3. <cbc.ca/news/canada/nova-scotia/14-new-cases-of-covid-19-in-nova-scotia-total-now-207-1.5520605>.

56. Rankin, Andrew. 2020. "N.S. premier's 'get the blazes out there' slogan ill-advised in face of Northwood tragedy: professor." *Saltwire,* June 25. <saltwire.com/news/provincial/ns-premiers-get-the-blazes-out-there-slogan-ill-advised-in-face-of-northwood-tragedy-professor-466542/>.

57. McKendrick, Devon. 2020. "'This is disrespectful': Premier passionately calls on people to follow proper COVID-19 practices." *CTV News Winnipeg,* April 1. <winnipeg.ctvnews.ca/this-is-disrespectful-premier-passionately-calls-on-people-to-follow-proper-covid-19-practices-1.4877913>.

58. Paling, Emma. 2020. "Angry Doug Ford Demands More COVID-19 Testing." *Huffington Post,* April 4. <huffingtonpost.ca/entry/doug-ford-angry-coronavirus-testing_ca_5e8e1f0dc5b6d641a6b8e7c3>.

59. Herhalt, Chris. 2020. "'A bunch of yahoos,' Ont. premier says of people protesting COVID-19 emergency measures." *CTV News Toronto,* April 25. <toronto.ctvnews.ca/a-bunch-of-yahoos-ont-premier-says-of-people-protesting-covid-19-emergency-measures-1.4911861>.

60. O'Neil, Lauren. 2020. "Doug Ford just called COVID-19 crappy and then apologized for his language." *BlogTO,* October 14. <blogto.com/city/2020/10/doug-ford-covid-19-situation-crappy/>.

61. Stone, Laura. 2020. "Sign-language interpreter takes on Premier Ford's 'angry dad' approach as he pushes for accessibility." *Globe and Mail,* April 1. <theglobeandmail.com/canada/article-sign-language-interpreter-takes-on-premier-fords-angry-dad-approach/>.

62. *CBC News.* 2020. "Families, advocates slam Ontario's Bill-218, calling it a 'powerful weapon' for LTCs to fend off liability." November 11. <cbc.ca/news/canada/toronto/bill218-liability-ontario-long-term-care-1.5798256>.

63. *National Post.* 2020. "Manitoba moves into 'critical' COVID territory, imposes strict lockdowns to take effect on Thursday." November 10. <nationalpost.com/news/canada/manitoba-moves-into-critical-covid-territory-imposes-strict-lockdowns-to-take-effect-on-thursday>.

64. Hoye, Bryce. 2020. "Shaming COVID-19 rule-breakers for spike unwise and disingenuous of Manitoba premier, critics say." *CBC News Manitoba,* October 28. <cbc.ca/news/canada/manitoba/manitoba-pallister-covid-19-criticism-1.5779417>.

65. Waylen, Georgina. 2021. "How hypermasculine leadership may have affected early Covid-19 policy responses." *European Politics and Policy, London School of Economics,* June 30. <blogs.lse.ac.uk/europpblog/2021/06/30/how-hypermasculine-leadership-may-have-affected-early-covid-19-policy-responses/>.

66. Ibid.

67. Lynn, Josh. 2021. "Emergency public health order 'may benefit' northern Sask.

communities as COVID-19 cases climb, official says." *CTV News Saskatoon*, July 31. <saskatoon.ctvnews.ca/emergency-public-health-order-may-benefit-northern-sask-communities-as-covid-19-cases-climb-official-says-1.5530683>.

68. Statistics Canada. 2016. "Athabasca Health Authority [Health region, December 2017], Saskatchewan and Saskatchewan [Province]." *Census Profile, 2016 Census*. <www12.statcan.gc.ca/census-recensement/2016/dp-pd/prof/details/page.cfm?Lang=E&Geo1=HR&Code1=4713&Geo2=PR&Code2=47&SearchText=Athabasca Health Authority&SearchType=Begins&SearchPR=01&B1=All&GeoLevel=PR&GeoCode=4713&TABID=1&type=0>.

January 2021

1. Leo, David. 2021. "Canada coronavirus cases surpass 585K as more politicians admit to holiday travel." *Global News*, January 2. <globalnews.ca/news/7552010/coronavirus-canada-update-jan-2/>.

2. Holly Witteman (@hwitteman). 2021. "I am hearing talk of "pandemic fatigue" in media pieces and I wonder if it might be helpful for such discussions to include people with chronic illnesses and disabilities." Twitter, September 21. <twitter.com/hwitteman/status/1308097316008714249?s=20>.

3. Chouinard, Valérie. 2020. "Jonathan Marchand a passé la nuit devant le parlement." *TVA*, August 13. <tvanouvelles.ca/2020/08/13/jonathan-marchand-a-passe-la-nuit-devant-le-parlement>.

4. Institut national de santé publique du Québec. 2021. "Données COVID-19 au Québec." March 2. <inspq.qc.ca/covid-19/donnees>.

5. CBC Montreal. 2020. "After 5 nights in a cage, Québec man reaches agreement with government." August 17. <cbc.ca/news/canada/montreal/chsld-jonathan-marchand-camp-national-assembly-1.5689088>.

6. Duval, Alexandre. 2020. "De retour en CHSLD, Jonathan Marchand constate « l'enfer bureaucratique»." *Radio-Canada Québec*, August 21. <ici.radio-canada.ca/nouvelle/1728107/jonathan-marchand-retour-chsld-enfer-bureaucratique-handicapes-assistance-personnelle-autodirigee>.

7. Duval, Alexandre. 2020. "Toujours sans aide personnalisée : « À ce rythme-là, j'ai le temps de mourir 4 fois »." *Radio-Canada Québec*, December 8. <ici.radio-canada.ca/nouvelle/1755285/jonathan-marchand-personnes-handicapees-projet-de-loi-assistance-personnelle-autodirigee-chsld-adultes>.

8. Linton, Megan. 2021. "Unregulated, for-profit Custodial Institutions for Disabled People house at least 4700 people in Ontario require immediate vaccination." Disability Justice Network of Ontario, February 24.

9. Nolen, Stephanie. 2021. "Remembering Northwood's COVID-19 dead." *The Coast*, April 15. <thecoast.ca/halifax/remembering-northwoods-covid-19-dead/Content?oid=26222525>.

10. Loreto, Nora. 2021. "The COVID outbreaks that Ontario wasn't counting." *Maclean's*, July 1. <macleans.ca/news/canada/the-covid-outbreaks-that-ontario-wasnt-counting/>.

11. McQuigge, Michelle. 2020. "Disabled Canadians feel excluded from COVID-19 messaging." *CTV News*, March 18. <ctvnews.ca/health/coronavirus/disabled-canadians-feel-excluded-from-covid-19-messaging-1.4857691>.

12. DeClerq, Katherine. 2020. "Sixth death reported at facility for vulnerable adults dealing with major COVID-19 outbreak." *CTV News Toronto*, April 28. <toronto.ctvnews.ca/sixth-death-reported-at-facility-for-vulnerable-adults-dealing-with-major-covid-19-outbreak-1.4914834>.

13. Loreto, Nora. 2021. "The COVID outbreaks that Ontario wasn't counting." *Maclean's*, July

1. <macleans.ca/news/canada/the-covid-outbreaks-that-ontario-wasnt-counting/>.

14. Kinross, Louise. 2021. "Families of group-home residents fight 'barbaric COVID-19 restrictions." *Bloom Blog,* June 15. <hollandbloorview.ca/stories-news-events/BLOOM-Blog/families-group-home-residents-fight-barbaric-covid-19-restrictions>.

15. Reid, Tashauna. 2020. "Canadians with disabilities left with few alternatives amid COVID-19 shutdowns." *CBC News,* April 9. <cbc.ca/news/health/covid-19-impact-on-canadians-with-disabilities-1.5525332>.

16. Craggs, Samantha. 2021. "45-year-old Ontario farmer is among the young and healthy being devastated by COVID-19." *CBC News Hamilton,* April 23. <cbc.ca/news/canada/hamilton/mike-vannetten-1.5999647>.

17. Agahi, Emad. 2021. "BC family still searching for answers to how healthy 46-year-old dad died of COVID-19." *Global News,* April 30. <globalnews.ca/news/7825096/BC-family-covid-death-answers/>.

18. Government of Alberta. 2021. "COVID-19 Alberta Statistics." July 21. <alberta.ca/stats/covid-19-alberta-statistics.htm#comorbidities>.

19. Ezekowitz, Justin A., et al. 2017. "Ethnicity." *2017 Comprehensive Update of the CCS Guidelines for the Management of Heart Failure.* Can J Cardiol, 33: 1342–1433. <ccs.ca/eguidelines/Content/Topics/HeartFailure/752%20Ethnicity.htm>.

20. Lim, Jolson. 2020. "Too few Canadians with disabilities got tax-free COVID benefit, minister charges." *iPolitics,* November 5. <ipolitics.ca/2020/11/05/too-few-canadians-with-disabilities-got-tax-free-covid-benefit-minister-charges>.

21. Diagnostic and Interventional Cardiology. 2020. "ACC COVID-19 Clinical Guidance For the Cardiovascular Care Team." March 9. <dicardiology.com/article/acc-covid-19-clinical-guidance-cardiovascular-care-team>.

22. Alberta Health Services. 2021. "COVID-19 Alberta statistics." February 28. <alberta.ca/stats/covid-19-alberta-statistics.htm#comorbidities>.

23. Fatah, Natasha (@NatashaFarah). 2021. "Why aren't people with disabilities front of the line for the Covid-19 vaccine?" Twitter, February 14. <mobile.twitter.com/NatashaFatah/status/1361041105475825671>.

24. *BBC News.* 2021. "COVID: Disabled people account for six in 10 deaths in England last year – ONS." February 11. <bbc.com/news/uk-56033813>.

25. Ginsburg, Faye, Mara Mills, and Rayna Rapp. 2020. "From Quality of Life to Disability Justice: Imagining a Post-Covid Future." *Somatosphere,* June 2. <somatosphere.net/2020/from-quality-of-life-to-disability-justice.html/>.

26. Gabrielle Peters, Gabrielle (@mssinenomine). 2021. Twitter, May 15. <twitter.com/mssinenomine/status/1393747103415824387?s=20>.

27. PROOF Food Insecurity Policy Research. n.d. ""Household Food Insecurity in Canada" <http://proof.utoronto.ca/food-insecurity/>.

28. Poisson, Jayme. 2020. "When social distancing is a matter of life and death." *CBC Frontburner,* March 16. <cbc.ca/radio/frontburner/when-social-distancing-is-a-matter-of-life-and-death-1.5499767>.

29. Fatah, Natasha (@NatashaFarah). 2021. "Why aren't people with disabilities front of the line for the Covid-19 vaccine?" Twitter, February 14. <mobile.twitter.com/NatashaFatah/status/1361041105475825671>.

30. Wong, Alice. 2020. "I'm disabled and need a ventilator to live. Am I expendable during this pandemic?" *Vox,* April 4. <vox.com/platform/amp/first-person/2020/4/4/21204261/coronavirus-covid-19-disabled-people-disabilities-triage>.

31. Ibid.

32. Sins Invalid. 2020. "Social Distancing and Crip Survival: A Disability Centered Response to COVID-19." March 19. <sinsinvalid.org/news-1/2020/3/19/social-distancing-and-crip-survival-a-disability-centered-response-to-covid-19>.

33. McQuigge, Michelle. 2020. "Federal government names group to ensure disabled Canadians included in COVID-19 response." *Globe and Mail,* April 10. <theglobeandmail.com/canada/article-federal-government-names-group-to-ensure-disabled-canadians-included-2/>.

34. Employment and Social Development Canada. 2020. "COVID-19 Disability Advisory Group Report – 2020." December 4. <canada.ca/en/employment-social-development/corporate/disability-advisory-group/reports/2020-advisory-group-report.html>.

35. Open Parliament. 2021. "Vote #72 on March 11th, 2021." March 11. <openparliament.ca/votes/43-2/72/>.

36. Employment and Social Development Canada. 2020. "COVID-19 Disability Advisory Group Report – 2020." December 4. <canada.ca/en/employment-social-development/corporate/disability-advisory-group/reports/2020-advisory-group-report.html>.

37. Reid, Tashauna. 2020. "Canadians with disabilities left with few alternatives amid COVID-19 shutdowns." *CBC News,* April 9. <cbc.ca/news/health/covid-19-impact-on-canadians-with-disabilities-1.5525332>.

38. Employment and Social Development Canada. 2020. "COVID-19 Disability Advisory Group Report – 2020." December 4. <canada.ca/en/employment-social-development/corporate/disability-advisory-group/reports/2020-advisory-group-report.html>.

39. McQuigge, Michelle. 2020. "Federal government names group to ensure disabled Canadians included in COVID-19 response." *Globe and Mail,* April 10. <theglobeandmail.com/canada/article-federal-government-names-group-to-ensure-disabled-canadians-included-2/>.

40. *CTV News.* 2020. "Pandemic-related disability support to cost feds $792 million, PBO says." August 26. <ctvnews.ca/politics/pandemic-related-disability-support-to-cost-feds-792-million-pbo-says-1.5079818>.

41. Lim, Jolson. 2020. "Too few Canadians with disabilities got tax-free COVID benefit, minister charges." *iPolitics,* November 5. <ipolitics.ca/2020/11/05/too-few-canadians-with-disabilities-got-tax-free-covid-benefit-minister-charges>.

42. Doan, Phil. 2020. "Canada's emergency relief leaves out those on social assistance." *Kitchener Today,* April 6. <kitchenertoday.com/local-news/canadas-emergency-relief-leaves-out-those-on-social-assistance-2230704>.

43. Kennedy, Brendan. 2021. "Province playing 'accounting games' with spending on social assistance." *Toronto Star,* February 10. <thestar.com/news/gta/2021/02/09/province-playing-accounting-games-with-spending-on-social-assistance.html>.

44. Blackwell, Tom. 2020. "Social assistance recipients allowed to top up with CERB payments, depending on province they live in." *National Post,* May 26. <nationalpost.com/news/social-assistance-recipients-permitted-to-double-dip-on-cerb-payments-depending-on-province-they-live-in>.

45. Robson, Fletcher. 2020. "Alberta is providing social assistance to 10,000 fewer people, primarily due to CERB." *CBC News Calgary,* September 3. <cbc.ca/news/canada/calgary/alberta-social-assistance-decline-income-support-cerb-1.5709769>.

46. Hudes, Sammy. 2021. "Budget 2021: UCP backs off from threat of widespread cuts to AISH." *Calgary Herald,* February 26. <calgaryherald.com/news/politics/budget-2021-ucp-backs-off-from-threat-of-widespread-cuts-to-aish>.

47. Eneas, Bryan. 2020. "Clawing back of CERB payments will hurt poorest in Sask.: Anti-poverty advocate." *CBC News Saskatchewan,* September 24. <cbc.ca/news/canada/saskatchewan/clawing-back-cerb-hurt-poorest-1.5737345>.

48. Fresh Start Finance. 2021. "Do You Qualify For SAID Disability Benefits In Saskatchewan?" January 24. <freshstartfinance.ca/blog/finance-tips/do-you-qualify-for-said-disability-benefits-in-saskatchewan>.

49. Bricker, Darrell. 2021. "COVID Continues to Take Heavy Toll

on Canadians' Mental Health." *Ipsos*, February 20. <ipsos.com/en-ca/covid-continues-take-heavy-toll-canadians-mental-health>.

50. Ibrahim, Hadeel. 2020. "Expelled Saint John councillor says he's been in Mexico for mental health reasons." CBC *News New Brunswick*, February 24. <cbc.ca/news/canada/new-brunswick/sean-casey-saint-john-coucillor-1.5924346>.

51. McIvor, Dave, and Sam Thompson. 2021. "Positive COVID-19 diagnosis can impact mental health: counsellor." *Global News*, February 10. <globalnews.ca/news/7632643/positive-covid-19-diagnosis-can-impact-mental-health-counsellor/>.

52. Smith, Callum. 2021. "'Stay in touch,' exercise, breathe: Combating mental health challenges during COVID-19." *Global News*, February 1. <globalnews.ca/news/7612403/mental-health-challenges-coronavirus/>.

53. Szperling, Peter. 2021. "CHEO sees 50 per cent increase in kids needing emergency assessments for eating disorders during pandemic." CTV *News Ottawa*, January 27. <ottawa.ctvnews.ca/cheo-sees-50-per-cent-increase-in-kids-needing-emergency-assessments-for-eating-disorders-during-pandemic-1.5285032>.

54. Jayasinha, Ranmalie, and Patricia Conrod. 2021. "Falling through the safety net: Youth are at the heart of Canada's mental health crisis." *The Conversation*, January 27. <theconversation.com/falling-through-the-safety-net-youth-are-at-the-heart-of-canadas-mental-health-crisis-152525>.

55. Cousins, Ben. 2020. "5 tips for handling your mental health during a second wave of COVID-19." CTV *News*, September 29. <ctvnews.ca/health/5-tips-for-handling-your-mental-health-during-a-second-wave-of-covid-19-1.5125651>.

56. Silver, Janet E. 2020. "As COVID cases rise, so do calls for more mental-health funding." *iPolitics*, October 8. <ipolitics.ca/2020/10/08/as-covid-cases-rise-so-do-calls-for-more-mental-health-funding/>.

57. Ibid.

58. CTV *Vancouver Island*. 2020. "B.C. schools receive $2-million cash boost to promote mental health." September 2. <vancouverisland.ctvnews.ca/b-c-schools-receive-2-million-cash-boost-to-promote-mental-health-1.5089626>.

59. Cave, Rachel. 2021. "N.B. health minister to announce addictions, mental health plan." CBC *News New Brunswick*, February 23. <cbc.ca/news/canada/new-brunswick/mental-health-drug-addiction-1.5923897>.

60. Brown, Laura. 2020. "Horizon Health to review what happened the day teen sought mental health help at Fredericton ER." CTV *News Atlantic*, February 26. <atlantic.ctvnews.ca/horizon-health-to-review-what-happened-the-day-teen-sought-mental-health-help-at-fredericton-er-1.5326007>.

February 2021

1. *National Post*. 2021. "The latest numbers on COVID-19 in Canada for Tuesday, Feb. 2, 2021." February 2. <nationalpost.com/pmn/news-pmn/canada-news-pmn/the-latest-numbers-on-covid-19-in-canada-for-tuesday-feb-2-2021-2>.

2. Loreto, Nora. 2020. "Search Terms at CTV, CBC News." Twitter, December 15. <https://twitter.com/nolore/status/1338957701167058944?lang=en>.

3. McCormick, Emily. 2021. "Amazon earnings: Q4 sales topped $100 billion for the first time, Bezos to step down as CEO." *Yahoo Finance*, February 2. <ca.finance.yahoo.com/news/amazon-reports-4q-2020-earnings-results-152012181.html>.

4. Amazon Canada. 2020. "Thank you to Amazon customers, employees, and selling partners for a record-breaking holiday season." December 28. <press.aboutamazon.com/news-releases/news-release-details/thank-you-amazon-customers-employees-and-selling-partners-record>.

5. Mann, Helen. 2020. "Ontario lockdown doesn't do anything to help warehouse workers, says advocate." *As It Happens,* December 22. <cbc.ca/radio/asithappens/as-it-happens-tuesday-edition-1.5851623/ontario-lockdown-doesn-t-do-anything-to-help-warehouse-workers-says-advocate-1.5852114>.

6. Slepian, Katya. 2020. "Physical distancing at work a challenge for 50% of British Columbians: CDC survey." *Salmon Arm Observer,* December 8. <saobserver.net/news/physical-distancing-at-work-a-challenge-for-50-of-british-columbians-cdc-survey/>.

7. Gordon, Sean. 2020. "In Québec, the battle against COVID-19 shifts to workplaces." CBC *News Montreal,* October 23. <cbc.ca/news/canada/montreal/Québec-covid-19-workplace-outbreaks-1.5773180>.

8. Gyulai, Linda. 2020. "Retail stores see most workplace COVID-19 outbreaks in Montreal." *Montreal Gazette,* September 30. <montrealgazette.com/news/local-news/retail-stores-see-most-workplace-covid-19-outbreaks-in-montreal>.

9. Gourde, Eric. 2020. "Pourquoi tout Chaudière-Appalaches est au rouge." *La Voix du Sud,* November 1. <lavoixdusud.com/2020/11/01/pourquoi-tout-chaudiere-appalaches-est-au-rouge/>.

10. BC Centre for Disease Control. n.d. "COVID-19 Public Exposures." Accessed on October 16, 2020. <bccdc.ca/health-info/diseases-conditions/covid-19/public-exposures>.

11. Aslam, Sonia. 2020. "Some staff fired at Big White Ski Resort following massive COVID outbreak." *News 1130,* December 16. <citynews1130.com/2020/12/16/staff-fired-big-white-following-covid-outbreak/>.

12. Waters, Shannon. 2020. "Horgan blames workers for workplace Covid outbreaks." *Politics Today,* November 19. <politicstoday.news/british-columbia-today/horgan-blames-workers-for-workplace-covid-outbreaks>.

13. CBC *News British Columbia.* 2020. "Employer not doing enough to protect courthouse staff, union says, after 8 sheriffs test positive for COVID-19." November 27. <cbc.ca/news/canada/british-columbia/surre-bc-courthouse-covid-19-positive-1.5819163>.

14. Feith, Jesse. 2020. "Québec workplace COVID outbreaks outpacing those in schools and care centres." *Montreal Gazette,* December 9. <montrealgazette.com/news/local-news/Québec-workplace-covid-outbreaks-outpacing-those-in-schools-and-care-centres>.

15. Grant, Tavia. 2021. "When COVID-19 strikes workplaces, what does real transparency look like? Why disclosure is rare, but revealing." *Globe and Mail,* March 18. <theglobeandmail.com/canada/article-when-covid-19-strikes-workplaces-what-does-real-transparency-look-like>.

16. Ibid.

17. Tam, Stephanie, Shivani Sood, and Chris Johnston. 2021. "Impact of COVID-19 on small businesses in Canada, first quarter of 2021." *Statistics Canada.* <statcan.gc.ca/n1/pub/45-28-0001/2021001/article/00009-eng.htm>.

18. O'Toole, Erin (@erinotoole). 2020. "Spotted in Cape Breton. I'm proud to have the support of small business owners." Twitter, August 26. <twitter.com/erinotoole/status/1298714872838893573?s=20>.

19. Nardi, Christopher. 2020. "Tories ask CRA to pause audits of wage subsidy recipients during pandemic. Experts say that's a bad idea." *National Post,* November 24. <nationalpost.com/news/politics/tories-ask-cra-to-pause-audits-of-wage-subsidy-recipients-during-pandemic-experts-say-thats-a-bad-idea>.

20. NDP (@NDP). 2021. "Small businesses are the backbone of our economy." Twitter, March 3. <twitter.com/ NDP/status/1367173073384988672?s=20>.

21. New Democratic Party of Canada. n.d. "Support small businesses. Tell Justin Trudeau

to stop favouring wealthy corporations." <ndp.ca/small-business>.

22. Sax, David. 2020. "COVID-19 has destroyed countless small businesses. But entrepreneurship has always been about rebirth." *Globe and Mail,* April 18. <theglobeandmail.com/opinion/article-coronavirus-has-decimated-small-business-but-entrepreneurship-has/>.

23. Kerr, Jaren. 2020. "Caledon's small businesses fear decimation from lockdown." *Globe and Mail,* December 11. <theglobeandmail.com/canada/toronto/article-caledons-small-businesses-fear-decimation-from-lockdown/>.

24. Deschamps, Tara. 2020. "Small businesses seek changes to Ontario lockdown rules as big box stores remain open." *Toronto Star,* November 23. <thestar.com/business/2020/11/23/small-businesses-seek-changes-to-ontario-lockdown-rules-as-big-box-stores-remain-open.html>.

25. Kelly, Dan. 2020. "CEBA, CEWS and rent assistance changes — everything you need to know." CFIB, October 30. YouTube Video. <youtu.be/YgmfxxWzZdY>.

26. Franklin, Michael. 2020. "Many small businesses in Canada 'won't survive' drop in revenue due to COVID-19: CFIB." *CTV News Calgary,* March 17. <calgary.ctvnews.ca/many-small-businesses-in-canada-won-t-survive-drop-in-revenue-due-to-covid-19-cfib-1.4856673>.

27. CFIB. n.d. "Investigating the impact of COVID-19 on independent business." Accessed December 25, 2020. <https://www.cfib-fcei.ca/en/research/survey-results/investigating-the-impact-of-covid-19-on-independent-business-archive>.

28. Government of Ontario. n.d. "Ongoing outbreaks." Ontario COVID-19 outbreaks data, December 15, 2020. <data.ontario.ca/dataset/ontario-covid-19-outbreaks-data/resource/66d15cce-bfee-4f91-9e6e-0ea79ec52b3d>.

29. Blackwell, Tom. 2020. "More than 400 COVID-19 cases at Amazon warehouses in Ontario amid concern over industrial spread of virus." *The Province,* December 18. <theprovince.com/news/more-than-400-covid-19-cases-at-amazon-warehouses-in-ontario-amid-concern-about-industrial-spread-of-virus>.

30. Alberta Health Services. n.d. "COVID-19 school status map." <web.archive.org/web/20201215011948/alberta.ca/schools/covid-19-school-status-map.htm>.

31. Alberta Health Services. n.d. "Outbreaks in Alberta." Accessed December 15, 2020. <alberta.ca/covid-19-alberta-data.aspx>.

32. Health Canada. n.d. "Coronavirus disease 2019 (COVID-19): Epidemiology update." Accessed December 15, 2020. <health-infobase.canada.ca/covid-19/epidemiological-summary-covid-19-cases.html>.

33. CBC News Edmonton. 2020. "'We have reached a precarious point': Alberta now has 13,166 active cases of COVID-19." November 23. <cbc.ca/news/canada/edmonton/alberta-covid-19-coronavirus-hinshaw-ndp-notley-1.5812610>.

34. Alberta Health Services. n.d. "Outbreaks in Alberta." Accessed December 15, 2020. <alberta.ca/covid-19-alberta-data.aspx>.

35. Ibid.

36. Marotta, Stefanie. 2020. "Ontario, Québec see COVID-19 outbreaks at workplaces climb." *Globe and Mail,* December 4. <theglobeandmail.com/canada/article-ontario-Québec-see-covid-19-outbreaks-at-workplaces-climb/>.

37. Mann, Helen. 2020. "Ontario lockdown doesn't do anything to help warehouse workers, says advocate." *As It Happens,* December 22. <cbc.ca/radio/asithappens/as-it-happens-tuesday-edition-1.5851623/ontario-lockdown-doesn-t-do-anything-to-help-warehouse-workers-says-advocate-1.5852114>.

38. Mojtehedzadeh, Sara, and Andrew Bailey. 2021. "Who is an essential worker in the GTA? Millions of us, data shows. This is life — outside lockdown — in five graphs." *Toronto Star,* February 2. <thestar.com/news/gta/2021/02/02/

who-is-an-essential-worker-in-the-gta-millions-of-us-data-shows-this-is-life-outside-lockdown-in-five-graphs.html>.

39. Ibid.

40. Marotta, Stefanie. 2020. "Ontario's Peel region sees surge in workplace COVID-19 infections." *Globe and Mail,* November 17. <theglobeandmail.com/canada/article-ontarios-peel-region-sees-surge-in-workplace-covid-19-infections/>.

41. Ibid.

42. *BBC News.* 2020. "Nearly 20,000 Covid-19 cases among Amazon workers." October 2. <bbc.com/news/business-54381928>.

43. Mojtehedzadeh, Sara. 2020. "Amazon warehouse workers in Canada saw injury rates double. Then COVID hit. Inside a hidden safety crisis." *Toronto Star,* December 10. <thestar.com/news/gta/2020/12/10/amazon-warehouse-workers-saw-injury-rates-double-then-covid-hit-inside-a-hidden-safety-crisis.html>.

44. Blackwell, Tom. 2020. "More than 400 COVID-19 cases at Amazon warehouses in Ontario amid concern over industrial spread of virus." *The Province,* December 18. <theprovince.com/news/more-than-400-covid-19-cases-at-amazon-warehouses-in-ontario-amid-concern-about-industrial-spread-of-virus>.

45. McKenzie-Sutter, Holly. 2021. "Ontario probes possible labour violations at Amazon site shut down over COVID-19 outbreak." *CBC News Toronto,* March 15. <cbc.ca/news/canada/toronto/ontario-labour-ministry-investigating-amazon-site-outbreak-covid-19-1.5950534>.

46. Marotta, Stefanie. 2020. "Ontario, Québec see COVID-19 outbreaks at workplaces climb." *Globe and Mail,* December 4. <theglobeandmail.com/canada/article-ontario-Québec-see-covid-19-outbreaks-at-workplaces-climb/>.

47. Caron, Roxanne. 2020. "Plus de 775 interventions de la CNESST liées à la COVID-19 en Montérégie-Est." *La Voix de l'Est,* December 7. <lavoixdelest.ca/actualites/plus-de-775-interventions-de-la-cnesst-liees-a-la-covid-19-en-monteregie-est-504c1d5 463674f44b0b9c9625fb3c288>.

48. Yourex-West, Heather. 2021. "Inside the oilsands site that has seen Canada's largest workplace COVID-19." *Global News,* May 11. <globalnews.ca/news/7852937/oil-sands-site-canada-largest-workplace-covid-outbreak/>.

49. *CBC News Edmonton.* 2021. "Oilsands workers inside Alberta's largest COVID-19 outbreak fear for their safety." May 12. <cbc.ca/news/canada/edmonton/cnrl-horizon-oilsands-covid-outbreak-1.6024267>.

50. Mertz, Emily. 2021. "Alberta oil sands group starts offering on-site COVID-19 vaccines as CNRL confirms 2 deaths." *Global News,* May 6. <globalnews.ca/news/7839664/alberta-oil-sands-on-site-covid-19-vaccines-cnrl-deaths-union-shutdown>.

51. Loreto, Nora. 2021. "Deaths: workplace outbreaks." Google Spreadsheets. <docs.google.com/spreadsheets/d/1M_RzojK0vwF9nAozI7aoyLpPU8EA1JEqO6rq0g1iebU/edit#gid=404463485>.

52. Windsor-Shellard, Ben, and Rabiya Nasir. 2021. "Coronavirus (COVID-19) related deaths by occupation, England and Wales: deaths registered between 9 March and 28 December 2020." *Office for National Statistics,* January 25. <ons.gov.uk/peoplepopulationandcommunity/healthandsocialcare/causesofdeath/bulletins/coronaviruscovid19relateddeathsbyoccupationenglandandwales/deathsregisteredbetween9marchand28december2020>.

53. Workers' Action Centre. 2020. "9-weeks of paid holiday for Premier Ford, zero paid sick days for frontline workers, as Conservative Government votes to adjourn the parliament two days early." December 9. <workersactioncentre.org/9-weeks-of-paid-holiday-for-premier-ford-zero-paid-sick-days-for-frontline-workers/>.

54. Tam, Stephanie, Shivani Sood, and Chris Johnston. 2021. "Impact of COVID-19 on

small businesses in Canada, first quarter of 2021." Statistics Canada, March 10. <www150.statcan.gc.ca/n1/pub/45-28-0001/2021001/article/00009-eng.htm>.

55. *Insauga.* 2020. "10 Pearson Airport taxi and limo drivers dead: union president." May 6. <insauga.com/10-pearson-airport-taxi-and-limo-drivers-dead-union-president>.

56. Greenaway, Kathryn. 2020. "As Montreal tops 3,000 COVID deaths, taxi drivers are on the front lines." *Montreal Gazette,* June 5. <montrealgazette.com/news/local-news/taxi-drivers-also-working-on-the-covid-19-front-lines>.

57. Frisque, Graeme. 2020. "Toronto Pearson Airport taxis and limos getting Plexiglas dividers in response to COVID-19." *Mississauga.com,* June 24. <mississauga.com/news-story/10040305-toronto-pearson-airport-taxis-and-limos-getting-plexiglas-dividers-in-response-to-covid-19/>.

58. Vega, Manuela. 2020. "Airport Taxi Association accepts COVID-19 relief from Pearson airport in Mississauga after initially rejecting it." *Mississauga.com,* August 20. <mississauga.com/news-story/10141549-airport-taxi-association-accepts-covid-19-relief-from-pearson-airport-in-mississauga-after-initially-rejecting-it>.

59. Shinuda, Jonah. 2020. "Federal government identifies multiple flights that landed at Pearson Airport with COVID-19." *InSauga,* November 28. <insauga.com/federal-government-identifies-multiple-flights-that-landed-at-pearson-airport-with-covid-19>.

60. Aversa, Angelo. 2020. "'My job is not very safe': Taxi driver fears he contracted COVID from passenger." *CTV News Windsor,* December 22. <windsor.ctvnews.ca/my-job-is-not-very-safe-taxi-driver-fears-he-contracted-covid-from-passenger-1.5241981>.

61. Sellar, Cody. 2020. "A taxing pandemic for taxi drivers." *Winnipeg Free Press,* December 7. <winnipegfreepress.com/special/coronavirus/a-taxing-pandemicfor-taxi-drivers-573314461.html>.

62. White-Crummey, Arthur. 2021. "Newcomer groups face cash crunch and high need during pandemic." *Regina Leader-Post,* January 16. <leaderpost.com/news/saskatchewan/newcomer-groups-face-cash-crunch-and-high-need-during-pandemic>.

63. Slugoski, Kendra. 2020. "Edmonton taxi, Uber drivers concerned with taking passengers to COVID-19 tests." *Global News Edmonton,* December 14. <globalnews.ca/video/7522386/edmonton-taxi-uber-drivers-concerned-with-taking-passengers-to-covid-19-tests>.

64. *CBC News Toronto.* 2020. "Beck Taxi says city shouldn't ask cabbies to transport people with probable or confirmed cases of COVID-19." November 24. <cbc.ca/news/canada/toronto/beck-taxi-transportation-covid-19-cab-drivers-city-vehicles-risk-protection-1.5815251>.

65. Freeman, Joshua. 2020. "Taxi drivers outraged after Toronto initially tells people to cab to COVID-19 testing sites." *CTV News Toronto,* April 17. <toronto.ctvnews.ca/taxi-drivers-outraged-after-toronto-initially-tells-people-to-cab-to-covid-19-testing-sites-1.4901445>.

66. Loreto, Nora. 2021. "Deaths: workplace outbreaks." Google Spreadsheets. <docs.google.com/spreadsheets/d/1M_RzojK0vwF9nAozI7aoyLpPU8EA1JEqO6rq0g1iebU/edit#gid=404463485>.

67. Riebe, Natasha. 2021. "Edmonton bus drivers 'strongly encouraged' but not required to wear masks, city says." *CBC News Edmonton,* January 12. <https://www.cbc.ca/news/canada/edmonton/city-council-covid-19-bus-drivers-1.5869446>.

68. *CBC News London.* 2020. "Watch this video of a London bus driver getting shoved after asking rider to wear a mask." October 22. <cbc.ca/news/canada/london/watch-this-video-of-a-london-bus-driver-getting-shoved-after-asking-rider-to-wear-a-mask-1.5772288>.

69. Abraham, Julian. 2020. "'Anxiety is through the roof': Union president says Halifax Transit drivers are in danger during pandemic." *CTV News Atlantic,* November 25.

<atlantic.ctvnews.ca/anxiety-is-through-the-roof-union-president-says-halifax-transit-drivers-are-in-danger-during-pandemic-1.5204382>.
70. Seville, Lisa Riordan. 2020. "These are the most dangerous jobs you can have in the age of coronavirus." NBC, May 8. <nbcnews.com/health/health-news/these-are-most-dangerous-jobs-you-can-have-age-coronavirus-n1201496>.
71. Mathai, Varghese, Asimanshu Das, Jeffrey Bailey and Kenneth Breuer. "Airflows inside passenger cars and implications for air-borne disease transmission." *Science Advances,* 7, 1 (January 1). <science.org/doi/10.1126/sciadv.abe0166>.

March 2021
1. Boynton, Sean. 2021. "Canada adds over 2,500 new coronavirus cases as vaccine rollout takes shape." *Global News,* March 1. <globalnews.ca/news/7671162/canada-coronavirus-update-march-1-2021/>.
2. Fenlon, Brodie. 2020. "Why CBC News is making changes to local programming during the COVID-19 crisis." *CBC Editor's Blog,* March 18. <cbc.ca/news/editorsblog/editors-blog-local-programming-1.5502141>.
3. Emmanuel, Rachel. 2020. "CBC works to restore local coverage suspended amid COVID-19 outbreak." *iPolitics,* March 26. <ipolitics.ca/2020/03/26/cbc-works-to-restore-local-coverage-suspended-amid-covid-19-outbreak/>.
4. Faguy, Steve. 2020. "CBC suspends local TV newscasts amid COVID-19 outbreak." *Fagstein,* March 18. <blog.fagstein.com/2020/03/18/cbc-suspends-local-tv-newscasts/>.
5. Ibid.
6. Ibid.
7. *J-Source.* 2020. "COVID-19 Media Impact Map for Canada." October 22. <j-source.ca/article/covid-19-media-impact-map-for-canada-update-oct-22/>.
8. Lonergan, Patricia. 2020. "Media layoffs during COVID-19: how the pandemic exposes existing industry problems." *News at UTM,* April 14. <utm.utoronto.ca/main-news/media-layoffs-during-covid-19-how-pandemic-exposes-existing-industry-problems>.
9. *Toronto Star.* 2020. "Torstar to eliminate 85 positions, reduce executive pay as ad revenue drops due to pandemic." April 6. <thestar.com/business/2020/04/06/torstar-to-eliminate-85-positions-reduce-executive-pay-as-ad-revenue-drops-due-to-pandemic.html>.
10. NordStar Capital Cision. 2020. "NordStar Completes Acquisition of Torstar." August 5. <newswire.ca/news-releases/nordstar-completes-acquisition-of-torstar-893486219.html>.
11. Wilson, Jim. 2020. "Torstar reverses planned job cuts." *HR Reporter,* October 2. <hrreporter.com/labour/news/torstar-reverses-planned-job-cuts/333859>.
12. Lindgren, April. 2020. "Local news is being decimated during one of its most important moments." *Policy Options,* May 27. <policyoptions.irpp.org/magazines/may-2020/local-news-is-being-decimated-during-one-of-its-most-important-moments/>.
13. Canadian Media Guild. 2020. "Union members stand together during painful layoffs at Vice." June 11. <cmg.ca/en/2020/06/11/union-members-stand-together-during-painful-layoffs-at-vice>.
14. NetNewsLedger. 2020. "Global News Layoffs Gut-Wrenching – Brent Jolly President CAJ." July 24. <netnewsledger.com/2020/07/24/global-news-layoffs-gut-wrenching-brent-jolly-president-caj/>.
15. Faguy, Steve. 2020. "Global Montreal replaces Jamie Orchard with Toronto-based anchor, cancels Focus Montreal." *Fagstein,* September 22. <blog.fagstein.com/2020/09/22/global-montreal-toronto-anchor/>.

16. Ashton-Beaucage, Devin. 2020. "COVID-19's impact on media in Canada." Friends of Canadian Broadcasting, September 14. <friends.ca/explore/article/covid-19s-impact-on-media-in-canada/>.

17. Rody, Bree. 2020. "Additional layoffs reported at Postmedia." *Media in Canada*, September 30. <mediaincanada.com/2020/09/30/additional-layoffs-reported-at-postmedia/>.

18. Rody, Bree. 2020. "Pelmorex sees more than a dozen layoffs." *Media in Canada*, October 9. <mediaincanada.com/2020/10/09/pelmorex-sees-more-than-a-dozen-layoffs/>.

19. Ashton-Beaucage, Devin. 2020. "COVID-19's impact on media in Canada." Friends of Canadian Broadcasting, September 14. <friends.ca/explore/article/covid-19s-impact-on-media-in-canada/>.

20. Dobby, Christine. 2021. "Rogers, Bell and Telus collected more than $240 million from Canada's wage-subsidy program — and Bell and Telus raised shareholder payouts." *Toronto Star,* February 8. <thestar.com/business/2021/02/08/top-telecoms-took-in-almost-a-quarter-billion-dollars-from-canadas-wage-subsidy-program-and-kept-paying-dividends.html>.

21. Ashton-Beaucage, Devin. 2020. "COVID-19's impact on media in Canada." Friends of Canadian Broadcasting, September 14. <friends.ca/explore/article/covid-19s-impact-on-media-in-canada/>.

22. Dawson, Tyler. 2020. "CBC to lay off dozens of journalists and management across multiple divisions." *National Post,* October 7. <nationalpost.com/news/canada/cbc-to-lay-off-dozens-of-journalists-and-management-across-multiple-divisions>.

23. Evans, Pete. 2020. "Bell cancels all-sports radio format on channels in Vancouver, Winnipeg and Hamilton." CBC *News Business,* February 9. <cbc.ca/news/business/bell-media-cuts-1.5907158>.

24. CBC *News Toronto.* 2020. "Bell Media cuts radio jobs, including on-air broadcast roles, in streamlining push." February 2. <cbc.ca/news/canada/toronto/bell-layoffs-1.5898421>.

25. Cision. 2021. "BCE reports 2020 Q4 and full-year results." February 4. <prnewswire.com/news-releases/bce-reports-2020-q4-and-full-year-results-301222121.html>.

26. Brown, Jesse. 2020. "The President of the CBC Lives In Brooklyn." *Canadaland,* December 11. <canadaland.com/the-president-of-the-cbc-lives-in-brooklyn/>.

27. *La Presse.* 2019. "La Cour approuve le plan de relance du Groupe Capitales Médias." December 23. <lapresse.ca/affaires/entreprises/2019-12-23/la-cour-approuve-le-plan-de-relance-du-groupe-capitales-medias>.

28. Lindgren, April. 2020. "Local news is being decimated during one of its most important moments." *Policy Options,* May 27. <policyoptions.irpp.org/magazines/may-2020/local-news-is-being-decimated-during-one-of-its-most-important-moments/>.

29. Ibid.

30. Scire, Sarah. 2020. "In Canada, a government program to support local news tries to determine who's most deserving." *Nieman Lab,* May 8. <niemanlab.org/2020/05/in-canada-a-government-program-to-support-local-news-tries-to-determine-whos-most-deserving/>.

31. Charlton, Jonathan. 2020. "La Loche the most concerning COVID-19 outbreak in Canada, epidemiologist says." CTV *News Saskatchewan,* April 30. <saskatoon.ctvnews.ca/la-loche-the-most-concerning-covid-19-outbreak-in-canada-epidemiologist-says-1.4919816>.

32. Malone, Kelly Geraldine. 2020. "Saskatchewan Indigenous community 'frustrated and angry' as it battles coronavirus outbreak." *Global News Regina,* July 2. <globalnews.ca/news/6925449/saskatchewan-indigenous-coronavirus-la-loche>.

33. Ibid.

34. Graney, Emma. 2020. "Kearl Lake coronavirus outbreak now linked to over 100

cases in four provinces." *Globe and Mail,* May 10. <theglobeandmail.com/business/article-kearl-lake-coronavirus-outbreak-now-linked-to-over-100-cases-in-four/>.

35. Tank, Phil. 2020. "Saskatchewan's worst COVID-19 outbreak ends in La Loche." *Saskatoon StarPhoenix,* July 16. <thestarphoenix.com/news/local-news/saskatchewans-worst-covid-19-outbreak-ends-in-la-loche>.

36. Arangio, Sergio. 2021. "Families speak out about deadly COVID outbreak at Extendicare Kapuskasing." CTV *Northern Ontario,* February 14. <northernontario.ctvnews.ca/families-speak-out-about-deadly-covid-outbreak-at-extendicare-kapuskasing-1.5308563>.

37. CBC *News Sudbury.* 2021. "Pierre Dorval talks about losing his dad and uncle in Extendicare Kapuskasing outbreak." February 12. <cbc.ca/news/canada/sudbury/extendicare-kapuskasing-pierre-dorval-covid-19-outbreak-1.5911051>.

38. Rivett, Paul, and Jordan Bitove. 2020. "Enough is enough: We demand change to the inhumane tragedy playing out in Ontario's long-term care homes." *Toronto Star,* December 31. <thestar.com/opinion/editorials/2020/12/30/enough-is-enough-we-demand-change-to-the-inhumane-tragedy-playing-out-in-ontarios-long-term-care-homes.html>.

39. Loreto, Nora (@nolore). 2020. "The Toronto Star, rather than having their own reporters track deaths, just lifted this number from Ontario health ministry data to make this front page." Twitter, December 31. <twitter.com/NoLore/status/1344678460892045314?s=20>.

40. Rinaldo, Sandy. "November 15, 2020." [Video.] CTV *National News.* <ctvnews.ca/video?clipId=2070509>.

41. Strauss, Matt (@strauss_matt). Twitter, November 24, 2020. <twitter.com/strauss_matt/status/1331272333047308288?s=20>.

42. Corbella, Licia. 2020. "Corbella: A look in the rear-view mirror necessary to decide future COVID-19 restrictions." *Calgary Herald,* November 23. <calgaryherald.com/opinion/columnists/corbella-facts-show-alberta-should-not-have-another-lockdown>.

43. Ibid.

44. Rieger, Sarah. "Calgary hospitals told to conserve oxygen, but doctors fear request is a red flag." CBC *News Calgary,* November 30. <cbc.ca/news/canada/calgary/oxygen-delivery-alberta-hospitals-covid-19-1.5822825>.

45. Rinaldo, Sandy. "November 15, 2020." [Video.] CTV *National News.* <ctvnews.ca/video?clipId=2070509>.

46. Vella, Erica. 2021. "Coronavirus: Toronto hospital worker dies from COVID-19." *Global News,* January 14. <globalnews.ca/video/7578038/coronavirus-toronto-hospital-worker-dies-from-covid-19>.

47. Vescera, Zak. 2021. "North Battleford healthcare worker dies after battle with COVID-19." *Saskatoon StarPhoenix,* February 18. <thestarphoenix.com/news/saskatchewan/north-battleford-health-care-worker-dies-of-covid-19>.

48. Paradis, Danielle. 2021. "The UCP knew the inequitable impacts of COVID-19 all along." *The Sprawl,* July 27. <sprawlalberta.com/ucp-knew-the-inequitable-impacts-of-covid-19-all-along>.

49. CBC *News Windsor.* 2021. "Windsor seniors' home worker who died of COVID-19 remembered as 'kind soul.'" February 10. <cbc.ca/news/canada/windsor/judy-hawkins-covid19-windsor-1.5908886>.

50. Oxford Living. n.d. "Our Team." Accessed February 19, 2021. <oxfordliving.ca/our-team/>.

51. Drevfjall, Ludvig. "A single nurse had to care for everyone at Lundy Manor, COVID-19 lawsuit alleges." *Thorold News,* May 6. <thoroldnews.com/coronavirus-covid-19-local-news/a-single-nurse-had-to-care-for-everyone-at-

lundy-manor-covid-19-lawsuit-alleges-2330104>.

52. Niagara Region Public Health. n.d. "Lundy Manor Retirement Residence Inspection Results." Accessed February 19, 2021. <niagararegion.ca/health/inspect/inspection. aspx?id=3579a90a-11cb-4b87-8359-1e39fad9e2a4>.

53. Favaro, Avis, Elizabeth St. Philip, and Alexandra Mae Jones. 2021. "'They're not machines:' Deaths of health-care workers underline the strain of COVID-19." CTV News, January 7. <ctvnews.ca/health/coronavirus/they-re-not-machines-deaths-of-health-care-workers-underline-the-strain-of-covid-19-1.5258509>.

54. Loreto, Nora. 2021. "Deaths: workplace outbreaks." Google Spreadsheets. <https://docs.google.com/spreadsheets/d/1M_RzojK0vwF9nAozI7aoyLp PU8EA1JEqO6rq0g1iebU/edit#gid=404463485>.

55. Informed Opinions. n.d. "Gender gap tracker" <gendergaptracker.informedopinions. org/>.

56. Graydon, Shari. 2021. "Pandemic reinforces need for media to better reflect women's diversity." Policy Options, February 8. <policyoptions.irpp.org/magazines/ february-2021/pandemic-reinforces-need-for-media-to-better-reflect-womens-diversity/>.

57. Green, Kiernan. 2020. "These Canadian News Sites Have Removed Paywalls From Coronavirus Coverage." J-Source, March 19. <j-source.ca/article/ these-canadian-news-sites-have-removed-paywalls-from-coronavirus-coverage/>.

58. Gentle, Irene. 2020. "Why we're offering free digital access to essential coronavirus information." Toronto Star, March 4. <thestar.com/news/canada/2020/03/04/why-were-offering-free-digital-access-to-essential-coronavirus-information.html>.

59. Brown, David. 2020. "Mary Brown's deal lifts pay wall at Postmedia." The Message, April 2. <the-message.ca/2020/04/02/mary-browns-deal-will-lift-pay-wall-at-postmedia/>.

60. Robinson, Nathan J. 2020. "The Truth Is Paywalled But The Lies Are Free." Current Affairs, August 2. <currentaffairs.org/2020/08/the-truth-is-paywalled-but-the-lies-are-free/>.

61. Sacerdote, Bruce, Ranjan Sehgal, and Molly Cook. 2020. "Why is all COVID-19 news bad news?" National Bureau of Economic Research Working Paper 28110. <nber.org/ system/files/working_papers/w28110/w28110.pdf>.

62. Global News. 2020. "Québec premier criticizes Montreal Gazette journalist's coronavirus reporting again." August 20. <globalnews.ca/news/7288970/ Québec-francois-legault-montreal-gazette-aaron-derfel/>.

63. Derfel, Aaron. 2021. "Analysis: Experts blast Legault for saying Québec is "resisting" third wave." Montreal Gazette, March 24. <montrealgazette.com/news/Québec/ analysis-experts-blast-legault-for-saying-Québec-is-resisting-third-wave>.

64. Derfel, Aaron. 2021. "Analysis: COVID-19 outbreaks in Montreal jump by 50 in a week." Montreal Gazette, March 31. <montrealgazette.com/news/local-news/ analysis-covid-19-outbreaks-in-montreal-jump-by-50-in-a-week>.

65. Derfel, Aaron. 2021. "Analysis: Why hasn't COVID's third wave flared up yet in Montreal?" Montreal Gazette, April 15. <https://montrealgazette.com/news/ local-news/analysis-why-hasnt-covids-third-wave-flared-up-yet-in-montreal>.

66. Derfel, Aaron. 2021. "Analysis: Super contagious Delta variant has public health experts worried." Montreal Gazette, June 5. <montrealgazette.com/news/local-news/ analysis-super-contagious-delta-variant-has-public-health-experts-worried>.

67. Derfel, Aaron. 2021. "Analysis: COVID-19 outbreaks down to 15 in Montreal, but threats remain." Montreal Gazette, July 14. <montrealgazette.com/news/local-news/ analysis-covid-19-outbreaks-down-to-15-in-montreal-but-threats-remain>.

68. Blades, Robin. 2021. "Protecting the brain against bad news." CMAJ, March 22. <cmaj. ca/content/193/12/E428>.

Conclusion

1.   Loreto, Nora. 2020. "As the coronavirus spreads, I'm glad we have universal health care in Canada." *Washington Post,* March 10. <washingtonpost.com/opinions/2020/03/10/how-could-us-better-handle-coronavirus-follow-canadas-example/>.

2.   Luck, Shaina. 2021. "Northwood contract talks stalled as other health-care unions seek strike vote." cbc *News Nova Scotia,* June 30. <cbc.ca/news/canada/nova-scotia/northwood-contract-talks-nova-scotia-1.6086204>.

3.   Da Silva, Danielle. 2021. "Manitoba poultry plant battles covid for second time." *Winnipeg Free Press,* June 30. <winnipegfreepress.com/special/coronavirus/manitoba-poultry-plant-battles-covid-for-second-time-574735602.html>.

4.   Tanguay, Sébastien. 2021. "Derrière un million de poulets euthanasias, un modele agricole qui bat de l'aile." *Radio-Canada Ici Québec,* June 25. <ici.radio-canada.ca/nouvelle/1803046/poulet-exceldor-modele-agricole-exploitation-intensive-conflit-greve>.

INDEX

Abdel-Nabi, Hadeel, 103
ableism, 3, 34, 250, 251, 271, 334
activists
    ableism, 334
    anti-Asian racism, 102
    anti-homelessness, 128
    anti-racist, 213
    Black activists, 98, 100, 105
    disabled people, 248–249, 257, 258,
    261, 263, 266
    feminists, 226
    housing activists, 111, 122, 126
    rent subsidies, 126
    sick leave, 169
    transit costs, 150
Air Canada, 146–148, 332
alert app, 11, 114–118, 123
Alivio, Rowena, 224–225
Allain, Julie, 268
Al-Othman, Fadel, 294
alpha variant, 45, 46, 206
Amalgamated Transit Union Local 508
    (Halifax), 296
Amazon facilities, 288, 292, 322
Amazon Fulfillment Centre (Bolton,
    ON), 274–276, 279, 288
Ambersley, Maureen, 319
American Sign Language, 251, 266
Andrew, Jill, 238–239
angry dad approach. *See* dad-premier
    phenomenon
anti-Asian racism, 20, 85, 88, 101–103,
    207
anti-Black racism, 84, 86, 87, 98, 105,
    133, 214, 239. *See also* Pazzano, Sam
anti-Chinese racism. *See* anti-Asian racism
anti-Indigenous racism, 239
anti-mask movement, 105, 212–215
anti-vaccine movement, 210, 212–215
Antonacci, J.P., 188

Antunes, Pedro, 145–146
Aquino, RJ (Tulayan Filipino Diaspora
    Society), 194
Arangio, Sergio, 311
Arruda, Horacio (Public Health Director
    QC), 240, 277
Arsalides, Mike, 45
Assured Income for the Severely Handi-
    capped (AISH), 265–266

back to school. *See also* schools
    congregant settings, 154
    and journalists, 154–155, 161–162,
    164–165
    and politicians, 154, 161
    protocols, 156, 159, 161–163, 164,
    173
    Québec, 155–156
    spring 2020, 160–162
    winter 2021, 171
Bailey, Andrew, 286
Bain, Beverly, 86–87, 97
Barrie, Ontario, 17
Basic Income Canada Network, 151
Battis, Todd, 241
Baxter, Mary, 177
B.C. Centre for Disease Control. *See*
    BCCDC
BCCDC, 55, 276, 277, 291
Beck Taxi, 295
Bégin, Nicolas (CNESST), 289
Bell, Roberta, 310
Bell Canada, 141, 150, 304
Benigo, Yoshua, 116
Berthiaume, Lee, 210
Bibb, Lisa, 188
Biddle, Robert, Jr., 192–193
Bignami, Simona, 325
Bischof, Harvey (OSSTF president), 162,
    172

387